Educating
Canadians

Educating Canadians

A Documentary History
of Public Education

Edited by Douglas A. Lawr and Robert D. Gidney
History of Education Department
Althouse College of Education
The University of Western Ontario

Van Nostrand Reinhold Ltd. Toronto
New York, Cincinnati, London, Melbourne

Copyright © 1973 by Van Nostrand Reinhold
Ltd., Toronto.

ISBN paper 0 442 34696 4
        cloth 0 442 34697 2
Library of Congress Number 72 6681

Design by Gottschalk & Ash Ltd.
Printed and bound in Canada by T. H. Best

The authors and publisher wish to acknowledge their gratitude to those who have given
permission for the use of copyrighted material
in this book. A complete listing of copyright
holders will be found on page 276.

Cover and jacket photograph by Joan Latchford

73 74 75 76 77 78 79 80 8 7 6 5 4 3 2 1

Foreword

This volume of documents is a welcome addition to the small but growing bibliography of the history of Canadian education. The editors have assembled a fascinating collection that at once reveals the rich diversity of educational traditions in Canada and the common assumptions about the goals of public education shared by most Canadians for more than a century. Professors Lawr and Gidney stress this latter point throughout the book, emphasizing the similarities in the origins, structures and aims of the ten provincial systems at every level from the elementary school to the university. By so doing they make an important point for all Canadian historians.

Much of the history of educational issues in Canada has been written from the vantage point of the politicians in the provincial legislatures and the federal parliament. This collection again presents their views but adds the thoughts of the schoolmen and of the administrators of the school systems. The latter, whether in British Columbia or in Quebec, whether Protestant or Roman Catholic, had more shared than differing convictions about the nature and purpose of public education. And this perspective adds to the understanding of the many "schools questions" which have bedevilled the history of Canada.

The readers of this book will also be reminded that schools are a barometer of the nation's public taste and its social order. This is not simply a record of the ideas of Canadians, past and present, about schools and schooling. The 1847 statement of the Reform Party of Nova Scotia that "popular ignorance is a public disgrace, and a source of weakness and danger" may have been a plea for a public school system. It was also an assertion of a belief in a particular way of life. That document, then, and the others in this volume, provide a glimpse into the thoughts of Canadians about their society, its past, its present state, its future aspirations, from Canada's colonial beginnings to the present day.

Robert Craig Brown
University of Toronto

Preface

This book originated in two frustrations. Like so many collections of readings, it began as an attempt to meet the difficulties we experienced in finding suitable teaching materials for our seminars and tutorials in Canadian educational history. It grew, as well, out of a second problem we encountered–that of presenting to our students the common issues at stake in a country where education is so often treated only in a provincial or a regional context. Thus we have attempted to accomplish two things in the following pages: to make available some of the more important or representative documents of Canadian educational history, and to emphasize the central issues faced by all the provinces as they established and then expanded their school systems.

We are well aware of the dangers of trying to write "national" history in a field so marked by regional diversity and we do not underestimate the differences among the provinces. We are, however, struck less by the variations among ten provincial school systems than by the similarities in their origins, their justifications, and their structure. We believe that it is easier to understand both the similarities and the differences once the common themes are grasped.

This book is a *selection* of documents. Though we have attempted wherever possible to maintain a reasonable degree of balance among the regions of the country, we have tried frist to find the best or the most representative documents for each theme or period, whatever their origins. We have not attempted to write a complete history of Canadian education; the book should be used in conjunction with other works on Canadian history and more particularly on Canadian educational history. We hope, however, that it contributes to an understanding of Canadian education–a subject we find both intrinsically interesting and useful in understanding why schools do what they do.

In the course of preparing the manuscript we have accumulated substantial intellectual debts and we hope the following acknowledgements will be accepted at least as token payment. Our colleagues at Althouse College–Professors William B. Hamilton, Judson Purdy, Hugh A. Stevenson, Douglas W. Ray and David J. Radcliffe have read and criticized parts of the manuscript, and have occasionally saved us from egregious errors. Any that may remain are ours alone. We are also indebted to our editor, Phyllis Buckley, of Van Nostrand Reinhold who sharp eye and good judgment saved us from many a pitfall. We are grateful to two former students, Mrs. Catharine Lambier and Miss Patricia McNaughten, who gave us valuable help in preparing the manuscript, and to the staff of the Althouse College Library for cheerfully providing us with services far beyond the call of duty. We would also like to thank Professor R. Craig Brown for his continuing interest in this rather neglected field of Canadian history. Above all, we must acknowledge the patience, tolerance, resourcefulness, and plain hard work of our wives, to whom we gratefully dedicate this work.

D.A.L.
R.D.G.

Contents

Introduction

Common traditions do not come easily to a country as large and as varied as Canada. Is it not presumptuous, then, to speak of "educating Canadians", as if our educational experiences were somehow widely shared across the country? Surely the diversity and division inherent in Canadian history are faithfully reproduced in the country's schools. How can one speak of French-Catholic and English-Protestant education in the same breath? The Roman Catholic Church in Quebec took over many of the educational responsibilities assumed by the state in English-speaking Canada. And even in English Canada, is education not compartmentalized into jealously guarded provincial jurisdictions? Religious minorities are treated differently in the schools of British Columbia, Ontario, and Newfoundland. And what of regionalism? Can any good come from studying the Maritime schools along with those of, say, Alberta?

There are certainly contrasts in our educational experience; yet they should not be allowed to obscure the similarities. The fact is that for over a century most Canadians have received whatever formal education they got from an institution commonly known as the public school. And the most remarkable feature of public education in Canada is not the contrasts that mark its provision, but the similarities. These similarities stem from three main sources: since the early nineteenth century Canadians have held common ideals about the value of education, they have faced common issues concerning the provision of schools, and they have met these issues with common responses. They have shared the belief that some kind of formal instruction was important for the proper development of the individual and the advancement of society.

But what kind of education was of most use? How should it be provided? And by whom? The common response to these questions was the public school organized into a highly regulated system to ensure that it would be educationally and financially responsible to the society that created it.

Once created, the public school systems across the country continued at the centre of our educational experience. For better or worse, nearly all our educational problems have had to be resolved in the public schools: how to provide education for all; how to extend educational opportunity fairly among the rich and the poor, the city and the village; how to ensure that public education meets the perceived needs of the country. In short, the public schools have developed in response to the intellectual currents of the times and to the changing conditions of Canadian society. And the conditions that affect the public schools have been, in many instances, independent of our usual political, regional, and even our cultural boundaries. The restrictions on educational expectations and opportunity for schooling that existed among various social classes and between urban and rural Canadians cut across religious and provincial lines. Irrespective of race or region, poor people received less schooling than the well-to-do, and urban children until recently, at least, have enjoyed more educational opportunities than their rural cousins. Throughout most of our educational history, a pupil in a one-room school on the prairies had more in common with his counterpart in rural Quebec than either of them had with students in the graded schools of Montreal or Winnipeg. These common Canadian conditions provide many unifying themes in our educational experience.

In the pre-public school era, education had very specific (and limited) purposes–to train a leadership elite for state and church. Few people were involved–only those with the ability and the means to take advantage of advanced education in the grammar schools, the classical colleges, or the universities. Little government provision was made for the education of the masses; the majority of the people were left to find instruction where they could–in the home, the workplace, the manse, the private school, or the community school. Because education had limited public purposes, there was limited provision for public schools.

By the middle of the nineteenth century, however, education had taken on a new importance and vastly expanded purposes. Widespread literacy was advocated as the answer to many of the afflictions society inherited: an enlightened, literate populace would be politically stable, socially cohesive, economically adaptable, and individually moral. Such a universal remedy could not be safely ignored by the state, and the governments of the various British North American colonies responded by assuming much greater responsibilities for the provision and control of education.

The means and ends of state intervention in this formative period of public elementary education were remarkably similar throughout British North America. It was generally acknowledged that if the full benefits of public schooling were to be realized two conditions had to be fulfilled: only the proper kind of education should be disseminated, and, secondly, it must be available to as many people as possible. To achieve the first prerequisite, centralized administrative boards or ministries of education were set up with Chief Super-

intendents and appointed Inspectors to regulate the licensing of teachers, the selection of curricula, and the choice of textbooks. To encourage local participation, the elected trustees were charged with certain duties pertaining to the management and upkeep of the local school. To clear the way for universal attendance, a compulsory school tax was levied on all property. Payment of this tax made it possible to remove the obstacle of tuition fees for the poor and discouraged the patronage of private schools by the rich.

Once the administrative and financial bases of a public school system were established, two issues still remained. What place would religion have in the new school arrangements, and to what extent would the older institutions of advanced education be incorporated into the public systems? After a generation of debate and dissension most of the English-speaking provinces decided that the requirements of the various denominations would be accommodated (with more or less satisfaction) in the state systems. Only in British Columbia were the schools completely non-sectarian. In Newfoundland and Quebec, the denominations emerged victorious. In Newfoundland, the administration of the schools was divided among several denominations. In Quebec, the state-supported public schools were also separated along religious lines, under the direction of Roman Catholic and Protestant Committees. For the most part, French-language secondary education also remained under the exclusive control of the Roman Catholic Church. In the rest of British North America the secondary institutions (but not the universities) were incorporated into the public school systems. And so, in a remarkably short time, the formative period of public education was over. By the time of Confederation, public systems were established with elementary schools for the masses and secondary institutions to prepare the intellectual elite for positions of leadership.

Once the structure of public education was established, the next step was to extend the purview of the schools to serve a greater variety of social and economic purposes, and at the end of the nineteenth century the time was ripe for just such an expansion, in a second outburst of educational enthusiasm. For there was much for the school to do, it seemed. With the coming of hundreds of thousands of non-English-speaking immigrants the national schools in the West were pressed into the service of assimilation. As the economy became more industrialized, the schools were asked to contribute to the country's development by providing the growing army of workers with the basis of a technical education. As society became less rural and more urban, many people worried about the social deterioration associated with city living conditions. Could the schools not reproduce for the urban child some of the responsibilities, experiences, and life-training once received in a more wholesome rural environment? As for rural schools, could they not be improved to equalize educational opportunity and enhance the quality of country life? In short, the schools must address themselves to the national, social, and economic realities of the day.

The demands for change were so extensive that it was felt by laymen and schoolmen alike that only a "New Education" would suffice to make the schools relevant to the twentieth century. Consequently, new subjects, like manual training and nature study, were introduced; new institutions—technical schools and consolidated school sections—were created. In some provinces the school-leaving age was pushed up to 16 years, so that more people might benefit from a longer period at school. Finally, a new pedagogy was developed to incorporate the new purposes and subjects into a complete educational experience. In effect, this new pedagogy attempted to replace the rather limited nineteenth-century concept of "school education" (basic skills, mental discipline) with one involving nothing less than the complete socialization of the child. Taken together, these school reforms proposed in the early decades of the new century did indeed constitute a "New Education".

Many obstacles, however, remained to slow the progress of public schooling along the lines set down by the New Education. The conservative, mental-discipline tradition persisted for decades, and its emphasis on the school as a place imparting a special kind of abstract learning was fundamentally opposed to the broad "education-for-life" pedagogy of the New Education. Furthermore, establishing new courses and new institutions was expensive, and economic conditions did not permit the outlay of a large percentage of the Gross National Product for schools until after the Second World War. These same economic conditions prevented widespread use of the schools. Until the 1950s most people left school after grades 8 or 9, and the university was very much an elitist institution. Educational change came slowly in the first half of the twentieth century.

Then came the sensational sixties–and the third (and final?) round of expansion began. Once again men spoke of a new education for a new age. Once again the school was charged with providing the means of achieving the good society: specialists to man our technology; greater educational opportunity to equalize our social structure; multicultural education for the minority groups; schools relevant to all students, not just the few who had traditionally used them for their economic and social advantage. But what set the 1960s apart from the other periods of "educational mania" was that this time the response was felt in the schools almost immediately. What had previously taken decades to achieve was done in a few years. Attendance figures rocketed; everyone, it seemed, was suddenly in school. The crush was felt most severely in the secondary and post-secondary institutions, which had retained much of their elitist past. The general prosperity of the sixties that permitted so many people to stay in school also enabled governments to meet the increased expenditure. New institutions like the community colleges sprang up across the country, and government money was eagerly sought after by the established universities. In the schools pedagogical reform once again became an issue. Educators first exploited the familiar methods of the New Education and then moved on into new pedagogical theories and practices.

In many ways, the 1960s marked the consummation of the public school tradition. The educational response was complete. With the school-leaving age pushed close to the post-secondary level, the public school now ran from the kindergarten to the university. More time and money were spent on schools than ever before. The public schools had taken over virtually all formal and most informal instruction; it was difficult to get a recognized education outside of them. But at what cost and with what effectiveness? In spite of the million dollar budgets of the sixties, it seemed to some observers that the public schools were as far from realizing their social and educational goals as they ever were. And for the first time a sizeable proportion of critics were not talking of the need for expansion and redirection, but of fundamental change to radically new types of educational experiences. By the end of the decade, it seemed as if an era in Canadian educational history had come to an end.

I

The Nature of Early Colonial Education

"Upper Canada is a new Country," Lieutenant-Governor Simcoe remarked in 1795, "but not a new people." His observation applies not only to Upper Canada, but to New France and later to all the colonies that made up British North America. French, British, or American, the colonists brought an established culture to the new land. Education, no less than politics or religion, was a part of that culture. Schools and colleges were founded in each of the colonies as quickly as the condition of a new society would permit. They were modelled upon institutions familiar at home, and they were intended to serve much the same purposes.

What characterized the educational traditions transplanted to the colonies? There were important differences among the traditions brought by people from different parts of Europe, Britain, and America; but there were also some fundamental similarities. Everywhere, education was voluntary, and hence the family played a crucial role in determining the amount of schooling a child would receive. Children might be sent to school for religious reasons, or to give them the skills to get on in the world; equally, they might not be sent at all. Because schooling depended upon the family, it was closely related to social class: in the main, advanced education was available only to those who could afford tuition fees and the cost of boarding their children away from home. Most children, if they received any formal education at all, never passed beyond the three Rs. Because schooling was voluntary, moreover, it was also characterized by variety. To meet their needs, parents used whatever means they had at their command: it might be a governess or a grammar school or a mercan-

tile academy; it might be a private-venture teacher, a Sunday school, or a school established and maintained by neighbourhood co-operation. By modern standards at least, the kinds of institutions that existed were remarkable for their heterogeneity in origin, financing, and purpose.

Colonial education was also characterized by its close links with the churches. Most denominations claimed the historic right to supervise the education of their members, and most needed institutions to train local people for both clerical and lay leadership. Hence it was the churches that founded the first colonial colleges, and their clergymen served as teachers in the early colleges, grammar schools, and academies. Some denominations, moreover–especially the Roman Catholic church–also attempted to maintain their own parish schools to provide an elementary education closely tied to religious teaching.

Finally, colonial education was characterized by the limited role of the state. Governments might reserve land or provide other means of endowing schools. They might provide the legal framework for the work of the churches or the local community in education. They might provide financial assistance to particular institutions, or even make regular annual grants to certain kinds of schools. Such measures were common in all the colonies by the early nineteenth century; indeed, they were perhaps inevitable in a new country where neither the churches nor the local communities were wealthy enough to support education by themselves. Nonetheless, governments did not administer or regulate education in the modern sense, nor did they take the initiative in establishing educational institutions. Their role was generally limited to

A. The Purposes of Schooling

assisting local initiative rather than providing leadership or control of educational development.

The documents in this chapter are designed to illustrate these common characteristics of early colonial education as it took root between the seventeenth and the early nineteenth century: its voluntarism, its variety, and the role of both governments and churches.

Why were schools established and maintained, often at considerable sacrifice and effort, in New France or in early British North America? One answer to that question was that education, and especially advanced education, was necessary to produce a civilized and competent elite, equipped to preserve and extend Christian civilization in the new world. The kind of education necessary to produce competent leaders was best described by Thomas McCulloch, a Presbyterian clergyman and teacher in early Nova Scotia (document A.1).

To preserve and extend a culture meant, in part at least, to preserve and extend its political institutions; and education, both elementary and advanced, could be a potent weapon in that struggle. It could, for example, help to secure British hegemony over a newly conquered French population (document A.2); equally, it could act as a bulwark against the infiltration of American republicanism and democracy into British North America (document A.3).

Schooling could also serve as a handmaiden of religion. Whether it was teaching the three Rs, or offering a more sophisticated level of learning, the churches considered education a means of promoting piety and winning converts (documents A.4 and A.5).

Clergymen, politicians, or editors were always more explicit about the purposes of schooling than the majority of people in the society. But the expectations of one small group of Upper Canadian villagers, and the curriculum necessary to achieve those expectations, are illustrated by their contract with a teacher in 1826 (document A.6).

A.1 The Nature and Uses of a Liberal Education

The original conformation and state of the human mind, connected with the peculiarity of those circumstances in which man is placed, evidently show that he has been designed for intellectual and moral improvement. Whether he possesses any innate sentiment or principle of knowledge, has been long the subject of philosophical dispute: But, that, in the first stages of his existence, he is destitute of that knowledge and government of himself, which are necessary for his preservation, good conduct, and happiness in life, has never been denied. With numerous wants and an important station in the scale of being assigned him, he neither knows how the first may be supplied, nor the ends and purposes of the last, fulfilled.

Under these disadvantages, however, the human mind possesses the *stamina* of subsequent improvements. Its operations indicate a susceptibility of receiving impressions and also a desire to receive them; and to supply its original want of intelligence and qualify itself for a course of activity and happiness, is the original tendency of these operations. In the structure of mind a principle of curiosity constitutes a prominent feature; and, in connexion with this principle, it is susceptible of various modes of acting which tend to gratify curiosity by the acquisition of knowledge.

. . . .

But, though the situation of every human being renders the acquisition of a certain degree of intelligence and activity unavoidable; no individual can, by his own observation and experience, acquire that intellectual and moral improvement for which man is designed. Besides, in the

A.1 Source: Thomas McCulloch, *The Nature and Uses of a Liberal Education* (Halifax, 1819), pp. 3-23

first stages of existence, a variety of circumstances combine to abstract attention from improvement to pleasure, and thus, to impede the enlargement of the intellectual faculties and deprave the heart. To guard against these evils, therefore, divine wisdom has placed man, during the early period of life, in a state of dependence; that the knowledge of parents might promote the improvement of children, and the wisdom of age counteract the follies of youth.

Accordingly, in all ages, this general arrangement of providence has been well understood. Wherever society has existed, the education of youth has been viewed as involving in it alike the improvement of the individual and the prosperity of the whole; and where public arrangements have been regulated by enlightened views, it has uniformly received a corresponding degree of attention. It may be also observed, that, in every age and country, the object of education has been radically the same. Considering the susceptibility of the human mind to receive impressions, it has been conducted upon the principle of removing from the presence of youth every thing tending to depravity of disposition, and of exhibiting whatever appeared to be good and useful and calculated to encourage imitation.

. . . .

In tracing the progress of education, the effects resulting from the invention of letters and the art of printing, ought not to be overlooked. By these means, the information of past ages is transmitted to the present; and every additional discovery and invention, communicated with ease to the various sections of civilized society. As tending to the diffusion of knowledge, therefore, their influence upon the intellectual and moral character of man, must have been great and important. Besides, wherever they have been introduced, they also appear to have altered considerably the object of public instruction. It thence became the employment of teachers to communicate to their pupils not only the principles of knowledge, but also those qualifications which might afford them access to the sources of intelligence, and enable them to transfer their knowledge to others: and, accordingly, reading, writing, and a few additional branches of learning most immediately connected with the ordinary business of life, everywhere constitute the general system of public education.

No civilized nation, however, has been satisfied with this degree of instruction. Both the wants of society, and that enlargement of the desire of knowledge which uniformly attends the diffusion of intelligence, have rendered an extension of the system of education a necessary appendage to the social state. To this object, accordingly, enlightened individuals and governments have turned their attention and founded seminaries, in which youth might receive a liberal education: and wherever such institutions have flourished, they have been viewed as ornaments of society and tests of the wisdom of those who maintained them, as barriers against barbarism, and the best rational means for the improvement of the world.

. . . .

Before proceeding to illustrate this subject, it might, perhaps, be requisite to specify in what a liberal education consists. But, without attempting to define a term which includes a variety of parts so extensive, at present I would only observe, that it denotes instruction in those branches of learning which are contemplated in this, and usually taught in similar, institutions. Its primary object is knowledge which could not be easily acquired in any other way: its ends, the improvement of man in intelligence and moral principle, as the basis of his subsequent duty and happiness. Viewing its object as knowledge, it is merely an enlargement of that system of discipline which commences its operation upon man with the first expansion of his intellectual powers. With respect to its ends, whether it be entitled to a high appreciation, must be ascertained by its utility.

. . . .

In society there are certain employments which have been denominated the learned professions; because a liberal education has been generally conceived to be requisite in order to a becoming discharge of their corresponding duties. These professions as they regard the protection of property, the preservation of health, and the moral excellence and happiness of man, are important in their objects. Whether they ought to be distinct offices, and as such, require a preparatory course of education, will best appear from a consideration of their nature: and I shall first direct your attention to the profession of the law.

. . . .

Many…circumstances which render an honourable practice of the law perplexing, might be enumerated. It is influenced by a multiplicity of particulars which escape the general observation of mankind. This might be illustrated by a reference to its forms and modes of expression, or to the fluctuating nature of customs and language. It might be shown from the frequency with which legal proceedings require, not merely an acquaintance with the principles of law, but, a knowledge of general science, chronology, and various other kinds of intelligence which comparatively few can attain: Or, I might turn your attention to that acuteness of thought, precision of language, and facility of expression, which those who must encounter the prejudiced and villainous part of the community, need. But it has already been sufficiently shown, that the profession of the law requires a species of knowledge which the greater part of mankind have neither leisure nor opportunity to obtain. This, then, will conduct us to the following conclusions: That the profession of the law as a distinct office is necessary; and that the education which qualifies for the discharge of its duties, is of essential importance to the interests of society.

Our attention may be next directed to the medical profession. Upon this part of the subject, however, few observations are requisite. The greater part of mankind are prone to prescribe; and, when assailed by disease, they are usually disposed to listen to advice. This originates in a persuasion that the aid of others may promote the restoration of health. Whether this object be entitled to a distinct office, will best appear by considering what knowledge is necessary in order to successfull practice.

That surgical operations require an acquaintance with the structure of the human frame and with the subsequent treatment of wounds, is sufficiently obvious: and it is, I believe, usually admitted, that the former cannot be accurately acquired without actual dissection. It is no less obvious, that, in order to a successful treatment of disease in general, the exact nature and stage of each, and also the composition and powers of medicine, must be ascertained. Judicious prescription, therefore, must be preceded by intelligence, various in its nature and remote from ordinary observation.

. . . .

In directing your attention next to the clerical office, I may observe that its existence as a separate employment in society, has not been left to human determination. Revealed religion has prescribed the offices of the church; and, consequently, in this case, duty consists in the observance of appointed order. It must be remarked, however, that scripture has established an inseparable connexion between qualification and office: a public instructor in the church must be *apt to teach*. This prerequisite, you will perceive, includes two particulars: He must be a man of information, and also possess a facility of communicating knowledge.

. . . .

The question, then, is not, whether a minister of the gospel need education, but, to what extent it is necessary; and every judicious clergyman, either self-taught or educated by others, will acquiesce in the remark, that, without extensive studies, adequate preparation for public teaching cannot be attained. This might be illustrated by showing you how a knowledge of various languages and of almost every other branch of literature, tends to the elucidation of Scripture; but, at present, I shall restrict myself to an illustration, the force of which you are more likely to feel. In a public teacher the power of communication is as requisite as the possession of knowledge; and when you consider the ends of religion, you will easily perceive, that accuracy of statement is vastly important. But where there is knowledge, a facility of communication is not always its attendant.–Were I to ask you, then, how this is attained, experience has prepared you to reply, only by years of painful application, aided alike by instruction and criticism.

Having taken this view of the learned professions, the additional remark, that a liberal education confers the intelligence requisite for the discharge of their various duties, would sufficiently show its importance. But, as the general scope of an academical course, is not well understood, it may not be unnecessary to state a few particulars respecting its nature and influence, and the mode in which it is conducted.

It is, I believe, generally imagined, that to communicate a knowledge of particulars which could not be easily obtained by any other means, is the principal design of the system of liberal education. But this constitutes only the minor part of its advantages; and were a student to leave College without any other acquisition, he would find himself exceedingly ill qualified for discharging the duties of a learned profession. The following observations will show you that it embraces a much more extensive range.

The object of education is not merely knowledge but science.

You are already aware, that, in the expansion of human intellect, individual objects and circumstances are the first materials of knowledge; and also, that, when the knowledge of these is attained, it conducts the mind to a species of intelligence, related to the individuals and yet distinct in its nature. A comparison of these having discovered their common quality, terms applicable to a whole genus and species, are introduced into language; and when a term of this kind is compared with its general quality, the knowledge of an abstract truth or principle is obtained. These principles are the primary objects of science, which, in its various parts, constitutes the material of a learned education. This, as it communicates knowledge, is valuable; but, as presenting knowledge in a scientific form, it is entitled to a higher appreciation. A general principle applies equally to what passes within our own observation and to every other case of the same nature. This might be illustrated by a reference to any department of science: but you already know the logical axiom, that whatever is true of the genus is true of the subordinate species and individuals. A liberal education, then, not only brings into view the knowledge of individual facts, but presents them arranged and classified

under general principles; and by these means knowledge is more easily retained; progress facilitated; and the basis of subsequent improvement, laid.

. . . .

Having made these remarks respecting the nature and influence of a liberal education, I may further observe, that, in the disposition of its parts, it is adapted to the gradual improvement of the mind. I have made this observation, particularly with the view of adverting to some branches of literature, which, as not bearing directly upon the business of a learned profession, have been conceived by many to be unnecessary additions. Of this number is the study of the ancient languages.

It is, I apprehend, the opinion of those who are unfriendly to the study of ancient languages, that it merely affords a knowledge of the words and modes of expression employed by particular nations. Admitting this to be the case, it may be very easily shown that this knowledge leads to important consequences. I have already observed, that, in order to entertain just views of a liberal education, it is necessary to consider man as a link in the chain of existence, equally connected with the past and succeeding ages. Now, it is upon an acquaintance with the past that present conduct is founded; and, consequently, the more extensive this knowledge is, the greater must be the intelligence of the mind. If any individual can, to his own experience, add the information acquired by others during former ages; his knowledge must be both more abundant and better established: and by the study of ancient languages, these ends are gained. By these means we associate, as it were, with the nations who used them; enter into their various transactions; mark their improvement in the arts and sciences; ascertain the nature of their religion, modes of living, and laws; and, thus, trace their progress from barbarism to a state of refinement. Such researches, beside the gratification which they afford to an inquisitive mind, promote individual intelligence, and, frequently, the improvement of the social state.

With respect to the Hebrew and Greek languages, I would merely remark, that no person who entertains just views of the nature of language, can conceive a knowledge of these to be of trivial importance to those persons whose office requires them to elucidate the scriptures. Upon the subject of the Latin, however, a few additional observations are requisite; because the study of this language being more general, is more frequently opposed. Premising, therefore, that opposition to this part of a liberal education, has usually proceeded from inadequate judges, I shall state to you some of those advantages which the study confers.

From knowledge acquired in the progress of education you are already aware, that, at one period, the power of the Romans, connected with their superior attainments in science and the arts of life, extended their language to almost every country of Europe. Wherever that nation enlarged their domain, they also endeavoured to introduce their improvements; and the introduction of their language to a certain extent, followed as an unavoidable consequence. It, thence, became partly the medium of social intercourse, and a necessary means for the acquisition of knowledge. Besides, the nations of Europe, at that time emerging from a state of barbarism, were destitute of terms, by which an enlarged system of knowledge could be expressed. On this account, along with the intelligence of the Romans, their language was also adopted; and, for many centuries, became the language of law, medicine, religion, and literature. This

measure, you will easily perceive, must have impeded the cultivation of modern languages; but its utility for the general diffusion of knowledge, has still continued its use to a certain extent in every European nation. From these remarks it is evident, that to the professional man who would secure to himself the intelligence of former ages or of distant nations, an acquaintance with this language must be a valuable attainment. Besides, it may be observed, that by custom its terms and modes of expression are so interwoven with the business of the learned professions, that the professional man who has not received this branch of education, can neither acquire nor communicate his knowledge with ease and advantage.

. . . .

From these remarks you will perceive the importance of this part of learning. At the same time they tend to illustrate the general point, that a liberal education in the disposition of its parts, is adapted to the gradual expansion of the intellectual powers. To this subject I would particularly direct your attention; because it is not in general considered according to its importance. Were the relation which the different parts of learning bear to the progressive enlargement of mind better understood; the general system of education, instead of meeting reproach, would, I am persuaded, be viewed with admiration, as a structure reared by the wisdom of ages. The profound speculations of science are, from their nature, not easily comprehended. To persons, therefore, who have not been habituated to observe that close connexion of thought which such investigations require, they must appear doubly intricate. Besides, it may be observed, that science as well as art, has its appropriate terms; and, consequently, ignorance of scientific terms behoved to increase their perplexity. But to obviate these difficulties, the arrangements of a liberal education are such, that the previous parts confer both a species of knowledge, and a degree of intelligence, which constitute a useful introduction to those that succeed. It is not necessary that I illustrate this remark by particular examples. You have only to consider what knowledge a learned profession requires, and by what means it may be most easily attained; and you will perceive that the introductory parts of a liberal education are of essential importance for the improvement of the mind, and also for the acquisition of that knowledge which bears upon the business of life.

. . . .

But beside the consideration of public utility, a liberal education is attended by many other consequences which render it a desirable attainment. The acquisition of knowledge is not without pain; but this is more than counterbalanced by those numerous sources of enjoyment which it unfolds to the mind: and intellectual pleasure is a species of gratification which few who feel, are willing to resign. Nor ought it to be overlooked, that intelligence, by enlarging the sphere of usefulness, amplifies also the pleasure of doing good. Besides, education communicates a dignity to the human character, which neither rank nor wealth is sufficient to purchase; and it may be farther observed, that, in this province, it presents prospects well calculated to concentrate the energies of your minds upon literary studies. The present state of the learned professions affords extensive scope to men of talents and literature. Various causes have as yet combined to impede the progress of education; and these offices have not been always filled by persons qualified to occupy stations so important. But this province now exhibits many proofs of a desire for literary improvement;

and very soon, in this as in other countries, ignorance will find its own station; and natural abilities cultivated by literary studies, raise their possessors to the first rank in society and to the principal offices of honour and profit.

A.2   The Political Role of Education

This is a letter from the British government to the Society for the Propagation of the Gospel regarding the provision of ministers and schoolteachers for one of the first English settlements in Nova Scotia. The S.P.G. was an Anglican missionary society.

To the Revd. Dr. Bearcroft,
Secry to the Society for the
Propagation of the Gospel in
Foreign Parts

Sir,

His Majesty having given Direction that a Number of persons should be sent to the Province of Nova Scotia in North America; I am directed by my Lords Commissioners for Trade and Plantations, to desire you will acquaint the Society for the Propagation of the Gospel in Foreign Parts, that it is proposed to settle the said Persons in six Townships, and that a particular Spot will be set apart in each of them for building a Church, and four hundred acres of Land adjacent thereto granted in perpetuity, free from the payment of any Quit Rent, to a Minister and his Successors, and two hundred in like manner to a Schoolmaster, their Lordships therefore recommend to the Society to name a Minister and School-master for each of the said Townships, hoping that they will give such En-

A.2 Source: Public Archives of Canada, MG11, A33, vol. 1432,
        Lords Commissioners for Trade to the Secretary,
        S.P.G., 6 April 1749.

couragement to them as the Society shall think proper until their Lands can be so far cultivated as to afford a Sufficient Support.

· ·

Their Lordships think proper that the Society should be informed that all the Inhabitants (except the Garrison of Annapolis) of the said Province, amounting to twenty thousand are French Roman Catholicks, and that there are a great Number of Priests resident among them who Act under the Directions of the French Bishop of Quebec.

At the same time their Lordships would recommend it to the consideration of the Society whether it may not be advisable among those to be sent to choose some among others of the Ministers and School-masters who by speaking the French Language may be particularly useful in cultivating a Sense of the true Protestant Religion among the said Inhabitants and educating their children in the Principles thereof.

I am
    Sir,
Your most obedient
    Humble Servant
[Signed] I. Pownall
Sollr. and Clerk of the Reports

Whitehall
April 6th 1749

A.3 The Political Importance of a University for Upper Canada

I have the honour to state, for Your Excellency's information, some of the reasons which, in my humble opinion, render it highly important that immediate steps should be taken to found

A.3 Source: Public Archives of Canada, RG5, AI, vol. 77, John Strachan to Lieutenant-Governor Maitland, 10 March 1826.

a University in this Province; and, as Your Excellency has also been pleased to call upon me to suggest what I consider to be in the power of His Majesty's Government towards commencing an Institution by which the youth now growing up in the Colony may have an opportunity of finishing their education under teachers of approved ability and tried attachment to the Parent State and the Established Church, I take the liberty to point out the way by which means may be obtained for accomplishing so desirable an object.

· ·

There is not, in either Province, any English Seminary above the rank of a good school, at which a liberal education can be obtained. Thus, the youth of nearly 300,000 Englishmen have no opportunity of receiving instruction within the Canadas in Law, Medicine or Divinity. The consequence is that many young men, coming forward to the learned professions, are obliged to look beyond the Province for the last two years of their education–undoubtedly the most important and critical of their lives. Very few are able, on account of the great expense, to go to England or Scotland; and the distance is so great, and the difficulties so many, that parental anxiety reluctantly trusts children so far from its observation and control. The youth are, therefore, in some degree compelled to look forward to the United States, where the means of education, though of a description far inferior to those of Great Britain, are yet superior to those within the Province, and a growing necessity is arising of sending them to finish their education in that country. Now, in the United States, a system prevails, unknown to, or unpractised, by any other nation. In all other countries morals and religion are made the basis of future instruction, and the first book put into the hands of children teach them the domestic, the social and the religious virtues; but in the United States politics pervade the whole system of instruction. The school books, from the very first elements, are stuffed with praises of their own institutions and breathe hatred to everything English. To such a country our youth may go, strongly attached to their native land and to all its establishments, but, by hearing them continually depreciated, and those of America praised, these attachments will, in many, be gradually weakened, and some may become fascinated with that liberty which has degenerated into licentiousness, and imbibe, perhaps, unconsciously, sentiments unfriendly to things of which Englishmen are proud. It is, indeed, easy to perceive the danger of sending our most prominent youth to a country to finish their education where they hear nothing in praise of their native land, and where everything bespeaks hatred and defiance, where her merits are considered defects, and all her noblest virtues and glories soiled by the poison of calumny; nor can it be expected that any of them, on their return, will give up their hearts and affections to their parent state with the same cordiality that they would have done had they been carefully nurtured within the British Dominions. What, indeed, can be more important to the true prosperity of the Province than the careful education of its youth? In what other way can we ever obtain a well instructed population by which to preserve our excellent Constitution and our connection with the British Empire, and give that respectable character to the country which arises from an intelligent magistracy, and from having public situations filled with men of ability and information? What has already been done to effect this purpose is highly creditable to the Province. The two primary steps have been taken, and the third, though the most important, is

opposed by no serious impediments which may not, it is hoped, be removed by Your Excellency, who has nothing more seriously at heart than the promotion of religion and education throughout the Province.

A.4 The Schools of the Sisters of Notre Dame

François, by the grace of God and of the Holy See, first Bishop of Quebec.
To all the faithful of New France, Greetings in Our Lord.

Our very dear daughter Marguerite Bourgeois, and our daughters living with her in the same community on the Island of Montreal, have informed us that they have served us without remuneration for several years as school mistresses on the said island of Montreal and in other places, bringing up young girls in the fear of God and the practice of Christian virtues, teaching them to read and write, and other things within their capabilities; that, following our authorization of 20 May 1669, they obtained *lettres d'établissement* from His Majesty dated the month of May 1671, confirmed by the Parliament of Paris, registered with the sovereign council of this country and in the registry of the clerk of the Island of Montreal; that they would be sufficiently supported and could subsist on the small farms and revenue they possess and by the work of their hands, without becoming a charge upon anyone; that they offer to work gratuitously as school mistresses on the island of Montreal or in other places where teachers are needed and which could provide the necessities of life for a school mistress, wherever we and our successors

A.4 Source: Proclamation of the Bishop of Quebec, 1676. H. Têtu and C.-O. Gagnon, eds., *Mandements, lettres pastorales, et circulaires des évêques de Québec* (Québec, 1887), vol. I, 99-100.

think necessary for the good of this Church; their hope is that it might please us to contribute to the stability of their establishment by giving it our approval, thus permitting them to continue their lives as school mistresses and to live together as Lay Sisters of the Congregation of Notre Dame, observing the rules that it might please us and our successors to prescribe.

After close consideration of the facts and realizing that the sound education of our children is one of the greatest things we can procure for the Church, and the best way of preserving and augmenting piety within Christian families; recognizing also the favour shown by our Lord in the past to Sister Bourgeois and her companions in their said duties in the schools where they have been employed, and wishing to encourage their zeal and contribute to their pious plan in any way within our power;

We have approved of in the past and do continue to approve of the establishment of the said Sister Bourgeois and her present companions and any future companions, thus permitting them to live within the community as Lay Sisters of the Congregation of Notre Dame, observing all regulations set down by us, and to continue their functions as school mistresses on the Island of Montreal or wherever we judge it necessary to send them, without their being able, at some future time, to claim to enter the religious life, which would be counter to our intentions and the hoped for conclusion of providing instruction for the children in rural parishes, in compliance with the letters patent granted Sister Bourgeois by His Majesty.

Delivered in Quebec under the seal and signature of ourselves and our secretary the sixth day of August, in the year sixteen hundred and seventy-six.

François, Bishop of Quebec.

A view of the Jesuit College and Church in Quebec City, c.1761.

A.5 Religion and Literacy: The Work of the Society for the Propagation of the Gospel in Foreign Parts

George Archbold, a missionary for the Society for the Propagation of the Gospel, is writing to ask for an increased stipend for his catechist.

The services that Mr. Milkham performed are of the most important kind, namely teaching children to read, since he has been here he has taught 170 children (most of whom commenced with him without a knowledge of the alphabet) to read the scriptures accompanied by catechetical instruction. The duty I required of him to perform is one of the most laborious and irksome kind that anyone could be engaged in for I think no drudgery can equal that of beginning with children from the alphabet–yet I found this much must be done or I could not get on–I felt I could not carry religion into the families of my Dutch parishioners, most of whom seem unable to read and whose associations and worldly propensities prevent them from paying a schoolmaster to instruct their children.... The result of my plan is now before you–a number of children have been instructed in the way that maketh wise unto salvation, the majority of whom belong to our church, who, except they had the advantage of a free school, would at this moment be utterly ignorant. It would have been a much easier task for Mr. Milkham to have gone from house to house exhorting and administering and reading to the people but what impression would this course produce amongst the ignorant and illiterate? none whatever–I clearly perceived that when the heads of families are unlettered they could only be reached through their children who must be taught to read in order to become proper mediums.... I employ a Schoolmaster in the Town at my own expense, to keep a School in a house which I leased, for the most part, out of my own funds. There are now in attendance from 40 to 50 boys daily–These are under my own eye–and the religious instruction imparted to them is from myself.

A.5 Source: Public Archives of Canada, S.P.G., "C" Mss., Archbold to the Bishop of Quebec, Cornwall (Upper Canada), 2 April 1838.

A.6 The Establishment of an Upper Canadian Common School, 1826

Contract between teacher and subscribers, 2 October 1826. Probably Charlotteville, Norfolk County, Ontario.

We the undersigned being deeply impressed with the necessity and utility of giving our children an education, by which they will be enabled to read the word of God and transact their own business–And being desirous and anxious of having a school taught for that desirable purpose –Therefore we mutually agree to engage C. D. Shiemerhorn to teach said school in a house built for that purpose in our district near Mr. Fairchilds for the term of six months–Said Scheimerhorn is to teach the different branches of *reading, writing, Arithmetic* and *english* Grammar if all are required–And as a compensation for his labors, We promise to pay him the sum of two dollars in grain per quarter for every schollar and the government money–Good and merchantable wheat to be valued at 6/N.Y. Cur. per bushel– It is to be remembered that said Scheimerhorn is to board himself during the term and as soon as the adequate number of schollars are procured he will commence the task of taking charge of children committed to him for instruction.

A.6 Source: Collection of the Norfolk Historical Society, pp. 2761-62.

B. Varieties of Early Schooling

What kind of schools were established in New France and in early British North America? Advanced education, in French Canada, was provided by the classical college. The natural way in which these institutions, like others, were transferred from the old world to the new is suggested by a comment of the superior of the Jesuit College at Quebec in 1711 (document B.1). The establishment of one of these colleges, its curriculum, and means of financial support are described in more detail in document B.2. The equivalent institutions in English Canada were the grammar schools and the universities–the former laying the foundation for an advanced education and the latter completing it. Documents B.3 and B.4 offer examples of attempts to create both grammar schools and colleges in late eighteenth-century Nova Scotia.

The classical college, the grammar school, and the university, however, catered only to a tiny minority of the population. Most children received their education, if they received any at all, in other kinds of schools. In both French and English Canada the most accessible school was usually the local common or parish school–that is, a school that taught the common branches of an English or French education: reading, writing, and arithmetic. It was usually begun through local initiative by a priest or clergyman or by a group of interested parents. Sometimes it was connected to the local church and supervised by the clergy or the parish council; sometimes it was non-denominational, a necessary compromise in a religiously mixed community. Its main source of financial support was usually voluntary subscription tuition fees. By the second or third decades of the nineteenth century, however, it was likely to receive a small grant from the government of the colony. The way in which many of these schools were locally organized, as well as the role of the government grant in maintaining them, is illustrated in document B.5, one of the early colonial elementary school acts.

Because of the thinness of settlement in most parts of rural New France or British North America, there was no alternative to the common or parish school; for better or worse, it was the only institution available. In the villages and towns, however, a variety of schools serving a multitude of purposes took root. Throughout New France's history, the religious orders provided much of the elementary and advanced education available –one early example was the work of the Sisters of Notre Dame, already introduced in the previous section of this chapter (document A.4). Private-venture schools flourished in most of the larger towns and villages, providing the appropriate education for girls and training boys in the skills of the counting-house, surveying, navigation, or engineering (documents B.6 and B.7). An alternative to the private-venture school was the joint-stock academy established by a group of subscribers (document B.8). Sometimes schools that began as a result of private or local initiative were later sustained through special government grants–for example, the early boarding school in the Red River colony, considered in document B.9. For those who could not, or would not, send their children to a day school, there were the Sunday schools, which in the early decades of the nineteenth century often taught reading as well as religion. And there was that most traditional of means, the apprenticeship indenture, which might include provision for the child to be taught the three Rs

"March of Intellect", an early common school in Adelaide Township, Ontario, sketched in 1845 by William Elliott, District Superintendent of Schools.

St. Paul's Church, parsonage and school house, Red River Settlement, 1858.

as well as a trade (document B.10). If anything characterized early colonial schooling, it was voluntarism and variety–the absence of universality, and the lack of uniformity in purposes, methods of provision, and means of finance.

B.1 The Transfer of Institutions
This is an extract from a letter written in 1711 by Father Joseph Germain, the Superior of the Jesuit College, on the state of the Canadian mission. The Jesuits founded the College at Quebec in 1635.

As regards the Quebec college, everything exists or is Done there as in our colleges in Europe –and perhaps with greater regularity, exactness, and Fruit than in many of our colleges in France. Classes are taught here in grammar, the humanities, rhetoric, mathematics, Philosophy, and Theology. The Pupils, although less numerous than in the large towns of Europe, nevertheless possess well-informed bodies and well-regulated minds; they are very industrious, Very docile, and capable of Making great progress in the study of letters and of virtue. I speak not of the savage children, whom our fathers educate in our missions; they likewise are not wanting in cleverness, and fail not to serve God well in their own manner of speaking and of living, according to their custom. But I refer to the French Children born in Canada, who speak the same language, who wear the same kind of clothes, and who follow the same studies as those in Paris. I say that they are very intelligent, have excellent dispositions, and are capable of succeeding well in everything that we can teach them.

B.1 Source: R. G. Thwaites, ed., *The Jesuit Relations and Allied Documents,* vol. 66, 209-11.

B.2 The Classical College at Nicolet
To His Excellency, Lieutenant General Sir John Coape Sherbrooke…

The humble petition of Joseph Octave Plessis, Catholic Bishop of Quebec, who respectfully submits it to Your Excellency.

When he took possession of his church in 1806, he found in his parish of Nicolet, District of Three Rivers, Province of Lower Canada, a newly-founded seminary begun partly through the efforts of his predecessor.

Realizing that there was no other establishment of this kind yet in the District of Three Rivers and that the children of this district had to go to seminaries in either Quebec or Montreal at great expense if they wanted an education, he believed it his duty to pay particular attention to this seminary and its advancement. In very few years he managed to gather enough teachers to give the children a general education.

The children are well instructed in the French, Latin, and English languages, geography, history, literature, poetry, rhetoric, philosophy, mathematics, and starting this year, Greek.

Upon leaving this school, as is the case upon leaving the seminaries of Quebec and Montreal, the pupils are capable of pursuing the profession they choose, be it the church, law, medicine, navigation, land-surveying, business, etc.

Your petitioner has supported this seminary until now and has enlarged its facilities so that there is now room for seventy boarders. He has been able to do this by being very careful and thrifty, and through the contributions of his friends and his own savings.

B.2 Source: Public Archives of Canada, C.O. 42/175, Sherbrooke to Bathurst, 16 November 1817, Encl: Memorial of Bishop J. O. Plessis, 27 October 1817.

Several citizens have let him know that, through larger contributions, they would furnish sufficient funds for an endowment for this seminary if they could see it firmly established by letters patent from His Majesty.

To facilitate obtaining these letters patent, your petitioner is willing to donate to the school, the house that the seminary is presently using. He acquired this property with his own money in the parish of Nicolet and it and its outbuildings are now valued at not less than three thousand pounds Provincial currency.

To begin the said endowment fund, your petitioner would also give the seminary, after paying the indemnity to the local seigneur, an extent of land of about two hundred and fifty acres, which also belongs to him in the said parish of Nicolet. A considerable portion of this land is under cultivation.

The humble desire of your petitioner is that the fund be administered and the education in the seminary be directed hereafter by a corporation of five members or trustees, composed of the Catholic Bishop of Quebec, his coadjutor, the Vicar General of the District of Three Rivers, the curé of the parish of Nicolet, and the eldest of the other curés in the District of Three Rivers, and by those who will succeed them in their respective posts.

These trustees should be authorized to acquire in the name of the seminary sufficient funds to give it an annual revenue of two thousand, five hundred pounds currency without ever exceeding that amount, to which end its records of receipts and expenditures should be inspected annually or triennially by such officers or agents as are duly appointed by His Majesty or by his representative in this Province.

Being more convinced than anyone of Your Excellency's lively interest in the progress of education and in the advancement of His Majesty's subjects in this province, your petitioner dares hope that Your Excellency will be willing to send this petition to the foot of the throne of His Majesty and obtain the requested letters. And your petitioner never ceases to pray etc. etc. etc.

Signed: J. O. Plessis
Quebec, 27 October, 1817.

B.3 The Founding of the Halifax Grammar School, 1789

This document originally appeared as an advertisement in a Halifax newspaper.

The provision which the wisdom of the Legislature has lately made for the foundation and support of a college in this province gives pleasure to every liberal mind and will certainly be followed by the most desirable effects. But there are still wanting inferior seminaries to prepare and qualify Youth for admission into the principal one, and to furnish such as pretend not to a complete collegiate education, with cheap and convenient means of attaining such useful knowledge as their future destination in life may admit or require.

It was matter of much regret in particular that in the very Capital of the Province no school hath been established for these purposes upon a plan sufficiently extensive or with adequate support. With a view to remedy this defect and in conformity with an Act of the Legislature formerly passed his Excellency the Lieutenant-Governor has been pleased to Nominate the Honourable Henry Newton, the Honourable

B.3 Source: Reprinted in J. W. Logan, "A History of the Halifax Grammar School...", *Nova Scotia Historical Society Collections*, vol. 23 (1934-36), 119-21.

Thomas Cochran, James Brenton, John Newton and Richard John Uniacke, Esqrs., as Trustees of a Grammar school forthwith to be erected in this town. These gentlemen have chosen Mr. William Cochran, formerly of Trinity College, Dublin, and lately professor of the Greek and Latin languages in the College at New York to be Master, Mr. George Glennie who was regularly educated in the University of Aberdeen to be Usher, and Mr. Thomas Brown, already well known in this place as an eminent writing master to be teacher of writing, Arithmetic, and Mathematics.

It is thought proper to give this early notification to the Public that until a suitable building can be provided the school will be opened without delay in the room where the Assembly of this Province meet, where youth will be instructed with the utmost assiduity and care in the English, French, Latin and Greek languages grammatically and from the first rudiments in writing, arithmetic, algebra and Geometry, with all the practical branches in the Mathematics, in Geography and the use of the globes with the art of constructing maps, and if it be required, in Astronomy, and Natural philosophy.

Particular care will be taken to train up the pupils in a just pronunciation and graceful elocution, for which purpose they will be frequently made to rehearse the Choicest pieces of English eloquence. There will be two public examinations of the school every year upon which occasions premiums will be given to those who excel in their respective classes. Several oratorical exercises will be performed and a separate premium given to the best speaker. The morals and health of the youth will be anxiously watched and the most unremitting exertions will be made to render this seminary a general benefit and worthy the patronage of the Public.

N.B. A dancing-master and music-master will attend those whose parents desire it.

B.4 The Need for a University in Nova Scotia, 1783

This is a letter from several of the leading political figures in Nova Scotia to Sir Guy Carleton, the Commander-in-Chief of the British forces in North America.

New York, October 18th, 1783.

Sir,–The province of Nova Scotia has been an object of great national importance, and as your Excellency's thoughts have been lately and are still engaged about measures to promote its population, prosperity and internal happiness, we flatter ourselves that a proposal which may contribute to the same salutary purposes will meet your approbation. The founding of a Colledge or Seminary of learning on a liberal plan in that province, where youth may receive a virtuous education and can be qualified for the learned professions, is, we humbly conceive, a measure of the greatest consequence, as it would diffuse religious literature, loyalty and good morals among His Majesty's subjects there.

. . . .

The plan that may be proper to adopt for this college, and the necessary regulations to support its credit and insure the benefits which may be expected from it, will require the maturest deliberation, and therefore it would be premature in the present stage of the business, and trespassing on your Excellency's time, to dwell minutely on the subject. Permit us to observe briefly, that so far as circumstances will admit, provision should be made for a president, for able professors in the different branches of

B.4 Source: Public Archives of Canada, MG11, N.S. A103, Carleton to Secretary of State Townshend, 24 November 1783.

science, and for a good grammar school, so that young gentlemen who are educated in this seminary and receive the usual degrees in the liberal arts, may be duly qualified for those degrees and for the professions to which their genius may respectively lead them.

The principal difficulty, and what calls for immediate attention, is to procure and establish funds that shall be adequate to these purposes, and here we conceive that recourse, in the first instance, should be had to government, whose interests will be essentially served, and whose countenance and aid may therefore be reasonably expected in founding and endowing this seminary.

If government should once patronize the scheme other sources of support will not be wanting. There are in Great Britain and Ireland many generous friends of science who, from motives of public spirit, will doubtless contribute to the design. When the business is brought forward it may be presumed that the Legislature of Nova Scotia, sensible of the many advantages which that province must derive from the institution, will afford it every aid in their power, and in the meantime lands might be appropriated there to the use of a college, and located in such a manner that they would rise in value and be productive of an annual income.

These short hints are, with deference, submitted to your Excellency as the best bridge of the steps that should be taken for accomplishing this desirable object, consistently with the enlarged and beneficent views of government respecting that province.

We have the honor to be, Sir,
Your Excellency's most obedient and most humble servants,

Charles Inglis,   Benjamin Moore,
H. Addison,   Charles Mongan,
Jonathan Odell,

To His Excellency Sir Guy Carleton.

B.5 An Act for Encouraging the Establishment of Schools throughout the Province: Nova Scotia, 1811.

WHEREAS *it is highly advantageous to the Youth of this Province, to afford them easy means of acquiring useful Knowledge in those essential parts of general education which are necessary to persons of every rank and station in civilized society; for obtaining therefore an object so desirable:*

Be it enacted by the Lieutenant-Governor, Council, and Assembly, That it shall and may be lawful for the Inhabitants, being Freeholders, or having an income, in real or personal Estate, of Forty shillings a year at the least, of such Townships, Districts or Settlements, in this Province, as may be desirous to have such Schools established therein, if such Township, District or Settlement, consist of thirty families or householders, to assemble on the first Monday in April or November, annually, during the continuance of this Act, for the purpose of voting, subscribing or raising, money, for the establishment and support of schools within such Township, District or Settlement, to the end that the Youth may be taught Orthography, Reading, Writing, and Arithmetic: *Provided nevertheless,* That the money so voted or subscribed shall not exceed two hundred pounds, nor less than fifty pounds, for one year, and if voted, it shall be by a majority of the inhabitants or householders then present being freeholders, or having an income of forty shillings a year, in real or personal estate, and

B.5 Source: *The Nova Scotia Royal Gazette*, 5 June 1811.

shall be assessed and collected in like manner as poor rates are by Law assessed and collected, and be paid into the hands of the Trustees for such school or schools, when appointed as hereinafter directed; and if the money shall be subscribed for the purposes aforesaid, the same shall be payable, and paid, to the said Trustees, for the purposes aforesaid; and, *Provided always*, That no such monies shall be voted by, assessed or Subscribed, by the inhabitants of such Townships, Districts or Settlement, unless the Overseers of the Poor, in the notice now by law required to be given for raising money for the Support of the Poor, shall also state that the subject of Establishing an English School and raising the money for the support thereof, is to be submitted at said meeting, which notice shall be given by the said Overseers at the request of any five freeholders of such Township, District or Settlement: and, *Provided also*, That no one school shall receive from the Province Treasury more than twenty-five pounds.

And be it further enacted, That it shall and may be lawful for such inhabitants of the several Townships, Districts and Settlements, at such meeting, to raise money, in manner aforesaid, for erecting, providing or repairing, one or more school-houses in their respective Townships, Districts and Settlements, and for procuring necessary furniture and utensils for the same, and also to define and settle the limits of such school or schools respectively.

And be it further enacted, That the Inhabitants or Householders in such Township, District or Settlement, as aforesaid, being free holders or having an income of forty shillings a year, in real or personal estate, who shall or may be desirous of having a school, or schools, established therein, shall nominate, at such meeting, six fit and proper persons, being free holders, to be Trustees of or for such school, whose names shall, by the Chairman of such meetings, be presented to the Court of General Sessions of the Peace for the County, of which such Township, District or Settlement, is part, out of which number the said Court of Sessions is hereby empowered and directed to appoint three, who shall be Trustees of and for such school, and shall and may serve during good behaviour, and residence within such Township, District or Settlement.

· ·

And be it further enacted, That it shall and may be lawful for the said Trustees to agree from time to time with proper persons, being duly licensed as by Law directed, to keep such school or schools in any Township, District or Settlement as aforesaid; and to fix the Salary to be allowed to each and every such School-Master, out of the money to be raised as hereinbefore directed, and that may be received from the Treasury of this Province, under the provisions of this Act, and the said Trustees are hereby required to use their best endeavours to cause the youth of the respective Townships, Districts and Settlements, regularly to attend the said schools, and to visit and inspect the said schools at least twice in each year during the continuance of this Act, and to enquire into the discipline and regulation thereof, and of the proficiency of the scholars, and to take care that the benefit of such schools shall be confined to the Youth of such persons as contribute to their support, if the money shall be raised by subscription.

And be it further enacted, That the said Trustees shall be and are hereby authorized and empowered, from time to time, and as often as they shall see fit, to enquire into the conduct or insufficiency of the master or teachers employed in such schools, and to report the same to the Court of Session, which shall have power to remove such master or teachers, if they find him or them negligent, insufficient, or of bad morals.

And, as an encouragement to the persons inhabiting the various Townships, Districts and Settlements, in the Province, to establish Schools therein, according to the former provision and directions of this Act:

Be it enacted, That as soon as it shall be certified in writing to the Governor, Lieutenant-Governor, or Commander in Chief, for the time being, by the Court of General Sessions of the Peace, in and for any county or district within this Province, that a School House has been actually built or provided for, and a School-master appointed thereto, in any of the said Townships, Districts or Settlements therein, and that money has been actually raised to the amount of fifty pounds, there shall be allowed for the further support of such school, the sum of twenty-five pounds per annum, and a like proportion for any larger sum not exceeding two hundred pounds, *provided*, no one school shall receive a sum larger than twenty-five pounds as aforesaid, the same to be drawn from the Treasury of the Province, by warrant from the Governor, Lieutenant-Governor, or Commander in Chief, for the time being, pursuant to the instructions and directions of his Majesty, in favour of the Trustees of such School, and to be by them applied in support thereof, according to the true intent and meaning of this Act.

And be it further enacted, That at the several Schools so to be established, when the same shall be in part provided for by assessment, the scholars shall be taught free from all expense whatever, other than their own books and stationery, and individual proportion of fuel.

And be it further enacted, That the said Trustees so as aforesaid to be appointed annually, to and with the said Court of General Sessions of the Peace in each county and district for all

monies by them received and dispersed to and for the use of such schools, and shall be subject to such rules and orders as the said Court shall from time to time make, touching the funds of the said several Schools or the application thereof.

And be it further enacted, That if any money shall be subscribed, granted or bequeathed, for the benefit of such Schools in this Province, by any person or persons whatsoever, the same shall be received and applied by the Trustees thereof, pursuant to the directions and provisions of this Act, and shall be considered as part of the sum which shall intitle such Township, District or Settlement to draw money from the Treasury, under the provisions of this Act.

And be it further enacted, That this Act shall continue and remain in full force and effect for three years from the publication thereof, and from thence to the end of the next Session of General Assembly, and no longer.

B.6 A Private-Venture School for Girls

York, Upper Canada.
Under the patronage of the Rt. Honorable Lady Sarah Maitland and the principal Ladies of Upper Canada

Mrs. Cockburn
(Successor to Mrs. Goodman)
Respectfully announces to her friends and the public, that she will commence her School Duties on the first Monday in June.

Mrs. Cockburn submits to their inspection, her School Terms which she trusts will be found so moderate that parents will be enabled to give young Ladies the requisite time to attain the desired acquirements.

B.6 Source: Advertisement in the *Upper Canada Gazette*, 30 May 1822.

TERMS PER QUARTER
For Education in the English Language, Grammatically, History, Geography, the use of the Globes, with plain and fancy Needle-work,   £2. 0. 0.
Writing and Ciphering,   0.10. 0.
The French Language,   1. 0. 0.
Drawing and Painting on Velvet,   1.10. 0.
For Board and Lodging,   8.10. 0.

Music, Dancing, Flower and Card-work, are also taught in the School and charged moderately.

Mrs. Cockburn will receive a Junior Class of little children from four to seven years of age, for five dollars per Quarter each.

ENTRANCE ONE GUINEA

Every Lady to provide a Table, and Tea-spoon, Knife and Fork, Sheets and Towels, and to pay for her own washing.

Three months notice is expected before any Lady leaves the School.—The terms of tuition, to day Scholars are the same as those to boarders; with half a Guinea entrance.

B.7 A Private-Venture School for Boys

Education for Young Gentlemen

WILLIAM GREEN Proposes opening an English School, for the Education of Youth on Monday, the 20th of April, in his house in Briton Street, near Captain Elmes's.—Where will be taught the following branches of Literature, in the most approved order from the best authors used in the principal Academies in Great Britain and Ireland,—*Viz.*

	Per Quarter
Reading	0/7/6
Do. with English Grammar, and the proper accent	0/10/0

B.7 Source: Advertisement in the *Saint John Gazette* (New Brunswick), 31 March 1789.

Writing	0/10/0
Arithmetic	0/12/6
Bookkeeping and Merchants Accounts	0/17/6

Geometry, Measuring, Surveying, Gauging, Navigation, Dialling, and other parts of Mathematicks according to agreement; also the use and projection of Maps and Charts after a natural, early and concise method without burden to the memory.

N.B. Those parents, etc., that will give him a preference in the tutorage of their children, may depend on the strictest attention being paid to their natural genius, and their moral abilities.

B.8 A Joint-Stock School in Quebec

To the Public

Union Hotel, 4th December 1818

At a Meeting of a number of the Citizens of Quebec it was Resolved, That

As the happiness of Society depends upon the principles and conduct of those that compose it—and those again, entirely depend upon the proper education of Youth; there cannot be too much attention paid to the *excellence, purity* and *extent* of the instruction communicated to them. With the middling ranks of Society, these must again be regulated by the expenses of Education, and a parent in Quebec may from the confined nature of his circumstances, be forced *(with the bitterest feelings)* only to bestow the one-half of the Education on his family, that he would have otherwise given them.

With an intention to obviate this difficulty, an association has been formed to procure Education for the children of its members, upon terms far more reasonable than what is common in Quebec.

B.8 Source: *Quebec Mercury*, 8 December 1818.

From the calculations they have made, they are happy to state that they will be able to communicate the various branches of polite and useful Education, at about one-third of the common expenses of it in this place.

The plan, with the fair calculation of the expense of carrying it into effect, may be seen at the warehouse of the President, Mr. John Shea, Buade Street, who has been requested by the association to receive the names of those who may find it their interest to become members. As the number of pupils must of necessity be limited, an early application will be necessary, as the vacancies that remain will soon be filled up. The Committee of management will be elected, and give a regular account of all their transactions annually.

A meeting of the Subscribers and those who approve of the principles of the Association, will be held in the Union Hotel, on Friday Evening, the 11th December 1818.

By order of the President.

GEORGE SCOTT, Secretary.

Quebec, Dec. 7th, 1818.

B.9 The Council of the Red River Colony Grants Financial Assistance to a Boarding School, 1835

The very great benefits that are likely to arise connected with the objects of morality, religion and education not only in Red River but through the Country at large, from the highly respectable and admirably conducted Boarding School, lately established for the instruction of the youth of both sexes under the management of the Revd. Mr. Jones, excites feelings of the most lively interest in its favor, and of great solicitude for its prosperity and success, which even in a business point of view are very desirable from the large

B.9 Source: E. H. Oliver, ed., *The Canadian North-West: Its Early Development and Legislative Records*...(Ottawa, 1915), vol. 2, 721-22.

amount of Capital it brings into circulation, while it is highly creditable to the Country and honourable to the Gentlemen who have come forward so handsomely in its support; but it is with unfeigned regret we observe that, owing to the heavy expense incurred by Mr. Jones in erecting the necessary buildings for this Seminary, it cannot possibly, at the present charge for board & education, afford remuneration adequate to the labour bestowed by Mr. Jones upon it and the outlay of money it has occasioned to him; and as an increased charge for Board and Education might operate to the prejudice of this Establishment in its infant state, it is Resolved

That an allowance be made to the Revd. Mr. Jones of £100 p. annum in aid of this highly promising establishment subject to the approbation of the Government and Committee, and it is further Resolved

That a vote of thanks be presented to Mr. and Mrs. Jones, for the readiness with which they entered into the views and wishes of the Gentlemen in the Country, when requested to undertake the formation of such an establishment, for the deep and lively interest they take in the improvement, and for the unremitting attention they pay to the health and comfort of the young folk entrusted to their care.

B.10 Schooling and Apprenticeship

This Indenture made the Fourteenth day of December in the year of our Lord 1846, *Witnesseth* that Thomas Tolmey Son of the Late John Tolmey of the Township of Lancaster in the County of Glengarry in the Eastern District in the Province of Canada, Farmer, (deceased) hath placed and bound himself of his own free and voluntary will and by and with the consent of

B.10 Source: Public Archives of Canada, MG24, 118, McPherson Papers, vol. I, Apprenticeship Indentures.

his Brother Alexander Tolmey apprentice to Kenneth McLennan of the Township of Lancaster aforesaid Weaver to be taught in the said Trade Science or Occupation of Weaving which the said Kenneth McLennan now useth and with him as an apprentice to dwell continue and serve for and during a period of three years and a half...the said apprentice having during all which said term of three years and a half his said master well and faithfully shall serve his secrets keep his lawful commands everywhere gladly do hurt his said Master he shall not willingly suffer to be done by others but the same to his power shall let or forthwith give notice thereof to his said master. The Goods of his said Master he shall not at any time embezil or waste nor lend them without his consent to any. From the Service of his said master he shall not at any time depart or absent himself without his said Masters leave but in all things as a good and faithful apprentice shall and will demean and behave himself towards his said Master all during the said term. And his said master for and in consideration of such faithful service to be performed by the said Apprentice the Trade Science or Occupation of a Weaver which he now useth with all things thereto belonging shall and will teach and instruct or otherwise cause to be well and sufficiently taught and instructed after the best way and manner that he can and shall and will also find and allow unto the said apprentice meat, drink, washing and Lodging mete and convenient for such an apprentice during the time aforesaid together with good wearing apparel Boots and Shoes as may be necessary...and also send him or cause him to be sent to an English School for a period of Four Callendar months... where he will be taught Reading. Writing, and Arithmetick and at the expiration of the said term shall and will give or cause to be given a Loom with a pair of Huddles and two Reeds.

In witness thereof...
Signed and Sealed in the presence of
James Sinster

His
Thomas X Tolmey
Mark

Kenneth McLennan

His
Alex. X Tolmey
Mark

II The Public Uses of Mass Education

In the middle decades of the nineteenth century, the methods of providing education in British North America changed dramatically. The traditional characteristics of education considered in the last chapter either disappeared or were greatly modified. The primary responsibility for the provision of elementary education passed from the family to the state. New school acts made schooling more available, and at the same time increased the degree of uniformity among schools. New demands were imposed upon the schools, and new administrative structures emerged to implement them. And as the role of governments expanded, church and state came into conflict over the control of education. The reason for these changes was the growth of a powerful ideology that gave the school a new importance in the social order.

The origins of that ideology were to be found in the political unrest and the economic and social dislocation that characterized the first half of the nineteenth century on both sides of the Atlantic. A new industrial society was emerging in Britain and in the northeastern United States, bringing new kinds of problems and new relationships between men. The French and American revolutions unleashed new political demands–for democracy, equality, and equal opportunity–throughout the western world. In Britain and the United States, cautious whigs and utopian socialists, evangelical Christians and infidel rationalists, political economists and philanthropists, all propounded new solutions to these problems, and more often than not they fell upon popular education as the cure for society's ills. The voices of educated opinion–journals like the *Edinburgh, Quarterly, Westminster*, and *North American* reviews–preached the new gospel in an astonishing number of articles in the 1820s, '30s, and '40s. Newspapers in British and American cities and those on the edge of the frontier picked up the theme. While there was little agreement on the ends to be reached, there was unanimity on the means. British conservatives believed the education of the masses would lend support to the religious establishment and create a spirit of rational subordination. American whigs hoped schooling would counteract the excesses of universal male suffrage. Malthusians hoped it would teach sexual restraint and thereby keep the population and the means of subsistence in balance. Political economists saw it as the best way to reconcile an emergent working class to the consequences of capitalism and technology. Owenites and other working-class publicists made it one of the great levers for creating a new society. For yet other men, education would end intemperance, eliminate crime, create social unity, spread the gospel, and encourage the arts and sciences. For Horace Mann in Massachusetts, it was "the great balance-wheel of the social machinery", and for the *Economist* in England, it was "the steam-engine of the moral world."

British North Americans, confronting their own problems, found it easy to adopt solutions preferred elsewhere. If the schoolmaster was abroad in Britain, if he could help solve the political and economic problems of Ireland or Massachusetts, why should he not be equally effective in British North America? Could popular education, for example, help resolve the political conflicts that plagued the colonies in the 1830s and '40s? Documents A.1 and A.2 show the close connection that different kinds of colonial liberals believed to exist between education and political reform. In contrast, the extract from the *Niagara Reporter* (document A.3) is an example of the conservative view that popular education could become the best defence against radicalism of all kinds. French Canadian opinion reflected the same division on ends and consensus on means. Louis-Joseph Papineau, the leading reformer in Lower Canada, contended in 1831 (document A.4) that education would give French Canadians the power to defeat the "foreign administration" that ruled them; in 1841, Charles Mondelet, a supporter of Lord Sydenham, argued that education was the best means of reconciling English and French (document A.5).

The uses of popular education, however, were not limited to political ends. Like many of his contemporaries, George Young, a leading Nova Scotian liberal, pointed out the connection between education and the moral and economic welfare of the colony (document A.6). His arguments illustrate how popular education became for British Americans, as for others, one of the great panaceas of the age.

A.1 Education against Oppression

What is chiefly wanted to consolidate and preserve British institutions and British principles in all her North American Colonies is Education. All reforms in government must begin by enlightening the people themselves. Our church and state government is exerting its utmost force to keep them in darkness; its colleges, its prelates, its district schools, its boards of education, all, all have one distinct tangible object in view; the very same object for which in darker ages "seats of learning" were founded by

A.1 Source: William Lyon Mackenzie, in the *Colonial Advocate*, 2 June 1831.

priests and tyrants–namely, to impart to "the chosen few" a sufficient fund of knowledge by which they might afterwards be enabled to rule over their more ignorant brethren. Therefore, my friends, encourage Education in every township, and seek not to put off the teacher of skill, talent and moral character, with a miserable pittance, but reward him liberally.

A.2 Education and Responsible Government

10. Q. What is meant by British Liberty?
A. That freedom of person, property, and opinion, which is consistent with common rights and public benefit. It is the natural right of man, as regards his fellow man. It has been secured by *solemn national acts in Great Britain.*
11. Q. What British Institutions more particularly represent or support the principle?
A. The Legislative Branches,–the Courts of Law, –the various Churches,–the Press,–the Schools.
. . . .
32. Q. What is Education?
A. It signifies a growth in knowledge, and in capability.
33. Q. Which are the means of Education?
A. The various schools,–the lecture tables,–the pulpits,–and the daily intercourse with nature and society, by which men make educational progress during life.
34. Q. State the effects to be reasonably expected from education.
A. Improvement in knowledge, power, morals, and religion,–and, consequently, improvement in citizenship, in self-respect, and respect for the various duties of society.

A.2 Source: The Reform Party of Nova Scotia, *A Brief Catechism of Liberal Principles*, 1847, reprinted in "Education for Responsible Government", introduced by D. C. Harvey, *Dalhousie Review*, 27, No. 3 (October, 1947), 338; 341-42, 350.

35.Q. Has the State, or Government, any obligations respecting education?

A. Yes, the people form the State. The people's knowledge and virtue constitute the chief riches of a State;–popular ignorance is a public disgrace, and source of weakness and danger. Consequently, the representatives of the energies of a people, the government, should secure the advantages of rudimental education for the people generally.

36.Q. State the Scholastic institutions of education.

A. Common Schools, Academies, and Colleges.

37.Q. State the objects, severally, of those institutions.

A. Common Schools are supposed to be devoted to those matters in which all men have a common interest, and with which they should have a common acquaintance. These are the rudimental branches of all knowledge,–reading, writing, science of language, science of computation, foundation of morals. Academies join to these studies, others of a more ornamental character;– and Colleges are supposed to include as many of the ornamental and scientific branches, as opportunities place within reach.

38.Q. State the public duty respecting these institutions respectively.

A. Clearly, to direct first and best energies for the provision of Common Schools. To assist in sustaining some Academies. To have, at least, one College, for a people, that various studies may not fall into disuse, that learning may not retrograde,–and that a depository and tribunal respecting general education may exist.

39.Q. State a relative view of these institutions, respecting the people generally.

A. Without the knowledge particularly imparted in Academies and Colleges, public intelligence and prosperity might advance;–without that of Common Schools a nation would decline;–he who has the latter may attain to the former, for the rudiments open the path to all improvement. They who can read and write and compute, may be said to have entered a path, to which there is no visible termination, and along which they may travel interminably. Academies and Colleges, make travelling, beyond a certain point, and to parts of communities, more easy and attractive.

....

90.Q. What do you learn, generally, from what you have expressed?

A. That politics, or the science of government, should moderately interest every British freeman;–that ignorance on the subject causes mistake and hostility, while removal of such ignorance, would tend to correct action and charitable temper. That Nova Scotia Liberalism signifies British freedom. That Liberty is a sacred heritage, and that its constituent parts should be carefully maintained. That a good Press, to the mind, like air to the body is the general medium of sound political life and action. That Education should have a basis formed of the simple rudiments of learning, and extensive as the population. That Responsible Government is British, and in accordance with common sense and Colonial prosperity; and that Elections are solemn expressions of opinion on political principles, and should be conducted in a manner worthy of intelligent freemen. The comprehending maxim is: Liberty, Intelligence, and Integrity, clearly understood, and well established on wise institutions, are the elements of political power and happiness.

A.3 Popular Education:
A Conservative View
Editorial in the *Niagara Reporter.*

Lord Durham has instituted an inquiry into the state of general education in Lower Canada, with a view to its extension. This is one of the most important questions that can be entertained by the Governor General; and if it succeeds in laying a foundation for an efficient system of popular instruction among the benighted habitants of that province, an enduring lustre will be added to his coronet, and generations yet unborn, will celebrate the anniversary of his arrival at Quebec, as the moral and intellectual resurrection-day of their country. An ample field, and but very slightly more cultivated, is open for the exertions of his Lordship's generous sympathies in this province. Improve the popular *mind*, and the popular *will* will be less refractory. Every new school that is established on a proper basis, is a new pillar of support to the fabric of social order and constitutional law. Every lesson of morality and religion which is imbibed by a people, weakens the chances of rebellion and insurrectionary violence; insomuch as tyrants *dare not oppress*, and demagogues *cannot delude*, an intelligent people. It is the still small voice of moral and religious instruction alone, that can check the violence of the political partisan, silence the declamation of the political agitator, and refute the sophistry of the modern political philosopher. Give the people education enough to convince them that they must be perfectly virtuous as well as perfectly wise, before they can safely assume the reins of an exclusive self-government, and they will repose quietly "under their own vine, and under their own figtree"–the balanced constitution framed for them by the wisdom of their forefathers, and tested and approved by the experience of many ages–instead of pursuing an illusory phantom of unattainable happiness through the intricacies of the captivating but fanciful theory of republicanism, which has hitherto failed as often as it has been tried, and which, according to all appearance, is again to be swept away by the torrent of ignorance and vice which is now bearing down on it with resistless force.

Let Lord Durham place the means of education in the hands of the people of these colonies, and that one act will redeem a thousand errors of administration in other matters. However much we may disapprove of what we sincerely believe to be his mistaken policy in one respect, we hesitate not to predict that if he succeed, (and we believe he will) in setting the machinery of popular education a-going, though he may not–indeed, cannot–live to see the full and magnificent result of a generous labour, he will confer a benefit on this important portion of the British Empire, which his warmest political admirers never anticipated, and entwine his own brow with a brighter wreath of immortality than in the proudest moments of his ambition, he ever dreamed of.

A.4 The Importance of Education
to French Canadians
This is an extract from a speech by Louis-Joseph Papineau.

In the age in which we live, the special concern of most civilized people is to diffuse the benefits of education–to facilitate instruction for all classes of society. This is the cause of the century. The most universal and uniform pro-

A.3 Source: Reprinted in the *Western Herald* (Sandwich, Upper Canada), 31 July 1838.

A.4 Source: Reported in *La Minerve*, 9 May 1831.

fession of faith is that education is one of the necessary conditions, a *sine-qua-non*, of social happiness.

French Canada will never, I hope, be unfaithful to this principle. The *Canadiens* will not be the only people stationary in the middle of this titanic struggle–in this race between the great nation from which they descend and the great nation to which they are joined, each one trying to surpass the other in the field of education.

· ·

If for some people, education is useful and glorious, for those who are drawn to free, constitutional governments, it is a necessity. For ourselves particularly, it is a vital necessity. We are friends of freedom and of the rights of our country. We are capable of preserving them only in as much as we are friends of education and carefully extend it to all classes of our society. We receive a constant influx of immigrants from the two countries which have made the greatest effort to educate their people–Great Britain and the United States. Three quarters, perhaps even more, of those who rule us come from these countries. Their preconceptions and preferences will always be contrary to ours–especially if they can say with some plausibility that they could not find anyone among us worthy of sharing the concerns of government. For a long time, this slander was the rallying cry of a party interested in making this lie which they think profits them, true. They seized power, they abused it and put impediments in the way of the desire for education shown by those they accused of ignorance. Thanks to our seminaries, there have always been men among our people who are better educated than those preferred by the ruling party. Each injustice of this kind is bound to aggravate. . . . For on the one hand, it destroys the motive for education and emulation among us. On the other hand, it iso-

lates and separates the people more and more from the administration. Finally this administration becomes foreign and odious to them, incapable of taking direction from the enlightened friends of the country it has persecuted, even when it recognizes its error and the necessity of correcting it. Its bias has been openly exhibited in the past. They are beginning to weaken. It is up to us to conquer them and finish their ruin by continuing the efforts started to put more schools everywhere.

· ·

Let the sacrifices made by this country not be lost, and let us gather the fruits expected from education. The sweetest of these fruits are the love of virtue, the use of outstanding talents, a constant respect for the rules of justice; knowledge of one's rights and those of others, the affirmed right to defend one's own without any wish to encroach on that of others; strong guarantees against the misuse of power, against the commission of abuses by those who govern, against the agitations and the unfounded discontent on the part of those who are governed. To have so many advantages makes it a duty of every citizen, great or small, rich or poor, to make every effort to get the best possible education for his family. Education is the richest heritage a father can leave his children. It is a gift that can not be entirely dissipated as good fortune can. If someone, because of momentary madness, loses sight of the advantages inherent in his education, sooner or later the words of wisdom heard in his youth, aided by unhappy lessons of experience, will bring him back to the path of duty. . . . Multiply the schools and you multiply proportionately the chances of obtaining this beneficial result. You bring together the ranks of society. You destroy

A.5 Source: Charles Mondelet, *Letters on Elementary and Practical Education* (Montreal, 1841), pp. 7-10.

the purely artificial, bad aristocrats and you create natural, good ones. For a just Providence has sown equally the seeds of talents and virtues in the hearts of children of all ranks and classes.

A.5 Education and the
⋅   Reconciliation of the Races

If, as I verily believe, and fondly anticipate, nothing can be more certainly conducive to the utter annihilation of national distinctions, and the prejudices, animosities and hatred they have engendered and fostered; than the working of my system of education, I have some right to expect and call for, from the public, a dispassionate attention to my suggestions.

We are all agreed that the state of anarchy we have lived in for some time past, is destructive of our happiness. Some of us trace our misfortunes to national distinctions which have been artfully speculated upon by some, to stir up the flame of discord; others look upon such an excited state of the public mind, as the effect and not the cause of the calamities we have been visited with. I deem it unnecessary to travel out of my way, to inquire into that subject; it is, I may say foreign to my plan; and such a discussion would, in all probability, revive, instead of allaying, the excitement which I hope to dispel by simply removing the *present* cause of its continuance.

. . . .

The want of a general and uniform system of Elementary and Practical Education, being extreme in Lower Canada, no time should be lost in adopting such means as are calculated to remedy so great an evil.

1. National distinctions and prejudices being, in the estimation of many persons, most formidable obstacles to the carrying into operation of a uniform system of education, means should at once be devised to surmount them.

2. Those means are perhaps of an easier execution than generally anticipated, the remedy consists simply in doing away with the fears now preying upon the minds of both the English and French population.

3. There is, no man will or can deny it, a mutual distrust prevailing in a very high degree, in respect of the language; the English population is impressed with the belief that the French Canadians are averse to and will oppose the spreading of the English language; the French Canadians, on the other hand, are apprehensive that efforts have been, and are about being made to wrest from them their vernacular, and to force them to speak the English language.

4. It is plain that the result of such fears, is a total mistrust and want of confidence the most dangerous, and very likely to become incurable, if not attended, properly attended to immediately.

5. Let there be established in each locality, as far as practicable, a French and an English school, either in one and the same building (which I think is a preferable mode) or in two distinct houses. The result is inevitable. The English parent seeing in the midst of the French settlements, English schools, will very naturally say to himself: "Surely, the French Canadians are not hostile to the spreading of the English language, it is better I should send my children to the French school, they will learn both languages and get on much better in the world." The French Canadian parent will at once find out that he is not forcibly to be robbed of his language, he will see the propriety of having his children taught the English language which will enable them to pave their way to useful ends; he will therefore send his children to the English school.

6. All reflecting men must be struck with one idea, that is, the now prevailing mutual distrust will vanish to make way for mutual confidence. Both

populations will cease to fear what they now dread so much, their anticipations and their hopes will not be visionary, there being nothing to oppose to facts: English and French schools working simultaneously, will be unanswerable arguments.

7. I have shewn, I trust, that one of the beneficial results of the simultaneous working of the English and French schools, will be the restoration of confidence between the two populations, as regards the language; much will already have been effected.

8. The children of both races, intermixing daily, as well for education as for other purposes, will be on friendly terms, play together, and visit one another. The parents whose distrust shall then have been dispelled, will have been humanized; their interest will also help them a little. They will not excite the children against one another, no more than they will grumble at their neighbours, because they happen to be of a different origin from their own.

. . . .

14. Let those who sincerely wish to see the English language in general use, tell me now, whether there is a better, a safer way of carrying out their views, than what I have suggested?

15. I do believe that, like the Anglo-Saxon race, the English language must eventually spread from the borders of the Atlantic, down to those of the Gulf of Mexico, and the confines of Guatemala and Mexico, and then directing its course westward, across the Rocky Mountains, reach the Pacific....

17. No man in his senses, will dream of having the English language exclusively spoken in the British possessions; all that the most sanguine may expect is, that it will be universally spoken. In the United States, though prevalent, it is not exclusive, no more than it is, and ever will be in

all well instructed communities where the rich and elegant French language will always be sought to be learnt.

18. No more is required to make of us all, one people, and to make us forget our origin. The moment the masses are enabled to convey their thoughts, meanings and wishes, by one and the same language, the end will be attained, and the sooner it is attained the better.

A.6 The Moral and Economic Consequences of Education

I come now to illustrate those [postulates] which make education the business and duty of the state. No Executive performs its obligations to the body politic, whose energies are not devoted to the instruction and amelioration of the mass.

1st–National wealth, it is true, is represented by matter–by products which are tangible –but these are produced by the operation of mind upon matter. Wealth is composed of matter, into which the skill and the labour of man has been incorporated. The improvement of the mind adds to the skill and manipulation of the hand, and thus enlarges its powers of production. The science and skill of the mechanic are a part of his annual income–of his powers of production–and clearly a part of his wealth, and of course of the wealth of the state. If the hand of one man can be formed and trained to do the labour of ten, the food he consumes gives a ten-fold value to the products of its industry. The cultivation of the mind increases skill, multiplies inventions, and gives new power and facility to the mechanic. The intellect of a nation becomes thus its richest mine of Gold.–It is ever ready, energetic, commandable; and therefore it is as imperative upon

A.6 Source: George R. Young, *On Colonial Literature, Science and Education...* (Halifax, 1842), vol. I, 135-44.

the government to cultivate and improve it, as it would be to call a new element of national wealth into existence, or to encourage one if discovered. –Some politicians now argue with some show and force of reasoning, that national wealth cannot be estimated, because there is no exact standard or measure by which we can value the combined energy, skill, and productive powers of the people–these are elements ever capable of being improved and stimulated, and thus increasing their returns by hundred-folds. The steam power of Great Britain, entirely the effect of mechanical skill, is equal to the labour of 200 millions–the annual products of the population has thus been increased ten-fold, in addition to all the brilliant results the engine is yet to accomplish. Another Watt, or Black, or Fulton, may yet spring from the form of a Parish or Industrial School, and give to practical Science a new scope, and break up new, deep, and ever increasing fountains of national wealth.

Upon the subject of education the Rev. Mr. Crawley published, in the Halifax Nova-Scotian for 1840, a series of letters entitled "the People's Interest". Although compelled to differ from the able Professor in some of his sectarian views, the earnest zeal these letters exhibit in favour of a general and practical system of education, founded on assessment, and the blending of religious and secular instructions–the two pillars on which an effective and useful system can alone be reared, –entitle him to respect, and I gladly avail myself here, as I intend to do in subsequent times, of some of his illustrations:–

"The mental field is surely as precious and as productive as any of the rich districts of our beautiful country, which the owners would grieve to throw into the hands of ignorant and miserable pretenders to husbandry, who should suffer them to become overrun with weeds, or spoiled for want of proper tillage. It is the mental field which the friends of education are called on to cultivate. The enlightened among them fail not to see in it a noble and invaluable object. Forth from that field with correct and judicious cultivation, they see proceeding their country's best and dearest hopes–increased energy, enterprise and talent–greater elevation of mind–greater refinement of manners–greater commercial, social, and political prosperity. Thence come the men who shall not be ashamed to take their rank with the wise, the learned, the ingenious, the distinguished, of other nations, the intellectual ornaments of the country, the able Statesmen, the practical men of science, and men of enlightened minds, blending science with art–in every department of modern avocation, which, modern improvement, with rapid strides, is multiplying."

2d.–The Government enact laws to control and subjugate the passions and vices of the people, by the influence of penalties and punishments. This is the direct–the imperative check upon crime. It is enforced by the whip, the pillory, the gaol–by punishments leading to fear and degradation. Is it not bound by higher responsibilities to apply the moral–the indirect check–To prevent rather than to cure or to punish? Sound education has this effect,–it softens the angry passions of our nature–it improves our virtuous tendencies. By education the Government will make the people more industrious, more moral, more cheerful and contented. If it be the duty of rulers to build gaols and workhouses, it is surely not less their duty to build schools, and open institutes and museums, to prevent the former from being filled. The spirit and policy of Prison discipline, is to discharge the convict with a loathing detestation of his crime–of the punishments and confinement it produced–teach him this when a boy–inspire him with these feelings *not after*, but *before* he commits the crime, and undergoes its disgrace and punishment. Let him be improved so as to avoid the workhouse–in place of delaying his instruction until he has fallen, and he cannot return to society, with the virtues of a later training, without the blemish and the load of his former transgressions ever resting, like a shadow on his forehead, disturbing his peace of mind, and depressing his notions of self-respect, by the stings of a loaded and guilty conscience. To awaken him to a sense of his former errors, and to send him back to society a reformed man, is ever attended with painful and withering reflections. How much wiser to save him all, by giving him a distaste for crime when a child.

3rd.–But as Colonists of Great Britain we must now recollect that we can no longer look upon this as a broad question, to be decided upon abstract and philosophical principles. The subjects of the British empire stand in that position that they must feel, and be pressed forward, by the influence of others. To acquire and maintain a pre-eminence in intelligence–in morals–in the arts and manufactures we must turn to the policy of other and rival states, and examine the progress of their exertions. The nations of the continent of Europe are now prosecuting a noble rivalry, in the moral improvement of the people, and in the spread of the arts, tending equally to increase their national resources, and the sum of human happiness. In France, Prussia, Germany, and in this New World, in the United States of America, education has been established as a national system. They have Ministers and Boards of education, and they are now held up, not as foils, but mirrors,–as examples to follow. In this branch of state policy the mother country and ourselves are behind–not before our sister nations....In France, Prussia, and Germany, the attention of the people and of the governments, are now directed to the spread and improvement of the arts and manufactures. In many they have already reached a superior skill. In some the supply not only meets the domestic demand, but affords a surplus to supply other nations. The domestic demand is guarded by a tariff and system of protective duties. They now compete with our motherland, in the markets of America, India, Asia Minor, and the Mediterranean. The United States have of late years made rapid progress and effected vast improvements in Manufactures; and in those of cotton, and several other of coarser fabric they supply not only their own people and the markets of South America, but even Greece and Asia Minor. The best improvements in Cotton Machinery have been the invention of American artists. Their tariff is sufficiently heavy to keep the domestic demand, exclusively, in many branches, to the domestic manufacturer. In the appliances, in skill, in invention, in the wide circle of the fine and useful arts, Great Britain, if she wishes to retain her supremacy and pre-eminence, must begin at the foundation, and, by introducing a system of national education, push skill and invention to the highest attainable limits. By making the system general, so as to embrace all, every mind and every talent is more likely to be developed, and the national powers of production to be of course encreased. The application of this reasoning is clear and obvious. In these Colonies we are placed in direct competition with the resources and skill, and in the products of our labour, with those of the New England States. We are bound not only to equal them in our systems of education, but, if we can, to surpass them; and thus to retain and secure that superiority which the forms, and the spirit of our political institutions, confer upon us, and which a broad and general system of Colonial education can alone render firm and enduring.

III   The Emerging Structure of Public Education

Architectural plans for a rural school house, recommended by J. George Hodgins, Toronto, 1857-58.

PLAN NO. 3.—FRONT PROSPECTIVE WITH GROUNDS &c.—FIG. I.

This plan is designed for sixty-four pupils. By placing seats opposite the flues, if required, it will contain that number of pupils, and will answer for a small village or thinly settled rural vicinity. The platform and black-board should be extended to the book closets, on each side of the Teacher's desk, in the places of the two seats for four

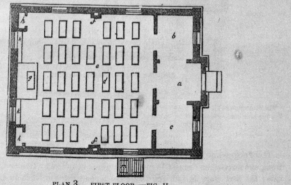

PLAN 3.   FIRST FLOOR.—FIG. II.

a. Lobby and entrance for both sexes.
b. Boys' clothes room to be used for recitation. 8 by 10 feet.
c. Girls' clothes room to be used for recitation. 8 by 10 feet.
d. Seats for two pupils each.
e. Passages two feet wide.

ff. Flues, one intended for smoke, and the other for ventilation.
g. Teacher's desk on a platform 5 by 8 feet.
h. Closet for books, &c.
k. Seats for four pupils each.
m. Entrance to the cellar.

A. Centralization

If education was indeed a universal remedy, the state had a supreme stake in its future. Popular education was, its advocates maintained, in the national interest; and thus, in George Young's words, "no Executive performs its obligations to the body politic, whose energies are not devoted to the instruction and amelioration of the mass."

In the middle decades of the nineteenth century, the argument was persuasive. Governments in western Europe, Britain, and North America passed a remarkably large volume of educational legislation. New state school systems were established and older systems like those of Prussia and Holland were modernized and extended.

The machinery used in different places to systematize the schools varied in detail but the general pattern of state intervention was the same. Central boards or ministries of education were established to exercise some degree of control over curricula, textbooks, and the certification of teachers. Chief executive officers were appointed to administer the law, and inspectorates created to visit the schools and see that the law was enforced. Government grants to education were enlarged, and the traditional voluntary methods of local school financing were superseded by property taxation. The logic of the argument was indisputable: if schooling was in the national interest, it was the responsibility of the state to encourage and guide it; if it was of universal benefit, it must be supported by all, open to all, and attended by all. The readings in this chapter are designed to cast light upon the structure of public education that developed in the British North American colonies and the arguments used to justify that structure.

Why was it necessary to create a strong central authority to direct the work of the elementary schools, to impose uniformity, to select the textbooks, and to certify teachers? As early as 1846, Egerton Ryerson, the new superintendent of education in Upper Canada and a man who was to become Canada's most influential nineteenth-century schoolman, argued that only a strong central authority could create an efficient and effective system of elementary education (document A.1). Though the arguments for centralization were first stated by educational reformers like Ryerson, they quickly became the common property of politicians, editors, and other men interested in improving the schools. In 1853, for example, a representative committee of the Lower Canadian House of Assembly concluded that no improvement in the schools of the province could be expected until firm central leadership and control were established (document A.2).

Efficiency, however, was not the only reason for the centralization of control over education. There were political reasons as well. The central authority, for example, had to be able to choose the textbooks used in the schools not only in order to improve their quality, but to ensure that they contained no subversive political or social ideas (document A.3). There was also the suspicion–common among those who made policy in British North America–that centralization was necessary because local people were not altogether sensible or responsible enough to run their own affairs; typically, the Attorney General of Nova Scotia, replying to critics of the new education bill of 1864, contended for this reason that the inspectorate must be appointed by the central rather than the local authority (document A.4).

The unanimity that existed among British North Americans about the kind of machinery needed to create an effective school system led to a remarkable degree of similarity in the provincial school acts. By the 1870s in most of English Canada the power to direct the development of education rested entirely in the hands of the provincial governments. The emerging structure of public education in these provinces is illustrated by the extracts from the British Columbia School Act of 1872 (document A.5). In Quebec the powers of the central authority were shared by church and state. (The relevant sections of the Quebec school acts of the 1860s and '70s, and the North West Territories School Ordinance of 1901–all of which provide examples of the degree of centralization in educational administration–are printed in another section of this chapter [documents C.5 and C.6] in order to place them in the context of the religious question in those provinces.) Whatever the exact composition of the central authority in the different provinces, however, its powers were remarkable. It determined the character and content of nearly every aspect of schooling. It had at its disposal a wide variety of means to enforce its will. And it left local people with only the most limited role in making, or even influencing, the policy of their schools.

A.1 The Necessity for a Central Educational Authority

Control and Inspection. If "it is the Master which makes the School," it is the Government that makes the system. What the Master is to the one, the Government must be to the other–the director, the animating spirit of it.

As proper rules, and a judicious course of instruction, prescribed for a School, would be of little use without a competent and diligent Master to execute the one, and impart the other; so the enactment of a Common School Law, however complete in its provisions, and the sanctioning of a course of instruction, however practical and comprehensive, will contribute little for the education of the people, without the parental, vigilant and energetic oversight of the Government. If it is the duty of the Government to legislate on the subject of Public Instruction, it must be its duty to see its laws executed. To pass a public law, and then abandon, or, what is equivalent, neglect the execution of it, is a solecism in Government. Yet this is the very absurdity which some Governments have long practised; and this is the primary cause why education has not advanced under such Governments. After having enacted a law, or laws, on the subject of Schools, they have left them,–as a cast off orphan,–to the neglect, or the care, as it might happen, of individuals, or neighbourhoods or Towns,–among whom the law has remained a dead letter, or has lingered on a feeble existence, according as the principal persons in each locality might be disposed to act, or not act, in a matter so vitally important to the entire interests and highest prosperity of the Country.

If Government exists for the prosperity of the public family, then every thing relating to educational instruction demands its practical care, as well as its legislative interference. Yet not a few persons have spoken, and written, as if the Government had nothing to do in a Department of its creation, which, more than any other, involves the heart and strength and happiness of the people, not to say the existence of a free Con-

A.1 Source: Egerton Ryerson, "Report on a System of Public Elementary Instruction for Upper Canada", in J.G. Hodgins, ed., *Documentary History of Education in Upper Canada* (Toronto, 1896-1910), vol. 6, 205-6.

stitution and system of laws, than merely to pass a Statute and make certain appropriations,–leaving the application, or misapplication, of public moneys, and every thing practical and essential in the administration of the law, to various localities, as so many isolated, or independent, Democracies.

Under such circumstances, there can be no System of Public Instruction; there may be one law, but the systems, or rather practices, may be as various as the smallest Municipal divisions. To be a State system of Public Instruction, there must be a State control as well as a State law.

The conviction of the important truth and duty involved in these remarks, has led to one of the most important improvements which have, during the present century, taken place in the science of Government,–the appointment of Officers, as well as the enactment of Laws for the Education of the whole people. Hence there is not a State in Europe, from despotic Russia, down to the smallest Canton of republican Switzerland, which has not its Council, or Board, or Minister, or Superintendent, or Prefect of Public Instruction,–exercising an active and provident oversight; co-extensive with the provisions of the Law and the community concerned. The most advanced of the neighbouring United States have found it necessary to adopt this as well as other, educational improvements of European civilization. And it is now generally admitted, that the education of the people is more dependent upon the administration, than upon the provisions of the Laws relating to Public Instruction.

. . . .

...So far as I have been able to ascertain, from the examples of enlightened Governments, and so far as I can judge from the nature of the case, I think the oversight of the Government should be directed chiefly to these objects:

(1) To see that the Legislative grants are faithfully and judiciously expended according to the intentions of the Legislature; that the conditions on which the appropriations have been made, are in all cases duly fulfilled.

(2) To see that the general principles of the Law, as well as the objects of its appropriations, are, in no instance contravened.

(3) To prepare the Regulations which relate to the general character and management of the Schools, and the qualifications and character of the Teachers,–leaving the employment of them to the people, and a large discretion as to modes of teaching.

(4) To provide or recommend Books, from the catalogue of which Trustees, or Committees, may be enabled to select suitable ones for the use of their Schools.

(5) To prepare and recommend suitable plans of School-houses, and their Furniture and Appendages, as one of the most important subsidiary means of securing good Schools,–a subject upon which it is intended by me, on a future occasion, to present a Special Report.

(6) To employ every constitutional means to excite a spirit of intellectual activity and inquiry, and to satisfy it, as far as possible, by aiding in the establishment and selection of School libraries and other means of diffusing useful knowledge.

(7) Finally, and especially, to see that an efficient System of Inspection is exercised over all of the Schools. This involves the examination and licensing of Teachers,–visiting the Schools,– discovering errors, and suggesting remedies, as to the organization, classification, and methods of teaching in the Schools,–giving counsel and instruction as to their management,–carefully examining the pupils,–animating Teachers, Trustees and parents, by conversations, addresses, etcetera,

whenever practicable, imparting vigor, by every available means, to the whole School System. What the Government is to the System, and what the Teacher is to the School, the local Inspector, or Superintendent of Schools, should be within the limits of his District.

A.2 Educational Reform and Centralization in Lower Canada

It is impossible not to admit, with nearly all those who have given their testimony, that the school system does not work in such a manner as to give to the youth sufficient instruction suitable to the industrial interests of the country. It is urgent that this state of things should not be allowed to continue for some years more; for it is to be apprehended that the real friends of education, discouraged by an unfruitful labour, will abandon the struggle, and leave the field free to ignorance and careless routine.

The causes which have prevented the progress of education and still retard it, have only to be pointed out to demonstrate at the same time the means which the Legislature ought to adopt to make our school system work with more efficiency, and cause it to produce more generous and satisfactory results. These causes would disappear by the application of new powers organized to control them.

No school system can work well, without an active, energetic, intelligent management, having the right of taking the initiative and of solving all difficulties that occur. A management having but the right to advise, is in Lower Canada an anomaly, and an absurdity. It ought

A.2 Source: "Report of the Select Committee appointed to inquire into the State of Education in Lower Canada...." (Sicotte Committee), *Journals of the Legislative Assembly of Canada*, 1852-53, Appendix J.J.

to have the power of enforcing the execution of the law. There ought to be a great deal of coercion in the powers accorded to the management, otherwise it will always go on weakening in public opinion, until it becomes, like the present one, completely inefficacious.

Surveillance ought to exist everywhere, and on the spot. This surveillance ought to be exercised by the Inspectors, conjointly with the local authorities, who ought to control the first, as they ought in their turn to be controlled by the Inspectors. The inspection of the schools by persons who are competent and independent of local influence, is necessary in all good school systems. The Inspectors ought to be less numerous, but better paid and rewarded, to admit of devoting all their time to the duties of their office.

One of the Inspectors ought to be appointed, in each judicial district, president of the board of examiners of such district. These presidents would form with the Superintendent a *Council of Instruction*, whose duties would be to prepare annually statistics on education, to facilitate the working of the law; to prepare modifications which might become necessary; to decide finally all contestations and difficulties submitted to it by the local authorities and occurring between them and the Inspectors. This council ought to meet four times a year, at least, to examine the reports of the Inspectors and local authorities, and deliberate on the interests of education, in order to cause the obstacles to the working of the law to disappear without delay.

The local authorities ought only to be composed of men qualified, by at least an elementary education, and the number of Commissioners ought to be reduced to three.

Normal Schools ought to be opened without delay at Quebec and Montreal, for forming teachers for primary and secondary instruction. It is impossible to anticipate satisfactory results from any system of primary instruction, if the persons who are called to give instruction are incapable and ignorant. It is the first thing to be done as most indispensable.

Protection ought to be accorded to the teachers for their salary, as well as respects the payment as the sufficiency. Assistance ought to be afforded in old age, to such as have been engaged in teaching for at least 30 years.

Uniformity in the books ought to be imperative, and strictly watched over.

The Council of Instruction ought to designate the books to be studied, and be authorized to have them printed either here or abroad. An allowance ought to be made every year for the purpose.

The teaching ought to be methodical, universal and as laid down in the orders issued by the council, or in the law.

A.3 Central Control of Textbooks: the Political Reasons

But, while the Constitution of the Provincial Board of Education has been ostensibly objected to, I believe that the real objection is rather against that with which the Board has been identified, namely, the prohibition of United States School Books in our Common Schools. It seems to be supposed that, if there were no Board of Education to recommend Text Books to be used in Schools, there would be no exclusion of American Books from the Schools. The extent to which these Books have been introduced into our Schools during the last ten years is almost incredi-

A.3 Source: Egerton Ryerson, "Special Report" to the Governor and Legislature of 1847, in J. G. Hodgins, ed., *Documentary History of Education in Upper Canada* (Toronto, 1896-1910), vol. 7, 110.

ble. I believe that nearly one half of the Books used in our Schools are from the United States. I have been informed by a Gentleman, who had attended the Examination of a Common School, some months since, in the interior of the Home District, that out of twenty-seven different School Books in the School, twenty-five of them were American. These Books are recommended by their adaptation to Elementary Schools, by their style and cheapness, in comparison of School Books heretofore printed in Canada. Many persons have become concerned in the trade of these Books; and many Teachers have acquired a partiality for them. Yet no one finds it convenient to come forth publicly and advocate the use of American Books in Canadian Schools. It is found more convenient to attack the supposed instrument of their exclusion. Hence the attacks upon the Board of Education for Upper Canada, and the Chief Superintendent of Schools, in respect to School Text Books. The fact, however, is that American School Books, unless permitted by the Board are excluded by the 30th Section of the Statute of 1846; whereas, the Provincial Board of Education is constituted by the 3rd Section. In regard to the exclusion of American Books from our Schools, I have explained, as I have had opportunity, that it is not because they are foreign books simply, that they are excluded, although it is patriotic to use our own in preference to foreign publications; but because they are, with very few exceptions, anti-British, in every sense of the word. They are unlike the School Books of any other enlightened people, so far as I have the means of knowing. The School Books of Germany, France and Great Britain contain nothing hostile to institutions, or derogatory to the character, of any other nation. I know not of a single English School Book in which there is even an allusion to the

United States not calculated to excite a feeling of respect for their inhabitants and government. It is not so with American School Books. With very few exceptions they abound with statements and allusions prejudicial to the institutions and character of the British Nation. It may be said that such statements and allusions are "few and far between," and exert no injurious influence upon the minds of children and their parents. But, surely, no School Book would be tolerated which should contain statements and allusions "few and far between" against the character and institutions of our Common Christianity. And why should books be authorized, or used in our Schools, inveighing against the character and institutions of our common Country? And, as to the influence of such publications, I believe, though silent and unperceptible in its operations, it is more extensive and powerful than is generally supposed. I believe such School Books are one element of powerful influence against the established Government of the Country.

From facts, which have come to my knowledge, I believe it will be found, on inquiry, that in precisely those parts of Upper Canada where United States School Books had been used most extensively, there the spirit of the insurrection in 1837 and 1838, was most prevalent.

A.4 Local or Central Control of The Inspectorate?

Hon. Atty. Gen.–It seems to me that we do not sufficiently consider the principle that should guide us in considering these subjects. The discussions both of yesterday and today are such as naturally, perhaps necessarily, result from a system of self-government in a small community such as Nova Scotia. Divided as a small com-

A.4 Source: Nova Scotia, *Parliamentary Debates*, House of Assembly, 28 February 1864.

munity is, under our principles of government, the Administration must have of necessity a very large and powerful influence in the regulation of the affairs of the country. In many instances it is necessary that they should have this power for the useful exercise of those functions which they are called upon to perform. But the moment you come to bring the principle into operation you find yourselves met precisely by the objections which have been made today. Those who are in opposition dread the accumulation of power in the hands of the Government, and they pass by in the discussion of questions like this, what should be the primary considerations entirely. What ought to be the primary consideration here? How are you to get the most efficient Inspectors of Schools. But the investigation has gone off into a very different line. How are you to get such an arrangement as will give the least power to the government and do the least injury to the opposition in a political aspect. It is natural such an argument should be urged. The House, however, must exercise its own discretion and act contrary to all such considerations. No one can doubt for a moment that upon the efficient character of the Inspectors depends the benefit of the bill now to be passed. If you can obtain efficient Inspectors of Schools you have made an improvement in the Educational Institutions most largely in advance of anything that exists now. Now I put it to any gentleman that hears me if there can be the slightest hesitation in his judgment as to the parties most calculated to appoint efficient Inspectors–men having intelligence, education, manner, and energy. That is the kind of men we want. Now the School Boards, except in cases where you appoint clergymen–and I do not know to what extent this is done throughout the Province–are not likely to be so constituted as to make selections of the character I wish.

Even if competent to do so, it is not likely they will be ready to sacrifice the several considerations that press upon them, in order to secure the best men. There will be so many influences brought to bear upon them that they will be in most instances led astray. In the appointment of Commissioners themselves there is felt a great deal of difficulty. You are obliged to make your selections with a view to various considerations that are secondary to the main point. You ought to appoint the best Commissioners, in respect to their capacity; but you cannot do it. You have to consider their political principles as well as religious tenets. Under all the circumstances, in fact, it is impossible to select the best men.–You are so fettered by various considerations that it is extremely difficult to get suitable Boards, to whom you would be willing to entrust the appointment of such important officers as Inspectors.

A.5 The Structure of Public Education

Board of Education.

3.   The Lieutenant-Governor in Council may, by Letters Patent under the Public Seal of the Province, appoint six fit and proper persons to be a Board of Education for the Province of British Columbia, and the persons so appointed shall respectively hold office during the pleasure of the Lieutenant-Governor; in the event of any one or more of the persons so appointed resigning, dying, or being removed from office, the vacancy or vacancies so occasioned may be filled up by new appointments in manner aforesaid.

Superintendent.

4.   The Lieutenant-Governor in Council may appoint a Superintendent of Education for the Province of British Columbia, who shall be ex

A.5 Source: *An Act Respecting Public Schools*, 1872. *Statutes of British Columbia*, 35 Vict. No. 16.

officio Chairman of the Board of Education, and such Superintendent shall hold office during the pleasure of the Lieutenant-Governor...

. . . .

Duties of Board of Education.

7.   It shall be the duty of the Board of Education–

. . . .

(3) To adopt all such lawful means in their power, as they deem expedient, to advance the interests and usefulness of Public Schools:

(4) To select, adopt, and prescribe a uniform series of text books to be used in the Public Schools of the Province, and to authorize the purchase and distribution thereof, by the Superintendent, among the different Public Schools, in such numbers and quantities as they may think fit:

(5) To make and establish rules and regulations for the conduct of Public Schools:

(6) To examine and give certificates of qualification to Teachers of Public Schools...

. . . .

(8) To appoint the Teacher or Teachers, in any School District, and to fix the salary or salaries of such Teacher or Teachers; and, upon good cause shown, to remove the same:

(9) To take charge and keep safely all apparatus to be purchased as hereinafter provided for school purposes in this Province, and to furnish, on the application of the Trustees of any District, endorsed by the Superintendent of Education, such apparatus as may be required for the School or Schools in such District;

(10) To purchase such apparatus as in their judgement may be necessary for the use of the Public Schools in the Province:

. . . .

(12) To establish a High School in any District where they may deem it expedient so to do, wherein the classics, mathematics, and higher branches of Education shall be taught; and such school shall be subject to the same obligations and regulations as Public Schools generally.

. . . .

Duties of Superintendent.

8.   It shall be the duty of the Superintendent–
(1) To visit each Public School within his jurisdiction, once in each year at least, unless oftener required by the Board of Education, or for the adjustment of disputes:
(2) To examine, at each yearly visit, the state and condition of the school, as respects the progress of the pupils in learning, the order and discipline observed, the system of instruction pursued, the mode of keeping the school registers, the average attendance of pupils, the character and condition of the buildings and premises, and to give such advice as he may judge proper:
(3) To deliver, in each School District, at least once a year, a public lecture on some subject connected with the objects, principles, and means of practical education; and to do all in his power to persuade and animate parents, guardians, trustees, and teachers to improve the character and efficiency of the Public Schools, and to secure the sound education of the young generally:
(4) To see that the schools are managed and conducted according to law, to prevent the use of unauthorized, and to recommend the use of authorized, books in each school:
(5) To suspend the certificate of qualification of any Teacher granted by the Board of Education, for any cause which may appear to him to require it, until the next ensuing meeting of the Board of Education, of which meeting due notice shall be given by the said Superintendent to the Teacher suspended; and the Board of Education shall confirm or disallow the action of the Superintendent in suspending such Teacher, as a majority of the members of the Board present at such meeting shall think proper…

. . . .

(7) To make annually, on or before the 1st day of September, a report of the actual state of the Public Schools throughout the Province, showing the number of pupils taught in each School District, over the age of 5 years and under the age of 16, the branches taught and average attendance, the amount of moneys expended in connection with each school, the number of visits made by him, the salaries of Teachers, the number of qualified Teachers, their standing and sex, together with any other information that he may possess respecting the educational state and wants and advantages of each school and district in the Province, and such statements and suggestions for improving the Public Schools and school laws and promoting education generally, as he may deem useful and expedient:
(8) To be responsible for all moneys paid through him on behalf of the Public Schools, and to give such security as the Lieutenant-Governor may require:
(9) To prepare suitable forms and to give such instructions as he may judge necessary and proper for making all reports and conducting all proceedings under this Act, and to cause the same, with such general regulations as may be approved of by the Board of Education for the better organization and government of Public Schools, to be trans-

mitted to the officers required to execute the provisions of this Act:

. . . .

School Trustees.

9.   For each School District there shall be three Trustees, each of whom, after the first election of Trustees, shall hold office for three years and until his successor shall have been elected.

. . . .

30.   It shall be the duty of the Trustees of each School District to appoint one of themselves to be Secretary and Treasurer to the Corporation, who shall give such security as may be required by a majority of the Trustees, for the correct and safe keeping and forthcoming, when called for, of the papers and moneys belonging to the Corporation, and for the correct keeping of a record of their proceedings in a book procured for that purpose, and for the receiving and accounting for all school moneys which shall come into his hands, and for the disbursing of such moneys in the manner directed by the majority of the Trustees. The Trustees shall take possession and have the custody of and safe-keeping of all Public School property, which has been acquired or given for Public School purposes in such District, and shall have power to acquire and hold as a Corporation, by any title whatsoever, any land, moveable property or income for school purposes, and to apply the same according to the terms on which the same were acquired or received; to do whatever they shall judge expedient with regard to the building, repairing, renting, warming, furnishing, and keeping in order the District School House or Houses, and the furniture and appendages belonging thereto, and the school lands and inclosures held by them; to pay the Teacher or Teachers employed in their District the salary or salaries of such Teacher or Teachers, to visit, from time to time, each school under their charge, and

see that it is conducted according to the authorized regulations, and that such school is duly provided with a register; to see that no unauthorized books are used in the school, and that the pupils are duly supplied with a uniform series of authorized text books, sanctioned and recommended by the Board of Education; to exercise all the corporate powers vested in them by this Act; to cause to be prepared and read at the annual meeting of their District their annual school report for the year then terminating; and such report shall include, amongst other things, a full and detailed account of the receipt and expenditure of all school money received and expended in behalf of such District, for any purpose whatever, during such year; to prepare and transmit annually, on or before the fifteenth day of January, a report to the Superintendent of Education, signed by a majority of the Trustees, and shall specify therein–

(1) The whole time the school in their District was kept by a qualified Teacher, during the year ending the 31st day of December:

(2) The amount of money received for the School District, and the manner in which such money shall have been expended.

(3) The whole number of children residing in the School District over the age of five years and under sixteen; the number of children taught in the school or schools respectively in such District, distinguishing the sexes and the average attendance of pupils in both winter and summer:

(4) The branches of education taught in the school, the number of pupils in each branch, the text books used, the number of public school examinations, visits, and lectures, and by whom made or delivered, and such other information as may be required.

. . . .

Public School Teachers and their Duties.

84.   It shall be the duty of every Teacher of a Public School–

(1) To teach diligently and faithfully all the branches required to be taught in the School, according to the terms of his engagement with the Trustees, and according to the rules and regulations adopted by the Board of Education:

(2) To keep the daily, weekly, and monthly registers of the School:

(3) To maintain proper order and discipline in his School, according to the authorised forms and regulations:

(4) To keep a visitors' book (which the Trustees shall provide) and enter therein the visits made to his School, and to present such book to such visitor, and request him to make therein any remarks suggested by his visit:

(5) At all times, when desired by them, to give to Trustees and visitors access to the registers and visitors' book appertaining to the School, and upon his leaving the School to deliver up the same to the order of the Trustees:

(6) To have at the end of each half-year public examinations of his school, of which he shall give due notice to the Trustees of the school, and through his pupils to their parents and guardians:

(7) To furnish to the Superintendent of Education, when desired, any information which it may be in his power to give respecting any thing connected with the operation of his school, or in anywise affecting its interests or character.

General Provisions.

85.   All Public Schools established under the provisions of this Act, shall be conducted upon strictly non-sectarian principles. The highest morality shall be inculcated, but no religious dogmas or creed shall be taught. All Judges, Clergymen, Members of the Legislature, and others interested in education, shall be school visitors.

B. Financing and the Quest for Universal Attendance

Colonial governments in British North America had traditionally provided grants in aid of local schools and these grants remained an important part of school finance. But for both practical and ideological reasons, governments would not take upon themselves the whole burden of school finance. The state usually provided a stipend which paid part of the teacher's salary; the rest had to be raised by local people themselves, usually by tuition fees. Tuition fees, however, had three disadvantages. They put a premium on finding the cheapest teacher available: the lower the salary, the lower the fees. They made school financing unpredictable, since the number of children attending a school might vary greatly from season to season and year to year. And they excluded many children whose parents were unwilling or too poor to pay the fees. All this remained tolerable so long as schooling was a matter of individual or family concern. But once it was assumed that all children should attend school and that schools should function as effectively as possible, it became important to find a more efficient way of financing education. By the middle decades of the nineteenth century most British North Americans increasingly agreed that some form of compulsory assessment was the best solution to all three problems.

Compulsory taxation would make local school financing predictable, and would substantially enlarge the size of the school fund. But equally important, it would make tuition-free schools possible–a goal, it was believed, indispensable to the success of public education. The arguments for both assessment and free schools are set forth by Theodore Rand, who, as Superintendent of Education in Nova Scotia from 1864 to 1870 and in New Brun-

swick from 1871 to 1883, presided over the introduction of free schools in both provinces (document B.1).

The introduction of compulsory education followed logically, though it came far more slowly–in some provinces not until the twentieth century. If schools were of benefit to society and if they were supported by all its members, then all children should be required to attend, especially those young people who most needed the moral and intellectual training the school could offer (documents B.2 and B.3).

B.1 The Case for Free Schools

[One reason why I commend assessment as a] system of supporting common schools to your favorable consideration, is its cheapness to parents educating their children. I will select the example of one district, rather better than an average specimen; and the same mode of reasoning will apply to every district in Upper Canada, and with the same results. In one district there were reported 200 schools in operation in 1848; the average time of keeping open the schools was eight months; the average salaries of teachers was £45.7s. 1d.; the total amount of the money available for the teachers' salaries, including the legislative grant, council assessment and rate-bills, was £7,401.18s.4½d.; the whole number of pupils between the ages of five and sixteen years on the school registers, was 9,147; the total number of children between those ages resident in the district, 20,600; cost per pupil for eight months, about sixteen shillings. Here it will be seen that more than one-half of the children of school age in the district were not attending any school. Now, sup-

B.1 Source: Theodore Rand, "An Argument for Assessment and Free Schools", Nova Scotia, *House of Assembly Journals*, 1865, Appendix No. 9, Education Report for 1864, Appendix A.

pose the schools be kept open the whole year, instead of two thirds of it; suppose the male and female teachers to be equal in number, and the salaries of the former to average £60, and those of the latter £40; suppose the 20,600 children to be in the schools instead of 9,147 of them. The whole sum required for the salaries of teachers would be £10,000–the cost per pupil would be less than ten shillings–less than five shillings per inhabitant–which would be reduced still further by deducting the legislative school grant. Thus would a provision be made for the education of every child in the district for the whole year; there would be no trouble or dispute about school-rate bills; there would be no difficulty in getting good teachers; the character and efficiency of the schools would be as much improved as the attendance of pupils would be increased; every child would be educated, and educated by the contribution of every man according to his means.

This is also the most effectual method of providing the best, as well as the cheapest, school for the youth of each school section. Our schools are now often poor and feeble, because a large portion of the best educated inhabitants stand aloof from them, as unworthy of their support, as unfit to educate their children. Thus the Common Schools are frequently left to the care and support of the least instructed part of the population, and then are complained of as inferior in character and badly supported. The Free School system makes every man a supporter of the school according to his property. All persons–and especially the more wealthy–who are thus identified with the school, will feel interested in it; they will be anxious that their contributions to the school should be as effective as possible, and that they themselves may derive all possible benefit from it. When all the inhabitants of a school section thus become concerned in the school, its character and

efficiency will inevitably be advanced. The more wealthy contributors will seek to make the school fit and efficient for the English education of their own children: the Trustees will be under no fears from the disinclination or opposition of particular individuals in employing a suitable teacher and stipulating his salary: and thus is the foundation laid for a good school, adapted to all the youth of the section. The character of the school will be as much advanced as the expense of it to individual parents will be diminished; the son of the poor man, equally with the son of the rich man, will drink from the stream of knowledge at the common fountain, and will experience corresponding elevation of thought, sentiment, feeling and pursuit. Such a sight cannot fail to gladden the heart of Christian humanity.

The Free School system is the true, and, I think, only effectual remedy for the pernicious and pauperising system which is at present incident to our common schools. Many children are now kept from school on the alleged grounds of parental poverty. How far this excuse is well founded, is immaterial to the question in hand; of the fact of the excuse itself, and of its widespread, blasting influence, there can be no doubt. Now, while one class of poor children are altogether deprived of the benefits of all education by parental pride or indifference, the other class of them are educated as paupers or as ragged scholars. Is it not likely that children educated under this character will imbibe the spirit of it? If we would wish them to feel and act, and rely upon themselves as freemen when they grow up to manhood, let them be educated in that spirit when young. Such is the spirit of the Free School system. It banishes the very idea of pauperism from the school. No child comes there by sufferance, but every one comes there upon the ground of right. The poor man as well as the rich man pays for the support of the school according to his means; and the right of his son to the school is thus as legal as that of the rich man's son.

But against this system of Free Schools certain objections have been made, the principal of which I will briefly answer:

First objection.—"The common schools are not fit to educate the children of the higher classes of society, and therefore these classes ought not to be taxed for the support of the common schools."

Answer.—The argument of this objection is the very cause of the evil on which the objection itself is founded. The unnatural and unpatriotic separation of the wealthier classes from the common school has caused its inefficiency and alleged degradation. Had the wealthy classes been identified with the Common Schools equally with their poorer neighbors—as is the case in Free School countries—the Common School would have been fit for the education of their children, and proportionally better than it now is for the education of the children of the more numerous common classes of society. In Free School cities and states, the Common Schools are acknowledged to be the best elementary schools in such cities and states; so much so, that the Governor of the State of Massachusetts remarked at a late school celebration, that if he had the riches of an Astor, he would send all his children through the Common School to the highest institutions in the State.

Second objection.—"It is unjust to tax persons for the support of a school which they do not patronize, and from which they derive no individual benefit."

Answer.—If this objection be well founded, it puts an end to school taxes of every kind, and abolishes school and college endowments of every description; it annihilates all systems of public instruction, and leaves education and schools to individual caprice and inclination. This doctrine was tried in the Belgian Netherlands after the revolt of Belgium from Holland in 1830; and in the course of five years, educational desolation spread throughout the kingdom, and the Legislature had to interfere to prevent the population from sinking into semi-barbarism. But the principle of a public tax for schools has been avowed in every school assessment which has ever been imposed by our Legislature, or by any District Council; the same principle is acted upon in the endowment of a Provincial University—for such endowment is as much public property as any part of the public annual revenue of the country. The principle has been avowed and acted upon by every Republican State of America, as well as by the Province of Canada and the countries of Europe. The only question is as to the extent to which the principle should be applied—whether to raise a part or the whole of what is required to support the public school. On this point it may be remarked, that if the principle be applied at all, it should be applied in that way and to that extent which will best promote the object contemplated, namely, the sound education of the people; and experience, as well as the nature of the case, shows that the free system of supporting schools is the most, and indeed the only, effectual means of promoting the universal education of the people.

I observe again on this second objection, that what it assumes as fact is not true. It assumes that none are benefited by the Common School but those who patronise it. This is the lowest, narrowest, and most selfish view of the subject and indicates a mind the most contracted and grovelling. This view applied to a Provincial

University, implies that no persons are benefited by it except graduates; applied to criminal jurisprudence and its requisite officers and prisons, it supposes that no persons are benefited by them except those whose persons are rescued from the assaults of violence, or whose property is restored from the hands of theft; applied to canals, harbors, roads, &c., this view assumes that no persons derive any benefit from them except those who personally navigate or travel over them. The fact is, that whatever tends to diminish crime and lessen the expenses of criminal jurisprudence, enhances the value of the whole estate of a country or district; and is not this the tendency of good common school education? And who has not witnessed the expenditure of more money in the detection, conviction, and punishment of a single uneducated criminal, than would be necessary to educate in the common school half a dozen children? Is it not better to spend money upon the child than upon the culprit–to prevent crime than to punish it? Again, whatever adds to the security of property of all kinds increases its value; and does not the proper education of the people do so? Whatever also tends to develop the physical resources of a country, must add to the value of property; and is not this the tendency of the education of the people? Is not education in fact the power of the people to make all the resources of their country tributary to their interests and comforts? And is not this the most obvious and prominent distinguishing feature between an educated and uneducated people–the power of the former, and the powerlessness of the latter, to develop the resources of nature and Providence, and make them subservient to human interests and enjoyments? Can this be done without increasing the value of property? I verily believe, that in the sound and universal education of the people, the balance of gain financially is on the side of the wealthier classes. If the poorer classes gain in intellectual power, and in the resources of individual and social happiness, the richer classes gain proportionally, I think more than proportionally, in the enhanced value of their property. As an illustration, take any two neighbourhoods, equal in advantages of situation and natural fertility of soil; the one inhabited by an ignorant, and therefore unenterprising, grovelling, if not disorderly, population; the other peopled with a well educated, and therefore enterprising, intelligent, and industrious class of inhabitants. The difference in the value of all real estates in the two neighbourhoods is ten if not a hundred-fold greater than the amount of school-tax that has ever been imposed upon it. And yet it is the school that makes the difference in the two neighbourhoods; and the larger the field of experiment the more marked will be the difference. Hence, in Free School countries, where the experiment has been so tested as to become a system, there are no warmer advocates of it than men of the largest property and the greatest intelligence; the profoundest scholars and the ablest statesmen.

B.2 The Moral Necessity for Compulsory Attendance

But while resolute in enforcing the criminal code, it behoves us also in the interest of humanity, to cast our eyes around and see what are the germs from which this rank crop of crime proceeds. Against those who come from distant places to ply among us their criminal vocation we can protect ourselves only by our vigilance in detections, and by inflicting upon the offenders, when convicted, the utmost penalties of the law; but against a band of youths born and growing

B.2 Source: Charge of the Judge at the Assizes, Toronto, 1868, in J. G. Hodgins, ed., *Documentary History of Education in Upper Canada* (Toronto, 1896-1910), vol. 20, 266.

up in our midst, hardened in vice, other means are necessary, and we may well enquire whether the Law itself is not defective, and whether we ourselves are not to blame, in not providing adequate measures for nipping crime in the bud, and for the prevention of its growth.

While we may feel proud of the progress we have made in providing a Common School Education for our youth, and of the large sum which we annually devote to that purpose, we cannot but feel that there is a radical defect in that System which permits so many children of both sexes to wander as beggars and vagrants through our streets, despatched upon their daily errand of crime, to bring home to worthless Parents, to be dissipated in drunkenness, what they may lay their little pilfering hands upon, or what they may extract from the charity of the simple, by ready tales of orphanage, or of some imaginary calamity suddenly fallen on their Parents, instruction in which fictions of misery is all that they receive at home, impressed upon their memories by cruel tortures and privation lest they, poor children, should forget their lessons.

To rescue this class from the evil influence of wicked Parents, is an object well worthy the ambition and utmost energy of the humane, and contributing, as every industrious citizen largely does, from the fruits of his industry, towards the Educational Fund, he would seem to have a right to demand that the Law which compels him to contribute towards the education of the children of others, should, at the same time, compel all to accept the benefits of education thus provided. The interests of the public and of humanity alike justify such an interposition of the Law, which some seem to shrink from, as, in their judgement, an unwarrantable interference with the parental authority.

In such cases as those to which we allude,

the parental authority is the greatest evil to which these poor children are exposed; and the evil has grown to so great a magnitude as to make it a Christian duty in those who frame our laws to interpose for its removal.

B.3 The Economic Necessity for Compulsory Attendance

The employment of children and young persons in mills and factories is extensive, and largely on the increase, the supply being unequal to the demand, particularly in some localities, which may partially explain why those of such tender years are engaged. As to obtaining with accuracy the ages of the children employed, we found some difficulty, inasmuch as the employer has no record thereof, having no interest or obligation in so doing; consequently, in order to ascertain their ages, they were interrogated either by one of the Commissioners or some one in the factory. We are sorry to report that in very many instances the children, having no education whatever, could not tell their ages; this applies more particularly to those from twelve years downwards–some being found as young as eight and nine years. On making our enquiries of these children as to their age, a reluctance to answer was shown by some, who would not understand the reason of the question being asked by strangers, and in other cases the answers were so obviously exaggerated as to lead us to believe that they were not truthfully given; occasionally, when we could gain the confidence of the very young children, we took the opportunity of ascertaining, as far as possible, why they were at work so young, with answers as follows:–"Having no father, had to help mother to get a living."–"Would rather work

B.3 Source: Canada, *Report of the Commissioners appointed to enquire into the Working of Mills and Factories of the Dominion...*, 1882, pp. 2-3.

than go to school." Some are there from the cupidity of their parents who have good positions as mechanics; others from the idle habits of the parents, who live on the earnings of the children, this being confirmed in one instance where three children were at work having a father as above described. Your Commissioners found this too often the case in cities and factory districts. It must be borne in mind that the children invariably work as many hours as adults, and if not compelled, are requested to work overtime when circumstances so demand, which has not been unusual of late in most lines of manufactures. The appearance and condition of the children in the after part of the day, such as may be witnessed in the months of July and August, was anything but inviting or desirable. They have to be at the mills or factories at 6:30 a.m., necessitating their being up at from 5:30 to 6 o'clock for their morning meal, some having to walk a distance of half a mile or more to their work. This undeniably is too heavy a strain on children of tender years, and is utterly condemned by all except those who are being directly benefited by such labor, and which they attempt to justify on the grounds,–

Reasons for employing young Children

1st. That the labor is light.

2nd. That it is not practicable for those more advanced in years.

3rd. That their competitors in the trade use this kind of labor.

4th. As there is no law or restriction on the question, some use it, and others who might be more liberally inclined have to follow.

It must not be understood from the above that employers of such labor are more anxious to obtain it than some parents are to force it upon them; the testimony of not a few proprietors and managers at present employing this class of labor leads us to believe that they are quite willing to discontinue its use for the benefit of the children, provided that education be compulsory; as a demand is gaining for intelligent and educated labor in our mills and factories. Great difference of opinion exists as to the half-time system of children in factories as adopted in England, and proposed in the Bill of Dr. Bergin. That the children should have some education all admit, while how it is to be obtained and they continue at work is the ground of debate. Many serious difficulties would be encountered by the half-time system in this country; it would cause interruptions and derangements in our Public Schools if connected with them, and which are under the control of the Local Governments,–and it may be mentioned here that by an Act of the Ontario Legislature passed in 1874, it is enacted that "every child from the age of seven to twelve years shall have the right to attend some school, or be otherwise educated for four months in every year, and any parent or guardian who does not provide that every child between the ages aforesaid under his care shall attend some school or be otherwise educated as thus of right declared, shall be subject to the penalties hereinafter provided by this Act." We were unable to find any place in which this Act is enforced. Most of the employers of labor under fourteen years of age have stated to your Commissioners that they would rather discontinue the employment of such labor than submit to the obligations imposed by the aforesaid Bill. If education be not enforced the question arises whether the children are not better cared for by spending a portion at least of their time at work, rather than wasting it on the public streets.

It will be seen from our statistics at what kind of labor and the extent to which children are employed. We find, in some trades where piece-work is done and where children are em-

C. The Role of the Church in Public Education

ployed, that they are not engaged by the firm or managers of the shop or factory, but by the hands who take such piece work to do, who arrange with the children as to the value of the labor, and who are solely interested in procuring the cheapest labor possible, irrespective of any other consideration as to the interests or condition of the labor employed. As to the attendance at school of children under fourteen years employed in factories, there is no attempt to attend school at all, from the fact that the regulations under which they work would not allow it. We have observed with regret a serious lack of education in very many of the adult factory hands. In some parts of the country a large proportion are to be found who can neither read or write, and employers are seriously inconvenienced by this lack of education in those applying for work, necessitating the importation of educated labor when our own people should be trained for these positions.

On the whole, the "education mania" and the consequent intervention of the state in education met remarkably little opposition. Indeed, by the 1850s the progress of public education was viewed by contemporaries as one of the cardinal achievements of the age. But one issue did provoke serious conflict: how could the new claims of the state to direct the work of the schools be reconciled with the traditional claims of the church to superintend education?

By mid-century this hardly constituted a problem for most Protestants. It was not that they had opted for secularism: religion in the schools was as indispensable for them as for Roman Catholics, and in those areas of British North America where a settlement was of one faith, the denominational school took root and flourished. But most new settlements contained members of several religious groups. These communities, moreover, were often poor and population densities were low. The combination of religious pluralism and relative poverty made the establishment of several denominational schools impossible; there would be one school or none at all. The demands of the environment were reinforced by the tendency among many Protestants in the first half of the nineteenth century to minimize the doctrinal differences that had traditionally divided them. Thus low church Anglicans, Presbyterians, Methodists, and Baptists found it less and less difficult to send their children to the same local school–a school that reflected their "common Christianity" by beginning the day with prayer, a hymn, and Bible-reading from the King James Version, and by teaching "nonsectarian" moral and religious values.

Many, no doubt, saw non-denominationalism as an unsatisfactory but unavoidable compromise. Others, Egerton Ryerson among them, saw it as a positive good. Ryerson's classic statement of its promise, made in his *Report on a System of Public Instruction* in 1846 (document C.1), was to become its standard defence; and his argument illustrates how Protestants resolved the potential conflict between the claims of the state and the claims of religion. The kind of religious instruction offered in the non-denominational schools is suggested by the regulations on the subject drafted by Ryerson for the Ontario schools (document C.2).

The argument, however, was unacceptable to Roman Catholics, English or French. Catholic leaders opposed the policy of placing the control of education solely in the hands of the state–they objected, for example, to both the centralist and secularist tendencies of the Canadian Common School Bill of 1841 (document C.3). Equally, they opposed on principle the idea that education and doctrinal religion could be separated (document C.4). The result was that in most parts of Canada, Catholics struggled to establish their own schools under church control. The degree of success they had depended upon local political factors–on the power of Catholic votes in the legislature, and the amount of opposition their demands aroused among Protestants. In the Maritime provinces, Ontario, and later in Saskatchewan and Alberta, both church and state were forced to compromise. Catholic schools were recognized by law or custom as part of the public school system–the kind of legal accommodation reached in one part of Canada is illustrated by document C.5. In British Columbia, and eventually in Manitoba, denominationalism was defeated entirely: all public schools are non-denominational.

Only in Quebec and Newfoundland were the churches successful in preventing control of the schools from being lodged in the hands of the state. In Quebec, the majority of local schools had long been either Catholic or Protestant and that fact was reflected in all the important school legislation of the period. The tendency towards state control of education manifested in the forties and fifties, culminating in the Sicotte Report (see document A.2 in this chapter) and the Council of Public Instruction Act of 1856, was reversed in the sixties and seventies by the combined efforts of Protestants who feared Catholic domination and Catholics inspired by the new spirit of ultramontanism. Their victory was complete. Between 1869 and 1875 the state became the handmaiden of the churches in education. The government framed the necessary legislation to maintain the schools, administered the routine business and provided the finances, but it handed over control of the curriculum, appointment of inspectors, and teacher certification to the Protestant and Catholic Committees of the Council of Public Instruction.

The result was that Quebec developed a school system in this respect not like the others. It had a public system of elementary education divided into Catholic and Protestant sectors, and a system of central control equally divided between Catholic and Protestant groups. Yet the differences should not be overestimated. The schools of Quebec were financed in much the same way as in other provinces and the control of education was no less centralized. The difference was that many of the powers held by ministers and departments of education in other provinces were, in Quebec, exercised by the Protestant and Catholic Committees of the Council of Public Instruction. Document C.6 contains the most important clauses of the Quebec school acts of 1869 to 1888 which consolidated this system of "dual administration".

In the nineteenth century, at least, Newfoundland was the great exception to many generalizations about British North America, especially about the nature of educational provision. As in other colonies, the state had begun to play a growing role in education during the 1830s and 1840s. As elsewhere, Roman Catholic leaders opposed government intervention and any tendency towards non-denominationalism–and, as in Quebec, they were successful in obtaining both a share of the government grant for their own parish schools and their own administrative structure. What was different about Newfoundland in the middle decades of the nineteenth century was that the Protestant churches increasingly demanded that they, too, should be able to maintain their own parish schools. Many Newfoundland communities were united by one faith and the school was inevitably a parish school. In many respects, the influence of English legislation was greater–the first government grants were, for example, given directly to the churches or to their school societies. And, of no less importance, Anglicans were united as in no other colony behind a high church bishop, Edward Feild, who fought a long and vigorous battle to obtain grant-aided denominational schools. By the early 1870s the government had conceded nearly every point. The education grant was divided among a number of denominations, each of which maintained schools wherever it could; the administration of education was likewise divided. The most important clauses of the Newfoundland School Act of 1874, which established denominational control of education in that province, can be found in document C.7.

C.1 The Benefits of Non-denominationalism

By Religion and Morality I do not mean sectarianism in any form, but the general system of truth and morals taught in the Holy Scriptures. Sectarianism is not morality. To be zealous for a Sect, and to be conscientious in morals are widely different. To inculcate the peculiarities of a Sect, and to teach the fundamental principles of Religion and Morality are equally different. Indeed, schools might be named in which there is the most rigorous inculcation of an exclusive sectarianism, where there is a deplorable absence of the fruits of both Religion and Morality. As there may be a very careful teaching of some of the ornamental branches of learning, while the essential and practical departments of it are very carelessly, if at all, taught; so it notoriously occurs that scrupulous and ostentatious maintenance and teaching of the "mint, anise, and cummin," of a vain and grasping sectarianism is accompanied with an equally notorious disregard of the "weightier matters of the law"–of Religion and Morality.

Such teaching may, as it has done, raise up an army of pugilists and persecutors, but it is not the way to create a community of Christians. To teach a child the dogmas and spirit of a Sect, before he is taught the essential principles of Religion and Morality, is to invert the pyramid,–to reverse the order of nature,–to feed with the bones of controversy, instead of with the nourishing milk of Truth and Charity.

C.1 Source: Egerton Ryerson, "Report on a System of Public Elementary Instruction for Upper Canada," in J. G. Hodgins, ed., *Documentary History of Education in Upper Canada* (Toronto, 1896-1910), vol. 6, 147-48; 158.

In these remarks I mean no objection to schools in connection with a particular Religious Community,–wholly controlled by such Community, and where its Worship is observed and its Creeds taught. Nor would I intimate that such establishments may not, in many instances, be more efficient and more desirable than any other differently constituted; nor that the exertions to establish and maintain them are not most praiseworthy and ought not to be countenanced and supported. I refer not to the constitution and control of Schools, or Seminaries, but to a kind of teaching,–a teaching which can be better understood than defined,–a teaching which unchristianizes four-fifths, if not nine-tenths, of Christiandom,–a teaching which substitutes the form for the reality,–the symbol for the substance,–the dogma for the doctrine,–the passion for Sect, for the love of God and our neighbours;–a teaching which, as history can attest, is productive of ecclesiastical corruptions, superstition, infidelity, social disputes and civil contentions and is inimical alike to good government and public tranquility.

I can aver, from personal experience and practice, as well as from a very extended enquiry on this subject, that a much more comprehensive course of Biblical and Religious instruction can be given than there is likely to be opportunity for doing so in Elementary Schools, without any restraint, on the one side, or any tincture of sectarianism, on the other,–a course embracing the entire History of the Bible, its institutions, cardinal doctrines and morals, together with the evidences of its authenticity...

The misapplication and abuse of Religious Instruction in Schools have induced many to adopt a contrary error, and to object to it altogether, as an element of popular education.

The creed of our Government, as representing a Christian people of various forms of Religious Worship, is Christianity in the broadest and most comprehensive sense of the term. The practice of the Government should correspond with its creed. With the circumstantials of sectarianism it has nothing to do; they form no article of its creed; they involve no one commandment of the Moral Law, either of the Old, or New, Testament; it is under no obligation to provide for the teaching of them, whatever importance individuals may attach to them; its affording different parties facilities for teaching them is the utmost that can be required, or expected, of it. The members of the various sects are alike its subjects; they contribute alike to its defence and support; they are alike entitled to its protection and countenance.

The inhabitants of the Province at large, professing Christianity, and being fully represented in the Government by Members of a Responsible Council–Christianity, therefore, upon the most popular principles of Government, should be the basis of a Provincial System of Education...

The foregoing observations and illustrations apply, for the most part, to a population consisting of both Protestants and Roman Catholics. The law provides against interfering with the religious scruples of each class, in respect both to religious books and the means of establishing Separate Schools.

In School Districts where the whole population is either Protestant, or Roman Catholic, and where, consequently, the Schools come under the character of "Separate", there the principles of Religious Instruction can be carried out into as minute detail as may accord with the views and wishes of either class of the population; though I am persuaded all that is essential to the moral interests of youth may be taught in what are termed Mixed Schools.

The great importance of this subject and the erroneous, or imperfect, views which prevail respecting it; and the desire of explaining fully what I conceive to be the most essential element of a judicious system of Public Instruction, are my apology for dwelling upon it at so great length. Religious differences, and divisions, should rather be healed than inflamed; and the points of agreement, and the means of mutual co-operation, on the part of different Religious Persuasions, should, doubtless, be studied and promoted by a wise and beneficient Government, while it sacrifices neither to religious bigotry, nor infidelity, the cardinal and catholic principles of the Christian Religion.

C.2 Regulations on Religious and Moral Instruction in the Elementary Schools of Canada West

Section 5. Constitution and Government of Schools in respect to Religious and Moral Intruction.

As Christianity is the basis of our whole system of elementary education, that principle should pervade it throughout. Where it cannot be carried out in mixed schools to the satisfaction of both Roman Catholics and Protestants, the law provides for the establishment of separate schools. And the Common School Act, fourteenth section, securing individual rights as well as recognizing Christianity, provides, "That in any Model or Common School established under this Act, no child shall be required to read or

C.2 Source: *Annual Report of the Normal, Model, Grammar and Common Schools in Upper Canada for the Year 1853,* Appendix One. Regulations, pp. 170-71.

study in or from any religious book, or to join in any exercise of devotion or religion, which shall be objected to by his or her parents or guardians: Provided always, that within this limitation, pupils shall be allowed to receive such religious instruction as their parents or guardian shall desire, according to the general regulations which shall be provided according to law."

In the section of the Act just quoted, the principle of religious instruction in the schools is recognized, the restriction within which it is to be given is stated, and the exclusive right of each parent and guardian on the subject is secured, without any interposition from Trustees, Superintendents, or the Government itself.

The common school being a day, and not a boarding school, rules arising from domestic relations and duties are not required; and as the pupils are under the care of their parents and guardians on Sabbaths, no regulations are called for in respect to their attendance at public worship.

In regard to the nature and extent of the daily religious exercises of the School and the special religious instruction given to pupils, the Council of Public Instruction for Upper Canada makes the following Regulations and Recommendations:–

1. The public religious exercises of each school shall be a matter of mutual voluntary arrangement between the teacher and the parent or guardian of each pupil, as to whether he shall hear such pupil recite from the Scriptures, or Catechism, or other summary of religious doctrine and duty of the persuasion of such parent or guardian. Such recitations, however, are not to interfere with the regular exercises of the school.

2. But the principles of religion and morality should be inculcated upon all the pupils of the

school. What the Commissioners of National Education in Ireland state as existing in schools under their charge, should characterize the instruction given in each school in Upper Canada. The Commissioners state that "in the National Schools the importance of religion is constantly impressed upon the minds of children, through the works calculated to promote good principles and fill the heart with love for religion, but which are so compiled as not to clash with the doctrines of any particular class of Christians." In each school the teacher should exert his best endeavours, by both example and precept, to impress upon the minds of all children and youth committed to his care and instruction, the principles of piety, justice, and a sacred regard to truth, love to their country, humanity and universal benevolence, sobriety, industry, frugality, chastity, moderation and temperance, and those other virtues which are the ornament of society, and on which a free constitution of government is founded; and it is the duty of each teacher to endeavour to lead his pupils, as their age and capacities will admit, into a clear understanding of the tendency of the above mentioned virtues, in order to preserve and perfect the blessings of law and liberty, as well as to promote their future happiness, and also to point out to them the evil tendency of the opposite vices.

C.3 Catholic Education and the State
Protest against the Common School Bill of 1841, 10 August 1841.

[The Bishop and the Vicars General] wish to advise Your Lordship that they have read with

C.3 Source: Public Archives of Canada, RG5 C1, vol. 72, Bishop Gaulin of Kingston and the Vicars General of the Diocese of Montreal, to Governor General Sydenham.

astonishment and distress a Bill entitled "Bill to amend certain Acts therein mentioned and to aid in the establishment and maintenance of Elementary Schools in this Province", which Solicitor General Day has just presented for the approval of the Legislature, in the intention that it become law. It is their firm conviction that this Bill is greatly injurious to Catholics in general in the Province, and to the Catholic clergy in particular. Indeed, this Bill allows the Governor to establish a Chief Superintendent of all schools in the Province; for each Municipal District the said Superintendent will name, arbitrarily, a Board of Examiners composed of five persons. This Superintendent and these Examiners may be quite foreign or perhaps even unfriendly to Catholicism. We are far from thinking that such fears could be realised under Your Lordship's administration. But Your Lordship will perceive the legitimacy of these same apprehensions, should a less liberal and tolerant Executive be in authority. Should this occurrence come about, is it not legitimate to believe that the Superintendent, and in turn the Examiners, will be unfriendly to Catholics? Yet it is these Examiners who will decide what subjects will be studied in the schools, what textbooks will be used, and it is they who will establish the general rules for the conduct of these same schools. A law could not, surely, exist that would offer *Canadiens* no guarantees for the religious principles they profess? There could not then, accordingly, be a law more likely to stir up the universal discontent of Catholics and to revive fatal animosities. May we say to Your Lordship that there is a more expedient and more natural means of promoting the much-desired progress of elementary instruction in this Province. This would be, it seems to us, for the government to provide, by pecuniary means, for Catholic schools separate and distinct from those of other religious denominations, without detriment to the aid afforded by law to the latter. Moreover, just as the books in use in Catholic schools must be under the control of their Church, so must the teachers, in accordance with the ancient custom of the country, which has not been amended. We must express to Your Lordship our pain on seeing that in spite of the frequent acknowledgement made of the Catholic clergy's great merit in connection with the education of youth, the Bill of which we are speaking excludes the clergy in future from all influence and participation in this important object. It is very true that this Bill sometimes mentions Clergymen; but it is no less true that it will always be easy to ensure that these Clergymen are neither Catholic bishops nor Catholic priests....Such are, My Lord, the humble representations that our conscience commands us to make against the Bill in question; and if desired, we will obtain the explicit sentiments of all the Catholic clergy, whom we are sure will support us. The necessity for haste does not allow us to go into more detail on other clauses of the Bill. But we firmly hope that Your Lordship will not allow it to become law, in view of the opinion of Catholics and of other religious denominations, whose rights would be equally injured as its effects became manifest.

C.4 The Catholic View of Religion in Education

This statement of the Catholic position was signed by the Bishops of Quebec, Montreal, Kingston, St. Hyacinthe, Bytown, Toronto, and Trois-Rivières.

C.4 Source: Pastoral Letter of the Second Provincial Council of Quebec. 4 June 1854. *Mandements, lettres pastorales, circulaires et autres documents publiés dans le diocèse de* Montréal (Montréal, 1869) vol. 2, 455-57.

For the good of our country and of our blessed religion, it is important that Catholic young people receive a solid instruction based on orthodox doctrine. This instruction must be set on an equal footing, in terms of the knowledge and enlightenment it offers, with that of our brothers who do not have the happiness of following our blessed religion. We therefore strongly urge you to procure for our children the advantages of an education suited to their intelligence and their station so that through worthwhile books they may enlighten themselves, strengthen themselves in good, and learn to fulfil faithfully their duties as citizens and as Christians.

Nevertheless you must take precautions in choosing a school to give your children only teachers who combine an adequate instruction with regular and Christian conduct. Many parents can bitterly deplore the consequences of their negligence on this all-important point. The example and words of a teacher frequently leave profound impressions, for good or evil, on the spirit and heart of his pupils. If the master possesses a religious spirit and maintains moral conduct, his pupils will be drawn towards good by his lessons and examples. But if he is unconvincing, if his words are not worthy of his high station, you may be assured that some of his pupils will some day feel the deadly effects of the education received from such a teacher. The evil seed, fallen on virgin ground, will not always produce its fruit right away; it could, in the presence of Christian parents, remain dormant for a long time. But when the right occasion arises, the bad impressions left embedded in a young heart will reveal themselves, to the greatest astonishment of his family.

However, if mothers and fathers are careful to keep their children away from Catholic schools which do not give complete guarantees for principles and morals, they have even more reason to avoid the schools which are indifferent to religion; and still more should they fear the Protestant schools, where the children are exposed to falsifications of the word of God, where their young minds are invited to form their own doctrines after private reading of the texts; where every year the Catholic pupil hears attacks of every sort on the principles and dogmas of his faith before he has had the opportunity really to know and understand them. What result would there be from his attendance at such schools?–A strange confusion in his religious ideas, usually followed by a distressing indifference in matters of faith. Oh! We beg you, if you have the slightest concern for the salvation of our children, do not expose them to the disastrous effects of doubt and infidelity by allowing them to enter these institutions where they would learn to question the most positive dogmas of revelation.

There could be no excuse, even if these institutions were superior to Catholic ones, because faith is a blessing which must be more highly esteemed than all worldly advantages. Besides, our elementary schools are not below the standards attained by the Protestant schools, and as for institutions at a higher level, we do not see that we have anything to envy of our separated brothers. Alongside their best colleges in the provinces and even in the neighbouring states, we can happily place our Catholic seminaries; and, thanks to God, we can today offer our studious youth an institution which is beginning most auspiciously: Laval University, for which we ask the most bountiful blessings from the Holy Spirit.

C.5 Legal Provision for Separate Schools in Alberta and Saskatchewan

The North West Territories School Ordinance of 1901 was important because its provisions became part of the constitution when Alberta and Saskatchewan were made provinces in 1905.

Department of Education

3.   There shall be a department of the public service of the Territories called the Department of Education over which the member of the executive Council appointed by the Lieutenant-Governor-in-Council under seal of the Territories to discharge the functions of the Commissioner of Education for the time being shall preside.

(2) The Lieutenant-Governor-in-Council may appoint such officers, clerks and servants as are required for the proper conduct of the business of the department and for the purpose of this Ordinance all of whom shall hold office during pleasure.

4.   The department shall have the control and management of all kindergarten schools, public and *separate schools*, normal schools, teachers' institutes, and the education of the deaf, deaf mute and blind persons.

. . . .

Regulations of the Department

6.   The Commissioner with the approval of the Lieutenant-Governor-in-Council shall have power:

1. To make regulations of the department–
(a) For the classification, organization, government, examination and inspection of all schools hereinbefore mentioned;
(b) For the construction, furnishing and care of school buildings and the arrangement of school premises;

C.5 Source: *North West Territories Ordinances*, 1901, Chapter 29.

(c) For the examination, licensing and grading of teachers and for the examination of persons who may desire to enter professions or who may wish certificates of having completed courses of study in any school;

(d) For a teachers' reading course and teachers' institutes and conventions.

2. To authorize text and reference books for the use of the pupils and teachers in all schools hereinbefore mentioned as well as such maps, globes, charts, and other apparatus or equipment as may be required for giving proper instruction in such schools;

3. To prepare a list of books suitable for school libraries and to make regulations for the management of such libraries;

4. To make due provision for the training of teachers.

. . . .

Educational Council

8.   There shall be an educational council consisting of five persons at least two of whom shall be Roman Catholics to be appointed by the Lieutenant-Governor-in-Council; who shall receive such remuneration as the Lieutenant-Governor-in-Council shall determine.

. . . .

10.   All general regulations respecting the inspection of schools, the examination, training, licensing, and grading of teachers, courses of study, teachers' institutes, and text and reference books shall before being adopted or amended be referred to the council for its discussion and report.

11.   The council shall consider such matters as may be referred to it as hereinbefore provided or by the Commissioner and may also consider any question concerning the educational system of the Territories as to it may seem fit and shall report thereon to the Lieutenant-Governor-in-Council.

Formation of Public School Districts

12.   Any portion of the Territories may be erected into a public school district provided that–

(a) It does not exceed five miles in length or breadth exclusive of road allowances;

(b) It contains four persons actually resident therein who on the erection of the district would be liable to assessment and twelve children between the ages of five and sixteen inclusive;

Provided however that in special cases the Commissioner may permit the boundaries of any district to exceed five miles in length or breadth or either.

. . . .

Separate Schools

41.   The minority of ratepayers in any district whether Protestant or Roman Catholic may establish a separate school therein; and in such case the ratepayers establishing such Protestant or Roman Catholic separate school shall be liable only to assessments of such rates as they impose upon themselves in respect thereof.

42.   The petition for the erection of a separate school district shall be signed by three resident ratepayers of the religious faith indicated in the name of the proposed district; and shall be in the form prescribed by the commissioner.

43.   The persons qualified to vote for or against the erection of a separate school district shall be ratepayers of the district of the same religious faith Protestant or Roman Catholic as the petitioners.

44.   The notice calling a meeting of the ratepayers for the purpose of taking their vote on the petition for the erection of a separate school district shall be in the form prescribed by the commissioner and the proceedings subsequent to the posting of such notice shall be the same as prescribed in the formation of public school districts.

45.   After the establishment of a separate school

district under the provisions of this Ordinance such separate school districts and the board thereof shall possess and exercise all rights, powers and privileges and be subject to the same liabilities and method of government as is herein provided in respect of public school districts.

(2) Any person who is legally assessed or assessable for a public school shall not be liable to assessment for any separate school established therein.

C.6 The Structure of Public Education in Quebec after 1869

Department of Public Instruction.

. . . .

1882. A superintendent of public instruction is appointed by the Lieutenant-Governor in Council. He has charge of the Department of Public Instruction.

. . . .

1885. The superintendent possesses all the powers, functions, rights and obligations conferred or imposed upon him by the various articles enacted in this title and the provisions of these Revised Statutes respecting his office.

1886. The superintendent, in the exercise of his functions, is bound to comply with the directions of the Council of Public Instruction, or with those of the Roman Catholic or Protestant Committee, as the case may be.

. . . .

1888. The superintendent is, *ex-officio*, president of the Council of Public Instruction, member of each of the two Committees thereof, visitor-general of all public schools, member of the Council of Arts and Manufactures, and visitor of the schools of arts and manufactures.

. . . .

C.6 Source: *Revised Statutes of the Province of Quebec*(Quebec, 1888), vol. I, Title V, Public Instruction, Chs. 2-4.

1891. The superintendent shall draw up, in accordance with the directions of the Council of Public Instruction or of the Committees thereof, a detailed statement of the sums required for public instruction, and submit the same annually to the Government.

1892. It is specially the duty of the superintendent:

1. To receive from the Provincial Treasurer, in addition to the amounts appropriated for superior education, all sums of money appropriated for public school purposes, and to distribute the same among the school commissioners and trustees of the respective municipalities, according to law, and in proportion to the population of the same, as ascertained by the then last census;

2. To prepare and cause to be printed and distributed all necessary forms;

3. To prepare and cause to be printed recommendations and advice on the management of schools, for the school commissioners and trustees, and for the secretary-treasurers and teachers;

4. To keep correct books and distinct schedules of all the matters under his superintendence and control, so that all requisite information may be clearly and promptly obtained by the Government, the Legislature, or the school visitors;

5. To examine and control the accounts of all persons, corporations and associations accountable for any public moneys appropriated and distributed under the laws relating to schools, and to report whether the said moneys are *bona fide* applied for the purposes for which they were granted;

6. To lay annually before the three branches of the Legislature a detailed report of the actual state of education in the Province, tables of schools, numbers of children attending them, and other like matters;

7. To state in his yearly report to the Legis-

lature, what he has done with the amounts voted for education during the period to which such report relates;

. . . .

2. *Council of Public Instruction, and Committees thereof...*
1893. The Council of Public Instruction is composed of Roman Catholic and Protestant members, as follows:

1. The bishops, ordinaries, or administrators of the Roman Catholic dioceses and apostolic vicariates, situated either in whole or in part in the Province, who are members *ex-officio;*

2. An equal number of Roman Catholic laymen appointed by the Lieutenant-Governor in Council;

3. A number of Protestant members, equal to the number of Roman Catholic members appointed by the Lieutenant-Governor in Council, who are appointed in the same manner....
1894. The Council of Public Instruction is divided into two Committees, the one consisting of the Roman Catholic and the other of the Protestant members thereof....
1895. The superintendent is a member of the Council of Public Instruction and *ex-officio* the chairman thereof.

In the case of the absence or sickness of the superintendent, the Council shall appoint one of its members present to act as chairman of the meeting.

The superintendent is *ex-officio* a member of each Committee, but he is entitled to vote only in the Committee to which he, by religion, belongs....

. . . .

1911. Everything within the scope of the functions of the Council of Public Instruction, which specially concerns the schools and public instruction

generally of Roman Catholics, shall be within the exclusive jurisdiction of the Roman Catholic Committee of such Council.

In the same manner, everything within the scope of such functions, which specially concerns the schools and public instruction generally of Protestants, shall be within the exclusive jurisdiction of the Protestant Committee....
1912. It shall be the duty of the Council of Public Instruction, or of the Roman Catholic and Protestant Committees respectively, according as the provisions of the preceding articles may require, with the approval of the Lieutenant-Governor in Council:

1. To fix the time of their meetings and the mode of proceeding;

2. To make regulations respecting normal schools;

3. To make from time to time, regulations for the organization, government and discipline of public schools, and for the classification of schools and teachers;

4. To select and cause to be published, due regard being had in such selection to schools in which the teaching is in French and to those in which the teaching is in English, text-books, maps and globes to be used, to the exclusion of all others, in the elementary schools, model schools and academies under the control of school commissioners or trustees;

This provision shall not extend to the selection of books having reference to religion or morals, which selection shall be made as provided by paragraph 4 of article 2026.

5. To acquire copyright of books, maps, pieces of music or other publications, whether originals, copies, or compilations, published under their direction for the use of schools in the Province;

6. To cause to be inserted by the superin-

tendent, in a book to be kept for that purpose, in such manner and form as they may direct, the names and grades and classes of all teachers who have received diplomas from the boards of examiners, also the names of all teachers who, after having gone through the regular course of instruction in any normal school, have received diplomas from the superintendent.

To ensure compliance with this provision, it shall be the duty of the superintendent to cause to be laid, from time to time, before the Council, the names and classification of all persons admitted as teachers by the different boards of examiners since their establishment to the date of such statement, and the names of all teachers who have received from him diplomas after going through the proper course of instruction in any normal school....

. . . .

1915. For bad conduct, immorality or intemperance, the Roman Catholic or Protestant Committee, as the case may be, may revoke any diploma granted by any board of examiners to any teacher, or granted to any student of any normal school by the superintendent....

. . . .

1940. School inspectors, professors, directors and principals of normal schools, the secretaries and the members of boards of examiners, shall be appointed or removed by the Lieutenant-Governor in Council, on the recommendation of the Roman Catholic or Protestant Committee of the Council of Public Instruction, according as such appointments or removals concerns Roman Catholic or Protestant schools....

. . . .

3. School Municipalities

1970. There shall be held, in the manner hereinafter provided in each municipality, village, town and city in the Province, one or more public schools for the elementary instruction of youth, under the control of school commissioners, or, in the event of dissentient schools being established therein, under the control of trustees....

. . . .

1972. The inhabitants of any city, town or village municipality, shall, for the purposes of this title, (unless it is otherwise provided by any special act) be subject to the jurisdiction of the school commissioners or trustees, elected for the municipality of which the city, town or village forms part, and shall have the right of voting at the election of such school commissioners or trustees....

. . . .

1981. The school commissioners or trustees shall divide the municipality into school districts, and shall designate them by the numbers one, two, &c., and the limits assigned by them to each district shall be entered in the register of their proceedings.

. . . .

1990. Any number whatever of the proprietors, occupants, tenants and rate-payers of a township or parish, divided into two or more municipalities for school purposes, professing a religious faith different from that of the majority of the said township or parish, may dissent and maintain one or more dissentient schools situated anywhere in the said township or parish, by giving notice in writing to the chairman of the school commissioners of their respective municipalities, and electing three trustees for school purposes, as provided in articles 1997 and following of these Revised Statutes.

2. The trustees of the said dissentients shall either maintain under their immediate control, or subsidize, a school of their own religious faith

situated in the said township or parish.

    3. If the members of the religious minority, in any one of the school municipalities into which the said township or parish is divided desire to send their children to the school maintained by the said trustees without becoming dissentients, it shall be lawful for the school commissioners of such municipality to make an annual grant, from the school funds of the municipality to the said trustees, in aid of the said dissentient school....

....

2026. It is the duty of school commissioners and trustees:

    1. To appoint and engage, by resolution of the school corporation and by written contract, teachers duly qualified to teach in the schools under their control;

    2. To cancel, after mature deliberation at a meeting called for the purpose, the engagements of teachers on account of incapacity, neglecting faithfully to perform their duties, insubordination, misconduct or immorality;

    3. To provide that the course of study authorized by the Roman Catholic or Protestant Committee, as the case may be, shall be followed in each school;

    4. To require that no other books be used in the schools under their control than those authorized by the Council of Public Instruction or either of the Committees thereof;

    The *curé*, or priest administering a Roman Catholic church shall, however, have the exclusive right of selecting the books having reference to religion and morals for the use of pupils of his religious faith.

    The Protestant Committee shall have similar powers respecting Protestant pupils.

    5. To establish general rules for the management of their schools, and to communicate them in writing to the teachers under their control;

    6. To fix the time of the annual public examination, and to attend the same;

    7. To name two or more from among themselves to visit each school under their control at least once in six months, and to report to the corporation of which they are members the state of the school and whether their regulations are strictly observed, also the progress of the scholars, the character and capacity of the teachers, and every other matter relating to the management of the schools;

    8. To comply, as regards the accounts and register to be kept by the secretary-treasurer, with all instructions, whether special or general, from time to time given them by the superintendent.

C.7 Denominationalism in Newfoundland

    Be it therefore enacted by the Governor, Legislative Council and Assembly, in Legislative Session convened:–

    I–That there shall be annually appropriated, out of such moneys as shall from time to time be in the hands of the Receiver General, unappropriated, a sum of money for Protestant Educational purposes, equal in proportion, according to population, to the sums of money by the said Acts appropriated for Roman Catholic Educational purposes...

    And the said sum, so appropriated by this Section for Protestant Educational purposes, shall be apportioned among the several Protestant Denominations according to population, to be expended by the several Boards of Education hereafter to be appointed in the Protestant Educational Districts mentioned in the said Acts, or as the said Educational Districts are hereby or may hereafter be altered.

....

C.7 Source: An Act to Amend the Acts for the Encouragement of Education... 1874. Newfoundland, *Statutes*, 37 Vict. Cap. V.

VII.–The Governor in Council shall nominate and appoint, in each of the Protestant Educational Districts in the said Acts mentioned, five or seven members of the Church of England–one of whom shall be the senior Clergyman of the said Church, actually resident or officiating in such District,–to form and be a Church of England Board of Education for such District. And the said Boards shall manage and expend all money hereby appropriated for Church of England Educational purposes.

VIII.–The Governor in Council shall nominate and appoint, in each of the Protestant Educational Districts in the said Acts mentioned, five or seven members of the Wesleyan Church–one of whom shall be the senior or superintendent Clergyman of the said Wesleyan Church, actually resident or officiating in such District, to form and be a Wesleyan Board of Education for such District; and the said Boards shall manage and expend all moneys hereby appropriated for Wesleyan Educational purposes.

IX.–The Educational Districts for Protestants of the Free Kirk of Scotland and the Congregationalists, shall be two, one of which shall extend from Harbor Main inclusive to Cape John, and shall be called "the Harbor Grace District;" and the other shall extend from Harbor Main exclusive to Cape Ray, and shall be called "the St. John's district;"–and the Governor in Council shall nominate and appoint five or seven members respectively of the said Free Kirk of Scotland and Congregationalists in each of such districts; and the meeting of such Boards shall be held at Harbor Grace and St. John's respectively; and the said Boards shall manage and expend all moneys hereby appropriated for the said Free Kirk of Scotland and Congregationalists in the respective districts.

X.–There shall be one Educational District for Protestants of the Kirk of Scotland, which shall include this Island and the Labrador; and in lieu of the sum to which the members of the Kirk of Scotland are entitled for Educational purposes, according to this Act, the same amount –viz., Forty pounds sterling, equal to One hundred and eighty-four dollars and sixty cents, as was granted by Act 21 Vic., Cap. 7, to the Commercial School at St. John's for Presbyterians, shall be annually appropriated, and the said sum shall be managed and expended by a Board of five or seven members of the Kirk of Scotland, to be appointed by the Governor in Council for the purpose of maintaining a School in St. John's.

XI.–All the provisions respecting Boards of Education contained in the said in part recited Acts, so far as the same are applicable, shall be in force and effect as regards the Boards of Education to be appointed under this Act.

. . . .

XIV.–The Governor in Council shall nominate and appoint two Protestant Inspectors of Schools,–one of whom shall be a member of the Church of England, for the Inspection of Church of England Schools, and the other shall be a member of the Wesleyan Church, for the Inspection of Wesleyan Schools; and such Inspectors shall also alternately inspect the other Protestant Schools provided for by this Act, and in addition to the duties imposed by the said Act, 21st Victoria, Cap. 7, the Inspectors shall classify each School, in one of three classes.

. . . .

XVIII.–If any Board of Education, appointed under this Act, shall desire to offer a superior education in any School under the control of such Board, and the Board shall provide a guarantee, to be approved of by the Governor in Council, for securing an adequate remuneration for an efficient Master for that purpose, such Board may establish in such School a higher grade of Education...

. . . .

XX.–This Act shall not come into operation until the First day of July, A. D. 1875, after a Census has been taken, upon which Census shall be based all the Denominational appropriations provided for by this Act. And the said appropriations shall be subject to re-adjustment upon the basis of each subsequent Decennial Census.

D. The Place of the Universities and Grammar Schools

During the second half of the nineteenth century, the grammar schools and academies (increasingly called high schools) were absorbed into the new state systems of education. In most of British North America the change occasioned little difficulty or debate. There were few genuinely independent grammar schools. They were financed in part by tuition fees but their clientele was never large or wealthy enough to maintain them by that means alone, and their continued existence or improvement had always depended upon government financial aid. Once it was accepted that the grammar schools should be integrated into the school system it was easily done by legislation, for few schools could have resisted such incorporation even had they wished to do so. Document D.1 presents some of the more common arguments used to justify the absorption of grammar schools into state systems.

Among the English population of Quebec, the same kind of transformation took place. Only among French Canadians where the classical colleges had private endowments not available elsewhere, and where the Catholic church would have resisted nationalization in any case, did secondary education remain beyond the direct control of the state. Catholic Quebec, indeed, had no state secondary schools until the 1920s.

The place of the universities within the education systems of English Canada was more complicated. Most of the early colleges had either been founded by religious denominations or were closely tied to them. The result was a multitude of small denominational colleges, often built and maintained at considerable sacrifice, but lacking the resources necessary to provide advanced education of the highest quality.

Governments tried to change this pattern in two ways. They attempted to establish single, provincial institutions large enough to support good libraries, laboratories, and a wide range of subjects impossible to offer in the small, geographically dispersed colleges. At the same time, they attempted to make these unitary institutions secular, or at least non-denominational. Their efforts often met with adamant opposition. In document D.2 the Presbyterians of Upper Canada state their reasons for rejecting Robert Baldwin's University Act of 1849: religious reasons are foremost, but they draw attention as well to the geographical disadvantages of a single institution in a colony like Upper Canada.

The fact that the denominational colleges were already established, and the conviction among many clergymen that religion and higher education were inseparable, meant that the only workable alternative in eastern Canada was university federation. Federation would allow the creation of a large institution consisting of a group of colleges, both church-related and non-denominational. Each college would continue to be a teaching centre, but some subjects and facilities would be shared. The colleges would refrain from exercising the right to give degrees, which would become the prerogative of the university itself. One of the earliest statements of the idea of federation—in this case applied to the problem in New Brunswick—is found in document D.3.

University federation became a common, though not a universal, English Canadian solution to the problem of providing higher education. In eastern Canada, however, the denominational college continued to exist alongside the federated university. In the new provinces and territories of the West, men took warning from the eastern example. They did not oppose the idea of federation or affiliation—that is, they accepted the idea that denominational colleges could be a part of a university—but where possible they refused to charter separate institutions, thus avoiding the dispersion of effort and resources that characterized higher education in the East. In document D.4, the President of the University of Saskatchewan describes the influence of the Canadian university tradition on higher education in the West, as seen from the vantage point of 1921.

D.1 The Absorption of the Grammar Schools

The arguments for absorption were stated by Egerton Ryerson, writing in 1849.

The District Grammar Schools were clearly intended to occupy an intermediate position between the Common Schools and the Colleges. Their object is distinct and peculiar; and so should be their organization. They are the first of the three stages in a system of liberal studies. As the College prepares for professional studies, so does the Grammar School prepare for the Colleges. Ought not the organization and system of instruction, therefore, in the Grammar Schools to have reference to the Colleges to which they are intended to be introductory? Or, should they be suffered to remain a compound of everything?

Do not the interests of classical learning require the existence of and endowment of special Schools for that purpose? Is not such the object of the District Grammar Schools? As they were partly endowed in 1797, for that object, ought they not to be made as efficient for its accom-

D.1 Source: Reprinted in J.G. Hodgins, ed., *Documentary History of Education in Upper Canada* (Toronto, 1896-1910), vol. 8, 290-91.

plishment as possible? Can that be the case, as long as Grammar Schools are allowed to teach everything, that is taught in the Common Schools? Are not the subjects peculiar to a Grammar School ample to occupy the time and employ the energies of any one man?

. . . .

...Surely, it never could have been intended, that Grammar Schools should occupy the same ground as Common Schools,–should compete with them: thus lowering the character and impairing the efficiency of both the Grammar and the neighbouring Common Schools. It is the bearing of this question on the interests of Common Schools that is the reason for thus discussing matters relating to any class of seminaries in the Province, not managed under the provisions of the Common School law. The following suggestions are, however, offered:-

1. Whether a formal and thorough inquiry (by Commission, or otherwise,) into the state and character of the District Grammar Schools, in Upper Canada ought not to be instituted. The facts that, notwithstanding the existence of from thirty to forty of these District Grammar Schools in Upper Canada,–of there being no less than sixty Grammar School Scholarships established in the Provincial University,–of the University being munificently endowed and provided with able Professors, and yet only eight students matriculating at the last Annual Convocation of 1849, a smaller number than annually enters the youngest of the Colleges in the newest States of the neighbouring Republic;–these facts, would appear to be quite sufficient to justify, if not demand, the most careful inquiry into the working of that class of Schools, on whose contributions the University depends for its numerical efficiency, as well as great numbers of youth for a sound elementary classical education.

2. Whether a Course of Studies and General Rules of Discipline should not be prepared and prescribed for the Grammar Schools,–fixing a standard below which pupils should not be admitted; thus stamping upon the Grammar Schools uniformity and definiteness of character, making them efficient in promoting the objects of their establishment, and preventing them, in any instance, from the useless, if not worse than useless, attempt at teaching a multitude of things imperfectly instead of teaching a few things efficiently.

3. Whether a thorough system of Governmental inspection ought not to be established and exercised over the Grammar Schools, as well as over Common Schools.

I am far from intimating an opinion that there are no efficient Grammar Schools in the Province, even under the present system, or rather absence of all system. There are several instances in which separate apartments for different classes of pupils are provided, and Assistants employed to teach the English branches. But such examples are rather exceptions to the general rule, than the rule itself. The general rule is, whether there be an Assistant, or not, to admit pupils of both sexes, and of all ages and attainments, from a, b,c, upwards, into Schools which ought to occupy a position distinct from, and superior to that of the Common Schools. Equally far be it from me to intimate, that there is any deficiency of qualifications on the part of Masters of Grammar Schools. But, I doubt not, that they will be the first to feel how much the efficiency and pleasures of their duties will be advanced by the introduction of a proper and uniform system, as they will be the first to confess, *"non omnia possumus omnes."*

The first building at
Dalhousic College,
Halifax, Nova Scotia.

D.2 The Case Against a Unitary Provincial Institution

The objections to the new University Act of 1849 and the reasons for maintaining Queen's College, according to its Royal Charter, may be comprised under the following heads:–

(1). The irreligious character of the Act of 1849, referred to. Not only is the teaching of Theology prohibited in the University of Toronto, but all forms of Divine Worship, all Public Prayer,–everything that can remind either Professors, or Students, of God, and the duties we owe to Him,–of our responsibility and obligations,–are rigidly and peremptorily excluded. And, as no test whatever is required of the Professors, not even belief in the existence of God, there is nothing in the Act to prevent Infidels, Atheists, or persons holding the most dangerous and pernicious principles, from being entrusted with the instruction of youth at that time of life, when evil impressions are most likely to be made upon their minds.

. . . .

(3). The Act is liable to this further objection, that, even although it made the best provision for the efficiency of the University, yet the confining of all the means of University education to one place, and one set of teachers, will, of itself, very much impair that efficiency. In education, more than in any other subject, a wholesome rivalry, a generous competition is of paramount importance; in this department of education the deadening effects of monopoly are more apparent than in any other. And, if such a system would be at once condemned, if

D.2 Source: "Statement of the Board of Trustees of the University of Queen's College, Kingston, of their reasons for resolving to Carry on that Institution...irrespective of the University Act of 1849", in J. G. Hodgins, ed., *Documentary History of Education in Upper Canada* (Toronto, 1896-1910) vol. 9, 184-88.

attempted to be applied to ordinary trade, or commerce, what reason can be assigned for applying it to a subject of such immensely higher importance as the education of our youth.

(4). To confine to one particular place the means of a higher education appears no less injudicious and impolitic than unjust. A Country of such immense extent, and increasing so rapidly in population, most assuredly requires more than one University. To require all the youth of the Province to travel to Toronto to obtain Education is, in fact, to pass sentence of exclusion against the greater part of them. Even in countries of far less extent, it is found indispensable to establish Universities in many different localities; as, for example, in Scotland, where four Universities have long existed and are all fully attended. Already the population of this Country is equal to that of Scotland, when her four Universities were established, and we cannot doubt that Canada will, at no very distant day, number a population far exceeding that which Scotland now contains.

(5). There is every reason to fear that, if Queen's College were to cease operations, as to its literary and philosophical department, the progress of nearly all those young men who are now studying with a view to the Ministry would be stopped. Of these there are now nearly twenty in different stages of advancement. Many of them from different causes could not attend at Toronto. At Queen's College every possible exertion is made to render attendance there as cheap as possible to students for the Presbyterian Church. They are entirely exempted from class fees, not only at the Divinity Classes but from the very commencement of their College course; and the Boarding Establishment, while possessing every needful comfort, is conducted with such strictical economy, that the expenses of the students per session amount only to a very moderate sum. The time of attendance is so arranged as to permit young men to teach, or be otherwise employed, during the summer. None of these advantages could be expected by them at the University of Toronto; the full amount of fees and dues would be enacted; they would have to board themselves in as expensive a manner as other students; and the times of attendance are such as to prevent any other occupation; so that none could attend but those who possess independent means, or whose friends are able to maintain them during the whole College course. Besides all this, the Bursaries, now pretty numerous, granted by individuals, or bodies interested in the welfare of the Presbyterian Church, would, in many cases, not be given to students attending an Institution like the University of Toronto, in which these individuals, or Bodies, might not place any confidence.

(6). The number of students at Queen's College, and the almost certain probability of further increase ought to induce us to maintain it. After the [Free Church] secession in 1844, only ten students attended; the number now is thirty-five, and the number anticipated next Session is fifty. The increase in the Preparatory School, which may be safely regarded as an indication of the future increase of the College, is most encouraging. In 1846, when the School re-opened, there were but six scholars. The number now attending is fifty,–nearly all engaged in such studies as will fit them for College; and from this source alone a constant annual influx of well prepared students may be expected. The fact that we can now point to upwards of eighty, and, probably next Session, to one hundred, of the youth of this Province, enjoying the benefits of a superior education in connection with Queen's College must undoubtedly tend to give the Institution very strong claims on the assistance of the

Legislature and the countenance of the community generally.

(7). The Roman Catholic Church has made Kingston the principal seat of their educational operations in Upper Canada, for which purpose it is admirably fitted by its central situation and the easy access to it from all parts of the Province. Should Queen's College be given up, as a Literary Institution, there would be no Protestant College in the whole vast distance from Montreal to Cobourg; and thus the whole of the superior education of those large sections of Country, of which Kingston is the natural capital, would be made over to a Roman Catholic Seminary.

(8). The manner in which the new Measure of 1849 has been received by the Country gives no hopes for its ultimate success. All the most numerous and influential Denominations of Christians have declared themselves most decidedly opposed to its principle. The adherents of the Church of Scotland, especially, look upon it with suspicion and dislike. Indeed, a Measure, so utterly opposed to Christianity, and so repugnant to the principles and practice of Presbyterianism, could never be expected to secure their confidence. The Church of Scotland has always held that education, from its lowest to its highest stage, ought to be founded on Religion, upon which all the real prosperity of individuals and Nations depends. And there is reason to believe, that not only the Members of that Church, but many parents who belong to other Religious Denominations, will prefer sending their children to Queen's College, rather than to one where every vestige of Religion is proscribed, and is studiously and purposely rejected.

D.3 Towards Unity in Higher Education: New Brunswick

11. In devising and maturing a proper sys-

tem of University Education, the question of religious instruction has not failed to engage the most earnest attention of the Commissioners. On this subject there should be no difference of opinion in a christian land and among a christian people. No youth can be properly educated who is not instructed in religion as well as in science and literature. The question is, not whether each youth shall be religiously instructed, but how far it is in the power, and therefore the duty of the Government to give such religious instruction? In a free country, the government is a reflection of the sentiments of the people and the executor of their will. As the government is not constituted to represent and inculcate the sentiments of any one religious persuasion, (in contradistinction to those of other religious persuasions,) so it would be false to its duty and character to attempt to do so. But the government, if not as representing the collective sentiments of all religious persuasions, yet as being at least the guardians of their equal rights, should require that the evidences, the truths, and the morals of Christianity, should lie at the foundation of all Public Collegiate instruction, and the spirit of christianity should pervade its whole administration. As to the teaching of what is peculiar to each religious persuasion, this clearly appertains to such religious persuasion and not to the government. It is confessedly the duty of each religious persuasion to provide for the religious instruction of its own youth; and the responsibility of performing or neglecting that duty rests with such religious persuasion, and not with the government. In a national or provincial College, therefore, like King's College, special provision should be made for allowing the authorities of each religious persuasion to give religious instruction during a part of one day in

D.3 Source: *Report of the Commissioners on King's College,*
Fredericton, 1854.

each week to such of its own youth as may be attending the College, and also to require such youth to attend at the time and place of such religious instruction, as also to attend their own place of worship at least once on Sabbath. This system of religious oversight and instruction has been in operation some years in regard to the Students of the Normal School at Toronto in Canada West; and the satisfactory and complete success of it there, has led to its recent introduction into the Toronto University College. The Clergy of the religious persuasions concerned, have shown a becoming readiness and fidelity in the performance of their duty; denominational rivalship, and the guilt and reproach of neglecting such a duty, together with the higher motives of moral obligation, have proved ample inducements to secure its performance.

12. Thus may King's College be non-denominational, yet facilities provided for giving denominational religious instruction to its Students by those whose proper province it is to give such instruction. There is no infringement of the religious rights or scruples of any class; yet there is a due regard to the interests and wishes of all classes.

. . . .

[We would make provision] likewise for the affiliation to the University of other seminaries of learning than King's College; so that a student matriculating in any of the courses of study recommended, may pursue his studies in any of the affiliated institutions, and come up before the Examiners appointed by the Senate, and on passing a satisfactory examination, receive his Degree or Diploma. Thus will the denominational seminaries, as well as other educational institutions of the country, become linked to the University in the bond of common relationship, cooperation, and interest; the independent self-government of those seminaries will not, in the slightest degree, be interfered with, while their exertions and usefulness will be encouraged and honored.

D.4 The Origins of the Western Universities

I think the careful observer will be surprised at the closeness of the approach of this University [Saskatchewan] to the Canadian type, notwithstanding the fewness of its years and the variety of the influences that have been at work. The Canadian stream of University life, or rather the two streams of University life, took their origin in two sources–both clerical in character–in the King's Colleges in Nova Scotia, New Brunswick and Toronto which copied Oxford, and the Seminary at Quebec which reflected Paris–possibly the inspirer also of Oxford.

The Oxford tradition was checked and marred by sectarian strife. Its opponents appealed to Scotland and New England for men and ideas until sectarian bitterness drove politicians and neutrals to the experiment made in London. There an examining University had been set up. It was non-sectarian in character and control, according equal liberty to all to teach when and how they pleased, provided they met a severe examination test. In Halifax, in Toronto and in Winnipeg, the London idea began an unequal struggle. It prepared the way for the conception of a University supported, controlled and devoted exclusively to the service of the state–a University at first resentful and antagonistic to ecclesiastical claims and criticisms, then indifferent, and now respectful and appreciative of religious rather than sectarian interests.

. . . .

D.4 Source: University of Saskatchewan, *The President's Report* 1920-21, pp. 11-12.

In Toronto, the struggle between the different University ideals has been keen and beneficent. In the Maritime Provinces, more bitter and destructive. The conception of the modern State University, absorbing but not destroying the best of the past, pervaded the report of the Toronto Commission of 1905 and was written into the Act of 1906. That Act has been reproduced with great particularity in the Alberta and Saskatchewan Acts of 1907 and later in the revised Acts of British Columbia and Manitoba. The Toronto Act represents an attempt to harmonize the Oxford and the Scottish traditions as they were represented in the denominational Colleges with the principles of State supremacy and support. It bears within it the imperfections due to the conflicts of the Churches and the local interests which supported them. The new Western Universities of British Columbia, Alberta and Saskatchewan were free from such embarrassments and began their existence with a single aim–to serve the State, unmindful of sectarian bias and urban rivalries. Hitherto they have resisted all attempts to embroil them in sectarian strife or to divide them into fragments to be flung to ravenous towns. Their rapid growth in influence and in service has been due to their singleness of purpose, their undivided efforts and to the large and liberal measure of State support with State control which they have received.

With this background, Saskatchewan University has elaborated a system of government, has formulated courses of study, has established standards of scholarship, has adopted methods of instruction, and has reached out to serve the different interests of the Province in a manner which, we believe, the competent observer will declare to be faithful to the best traditions of the Universities of Canada.

IV

The System at Work: Victorian Education In Theory and Practice

In Canada it may appear to be something of a misnomer to speak of a "national" system of education. The British North America Act placed the control of education under provincial jurisdiction: in law, there are as many school systems as there are provinces. Yet going to school in English Canada provided much the same kind of experience in Nova Scotia or Ontario or British Columbia; and the differences that existed between French and English institutions should not be allowed to obscure the many similarities. During the middle decades of the nineteenth century, eastern Canadian school systems developed relatively independently of each other, but they all looked much the same. And because of the "cultural imperialism" of the older parts of Canada, similar institutions took root in the prairies and British Columbia. Men born and raised in Ontario or Quebec or Nova Scotia carried their

ideas and institutions with them when they emigrated. Thus, the first western school acts were transcripts of those in the east. The new western universities were often modelled on eastern institutions; the same is true of the western classical colleges begun by French Canadians. The departments of education and the schools were staffed by easterners; and from the nineties, leading schoolmen met in national associations to share their ideas. The problems of public education, then, no less than the achievements, were much the same in all parts of the country.

One reason for these similarities was that Canadians shared many common assumptions about the purposes and organization of education. Some of these assumptions–the justifications for state intervention in education, and for a particular kind of administrative structure–have already been examined in

George Jay Elementary School, Victoria, B.C., in 1910.

A. The Theory of Mental Discipline

Chapters II and III. Two others deserve attention. The first of these is the theory of learning that explained how formal education prepared a child for adult life; the second is the Victorian Canadian view of the relationship between elementary and more advanced kinds of schooling. Together, these several assumptions formed a kind of public school consensus about purposes, structure, and pedagogy which shaped the institutions inherited by later generations of Canadians and which also provided the conventional wisdom that later school reformers would attack.

There was a second important reason, however, for the similarity among Canadian school systems, and it had little to do with educational issues. In every province there were social and economic factors that determined who would go to school and for how long. One of these was the impact of social class on educational opportunity. Another was the gap between urban and rural life. Considerations such as these were no less important than educational ideas in determining the nature of Victorian education in Canada.

The terminal date in this chapter is deliberately vague. We are concerned here with the nature of a system that grew to maturity during the Victorian age and that characterized Canadian education until both the schools and the society were changed by the impact of war, industrialization, and urbanization during the early twentieth century.

How could schooling do what it was supposed to do? How could it raise good citizens, temperate and industrious men and women, civilized leaders for society? The answer lay in a theory of learning which dominated debate about the most suitable kind of curriculum. That theory–usually known as mental discipline–is explained in documents A.1 and A.2.

The theory applied to all levels of schooling and at each level it influenced the selection of subjects to be taught. It provided a justification for both the "general education" of students in the elementary schools (document A.3), and for the dominance of a small group of academic subjects–especially the classics–in the secondary school and college curriculum (document A.4).

A.1 Mental Discipline and the Training of the Intellect

Sir William Peterson, a Scotsman and graduate of Edinburgh, Gottingen, and Oxford universities, was Principal of McGill University from 1895 to 1919. The extract reproduced here is from an address he gave in 1904.

It ought never to be forgotten, to begin with, that all education should be a training of faculty. Its essential aim should be "to develop and train the natural powers of the mind; to make it quick, observing, apprehensive, accurate, logical; able to understand argument; able to search out facts for itself, and draw from them the proper conclusions; to reason, and to understand reasoning; in one word, to think" (Professor G. G. Ramsay). It is almost a platitude to say that the real test of efficiency in education is not the accumulation of

A.1 Source: Sir William Peterson, "National Education", Ontario Educational Association *Proceedings* (1904), pp. 74-76.

data or the acquisition of knowledge, but the development of intellectual power. What seems to be more in need of emphasis–especially in view of the clamor for what are known as "soft subjects"–is that in the elementary stages this cannot be attained without a certain amount of drudgery. Only through earnest application–bestowed sometimes even on what may seem to be an uncongenial subject–will the pupil form those habits of attention, concentration, accuracy and thoroughness which form the indispensable foundation of further progress. Competent critics have not hesitated to say that smattering and superficiality are the curse of our school education. We plume ourselves on being "alive" and "up-to-date", and we use high-sounding phrases about "relating the work of the class-room to the work of life." This leads to the introduction into the curriculum of stenography and typewriting, which are hailed as being much more "vivid and vital" than any "dead languages." But should we not lay to heart the warnings addressed to us by those who are entitled to speak with authority on the subject? Let me quote two from England and one from the United States. "Do not overload the curriculum," said Sir Joshua Fitch, "by multiplying the number of necessary subjects, but hold fast resolutely by the recognized and staple subjects which experience has shown to have the best formative value; secure a definite proportion of hours to those subjects, and for the rest of the available time provide as many forms of intellectual and other activity as your appliances and teaching staff have at command." And again: "The mental gymnastic afforded by a complete devotion to one chosen subject, which taxes all the powers of the student to the utmost, is far superior to that furnished by a half-hearted study of a dozen incongruous things. When the training has once been received, the mind, strengthened rather than cramped by the limits within which it has been working, may expatiate with profit over a wider field; but the training is the main thing" (Professor A. S. Wilkins). Or take this from a report of one of the American Committees of Twelve: "(The tendency to lengthen the Latin course by extending it down into the elementary schools) had its origin in a growing conviction that the ends of education, at least in the earlier stages are best subserved by the concentration of effort upon a limited number of leading studies, properly correlated, rather than by the scattering of energies over an indefinite range of loosely related subjects."

The view thus set forth should, I take it, be accepted as one of the fixed principles of National Education everywhere, and it may confidently be set against much current talk. Making every allowance for adjustment of details in different localities, and for different classes of pupils, there is surely an *a priori* probability that the subjects which *modern* Universities require for entrance are, in the main, the subjects which ought to form the staple of a good general education.

But, say the critics, this is to assume that "what is good preparation for entrance into the Freshman class in College is equally good for the boy who is to be a farmer, or the girl who is to manage a farm home…To teach in the elementary schools what is simply taken up in College or University is not sound in principle. The old academic methods are out of place with young children." This is only partially true. Special teaching must, of course, be provided in connection with special courses, but farmers need, just as much as others, training in habits of accuracy, and much of what is valuable in the traditional curriculum will be quite as valuable for them as for others. There are some subjects that must be adhered to for all pupils; it is the methods of teaching that will always afford room for improvement.

A.2 The Moral Significance of Intellectual Exercises

The intellectual exercises of the school have ...a moral significance that is sometimes strangely overlooked. There can be no intellectual advance without attention. But on the moral side attention demands earnestness and concentration of purpose. If continued, as it must be in the more difficult parts of the intellectual training, the child acquires in this painstaking application the moral qualities of perseverance, patience and self-denial. If the intellectual training is successful in arousing, quickening and establishing a genuine interest in the discovery of truth, the child gets a glimpse of the significance of the ideal. He learns the lesson of self-control, self-expression and self-development in devotion to the claims of truth, which is higher than selfishness, higher than mere likings, aversions and individual waywardness and caprice.

This attitude to truth is invaluable in leading to a similar recognition of the claims of beauty goodness and righteousness.

It is evident that the habits above mentioned are not merely intellectual achievements. They are moral elements incorporated into the life and forming part of the character of the child.

. . . .

Intellectual training has been already dealt with in general terms. The moral value of a genuine interest in study must not be overlooked. To work assiduously to pass an examination may train the pupil to overcome lazy tendencies. Although there may be concentration of purpose without true morality, for an evil end may be persistently pursued, it is nevertheless true that there can be no strength of character, no advance in

A.2 Source: James G. Hume, "Moral Training in Public Schools", Ontario Educational Association *Proceedings* (1898), pp. 233-34.

goodness, upon the basis of vacillating instability of disposition. In the prevention of copying an occasion is given to teach honesty, self-respect and self-reliance.

A.3 Mental Discipline and General Education in the Elementary Schools

This extract, part of the introduction to the revised elementary school course of studies in New Brunswick, was written by the Chief Superintendent of Education for that province, Theodore Rand.

An examination of the Course will shew that the following assumptions underlie its outline provisions:–

1.   That the public school is primarily an agency for the general education of all classes of youth,– a school designed to impart a common education useful to all and open to all.

2.   That the comprehensive and practical aim of the public school is to prepare the child to discharge the duties and meet the obligations of coming manhood, including his relations to the family, society, and the State,–relations involving the highest and most important activities of civilized life.

3.   That the elements in this elementary training are physical health, intelligence (intellectual furnishing and force), and character.

Examination will further shew that, on its intellectual side, the following principles, among others, have controlled the selection and order of the subjects of the outline Course:–

1.   That the aim of the education contemplated is two-fold: the full development of all the powers and faculties, and the acquisition of such knowledge as shall be of the greatest value in the ordin-

A.3 Source: "Report of the Chief Superintendent of Education for the Year 1880", *Journals of the Legislative Assembly of New Brunswick*, 1881.

ary vocations and in the discharge of daily duties.
2. That all the faculties of the mind should be
cultivated, in every department of school-work,
in the order of the growth and relative activity of
each faculty.

· ·

7. That the application to be made of the
knowledge gained–utility in its broadest sense–
should be duly recognized, thus preserving the
link between use and knowledge.
8. That the course of study for general education is of equal utility for all pupils, irrespective
of their future work or field of activity; and that
special adaptations for professional purposes
should be made only in the Standards of the High
School Course.

· ·

The public school exhausts neither the right
nor the duty of the State in education. It may establish higher institutions, and it may organize
or encourage special schools of an elementary
character to meet the wants of classes. The public
school is primarily an agency for the general education of all classes of youth. It is a common
school, furnishing a common education useful
alike to rich and poor, high and low. This primary
function of the public school is of the highest
practical importance and value. Its comprehensive aim is to prepare the child to discharge the
duties and meet the obligations of coming manhood, including his relations to the family, society, and the State,–relations involving the highest
and most important activities of civilized life.
The public school assumes that every child that
crosses its threshold to receive instruction is to
reach mature life and engage in manly duties, and
that his first and highest need is to have the elements of manhood within him developed, quickened, energized, and rightly directed.

This primary function of the public school
should not be subverted to provide technical instruction. This would sacrifice the more important to the less important. All experience shows
that, even for industrial purposes, no technical
training can compensate for the lack of general
education. "The hand becomes another hand
when guided by an intelligent mind." Thought
gives quickness and accuracy to the eye, and cun-
ning to the fingers. General intelligence not only
promotes industrial skill, but it creates a demand
for its products. It touches both of the great laws
of wealth. What a conserver of industrial skill
and enterprise is character! The common schools
of a country, if efficient as such, will necessarily contribute more to industrial skill and enterprise than any amount of mere technical or industrial training can furnish.

A.4 Mental Discipline and the Value of the Classics

This document is part of a pastoral letter by the
Archbishop of Quebec (P.F. Turgeon) announc-
ing the establishment of Laval University, and is
reproduced in a Pastoral Letter by the Bishop
of Montreal, dated 20 June 1853. It is specifically a defence of the classics, which, though
not the only subjects on the course of study,
were central to the purposes of the classical
colleges.

We are aware that the clergy and the colleges are widely criticized for their efforts to promote classical instruction. Certain critics say that
the time spent studying the classical languages is
wasted, and that it would be better spent acquiring a training in commerce, agriculture, or a

A.4 Source: Montréal (Diocèse), *Mandements, lettres pastorales, circulaires, et autres documents* (Montréal, 1869), vol. 2, p. 418, pp. 420-21.

trade. The classics, they add, exert a dangerous influence and they are not compatible with the sentiments of a dynamic century such as ours. Thus they conclude that our institutions of higher education should modify their curriculum, and put aside the classics in favour of an education that is less lofty but more easily acquired and more useful.

. . . .

But is it necessary to condemn a system of education which has proven its worth through its long usage, because some corrupt practices, which are easily corrected and easily foreseen, have crept in? Is it fair to force education to concern itself only with physical well-being, because material interests must have their place in a well-organized society? Man does not live by bread alone; the mind God gave him requires nourishment, as well as his body. Through the study of the great authors of ancient times, the mind fortifies itself. It nourishes itself upon doctrines put forward in these works. The mind expands and enlightens itself through daily contacts with these noble spirits. The mind enriches itself with the knowledge and enlightenment of past centuries. The mind, by adopting this heritage, would be able to reproduce it as required, marked by its own seal. But the intelligence of a child, like his body, can only develop itself gradually. You would suffocate it by giving it food fit only for minds already formed by culture. Before launching into the study of more abstract subjects, the wise teacher should prepare the mind little by little so that later on it can embrace these subjects easily and profitably. Indeed, reason and experience teach us that it is through the study of language that a young mind accustoms itself to co-ordinating and comparing its ideas–thus readying itself to receive the lessons of formal knowledge.

Due to the similarity of general language rules among civilized people, one should choose to teach to the young student the languages with the best developed principles of grammar–those which can facilitate the learning of most other languages. Once again, experience has shown that Greek and Latin possess undeniable advantages in this field. In fact, Greek and Latin are the mothers or originators of all modern languages in Europe. Indeed, for those who learn these two first, it is easy to learn the others. By their clarity, their force, their precision, they give, to those who would analyse and study them, powerful means of developing their intelligence and bringing to light their potential. Finally, they reveal to us the finest minds of antiquity, with the Homers, the Demosthenes, the Ciceros of the pagan civilizations; the Jeromes, the Augustines, the Basils, the Chrysostomes, of the Christian civilization. And certainly you would agree that there is much to gain from the society of men of such strength.

This is what was understood by our illustrious predecessors when they undertook to protect, favour and defend with all their power, these institutions where one grows familiar with the classical authors of Rome and Athens.

B.　The Social Function of Advanced Education

From the 1840s most Canadians agreed that all children should receive some schooling. But they also agreed that not all children could or should receive the same amount. The educational system consisted, in essence, of two interconnected parts: the elementary schools, and the secondary schools and universities. Document B.1 sets out the different purposes of the two levels of public education; document B.2 considers the function of the high school in more detail, but in doing so, emphasizes the connection between elementary and secondary education. The latter institution, A. H. MacKay argues, should be free, so that the talented minority, whatever their social origin, may attend.

In French Canada, the classical college provided both secondary and undergraduate education. In an article published in 1924 for English Canadian readers, Emile Chartier explains the origins and purpose of the institution, some of the differences in emphasis between French and English post-elementary education, and the similarities and differences in the curriculum between the Quebec English high school and the classical college. Once again, the differences should not be allowed to obscure the similarities of purpose, clientele, and content of the curriculum (document B.3).

B.1　The Function of Elementary and Secondary Education

The following remarks are from the joint report of the High School Inspectors of Ontario for 1873.

B.1 Source: *Annual Report of the Normal, Model, High and Public Schools of Ontario for the Year 1873*, Part III, pp. 8, 10.

The total number of pupils attending all the public and private High Schools of the Province may be set down as about one half of one per cent of the entire population. It is not to be expected that this percentage will be either much or rapidly increased, and it may accordingly be taken as a rough guide in estimating the probable natural and healthy attendance in a proposed High School district. It is undoubtedly the case at the present time, that in some of our cities and towns, and in some of our rural High School districts the number enrolled on the annual register exceeds one per cent of the population. But this state of things is in many cases abnormal, while in others it naturally arises from the superior wealth or intellectual culture of the inhabitants.

. . . .

The *raison d'être* of the High School system is entirely different from that of the Public School system. The object of the latter is to provide for every child of sound mind the means of obtaining a minimum amount of knowledge and mental training; the object of the former is to provide for a comparatively small fraction of the population the elements of a liberal culture. The Public Schools exist to sow intelligence widely, the High Schools to plough deeply a small portion of mental soil. The all-important aim of the former is to reach every child; the all-important aim of the latter is to combine thorough training with breadth of mental vision. In the former case the number of pupils instructed should be mainly regarded by the community, in the latter, the quality of the instruction. The quality of instruction given in the Public Schools and the numbers attending the High Schools are not themselves unimportant matters, but their relative importance is different in the two classes of Schools....

In the High Schools are being educated, it is to be presumed, the leading men of the next generation, its clergymen, its lawyers, its doctors, its editors, the men who will make farming a science, its engineers and machinists, its prominent manufacturers and merchants, and its teachers. It is important that they at least as the advisors and guides of the future should receive a wide culture and know what thoroughness is.

B.2 The Functions of the High School
A. H. MacKay, the author of this document, was Superintendent of Education for Nova Scotia, 1890-1925.

The scope of the High School may first be approximately delineated, on the one hand, by the common school, which in Nova Scotia covers approximately an eight years' course of post-kindergarten and pre-High School work. The ages of pupils at this *terminus a quo* will most commonly be found ranging from 13 to 15. The *terminus ad quem* may be the ordinary vocations of life, or the teaching profession, either one, two, three or four years after, or the university, medical, theological, law or engineering colleges three or four years after. The common school should have work to do for those below 13. The superior limit should of course be unrestricted as to age. I would not fix a minimum age limit; but I think the entrance examination should be on work requiring, as a general rule, an age as mature as has been mentioned–from 13 to 15.

We may next ask the question: While common school education is admittedly so valuable for the public weal that no one now questions the duty of the State to encourage it by making it free, does education lose its value intrinsically or relatively after it passes the common school stage, so that it should then cease to be free? To this my an-

B.2 Source: A. H. MacKay, 'The True Scope and Function of the High School", Dominion Educational Association *Proceedings* (1892), pp. 63-65.

swer would be: There is a higher education which is even more valuable for the general good, the education of the educators and of the directors of every phase of activity affecting the well-being of the country. This higher education, in so far as it can be conducted on general lines, at least, should also be free.

It may be said, What! do you propose to give High School training to every boy and girl in the country? Would not such a system affect us injuriously from an industrial point of view? Would not boys well adapted for manual labor be made good for nothing by striving to do intellectual labor instead, and so be made good for nothing at the expense of the country?–the country losing his remunerative labor and the cost of schooling him, both together? I would answer: Yes, if the High School is merely a road to some of the learned professions, as theology, law, medicine, and the like. But I would answer: No, if the High School is directing the development of what tends to elevate and advance the country in every direction in which it may advance. There are so many attractions compared with the hard work of the student besetting the young on every side, that the majority cannot complete the common school course. They long for some form of active employment. The school life is not adapted to their mental or physical habits. Experience proves that the average High School work is in this sense too hard for the great majority of mankind–even for those who are not compelled to work early for their bread. There is therefore no danger of the High School becoming too crowded with those not adapted for High School work. The cost of board is protection enough.

There is also another great public advantage in the free High School system. It puts genius in the poor man's child more nearly on a par with that of the rich man. The rich man still has the advantage, as his children need not be required to help in the earning of their daily bread. High School fees means discrimination against the child because he is born poor.

The High School is the natural channel through which must rise our university men, our professional men, our directors of the more abstruse and technical industries, our legislators;– in a word, the rulers of our country in each of its interests or departments are likely with few exceptions to pass through the High School. It is an advantage to the country to have those with talent or genius directing its affairs. Experience shows that some of the most remarkable leaders of thought and action arise from the humbler ranks of the poor and middle classes. Do not place a tax of fees on these which would bear more heavily on them than on the children of the rich, and which would, therefore, tend to reduce the number of those fitted to lead and to stimulate useful activity in the State, and to keep out of the virtual ruling class those who perhaps more than any others contribute to the stability of society. When the virtual rulers of a country are drawn from the wealthier classes, we have a governing caste which does not always understand nor reconcile the democracy. Then come strains which may eventually cause the bonds of the commonwealth to snap, and anarchy or revolution to reign until the disturbing elements are consumed. But with every facility given to men of genius to rise from every rank to the ruling caste, we shall have a vast ruling syndicate in full sympathy with all classes and conditions. Those most materially helped by a free High School system are thus most likely to be the strongest strands knitting the democracy in happy and profitable union with the always necessary aristocracy.

B.3 The Classical Colleges of Quebec

Canon Emile Chartier was Vice-Rector of the University of Montreal at the time this paper was written.

In the French universities, the old Faculty of Arts, which formed part of superior education, has disappeared. It has been superseded, in Montreal as in France, by the three Faculties of Philosophy, of Letters and of Pure Science.

The faculty of Arts of the English, Anglo-Canadian and American universities, leading to a B.A. degree, has however its equivalent in our university, where it comes within the province of secondary education. It consists of the several affiliated colleges.[1]

Institutions of this nature have always been considered so necessary by Canadians of French origin that they have multiplied them throughout their history. Quebec College, founded in 1635 by the Jesuits, was continued by the Quebec Seminary in 1668. From 1760 to 1840, eight others appeared: Montreal (1767), Nicolet (1803), Saint Hyacinth (1811), Saint Boniface (1818), Sainte-Thérèse and Chambly (1825), Sainte-Anne de la Pocatière (1827), l'Assomption (1832). From 1840 to 1867, ten more colleges were launched: Joliette (1846), Saint-Laurent (1847), Bytown or Ottawa (1848), Bourget (in Rigaud) and Saint Mary's in Montreal (1850), Levis and Sainte-Marie de Monnoir (1853), Memramcook (1854),

[1]There is however a double difference. The English universities only count as forming part of their Faculty of Arts, the last four years of the Arts or College Course; we include in our Faculty of Arts the first four years of the course (about equal to their High School). In their Faculty of Arts, the English only confer the B.A. degree; in theirs, the French grant the three Bachelors' degrees, B.L., B.Sc., and B.A., and to obtain any of these three, eight complete years of classical studies are always required.

B.3 Source: Emile Chartier, "The Classical Colleges of Quebec", *Queen's Quarterly*, 31, 3(January, 1924), 270-76, 280-83, 285-86.

Three Rivers (1860), and Rimouski (1862). Ten others were opened between 1867 and 1914: Chicoutimi (1873), Sherbrooke (1875), Pointe-de-l'Eglise (1890), Valleyfield (1893), Caraquet (1899), Notre-Dame Ladies' College in Montreal (1908), Saint John's and Saint Alexander's-by-the-Gatineau or Ironside (1911), Nominingue–Mont Laurier and North Cobalt (1912), Sudbury and Edmonton (1913). Even the war, from 1914 to 1918, did not prevent the foundation of two more colleges: Saskatoon and Gravelbourg. Barring two of these institutions which have since disappeared (Chambly and Sainte-Marie de Monnoir), there remain thirty-one colleges established and supported by the French element.

Of these thirty-one, the Province of Quebec counts within its own boundaries twenty-one. Nine are affiliated to Laval University.... Twelve, affiliated to Laval until 1922, have been attached since that date to the new Montreal University ....

. . . .

All are the issue of religious inspiration, all depend on ecclesiastical authority, all are under the direction of the diocesan clergy or of a religious community, all have the boarding-school regime and a double object: primarily to fit recruits for the clergy and, subsidiarily, to train members for the liberal and professional careers.

Most of our colleges are the development of a Latin School, organized in his presbytery by some country parish priest. The priest seems to have guessed that his parish would some day become an episcopal see, and his provisions have often come true. These rectors had thus sown the seed of the seminary which the Council of Trent imposes upon all bishoprics. By force of events, as the rectories were the sole institutions of secondary education, parents sent to them their sons without distinction as to which career the latter were destined. Thus, the rectories became college-

seminaries, where the future laity received its education in common with the future clergymen. This community of college life explains the intimate union which has existed at all times, in Quebec, between the lay and ecclesiastical elements. It is this community of college life which has maintained the influence on the multitude of all the cultured men and which has produced the pacific disposition, the broad-mindedness and the industrious spirit which are credited to the Province of Quebec even by observers most estranged from its creed and its language. Thus, to train both a religious and civil elite was the main intention of the founders.

. . . .

The character of most of our colleges at present is distinctly idealistic. A few, such as Sherbrooke, have annexed a course in industry. Others, Saint Ann's for instance, include an agricultural school. Nearly half of them begin with a three or four years' commercial course. In all of them, however, midway and at the summit of the studies is the old programme based on Greek, Latin, French, English and scholastic philosophy. In this, none has changed anything whatsoever in the ideal of the initiators.

To render the organization of our classical course more easy to understand, we will compare it to the organization of English and American universities.[1] We do not wish to pronounce here on the relative value of the training received in our colleges and that received elsewhere. We will simply note the distinguishing characteristic which we mean our secondary teaching to maintain. To the training obtained by science and mathematics, which specialize in the early years,

[1] The Equivalence concerns the French classical institutions (8 years) and the English High Schools (4 years) with the English College or Arts Course (4 years) of Quebec. The New York count, unit or credit, has been taken as a common basis; it covers one hour's teaching per day during 40 weeks of five days.

we prefer the more disinterested and more general culture by means of history, literature and scholastic philosophy.

The studies preparatory to the B.A. degree comprise a course of eight school years, following seven years of primary schooling. The academic year lasts approximately from the 1st of September to the 20th of June. The distribution of the subjects and the time allotted to each is indicated on the following schedules:

. . . .

SUMMARY (divided into 4 and 4 years)

Literary Training	Years 1-4 Eng. Fren.		Years 5-8 Eng. Fren.		Years 1-8 Eng. Fren.	
Mother tongue	13¼	16¼	6	5	19¼	21¼
Second language	11¼	12	8	6	19¼	18
Literature	4½	3¾	13	10	17½	13¾
Latin	16½	26¼	8	7½	24½	33¾
Greek	7¾	7½	4	5	11¾	12¼
History	6¾	11¼	5	5	11¾	17¼
Geography	2½	11¼			2½	11¼
Totals	62½	88¼	44	39½	106½	127¾

Scientific Training

	Years 1-4 Eng. Fren.		Years 5-8 Eng. Fren.		Years 1-8 Eng. Fren.	
Chemistry	3		7	4	19	4
Mathematics	20¼	9½	4	11½	24¼	21
Physics			4	5	4	5
Science (natural)				4		4
Philosophy			8	19	8	19
Totals	23¼	9½	23	43½	46¼	53

General Summary

	Years 1-4 Eng. Fren.		Years 5-8 Eng. Fren.		Years 1-8 Eng. Fren.	
Literary	62½	88¼	44	39½	106½	127¾
Scientific	23¼	9½	23	43½	46¼	53
Special Subjects	9¼				9¼	
Total sum	95	97¾	67	83	162	180¾

This comparison leads to certain rather unexpected conclusions:

(a) In the English as in the French educational institutions, the programme of work for the first six years includes on the literary side, the teaching of Greek, Latin, French, English, General History and History of Literature, Literary Composition and Geography; on the science side it includes the study of Mathematics in both and, in addition, that of Chemistry in the English course. Neither of the two programmes includes Philosophy or Natural Science (such as Botany), before the seventh year;

(b) In the English institutions, the science teaching during the first six years is almost the double of what it is during the last two years. Inversely, in the French colleges it is three times greater during the last two years than during the first six years;

(c) On the other hand, the teaching of literary subjects in the French colleges is five times greater during the first six years than during the last two years; while in the English institutions literary subjects during the last two years take up three times what they do during the first six years;

(d) In short, during the first six years, the French colleges attach more importance to their literary studies, the English to their science; during the last two years, the English institutions pay more attention to their literary studies, the French to their science.

Or, to put it in other words: it is easily noticeable that the French and English systems differ radically in this, viz., that the latter have a fairly even mixture of their scientific and literary subjects throughout, with perhaps more science than literature at first and then vice-versa, while the French system consists in taking chiefly literary subjects first, and then practically all the science in the final years. Which system is superior is not for us to say, but the fact is that each results in a general mental training of very high value, and in the total the sum of credits to each of the subjects is remarkably similar.

. . . .

It pleases us to submit to further judgment on the merits of the rigorous discipline and atmosphere of labour which shrouds each of these colleges. Both these characteristics are prominent in the following college boys' time-table:

Ordinary school days

5.15–Rise
5.40–Morning prayers and meditation
6.00–Study, 45 min.
6.45–Mass and daily communion
7.30–Breakfast and recreation
8.00–Class, 2 hrs.
10.00–Recreation
10.30–Study, 1¼ hrs.
11.45–Self-examination
12.00–Dinner
12.30–Recreation
1.30–Study, ½ hr.
2.00–Class, 2 hrs.
4.00–Recreation
4.30–Study (weekly confession on Saturdays) 1½ hr.
6.00–Chaplet and spiritual reading
6.30–Supper
7.00–Short visit to the Blessed Sacrament and recreation
8.00–Evening prayers
8.15–Study or confession
9.00–Bedtime

. . . .

To measure even more the value of this preparation, we appeal to an argument which, though negative, is none the less expressive. It consists in the results of the annual examinations for the B.A. degree to which may be admitted only those who have completed to the last day the eight years' classical studies, after their seven years of preliminary schooling.... However, a few preliminary explanations are necessary to give a clear idea of our organization leading to the B.A. degree. These de-

tails will prevent from being accredited the idle talk which has so often been uttered on our account in misinformed circles.

With us, the six years of literary studies (from the 6th Form to Rhetoric inclusive) end with an examination on Letters and the two years of science-philosophy close with an examination on Science. Together, these two constitute the Bachelor's examination.

Amongst the subjects of these two tests, on Letters and on Science respectively, some are termed Collegiate or Local and the others University subjects.

The Collegiate or Local subjects, for the literary portion, are General History, History of Canada, Geography, Principles of Composition, Literary History and Religion; for the scientific portion, Natural History, Astronomy, Chemistry and Religion. The examination on these subjects is passed in each affiliated college, according to the University programme and regulations, but under the supervision and on the responsibility of the local superiors. The results of these examinations do not count for the diploma, but are the entrance requirements to the university tests.

The University subjects are, for Letters: Essay, Latin Version, Latin Theme, Greek Version, French or English Theme; for Science: Mathematics, Physics, Philosophy (Logic, Ethics and Metaphysics).

The University selects, among the questions submitted by the affiliated Colleges, those which form the University examination. This test, supervised by the professors of the Faculty of Arts, takes place in all the colleges, on the same questions, at the same date (determined by the Rector in consultation with the superiors). It lasts twenty-nine hours. The candidates bring with them neither books, nor notes, not even paper; they are furnished with everything they need on the spot.

Their names must not appear on the papers; they use figures instead and their names are only revealed after the corrections are finished.

Immediately after the examination, the tests are sent to the University. They are corrected by a committee composed of professors of the Faculty of Arts. The results, with the corrected papers, remain with the University to be filed for reference.

The result of the University examinations alone entitles to the degrees of B.A., B.Sc., or B.L., as the case may be. The candidate becomes Bachelor of Arts if he be credited with 60% of the points on the total of the University tests for both Letters and Science. The candidate becomes Bachelor of Science if he be credited with (a) 60% on the total in Science, (b) 50% on the total in Letters. The candidate becomes Bachelor in Letters if he be credited with (a) 60% on the total in Letters, (b) 50% on the total in Science.

· ·

These explanations concerning our Bachelors' degrees being given, here is the argument of which we were speaking. In 1887, we believe, the Provincial Parliament passed a bill known as the Hall Act. In virtue of this law, the diploma awarded by the University to its Bachelors is equivalent to the Entrance Examinations (brevet) passed before the Boards of Examiners constituted by the different professions. The equivalence was at first admitted for the study of law and medicine. Later, it was extended to the professions of dental surgery, civil engineering, surveying and architecture....

· ·

A polemic has recently arisen concerning the "Brevet" or entrance examination to the liberal studies. A Montreal newspaper declared the B.A. could be obtained in the classical colleges between the ages of 16 and 18. It concluded there was an injustice on the part of the professional bodies towards the English minority. Statistics establish that pupils enter Humanities (Belles-lettres), which is the form corresponding to the first year (Freshmen) of the College or Arts course in the English Universities, at the age of 17 2/3 years. The pupils in Senior Philosphy average, at the beginning of the Fall term, 20 years and 10 months. At the end of the year, the average age of the candidate to the B.A. is then 21 2/3 years. This equals, if it does not surpass, the average age of the candidates in the English Universities. This is another proof that pupils in our colleges take the time wanted to acquire general culture.

And it is really a question of general competence and culture which is at stake. This is too often forgotten when speaking of the colleges. They are neither machines for the turning out of paragons or of walking encyclopedias, nor are they schools preparatory to finance, or commerce, or arts and trades. Their object is to form a civil and religious elite, therefore intellectual, moral and social. The success they have achieved is highly attested by the history of our country, by their own private annals and by the official records.

C. Social Class and Educational Opportunity

The kind of schooling a child would receive in Victorian Canada was influenced by the purposes established for the schools, and by the effort of the departments of education to impose standardization and uniformity among schools of a like kind. But it was also influenced by two other important factors which often worked at cross-purposes to official aims and organization. The first of these factors was social class. The connection between level of schooling and social class is implicit in many of the preceding documents in this chapter. MacKay's argument for the free high school, for example, (document B.2), was part of a tradition of Canadian educational thought that stretched back at least as far as McCulloch and Strachan, and beyond that, to the Scottish conviction that the bright boy should have a chance at advanced education regardless of his social origins. Victorian Canadians believed that there was a "natural aristocracy" of talent, to be found among all classes, which should be encouraged to compete for the highest prizes of life. As the statistics from Ontario show (document C.I), enough children from parents in "agricultural" or "mechanical" occupation did reach high school to give the idea of a genuine "educational ladder" some substance of reality; the figures also show the way in which the high school was the gateway to white collar work. But it is equally true that only a fraction of the total number who entered elementary school ever entered high school, let alone completed it. And the extent to which social class was a determining factor in the ability of children to stay in school–that is, even to complete elementary school–is vividly demonstrated in the testimony given to the Royal Commission on the Relations of Capital and Labour in 1887 (document C.2).

C.1 Class and the Secondary School, 1901

C.1 Source: *Report of the Minister of Education, Province of Ontario, for the Year 1901*, pp. 48-53.

Representative High Schools and Collegiate Institutes	Destination of Pupils						Occupation of Parents				
	Number who entered mercantile life	Number who became occupied with agriculture	No. who entered the professions of law, medicine & the Church	Number who became teachers	No. who entered any other profession	No. who left for other occupations	Commerce	Agriculture	Mechanical occupations	Professions	Without occupation
High Schools											
Omemee	1	3	4	3	–	33	3	25	6	4	5
Orangeville	13	9	5	26	5	28	49	92	32	22	18
Oshawa	20	8	1	6	–	22	40	62	53	20	–
Paris	4	2	–	3	–	12	21	20	25	7	11
Parkhill	2	3	–	6	2	6	9	24	4	4	6
Pembroke	9	4	2	5	3	21	40	34	60	24	16
Petrolea	12	2	–	5	3	11	28	22	45	5	–
Picton	–	–	4	11	–	–	54	113	52	21	3
Port Arthur	20	10	–	5	–	2	20	10	20	5	5
Port Dover	6	3	1	3	3	8	12	33	14	7	13
Port Elgin	4	2	2	4	–	14	29	23	13	12	9
Port Hope	11	1	2	14	–	15	42	56	28	20	21
Collegiate Institutes											
Hamilton	70	20	10	45	4	30	319	84	148	102	10
Stratford	17	6	9	20	–	26	101	56	83	28	32
London	114	13	8	28	17	72	337	80	206	64	129
Owen Sound	18	11	15	53	4	40	138	87	92	37	23
Provincial Totals											
Totals, H.S.	564	424	169	633	139	837	2,075	3,763	2,303	823	769
Totals, C.I.	767	333	199	538	209	1,057	3,373	2,458	2,751	1,130	1,019
Grand totals, 1900	1,331	757	368	1,171	348	1,894	5,448	6,221	5,054	1,953	1,788
Grand totals, 1899	1,449	944	467	1,297	–	1,910	6,493	7,320	6,237	2,410	–
Percentages	18	13	7	15	6	30	26	30	25	10	9

C.2 The Impact of Social Class on School Attendance

The witness replying to the questions put by the members of the Commission is A. H. Mac-Kay, supervisor of schools for Halifax, Nova Scotia.

By Mr. Freed:-
Q.   Are the schools of Nova Scotia free?
A.   Yes. They are supported by assessment.

By the Chairman:-
Q.   There are no school fees?   A.   The schools are free to pupils residing in the section; but when a pupil moves from one section to another and does not acquire privileges in the latter section, he is required to pay fees there.

. . . .

Q.   Is the county academy free?   A.   Yes; it is free to all persons in the county. It has been free for two years.
Q.   Do the pupils in the schools provide their own books.   A.   They do.

. . . .

Q.   Are any school ages prescribed by the Government?   A.   The age of five years admits a child to school, but there is no limit upwards.
Q.   Can you tell us what proportion of children between five years and fifteen years of age are enrolled as attending school?   A.   I might do so by referring to the tables.
Q.   Can you tell us how it is in your own district?   A.   About one in six of the whole population.
Q.   What proportion are in attendance on school?   A.   Fifty-nine per cent, as far as I remember. I think this year it is sixty-two per cent.
Q.   Do many of the children quit school at an early age in order to go to work?   A.   A large

C.2 Source: Royal Commission on the Relations of Capital and Labor in Canada, *Report* (Ottawa, 1889), 5, pp. 83-88.

number of children leave school before they have finished the common school grade of education. I should think about seventy-five per cent of them leave school before they have finished the common school education. There are eight grades, and a good many children–perhaps more than seventy-five per cent–leave school before reaching the eighth grade; and fifty-six per cent before reaching the sixth grade.
Q.   Tell us the average age of the children who quit school to go to work before the sixth grade?
A.   I can only form a general estimate. I have never made any calculations on that point; but think the age would be between twelve and thirteen.

. . . .

By Mr. Heakes:-
Q.   Is the school law in the Province of Nova Scotia compulsory; does it make attendance at the schools compulsory?   A.   There is a law on the statute book which is optional with each section. If the trustees wish to put it in operation it makes the attendance compulsory for that section.
Q.   What is the age at which it applies?   A.   Between the ages of 7 and 12. That law has not been utilized generally throughout the province.

. . . .

Q.   Has it been adopted in the city of Halifax?
A.   No. We had the opportunity but on account of the city government differing from other sections it could not be utilized. It has been utilized in a few sections, but wherever it has been adopted it has been dropped. It has to be voted upon every year. It was adopted in Dartmouth and a census was taken of the children, but it was never carried out. The next year it was dropped. In the sections the matter is decided at the annual meeting, but in the city of Halifax it is decided by the city council.

. . . .

By Mr. Heakes:–

Q.   Have you any knowledge of children under the age of twelve working in the factories?   A. No; I have no specific knowledge of it, though I believe there are some.

Q.   Is the attendance of children of laboring men at the schools regular?   A.   No; it is very irregular. We have a bill before the Legislature now providing for the appointment of a truant officer in the city and for compulsory education, which we think will be found very complete.

By the Chairman:–

Q.   Will that be subject to local option?   A. No; it will apply only to the city of Halifax.

. . . .

Q.   Do you know if any class of the community, say the working class, withdraw their children from school through not having the means to keep them properly clothed and not having the means to buy books?   A.   I have reason to believe that a large number of children who attend school are prepared for doing so by charitable associations, and that a large number who are taken away from school are not able to continue any longer, or think they are not.

Q.   Do you think there would be a larger proportion of the children of the working classes in attendance at school if the books were free–purchased by the Government or by the municipality? A.   I do not think it would make much difference; it would, of course, make some. I think poverty strikes chiefly in the matter of clothing, and the necessity for earning something to contribute to the support of the other members of the family. The whole outfit of books required to pass through the common schools does not amount to more than $5 or $6, extending over a period of five, six or seven years, or from the time a child is five years old until he is thirteen.

D. The Gap between Urban and Rural Schooling

The second important factor determining the kind of schooling a child would receive was the difference between urban and rural schools. From the time that school systems were created, the cities and towns, in every part of Canada, had two important advantages: they could draw upon a larger clientele and they could depend upon a larger tax base than the rural areas. The consequences were important. City children, from the 1850s, could expect to attend a large "union" school where each grade would be taught by a different teacher and where school life was highly organized. If they completed elementary school, they could expect to have access to a nearby high school. Their teachers would be more likely to have more education themselves and to have some teacher training. And the pupils would be more likely to benefit from the (presumed) pedagogical advances of the era: grading, classrooms equipped with blackboards, maps, scientific apparatus, kindergartens, and new teaching methods.

In the rural areas, the story was different. Before the era of the school bus and paved roads, school sections in rural Canada were inevitably small–the limits determined by the distance a child could walk, which was usually thought to be a maximum of two miles to school. The small school section drew upon only a few families and hence had limited resources. The equipment compared badly with that of the urban school, it was often difficult to attract qualified teachers, and until the late nineteenth century there was no opportunity for rural children to attend high school unless parents could afford to send their children to board in a nearby town.

The contrasts between urban and rural schools were sharp ones. By the late 1850s, many urban schools already had begun to take on the familiar shape of modern elementary schools (document D.1). The laconic reports of two Inspectors, one from Quebec and the other from Prince Edward Island, illustrate vividly the contrast between urban and rural schools (documents D.2 and D.3). Yet Canada was still a predominantly rural country, and it was, as E. W. Nichols points out in document D.4, in the rural school that most Canadian children received what education they were likely to get until well into the twentieth century.

D.1 The Big City School in the 1850s
This is a description of the Toronto elementary schools in 1859.

As nearly all the children who attend the City Schools come from the industrial classes, the system of instruction pursued in the schools has been based upon practical considerations of utility, so as to impart to the pupils such a sound and useful English education as shall fit him or her to enter upon the daily pursuits of industrial or domestic life; and to accomplish these objects the following arrangements regulate the internal economy, and the mode of instruction, adopted and practised in the City Schools.

As it was necessary to have some one study recognized as the standard whereby classification and promotion should be arranged, it was considered that *reading* offered the most reliable and uniform guide in this particular. The *classes*, therefore, when designated as first, third, or fifth, for example, mean that the pupils of such classes make use of the first, third, or fifth National Reader.

D.1 Source: *Report on the Past History and Present Condition of the Common or Public Schools of the City of Toronto* (Toronto: City of Toronto Board of School Trustees, 1859), pp. 58-62.

Devlin School, Rainy River District, 1904.

Ontario Normal College and Collegiate Institute, Hamilton, c.1901.

In the six large schools there are separate male and female departments. Each department, where the number of pupils warrants it, has three divisions, but otherwise only two divisions, each with its own responsible teacher. In the two smaller or auxiliary schools, namely, the Trinity School, and the Western School, the attendance includes both boys and girls, under the charge of one teacher.

Each department of the six large schools being subdivided as above stated, it should be understood that the *first* or junior division, generally known as the gallery class, comprises those very young children who, commencing with the alphabet, are carried forward until they can spell and read in the First Book; they are also taught the first elements of geography and of arithmetic, as far as the simple rules of addition and subtraction, together with the multiplication table; and the teacher further instructs them in attempts to write on the slate. The mode of instruction in the gallery classes is chiefly simultaneous, and by *viva voce* teaching. Tablet lessons are used for spelling and reading; large maps supply the means of teaching geography; and the black board, together with the abacus or calculator, assist to teach arithmetic.

At certain periods, generally Easter and Mid-summer, the pupils are drafted, if found sufficiently advanced, from the gallery class into the second or intermediate division, where they commence to read in the Second Book, and so on through the sequel into the Third Book; they begin to learn to write with pen and ink, and are familiarized with easy dictation. Arithmetic on the slate as far as the compound rules, becomes a daily study; the elements of English Grammar and easy parsing lessons now come into practice. Geography, as far as the names of countries, cities, mountains, lakes, rivers, &c., is taught from maps.

The elements of history are now commenced; object lessons are used by the teacher to give the pupil some knowledge of natural history; and in the girls' department instruction is also given in needle-work.

After a specified period, and promotion depending of course upon proficiency, the pupil is now advanced to the third or highest division, which is under the immediate personal charge of the head master in the boys', and of the head mistress in the girls' department–but although the departments are distinct the one from the other, yet the studies pursued are in all material respects so much alike, that what is stated of one may be taken as applying to both. In this, viz.: the third or senior division, the pupil reads, and is taught to understand, the Fourth and Fifth Books; and in the highest class, Sullivan's Literary Class Book is used. Spelling orally, and frequent dictation both in prose and verse are resorted to, and the meaning of words is studied and their roots explained and traced. Arithmetic, including the compound rules to reduction, proportion, vulgar and decimal fractions and the extraction of roots, occupies close attention. The study of the English language is now extended into Syntax; parsing of simple sentences, and, in the higher classes, analytical parsing, are carefully studied. Writing from copy-lines having now reached its mechanical extent, the pupil's pen is practised in transcribing from books such subjects in prose and verse as are calculated to store the memory with some useful fact, or impart to the mind some moral lesson. Geography, though still taught to some extent from maps, now requires a text book and an atlas to assist the scholar's progress; and in addition to a thorough knowledge of the general features of the earth's surface, the pupil is instructed with regard to the physical geography, the productions, climate, form of government, manners and customs of the principal countries of the civilized world. Elementary history, which was commenced in the second division, is carried steadily onward from the general history of the world to that of Europe, while especial attention is given to the History of England, as our mother country, and to that of Canada as our adopted home. Pencil drawing is taught to all the scholars sufficiently advanced to undertake the study; and, where the tastes or the aptitude of the teacher points in that direction, vocal music is taught to all the pupils, and in some of the schools considerable proficiency is attained in this agreeable branch of popular education. In the boys' schools, book-keeping and practical mensuration are studied; and mathematics are taught to the higher classes as far as Equations, and the first two, or perhaps, three books of Euclid; while in the girls' school the higher branches of needle work, such as crochet, worsted work, and embroidery, take the place of mathematics; and at the Midsummer and Christmas Holidays, numerous interesting specimens of penmanship, maps (plain and coloured), pencil (and sometimes water-colour) drawings, and of plain and ornamental needle-work, are exhibited for the inspection of visitors.

According to the "General Regulations for Common Schools," as prescribed by the Council of Public Instruction, every alternate Saturday is declared to be a holiday, and for some time this regulation was carried out in the City Schools; but it was not found to work well–the Saturday *going to School* was too often forgotten by the pupils–the alternate attendance soon became almost nominal–and, in consequence, the Schools are now not open at all on Saturdays. As regards other holidays, it has been customary to give a week at Easter–a month in summer, usually in August–and a fortnight at Christmas.

The following "Time Table" exhibits at one view the daily and hourly occupations of the pupils of the third or senior division of each department. Each division has of course its own time table, but as the studies in the gallery class are altogether elementary, and those in the second division are in all material particulars analogous in character, if not in extent, to those of the third, it is thought unnecessary to publish the detailed studies of the first and second divisions, inasmuch as the arrangements set forth in the time table of the third or senior division will, it is assumed, sufficiently explain the general character of the course of study pursued in the City Schools: (see table on page opposite)

D.2 Protestant Schools in Quebec, 1905
A Quebec Protestant school inspector contrasts the urban and rural schools in that province.

It may be said at once that the Protestant schools in Montreal are in a good condition. The school board consists of enlightened and progressive men who give much time to their work, and through their own efforts and those of their officers administer the public funds wisely. Their schools are modern and hygienic in construction, and are well equipped with furniture and apparatus.

Most important of all, their teachers having been chosen from the best graduates of the Normal School, remain long in their positions and through training, experience, ability and devotion produce the best results in the education of the young.

In short, these schools will bear comparison with any in Canada.

D.2 Source: *Report of the Superintendent of Public Instruction for the Province of Quebec*, 1905-06, pp. xiii-xv.

Public Schools, City of Toronto.–Time Table, Male Department, Third Division–Hours of Study, from Nine A.M. to Noon; and from One to Four P.M.–Occupation of time.

From	To	Monday	Tuesday	Wednesday	Thursday	Friday
9.00	10.00	Reading, Scriptures with Sacred Geography	Reading–Derivations, 5th Book; Dictation, 4th Book.	Reading–Dictation, 5th Book; Science (Natural), 4th Book.	Reading–History, 5th Book; Political Economy, 4th Book.	Repetition and Elocution
10.00	10.50	Writing–Small Hand	Writing–Large Hand	Drawing	Writing and Book-keeping	Writing of Figures; Revision of Euclid
10.50	11.00	Forenoon Recess				
11.00	12.00	Arithmetic–Examine Simple Rules	Arithmetic–Compound Rules	Arithmetic–Proportion	Arithmetic–Fractions, &c.	Arithmetic–Repetition
12.00	1.00	Noon Intermission				
1.00	2.00	Grammar–Letter-writing (Composition)	Analysis of Sentences–Comp. of Sim. Nominatives	Grammar–Composition; Des. of Objects; Abstracts	Analysis of Sentences–Written Parsing or Comp.	Repetition of Grammar and Analysis; Composition
2.00	2.50	Geography of America–Map Drawing	History	Geography (General)–Map Drawing	History	Repetition; Geography Object Lesson
2.50	3.00	Afternoon Recess				
3.00	3.55	Arithmetic, Algebra, Euclid	Arithmetic, Algebra, Mental Arithmetic	Arithmetic, Euclid, Science (Natural)	Arithmetic, Algebra, Mental Arithmetic	Singing and Recitation of Poetry, &c.

N.B. The School to be opened and closed with Scripture Reading and Prayer. Books from the Library will be given out each Friday afternoon.

For the towns and villages, in which there are academies and model schools, the same may be said, with more reserve.

In the rural parts a widely different condition prevails in three particulars. Generally speaking, the schoolhouses are plain, cheerless and insufficiently furnished.

Owing to the small attendance, the ventilation is usually ample.

The teachers, with notable exceptions of course, may be described as birds of passage. Over three hundred of them have no diplomas at all, and many of the rest, although professionally trained, gain only the experience that comes to them while they wait for some other occupation or means of support. And finally, some schools have an annual term of six months or less.

It is then the condition of these rural schools that gives concern to all patriotic men who consider the educational question in this Province.

The wide difference between the city and town schools on one hand, and the rural schools on the other has its origin in social and economic conditions.

In one case we have within an area of a few square miles a large population and taxable property of great value.

The schools can be properly graded, and as many pupils may be assigned to one teacher as she can efficiently manage.

In the other case the population is sparse, the valuation is small.

There are over four hundred Protestant rural schools with an average attendance of about ten.

The city of Montreal, with all its resources, can afford only one teacher for forty pupils, but these schools are obliged to furnish one teacher for every ten children.

In order to keep the cost per pupil at a low figure school commissioners resort to two vicious devices.

They engage cheap and inefficient teachers, and they shorten the school term.

Three remedies should be applied to the cure of the evils prevalent in these rural schools.

(1) Consolidation should be effected wherever possible in order to bring the pupils of three or four weak schools under the instruction of one teacher.

(2) The government grants to these schools should be increased, and should be administered in such a way as to give assistance to the schools that most need it and whose supporters contribute most freely.

(3) The ratepayers should tax themselves at a higher rate than at present.

As a result of the increased funds better salaries could be paid and teachers would be encouraged to remain in their work, and the school term could be extended to at least eight months a year.

D.3 Rural Schools in Prince Edward Island, 1882

This is a report by Peter Curran, one of the school inspectors for the province.

I beg leave to submit for your consideration my Report of the schools within the Eastern Inspectoral District for the year 1882.

During the past twelve months I have made the usual half-yearly visits to all the schools in the Eastern District, with the exception of Boughton Island, which was vacant during the first half of the year, and reported to me as vacant by some of the people of Launching District when I visited their school in September.

On my first tour of inspection I found five vacant schools, three of which were in operation at the date of my second visit. During the last half year I found in all, fourteen vacant schools, four of which were visited in July, and eight in August. Some of these vacancies have since been filled. Only two districts have been without teachers during the whole year, namely, Goose River and Blackbush. Since July, 1879, these schools have been open during only part of one term.

A new schoolhouse has been built at Bear River, South, during the year, and new buildings were in course of erection at Mansfield and Gray's Road, when I last visited these districts. At the annual meeting in June last, money was voted for the building of schoolhouses in the following districts: Rollo Bay East, Upton, Egglinton and Donagh. New schoolhouses are needed at Mount Herbert, Albion, Caledonia, Green Marsh, Peake's Road, Glenoe, Dromore and Orwell Cove. The schoolhouse in the last named is in a fair state of repair, but is too small for the accommodation of the large number of children in attendance. The

D.3 Source: *Report of the Chief Superintendent of Education of Prince Edward Island*, 1882, Appendix C, pp. 53-55.

schoolhouses at Fortune Road and Mount Hope
have been finished on the inside, and those at
Priest Pond, Brown's Creek, and St. Peter's Road,
Lot 53, have undergone considerable repairs since
the date of my last Report.

At the time of my first visit, I found fifteen
schools closed. The number examined during the
first half year was one hundred and fifty-nine. On
my second circuit, seven schools were closed on
account of the prevalence of diptheria, two because of the sickness of teachers, and five from other
causes. Only one of the schools in operation during
the year was closed at the time of both visits. The
number of schools examined during the last six
months is one hundred and fifty-two. Of these,
six were taught by teachers of the first class, thirty-
six by second class teachers, and the remainder
were in charge of third class teachers. One of the
first class teachers left the profession at the end of
three months. The sum of $115 is received as sup-
plement by the remaining five, being an average
of $23 each. Eight of the second class teachers en-
gaged in July receive no supplement. Twenty-
eight receive on an average $25, or in all $700. Of
one hundred and ten teachers of the third class
whose schools were examined during the present
school year, thirty-five teach without supplement,
the remaining seventy-five receiving $1,433.50,
an average of $19.11 each. It will thus be seen, that
although there has been an increase of four first
class and four second class teachers over last year,
there has been a decrease in the average amount
received as supplement by each teacher, and also
in the total amount voted as supplement at the
last annual meeting.

Since the date of my last Report, nine
schools have been supplied with blackboards,
one with map of P.E. Island, seventeen with maps
of the World, and twenty-seven with maps of
Canada. There are thirty schools in which new

blackboards are needed; twenty-six require new
maps of the World, and ninety-eight are without
maps of the Dominion. This want of apparatus is
to be ascribed rather to the difficulty Trustees
find in collecting the amounts voted at the annual
meeting, than to unwillingness on the part of ratepayers to make provision for necessary school
requisites. In many districts there remains at the
close of the school year a part of the assessment
which Trustees have been unable to collect. Sup-
plements and the cost of fuel are usually paid first,
and the supplying of maps, blackboards, &c., is
thus deferred from time to time. In nearly all districts unprovided with these necessary appliances,
money was voted at the last or former annual
meetings for the purpose of supplying them. In a
few, the required amount was collected at the
time of my last visit, and probably they have
since been procured.

It will readily be understood that the want
of maps in these schools is a serious hinderance to
the teaching of Geography, but I regret to say that
in a few schools, the teachers make but little use
of those furnished. I have seen some pupils who
were said to have studied the greater part of Col-
lins' Geography, yet were unable to define the
terms, latitude, longitude, tropics, equator and
meridians. It is only after studying the text-book
for a considerable time that some teachers begin
to make use of maps.

Only one of the schools visited by me is supplied with a wall map of England. The maps found
in Campbell's Geography are used with good results in a number of schools in connection with
the study of English History. This branch has
been more generally attended to during the last,
than in any of the three preceding years. The
knowledge of the outlines of English History
shown at last examination by some children who
had not advanced beyond the Fourth Reading

Book, was very creditable. More attention appears to be given by some teachers to the wars carried on and the battles fought during each period, than to the constitutional changes, or the progress made by people in civilization, the sciences and useful arts.

With few exceptions, there is a marked improvement in the grading of pupils over last year. There is less inclination shown than formerly to push the pupils on to the study of higher branches, to the neglect of elementary subjects proper to the grades assigned to these pupils.

D.4 The Little White Schoolhouse

The schoolhouse itself...is of a dingy white; and the roof looks heavy, with a certain solidity about the eaves. If the concept of the builder had been translated into ancient architecture, it would be of Doric design; now it resembles rather an amiable toadstool, altered into rectangular form, with a stock nearly as large as the top. It stands end to the road, facing north, with two windows on the east side and three on the west; and as one looks from the door across the cultivated field, pasture and woodland, one is sure to notice a little pile of firewood in the immediate foreground to the right; the ash-barrel, too, is there or thereabouts.

. . . .

As one enters the school-room itself from the boys' ante-room one finds the teacher's platform, desk, and chair of state immediately to the right. Behind platform, desk and chair rises a formidable blackboard, and above the blackboard is suspended a solemn eight-day clock. Among its uses, the clock often records the approximate time; but its main value is as a focus for contemplation. Directly opposite the teacher's desk at the other end of the room stands the stove. How

D.4 Source: E. W. Nichols, "The Little White Schoolhouse", *Dalhousie Review*, 5(1925-26), 311-23.

many feet of pipe it possesses might be ascertained by measurement, but could not be conjectured without exaggeration. It looks a mile long. This pipe rises many feet above the stove, hooks itself into a wire support depending from the ceiling, and turns northward. Thither it sweeps in unimpeded majesty above the middle row of seats, and triumphantly pierces the wall into the chimney somewhere near the clock. Here and there in the journey it receives additional support from the ceiling.

There are three rows of seats, those nearest the windows containing seven seats each, and the middle one five. This diminution of number is accounted for by the teacher's desk at one end of the room and the stove at the other. Each seat accommodates two pupils. The eastern row is occupied by boys and the western by girls, while the middle row is debatable ground. Usually the boys possess the larger seats and the girls the smaller; for the seats increase in stature as they near the stove. A flat, smooth, comfortable board sprouts from the back of the stove, which has also often in bad weather a bench placed at either end. When a pupil asks to "go to the stove," he means to sit on one of the benches or on the projecting board; preferably the latter, since it furnishes a back for comfort and a neighbour for conference.

In addition to the one big blackboard–the blackboard of state–there is another painted on the plaster of the western wall, and the maps hang anywhere around the room. There is an old globe on a frame in one corner...There is a tall pointer in the south-west corner; near the southeast corner stands a bench supporting a water pail and a tin basin. Somewhere in the teacher's desk lies a heavy strap used in ethical instruction.

The community from which the pupils come is quite homogeneous, of British stock throughout. Everybody is white; practically everybody is

Baptist or Methodist; everybody except an occasional epicene–who is not highly esteemed–is strongly Tory or strongly Grit; everybody, with very rare exceptions, is bitterly respectable; everybody gets his living from the soil and the forest. The interests of these children are those of the parents. Theological discussion turns chiefly on the nature of baptism, and is not all unworthy of the subtlety of the Greek Fathers. Ethical argument is concerned with the relative wickedness of cards, dancing and tobacco. Political oratory is devoted to attacking and defending the doctrine of Protection and the character of the Dominion member. None of these questions is, perhaps, much inferior in genuine intellectual interest to the latest baseball score, the latest jazz on the gramophone, or the latest jangle over the radio. These minor differences in opinion against a common background give life and zest to all sorts of neighbourhood rows. In the usual absence of any real scandal, the gossip is pretty small stuff; but such as it is, the children capture it and drag it joyfully to school, to furnish occasion for further squabbles and make life more interesting.

. . . .

The teacher is usually a girl holding a "C" licence. The chief need of the school is for sound discipline and for sound elementary knowledge. Thus if the teacher can maintain order in the school-room and teach the pupils to read, write and cipher diligently and well, she is safe from interferences on the part of parents and trustees, and may add anything that she knows and that the pupil will endure. Her salary is diminutive; but so is her board bill. She is paid enough to buy food; and if some kind relative will help with her clothing, she may get through the year without debt. She has a respected position in the community; for the people hold the quaint opinion that education is a good in itself, provided it doesn't cost too much, and, in some measure, a practical necessity as well. If the teacher has been to Normal School, she may disparage this primitive notion; but she is more likely to yield to the gentle pressure of neighbourhood opinion, transmitted perhaps from Loyalist ancestors. And the parents will, for the most part, support her authority without question. Presumably there are as many meddlesome people here as elsewhere, and no doubt they think highly of their offspring; but their intimate contact with Nature, "who speaks with a blow, and gives no word of explanation", restrains them from too great an excess of humbug in dealing with the youth. These are taught to obey. If Johnny will not do what the teacher tells him, he may refuse at home to bring in the wood. If Jenny will not learn her lesson, she will perhaps refuse to learn to knit. Hence the teacher is not only allowed but upon occasion expected to apply corporal punishment; and when corporal punishment is never obtrusive, but always ready on demand, the business of the school flows for the most part smoothly.

That business consists in teaching twenty or thirty boys and girls, of various sizes from three feet to six, and various ages from five to twenty, whatever is required by the Nova Scotia curriculum. There is very little interference on the part of anybody outside. Once or twice during the year the inspector calls on his weary round; but he is a kindly man, and both teacher and pupils hold him in esteem. Everybody is firmly persuaded of the paramount importance of arithmetic. It is a prominent "note" of virtue that it does not allow its possessor to be swindled, and a man "good at figgers" will not allow any adversary to juggle them to his hurt. He will not get a mortgage on his farm. It is important to be able to read. One gets news from the papers, and there are interesting books. It is important to be able to write a good hand, for one writes only for someone else to read.

. . . .

Concerning the old school-books, a volume could be written. Of the primers in which one began to read, the only tale that remains in the head of one of the pupils of The Little White Schoolhouse is that of a cat that was fat, and lay on a mat, and eventually saw a rat. It was a tale not at all remote from life. Everyone had seen all the figures in the tale,–had seen the family cat often bringing in, somewhat contemptuously, the ordinary mouse, and sometimes standing proudly over the prostrate rat. And as for mats, everyone knows every step of their manufacture, from the time that the aged garment disappeared from use to reappear in all the majesty of reinvigorated youth and colour from the dye pot as from Medea's caldron, until after the regular mat festival the gorgeous blend of colours glowed upon the floor. Then came the *Royal Readers*, of pious memory.... There is the pathetic tale of Little Jim, and the thrilling tale of the child and the tiger. Boadicea is esteemed, and no one cares if her name should be Boudicca. Sir Ralph the Rover is a wicked man who has a sad adventure at the Inchcape Rock, and the snow at Hohenlinden is as white as the snow in the yard after a big storm. There is a famous story about a skater and the wolves, and how the man escaped from the beasts because he could turn more quickly on the ice than could the wolves. That is what the children will do if a wolf comes among them on the pond. He probably won't, but there are large, cross dogs, and wild cats are not unknown. Something interesting may happen. There is a pleasant account of Hudson's Bay traders, and everyone remembers the picture of the moccasin at the top of the page. There is Macaulay's story of the relief of Londonderry; and the whole class shares

the joy of the haggard wretches on the wall when the great boom broke, even if the *Mountjoy* had rebounded and stuck in the mud. Long passages from *The Lady of the Lake* are known by rote, not because they have been learned, but from the sheer impact of the printed word upon the eye and ringing verse upon the ear. There is no end to the interest of the *Royal Readers*.

Each lesson in the *Reader* is provided with a list of difficult words to be spelled, and meanings thereof to be memorized. The spellings are in heavy type, and the meanings in lighter type. One can "hear out" one's own spellings by covering with a blotter either the words or the meanings; but the favourite method is to persuade some friend to "hear them out", and it has been discovered by long experience that he who hears learns faster than he who recites.

After all, the old *Readers* furnish an opening into the world of letters, and the pupil who has mastered them faithfully is able to read as far in English literature, as his industry and taste and time permit. It is perhaps as little possible to leave The Little White Schoolhouse with a total incapacity and disinclination to read a decent book as it is to graduate from College in the same state. College courses may be used by the adroit as a vaccine against liberal culture; and it is still possible, in some places, "to obtain a degree" as President Lowell puts it, "and evade an education."

Of the old *Arithmetic*, one may not speak lightly. Many years ago there was a green one, later a yellow one, or it may be that the yellow one came first. Each furnished a joyous excursion through the mystical field of numbers. One admitted at the first, without undue scrutiny, a few simple propositions, that $2+2=4$ and $3 \times 3=9$, and the like, and with their support marched bravely through the thorny field of fractions and decimals, and the dense forest of interest and percentages. There were exciting problems about Yonge St., Toronto, and quieter investigations as to the length of time that it took six men to dig a ditch x feet long and y feet deep and z feet wide. After the green and the yellow came a series of little paper-covered books, culminating in a hard-covered thing known as *The Academic Arithmetic*. It, too, contained problems profitable for instruction and edification. And any *Arithmetic* has the merit that it can always be used at intervals of the cessation of other business. The slate and pencil are produced, and one gets comfortably involved in a calculation that may be easily prolonged until the bell rings without bringing one under the imputation of laziness.

Now and then some advanced pupils are initiated into algebra and geometry. The younger among them at times wonder whether x and y always mean the same, or if they sometimes change. And if they do change, why is it? It seems a complicated sort of tit-tat-toe. But geometry deals with figures that are much more obvious, and often beautiful to see; though it does sometimes seem ridiculous to spend an hour proving something, when the matter could be settled in a moment by a graduated ruler.

The *Geographies*–there are two, the big one and the little one– are excellent entertainment, even if they do contain tales difficult of belief. Nor is their beauty wholly obscured even when the teacher tries to keep the flock busy by requesting them to learn the counties of England or Ontario or Scotland or even Quebec. There was once a stout youth who had no strong impulse toward philosophical pursuits, and no aptitude for the printed word. He was asked to learn the counties of Quebec, and he did nothing else of a studious nature for some days. But the French names baffled him. One day, during a lull in activities, the teacher called on him to recite them. "Tolly-

ollyok, Willygiskel" he began, and stopped. He was not set to further research, and is to-day a prosperous and respected man of business.

Of *Histories* there are three in use. One is a small soft-covered book, known as *The Brief History of England*, filled with little nuggets of fact, and delightful lists of names and dates. This work is begun well down in the grades, and may be carried on indefinitely. There is a larger volume on the same subject, restricted to the eighth grade and the ninth, when a ninth grade appears. The third is a genial little history of Canada from Cabot to the present. This last contains some fascinating small maps, and occasional shifts from large to small type that catch the eye. There is abundance of time to study these various works, and everybody who can learn anything gets some notion of Canada and England from them. An occasional radical parent grumbles at the time that his child wastes over "dates and stuff" But the grumble is half hearted; for everybody has, or thinks he has, some ancestor or ancestors, and after all, in a way it is only learning about one's family affairs.

The subject of grammar occupies a peculiar place in The Little White Schoolhouse. There is a small and stern volume which may be permitted in the hands of pupils in the sixth grade, and accompanies them through the remainder of their course. It contains a reasonably succinct statement of English grammar from a functional point of view, and affords fairly rigorous practice in the logic of language. It is customary for those pupils who pursue this study to carry on their investigation during the last period of the day– from three till four–on Monday, Wednesday, and Friday. The Friday afternoon grammar may be omitted, as some teachers prefer to have that time for the speaking of pieces. It is a convention among the pupils to profess that grammar is without value. Yet they do not really hate it with especial hatred, and those who reach the dizzy height of the High School at Fox Brook or the County Academy find its lessons very valuable in their higher studies. But it must on no account influence one's daily speech. There is a *mos minorum* that requires each and all to speak as the community speaks; and the community on the whole, and apart from special occasions of display by licensed speakers, prefers a dialect terse, racy, rather highly figurative, and picturesquely ungrammatical superficially, though not far from correct English idiom in essential structure.

There is one exercise of the day that, though not strictly a part of the curriculum, is never omitted. Every morning, after the roll is called, the pupils read a chapter in the Bible, taking a verse each. The selection is usually from the New Testament. There is no comment or explanation. But no one can leave the school after a few years without having the doctrines, imagery, and phraseology of the Scripture firmly imprinted upon his mind. The elders all know the Bible too: and the language of the natives is, often, redolent of the King James version. There is no danger of anyone missing an apposite reference to Scripture characters. A curious glittering poverty of mind marks a generation that lacks this training.

There are other subjects of study, but these are the staples. Once or twice some pundit among teachers has taught some hesitating Latin or French. Drawing of some sort is often introduced, but is treated by the children rather as an amusement than as a serious pursuit. There are funny little books on hygiene, chiefly devoted to proving the evil effects of alcohol and tobacco on the human frame. These are not taken very seriously, as there are no steady drinkers in the community, and the tobacco users are respectable citizens who have no intention of making any change in their habits, or of listening to any impertinence about their pipes from anybody's children.

The Friday afternoon "recitations" occasionally bring in a stray parent or two; and the boy stands on the burning deck immediately before the teacher's desk with brief though unrelenting volubility; or a very small child brings in Mary's lamb, or lisps the poem about the little drops of water and little grains of sand that constitute this terrestrial globe. The annual "examination" is a larger affair, and often requires an elaborate "dialogue," as the pupils call the elementary plays that they learn for the occasion. Then the adults of the neighbourhood attend in large numbers, and watch with parental zeal the performances of their progeny. But the affair bears little enough relation to the serious work of the year.

. . . .

For The Little White Schoolhouse never quite loses its appeal. Here shall appear no paean of praise, no tear of sensibility, no exuberance of enthusiasm. It is a dingy little spot, with some solid merit, and no superficial attractions. And it is pleasant to reflect that the generations, as they come on, pass through its discipline; that they fall into the same mud holes, fight in the same anteroom, roam the same woods, parse the same sentences, stand upon the same burning deck, struggle with the same sums and the same dates. It is the university of the people, that turns rather primitive little savages into rather commonplace young Canadians. What one thinks of it depends on what one thinks of the commonplace Canadian.

V

Minority Education and Nationbuilding 1870-1970

The half century prior to World War I was a period of conscious Canadian nationbuilding. In 1867, the British North America Act united central Canada, Nova Scotia, and New Brunswick into a federal state, and laid the constitutional basis for a strong political nation. By 1873, six years after the first "Act of Confederation", this new nation had grown to include Prince Edward Island, Manitoba, British Columbia, and the vast expanse of the North West Territories. It literally stretched from sea to sea, and its more than 3½ million square miles of territory occupied half a continent.

A nation, however, is not just a political or geographical entity; a Canadian economic structure also had to be built. Generous settlement measures and aggressive immigration policies were devised to develop the agricultural regions of the West. A protective tariff was thrown around the country to help establish an industrial and manufacturing base in eastern Canada. Railways were built to join the various regions with "bonds of steel". Indeed, railways became the tangible symbols of Canadian nationbuilding, and by 1905 there were three transcontinentals spanning the country–often within sight of each other!

But there was more to nationbuilding than legislating political and economic structures into existence. Some very fundamental cultural issues also had to be resolved. Exactly what kind of a nation was being built? Was this new and greater Canda to be an "English" country with one bicultural province? Or would the cultural duality so evident in her population be recognized and preserved throughout her wide domain? Would the English-speaking majorities outside of Quebec impose their institutions upon the French-speaking minorities in the name of democracy? Or would the

guarantees in the country's constitution (the British North America Act) be a sufficient safeguard for minority rights? And what of the European and Asian immigrants settling in the West? Would their cultures and languages be allowed to persist in a multi-cultural nation, or would they be deliberately assimilated at the earliest opportunity?

These were the aspects of Canadian nationhood that could only be determined by the experience of living together. And since the preservation of culture and language was so intimately connected with education, these were also the issues that brought on a succession of "school questions" in the fifty years preceding World War I.

By 1916, these issues had been contested in almost every region of Canada. As a result, the shape of a national community–complete in its cultural as well as its political and economic dimensions–was clearly outlined. The place of cultural minorities, French-speaking or otherwise, was settled: the English-speaking view of Canadian nationality would prevail. Outside of Quebec, there would be one national culture and one national language. For those who held a different concept of Canadian nationality, it was a hard verdict to accept. Perhaps Henri Bourassa best summed up the disappointment and disillusionment of those who had argued for a bicultural nation with his bitter comment of 1915, when the country was at war with the German Empire: "Les ennemis de la langue française, de la civilisation française au Canada, ce ne sont pas les Boches des bords de la Sprée; ce sont les anglicisateurs anglo-canadiens....Ce sont surtout les Canadiens français aveulis et avilis par la conquête et par trois siècles de servitude coloniale."[1]

Nevertheless, the definition of Canadian nationality hammered out in this first period of Canadian nationbuilding was destined to persist, with only slight alterations, for the next half century.

By the 1960s, however, the basic principles of the national structure created in the nineteenth century were drawing heavy fire. There had never been complete agreement on any of the main courses–political, economic, or national—charted for Canadian development, but with the changing conditions and expectations of the 1960s the opposition coalesced into a sustained attack. The tradition of a strong central government laid down by the B.N.A. Act was challenged by the increasing social responsibilities and growing power of the provinces. The economic policies designed to further the industrialization of Canada were indicted for spawning regional inequalities and the "branch-plant" economy. In the nineteenth century, the main concern was building the physical structure of the Canadian nation; in the mid twentieth century, this structure was reassessed in respect to the quality of life it afforded Canadians.

The nineteenth-century definition of Canadian nationality was also under attack. Sparked by a resurgence of French-Canadian nationalism in the 1960s, many Canadians, both English- and French-speaking, felt that Canada would have to recognize, even emphasize, her cultural duality if she were to survive as a nation at all. Soon other minority

Collecting for the Red Cross, Manning Avenue School, Toronto, 1916.

A. National Schools: The Religious Question

groups emerged to press for recognition in what would have to be not a bicultural, but a multicultural nation. In short, to many Canadians in the 1960s, it seemed as if a new and different definition of Canadian nationality was required.

And once again the schools were pressed into the service of nationbuilding. As they had aided in the formation of the old, so too, it was asserted, would they assist in the birth of the new.

Each of the two "founding races" viewed the schools as essential institutions in the preservation and perpetuation of its culture in Canada. As a perceptive French chronicler of the Canadian scene, André Siegfried, observed around the turn of the century, the "education problem" involved nothing less than "the very destiny of two peoples and two civilizations" (document A.1). One of the main bulwarks of French-Canadian nationality was the Roman Catholic Church, which in Quebec played a central role in those schools designed to pass on a French and Catholic culture. But by 1900 every other Canadian province had an English-speaking, predominantly Protestant majority, which regarded sectarian schools as divisive. The "national schools" of the Protestant majorities were the non-denominational public schools. And so the stage for conflict was set: to what extent would the provincial majorities tolerate the "separate" schools of their Catholic minorities?

The provincial governments, however, did not have a completely free hand in the matter of sectarian education. Under certain, specified conditions the rights of denominational schools were protected by the terms of the Canadian constitution, the B.N.A. Act. Because of this legal sanction, interference with these schools led to a series of court battles, which culminated in the Manitoba School Question, 1890-1896 (document A.2). The results of this litigation, expressed here in the balanced and pallid prose of the courts, were explosive. To the French Catholic minority, Manitoba's successful abolition of publicly-supported Catholic schools eloquently stated the position of the minority Catholic culture in Canada (document A.3). It seemed as if some very fundamental assumptions about the

[1]Robert Rumilly, *Henri Bourassa, La Vie Publique d'un Grand Canadien* (Montréal: Les Éditions Chantecler Ltée, 1953), pp. 530-31.

Loretto Abbey, Toronto.

nature of their country had been attacked and routed.

A.1 National Schools: French Catholics and English Protestants

In a country like Canada the school must sooner or later become to a greater degree than elsewhere the principal stake to be struggled for by the opposing forces, national and religious. Therein is the framework of the future. Catholics and Protestants, French and English, ask themselves alike with anxiety what is being made of their children. Hence the intense fierceness of the discussions bearing upon this subject: what is at issue is not merely the lot of a ministry, a party, a method of government, but the very destiny of two peoples and two civilizations.

The problem of Canadian education is one of infinite complexity, but its essential elements are easy enough to set out and to grasp. We have two separate races, living together under the same laws, but not speaking the same language or practising the same religion. Each of these two races is so strongly attached to that which constitutes its individuality that it would not sacrifice the smallest particle of it to the cause of the unity of the nation. Now the dream of unity is cherished ardently by the British majority, which bears impatiently with the survival of the vanquished race. Naturally the minority resists, but as it is not able and has no wish to secede, the adversaries are forced to live on side by side as best they can in the consciousness that separation is impossible and that their union can never be complete. Herein is the secret of a problem which doubtless will never be solved to the satisfaction of both parties.

The French policy is clearly defined. As it is essential for the future that the children should retain the tongue and the creed of their parents, our compatriots are determined that French and the doctrines of Catholicism shall be taught under their own supervision in public schools set apart for them and subsidized by the state. There must be no question of secular education in this clearly defined and homogeneous world in which there are few who are not obedient servants of the Church.

The Protestants, on the other hand, look with disfavour upon these schools, which they accuse of being at once anglophobe and clerical, and which they tolerate rather than accept. They regard with envy their neighbours in the United States, where the cosmopolitan elements are swiftly assimilated, and where public opinion frowns upon those sections which are disinclined to learn English. Above all, they detest the influence of the clergy, and cannot reconcile themselves to patronizing even indirectly a system of teaching which is in the hands of the *curés*. Their predilection is in favour of a system of "free", "compulsory" education, which if not secular shall be neutral as regards the Christian forms of belief.

It is easy to see that these two views cannot be reconciled. Wherever it is possible the English refuse to subsidize the Catholic schools. On their side, the French retain an invincible mistrust of the schools of their rivals, and seldom or never send their children to them.

A.1 Source: André Siegfried, *The Race Question in Canada* (London, England: W. E. Nash, 1907), pp. 60-61.

A.2 The British North America Act and Denominational Schools

Article VI, Section 93,
British North America Act, 1867

As finally drafted and passed by the British Parliament, the educational provisions of the Canadian constitution read as follows:

In and for each Province the Legislature may exclusively make Laws in relation to Education, subject and according to the following provisions:

1.   Nothing in any such law shall prejudicially affect any Right or Privilege with respect to Denominational Schools which any Class of Persons have by Law in the Province at the Union:

2.   All the Powers and Privileges, and Duties at the Union by Law conferred and imposed in Upper Canada on the Separate Schools and School Trustees of the Queen's Roman Catholic Subjects shall be and the same are hereby extended to the Dissentient Schools of the Queen's Protestant and Roman Catholic Subjects in Quebec:

3.   Where in any Povince a System of Separate or Dissentient Schools exists by Law at the Union or is thereafter established by the Legislature of the Province, an Appeal shall lie to the Governor-General-in-Council from any Act or Decision of any Provincial Authority affecting any Right or Privilege of the Protestant or Roman Catholic Minority of the Queen's Subjects in relation to Education:

4.   In case any such Provincial Law as from Time to Time seems to the Governor-General-in-Council requisite for the due Execution of the Provisions of this Section is not made, or in case any decision of the Governor-General-in-Council on any Appeal under this Section is not duly executed by the proper Provincial Authority in that Behalf, then and in every such case, and as far only as the Circumstances of each Case require, the Parliament of Canada may make remedial Laws for the due Execution of the Provisions of this Section and of any Decision of the Governor-General-in-Council under this Section.[1]

Legal Interpretations of Section 93

The constitutional provisions for education are expressed in one general statement and four qualifying clauses or subsections. These will be examined in the light of court decisions which have interpreted them.

General Statement: "Christian Brothers" Case

"In and for each Province the Legislature may exclusively make Laws in relation to Education...." The emphasis here on the "exclusive" right of the provinces to legislate on educational matters was upheld in 1876 when a bill to incorporate the Christian Brothers as a Company of Teachers for the Dominion was referred by the Senate to the Supreme Court of Canada. The court ruled the bill to be unconstitutional and *ultra vires* of the federal government as infringing upon the powers of the provincial legislatures.[2]

Subsection 1: "New Brunswick" Case

"Nothing in any such law shall prejudicially affect any Right or Privilege with respect to Denominational Schools which any Class of Persons have *by Law in the Province at the Union.*" In this first subsection the italicized phrases have proved to be the significant ones in legal deci-

A.2 Source: John Cheal, *Investment in Canadian Youth* (Toronto: Macmillan, 1963), pp. 25-31. Eds: Note – Some of the original footnotes have been omitted.

[1] 30 Vict. Cap.3, Art.VI, S.93.

[2] L. William Coutlee, *Supreme Court Cases* (Toronto: The Carswell Co. Ltd., 1907), p. 2.

sions. This is illustrated by the *New Brunswick* case. In 1871 the New Brunswick legislature revoked provisions of a former Parish Schools Act under which Roman Catholics had enjoyed the privilege of giving religious instruction in their schools, and passed a Common School Act which required all schools receiving government aid to be non-sectarian and free.

"It was contended on the part of the petitioner that the Common Schools Act of 1871 by repealing the School Act of 1858 and requiring that schools shall be non-sectarian thereby deprived Roman Catholics not only of the right which the Act of 1858 had secured to them of having the Douay Bible read by their children in the mixed schools, but also of the privilege which they had under that Act, of creating schools of a character exclusively Roman Catholic in districts where the population was entirely Roman Catholic.... And therefore, that the Common Schools Act of 1871 does 'prejudicially affect' rights and privileges which were secured to Roman Catholics as a class in respect to Denominational Schools, and is therefore unconstitutional, as being in conflict with ss. 1 of sec. 93 of B.N.A. Act."[3]

The plaintiff in this case based the argument on the provisions in the first portion of subsection one. The court, however, based its judgment not on those rights or privileges that the Roman Catholic minority had enjoyed by practice, but those that had been provided for by law....
      ...the ruling of the Supreme Court of New Brunswick...held:

"That, neither the School Act of 1871, nor the School Act of 1858, which it repealed, provided for the establishment of Denominational Schools, and that neither of those Acts conferred any legal rights or privileges upon any class of persons or upon any one Denomination of Christians, in the government or control of the schools organized thereunder; and that the schools established in pursuance of the Act of 1858 were not Denominational, and therefore that the School Act of 1871, which declares that the schools conducted under *its* provisions shall be non-denominational is not *ultra vires* of the Legislature of New Brunswick."[4]

Consequently, New Brunswick and other provinces that had no legal provisions for separate schools before entering the union were not bound to provide publicly-supported schools for a religious minority. In some instances "gentlemen's agreements" have been worked out whereby pupils of a religious minority attend certain schools to which teachers of their own faith are appointed. Such arrangements are of an informal character, however, and have no support in law.

Subsections 3 and 4: "Manitoba" Case
The "Manitoba School Question" of 1890-6 tested not only Subsection 1 of Section 93, but also Subsections 3 and 4 which provided for appeals to the federal government and remedial action by that government to overrule provincial legislation that denies the minority rights....
      The background of...the "Manitoba School Question" is well summed up in the following excerpt from the Manitoba Law Reports:

[3] I Pugs. N.B.R. 273.

[4] Ibid.

"The territory now constituting the Province of Manitoba was admitted into the Canadian Confederation by virtue of the Manitoba Act, 33 Vic., c.3, (D.1870) and an Order-in-Council issued in pursuance thereof. Prior to the passage of said Act there were in the territory a number of effective schools for children. These schools were all denominational schools, some being controlled by the Roman Catholic Church, and others by various Protestant denominations. These schools were supported by the various churches, and by voluntary contributions. There were no public schools in the sense of state schools, and no taxes were levied to support such schools....

The Legislature of the new Province in the year 1871 established a system of public schools by which there was one Board of Education divided into two sections–a Protestant section and a Roman Catholic section. The school sections throughout the Province were divided into Protestant and Catholic. The Protestant schools were under the control of the Protestant section of the Board, and the Roman Catholic schools under the control of the Roman Catholic section of the Board. Taxes were levied for the support of the Protestant schools on the property of Protestants alone, and for the support of Roman Catholic schools on the property of Roman Catholics alone. The grant made annually by the Legislature was apportioned between the two classes of schools. This system under various statutes was retained until the year 1890. In 1890 the Public Schools Act, 53 Vic., c.38 (M) was passed, by which all previous statutes relating to education were repealed and a system of non-sectarian schools was established, for the support of which all ratepayers, both Roman Catholic and Protestant were alike taxed."[5]

[5]Manitoba Law Reports, 7, p. 273.

In regard to education, the Manitoba Act had adopted wording similar to that in Section 93 of the B.N.A. Act. There were two significant differences, however. One was the addition of the words "or practice" to subsection one so that it read, "Nothing in any such law shall prejudicially affect any right or privilege with respect to Denominational Schools which any class of Persons have *by Law or Practice* in the Province at the Union." The second change was the omission in Subsection 3 of the words "or is established" which provided protection against the loss of privileges granted after joining the Union.

From the Act of 1890 two lawsuits arose. The first, *City of Winnipeg v. Barrett*, was based on the claim that the Act had prejudicially affected the rights and privileges respecting denominational schools that Roman Catholics had enjoyed at the time the province of Manitoba entered the Union. The emphasis was on rights enjoyed "by practice" since the province, being new, had no schools that existed "by law". However, the Manitoba Supreme Court declared: "The right... that Roman Catholics had before the Union, to establish denominational schools and to attend them and to compete as regards their schools, on equal terms with other denominations, or Protestants generally, has not been taken away and can be exercised now as fully as it could have been before the Union." The court also recorded that Sir John A. Macdonald, in his report on the New Brunswick Common Schools Act, had expressed the opinion that the subsections of Section 93 "applied exclusively to the denominational, separate or dissentient schools, and did not in any way affect or lessen the powers of Provincial Legislatures to pass laws respecting the general educational systems of the Provinces".

The case then went to the Supreme Court of Canada, where the judgment of the Manitoba courts was unanimously reversed. The Supreme Court took the position that "if they have their own schools they will be taxed for the support of the public schools and will thus be 'prejudicially affected' in their rights." This court gave particular significance to the phrase "or practice" in the Manitoba Act and stated, "There were at that time in actual operation or practice a system of denominational schools in Manitoba well established and the *de facto* rights and privileges of which were enjoyed by a large class of persons."

Finally, the case was appealed to the Judicial Committee of the House of Lords (the Privy Council). In its judgment this tribunal stated:

"In their Lordships' opinion, it would be going much too far to hold that the establishment of a national system of education upon an unsectarian basis is so inconsistent with the right to set up and maintain denominational schools that the two things cannot exist together, or that the existence of one necessarily implies or involves immunity from taxation for the purpose of the other. They cannot assent to the view, which seems to be indicated by one of the members of the Supreme Court, that public schools under the Act of 1890 are in reality Protestant schools."[6]

The Privy Council, therefore, sustained the decision of the Manitoba courts that the Public Schools Act was valid.

The *Barrett* case was followed by the case of *Brophy v. Attorney-General of Manitoba*, 1895. The religious minority appealed to the federal cabinet for remedial legislation as provided in Subsections 3 and 4 of Section 93. Because of the omission in the Manitoba Act of the words "or is established", which were in the B.N.A. Act,

the Dominion government was in doubt as to its competency to hear an appeal. It therefore requested an opinion from the Supreme Court and received the decision that no appeal lay. The case was then taken to the Privy Council which held that the Province of Manitoba was acting within its powers in repealing the earlier legislation, but that the minority still had the right to appeal as provided in Section 93.

After the decision of the Judicial Committee was given the [federal government] proceeded to hear the appeal.... The result of their deliberations was the passage of [a remedial order]. By this order they required the Province of Manitoba to restore to the minority the following alleged rights:–

(a)   The right to build, maintain, equip, manage, conduct and support Roman Catholic schools in the manner provided for by the said statutes which were repealed by the two acts of 1890 aforesaid.
(b)   The right to share proportionately in any grant made out of the public funds for the purpose of education.
(c)   The right of exemption of such Roman Catholics as contributed to Roman Catholic schools from all payment or contribution to the support of any other schools."[7]

The government of Manitoba submitted an answer to the Dominion government in which it pointed out "that the remedial order demanded the restoration of the old school laws which had been found inefficient; that the policy of 1890 had been adopted after a careful examination of the system previously prevailing; that, under the old system, many people grew up in a state of

---

[6] J.C. 1892, p. 446.

[7] F. C. Wade, *The Manitoba School Question* (Winnipeg: Manitoba Institution for Deaf and Dumb, 1895), p. 4.

illiteracy; that, apart from the objections to separate schools on principle, the weight of school taxation and the sparseness of settlement made it impossible to carry on a double system of schools."

When the Manitoba legislature failed to act on the Dominion government's remedial order, a bill was introduced into the 1896 session of Parliament to compel this action. The bill was delayed in its passage through Parliament until the session prorogued without the bill being passed. Before the next session a federal election was held in which the government was defeated, mainly over this issue. As a result Manitoba has continued to provide for only a public school system and no further remedial legislation has been introduced into the Dominion Parliament.

At this point it may be well to summarize the decisions in the *New Brunswick* and *Manitoba* cases and the *Christian Brothers* case:
1.   Legislation in the field of education is the exclusive prerogative of provincial governments.
2.   Religious minorities may claim only those rights and privileges to which they were entitled by law when the province entered the Union.
3.   Minorities have the right of appeal to the federal government in cases where they feel these rights have been prejudicially affected.
4.   The federal government has the legal right to pass remedial legislation overruling provincial legislation in cases where such appeals are sustained.
5.   However, as a result of the federal government's experience in the Manitoba issue, it would seem highly inexpedient for any such government to overrule the decisions of a provincial legislature with respect to education in its own province.

A.3 The Minority Replies: Catholic and French Reaction

Let me draw the attention of this House to the pastoral recently issued by the archbishops and bishops of the ecclesiastical provinces of Quebec, Montreal and Ottawa, and addressed to the clergy, secular and regular, and all the faithful of these provinces, in which we find the following passages:–

"Consequently, it is with great surprise and profound grief we learn that, even here in our own country where religious liberty is loudly proclaimed, legalized attempts have been made to introduce that censurable and censured system of unsectarian schools, in order to deprive the church of a right which is inseparable from the free exercise of Catholic worship, guaranteed by the faith of the treaties. In another province of this land, inhabited by Catholics, they are trying once more an underhand and satanic persecution against the sacred rights of the Church. It was with emotion of heart we heard the Venerable Archbishop of St. Boniface raise his voice once more against this iniquity. In a pastoral letter, dated the 15th of last August, the illustrious prelate makes known this perfidious stratagem for perverting youth, forewarns his flock against it, and lets them see how odious it is.

A trial of a novel kind has come upon us. In a land where freedom of religion is so loudly proclaimed, fetters have been placed on that liberty. Our social and political institutions warranted protection to all our rights, and now, behold the same rights trampled upon by the very persons who should safeguard them. Here you are exposed to persecution–not a bloody persecution which attacks the body or external life, but a persecu-

A.3 Source: C. R. Devlin, Canada, House of Commons, *Debates*, 1891, vol. 31, 120-21.

tion most cunningly masked, which attacks the intellect, hinders it from being enlightened by Christian light and guided by the reflections of its divine splendours."

Now, even since then we know that the attention of the Government has been drawn to this matter by the French press of the country, notably by the *Courrier de Canada*, which in more than one brilliant article sounded the note of alarm. The attention of the Government has also been called by *La Minerve, La Presse*, and many other French Conservative organs of importance to this question, but all in vain: and ever since the expiration of the time when disallowance [of the Manitoba Public Schools Act] might have been applied for, a stronger feeling of indignation has prevailed. I could give you, in a few words, an expression of that opinion, which is certainly strong:

"It seems evident that the Manitoba Acts will not be disallowed.

It is a misfortune, and a greater misfortune than it is perhaps believed.

Not only does the sanction of the injustice perpetrated by the odious Martin[1] deprive our compatriots and co-religionists of the use of their language, and of the right to have their children educated in Catholic schools, but it violently shakes Confederation.

The compact of 1867 cannot for a long time stand such shocks.

French Canadians and Catholics, who have always been the most faithful observers and the most constant supporters of the British North America Act, will know henceforth how little the constitution protects their most sacred rights,

since a fanatical majority may trample upon them with impunity.

The results may not immediately be felt. The people's feelings are somewhat blunted presently. People undergo the reaction of the violent crisis which they have had to go through of late. The weak and undignified stand of their natural leaders has disconcerted and discouraged them."

That is pretty strong language, but it is taken from a Conservative organ. Strong though it be, it is none the less, I believe, a faithful presentation of the sentiments entertained by the great majority of the population of the Province of Quebec.

[1]Joseph Martin, Manitoba's Attorney-General (1888-1891) was the originator and a strong supporter of the Public Schools Act.–ED.

B. National Schools: The Language Question

The second part of the national school question involved a conflict over the place of French as a language of instruction in the nation's schools. The language question struck to the very heart of the problem of Canadian nationhood. Was Canada an English-speaking country with a bilingual province (Quebec), or would the principle of bilingualism be recognized in the schools across the country? Although the question was crucial, there were no language provisions in the B.N.A. Act pertaining to schools, and the provincial Departments of Education were free to deal with the issue as they saw fit.

Many French-speaking spokesmen sought to make not only Quebec, but the whole of Canada their homeland. This meant that French-language instruction would have to be available to French Canadians wherever they might live in the country. Since the letter of the law was silent on the matter of language rights in schools, they buttressed their case with an appeal to history and to the "faith" and the "spirit" of the treaties that united French and English in Canada (document B.1).

Many Anglo-Canadians, however, disagreed with the principle of bilingualism. To them, the English language was the one great unifying force in the country. Consequently, when thousands of Europeans settled in the West in the first decade of the twentieth century, the English language and the "national school" were seen as the primary means of assimilating them into the Canadian nationality (document B.2). And although the French-Canadian population amounted to 28 per cent of the total, the French-speaking minorities in the West were regarded in the same light as the Ruthenians, who accounted for only .9 per cent of the population–they were all foreign elements to be assimilated.

In the East, European immigration was light and the language issue was strictly a contest between French and English. In 1912 the Ontario Department of Education issued "Regulation 17" which prohibited the use of French as a language of instruction in all but the primary grades. The regulation applied to all schools, both "public" and "separate". Had the measure been enforced to the letter, it would have cut off a quarter of a million Franco-Ontarians from French-language instruction in their schools. Regulation 17 drew sharp criticism from French Canadians in both Ontario and Quebec. In document B.3, the Toronto *Globe* (which called itself "Canada's national newspaper") answers these critics by articulating some of the English-Canadian arguments for monolingualism.

B.1 The Case for French-language Schools

My subject presents itself under three aspects. First, what are the rights of the French language in Canada; second, to examine how those rights have been respected and practised; and finally, if bi-lingualism is a danger or a source of strength to our country. Of course one could find the first right of the French language in any country or any language in natural law–the right of a man to speak the language taught him by his mother. But in this country the position is different. I have referred back to the treaties of 1759, 1760 and 1763, the Treaty of Paris, and I find no grounds there for the legal right to the use of the French language in Canada. But after the con-

B.1 Source: Armand Lavergne, M.L.A., "The Position of the French Language in Canada", *Addresses Delivered Before the Canadian Club of Montreal*, 1911-1912, pp. 65-70.

quest, as a matter of fact and of necessity, French was used in Canada from the very beginning. It was first used officially in 1791 when the first Legislature was opened in Quebec. Some members suggested that English being the language of the Empire should alone be used in the Legislature at Quebec. But Papineau, the Speaker of that Legislature, argued that French being the language of the majority should be recognized officially. And his services to the Crown during the preceding war, coupled with his strong personality, enabled him to carry that principle, and for the first time since the conquest French was officially used in 1791. When the Union came, on the instructions of Lord Durham, French was debarred as an official language; but a man whom every Canadian is proud of and whose memory is respected by every party in this country, Lafontaine, insisted on speaking French, saying that he did so because it was against the law, that it was a bad law and should be repealed. And in 1844 it was repealed, and French was recognized as an official language equally with English.

But all these different treaties finished in 1867. When Confederation was formed it was put into the British North America Act as part of the constitution of the country. Clause 23 of that Act gives the right to members of the Houses of Parliament and the Legislature at Quebec to speak either French or English and also any Court in Canada may use either language, and in Quebec Acts of Parliament and the Legislature must be put in both languages.

That is the law of our constitution. I will not give you my own opinion but will give you the opinion of one of the founders of Confederation, Sir John Macdonald. On February 17th, 1890, speaking in the House of Commons in answer to D'Alton McCarthy, who had moved for the abolition of French in the North West, he said that if any attempt should be made in certain quarters to oppress one language or make it inferior to the other, it would not only be foolish, but wicked, even though such a thing should be possible. Sir John said that under the Constitution all British were equal, with equal rights of every kind, language, religion, property and person,–that there was no paramount race and no conquered race, but all were equally British subjects.

The words of Sir John Macdonald, it seems to me, express the very spirit of our Constitution, that all British subjects in this country have equal rights in the matter of language. We find, therefore, that this Confederation is based upon compromise, where the two races quit fighting and formed a union under a well understood principle, that both races and languages should be equal. The mover of the B.N.A. Act in the Imperial House expressed this more clearly and eloquently than I can. Lord Carnarvon, in moving it in 1866, said, "Lower Canada too is jealous of its customs and traditions and institutions and language and will enter the Union only on the understanding that she retain them." So that Union formed in 1867 was on that distinct principle, which was carried into fruit in the Constitution. It is, therefore, I hope, admitted that the principle of equality is evident as that upon which our Confederation rests.

Has this been truly carried into practice? You may say it has been by using the French language in this country; but although it is equally official it has suffered many grievances, some serious, others less serious but still humiliating to the minority, and tending to prevent a good understanding between the French and English speaking Canadians.

First of all amongst the more serious grievances of the French, I would say that whilst in the Province of Quebec, the minority receive at the hands of the majority not only the most just but the most generous treatment that a minority has ever received at the hands of the majority–yet in the other Provinces, where the rights of the French were guaranteed them either by the word of the Sovereign, the Bill of Rights (as in Manitoba, granted in 1870), or the House of Commons (as in the North West Territories in 1875), or in Ontario where there is no law to give legal status to the French...while, I say, in Quebec we give the minority just, fair and generous treatment, the French minorities in the other Provinces have seen successively their privileges curtailed in Prince Edward Island, Nova Scotia, New Brunswick and Manitoba and the North West Territories, and there is talk of still further curtailing them in Manitoba [and Ontario] to-day.

This is not a matter of schools, to have the people of this country admitting the principle of national schools. To me it seems strange from a religious or national point of view to say that schools can be regarded as national, which are opposed to the belief of 40 per cent of the population and to the language of 30 per cent. Is there ...a British principle...[that] goes against the non-sectarian schools, a principle not recognized in England and with but one object–to cut off the child from the faith of its father and the language of its mother? What would be the consequence if Quebec were to retaliate and treat the minority in this Province as the French minorities are treated in the other Provinces? I say it would be an injustice, and although I am supposed to be an extremist, as long as I had a voice left I would raise it against such an injustice to the minority in Quebec.If such a thing were done in Quebec, "Ulster would fight, and," I think, "Ulster would be right."

. . . .

I understand to a certain extent the sentiment of those who think it would be better to have only one language in this country. I would not say that I share that view, but I understand and respect it. But did it ever strike you that the French population of this country might have similar ideas? I have been told that there is in this country a school which says that Canada must be English even at the cost of ceasing to be British. This argument I will not admit. It is too late for it. You cannot tear up history, and surely there is not an English speaking party or man here who would say that French has to be conquered. The English have come here and we have had our fights, but we cannot tear up history. We are both here to stay–why not learn to understand each other immediately? I see no danger in the duality of our language; quite the contrary. Take, for example, Switzerland...where a real liberty has been preserved although the people speak three different languages. Then take Belgium. Is there a country which can compare proportionately in its world-wide business and trade with Belgium? and there they speak two languages which are officially recognized to the minutest details. Therefore it seems to me that the duality of our country, far from being a danger, is really a source of strength; and the more we preserve it the more strongly we shall preserve our country, with a two-edged sword to fight its battles.

B.2 The English Language and the Immigrant

A great deal has been said and much has been written regarding the great national task of

B.2 Source: J. T. M. Anderson [Inspector of Schools, Saskatchewan], *The Education of the New-Canadian, A Treatise on Canada's Greatest Education Problem* (London and Toronto: J. M. Dent and Sons, Ltd., 1918), pp. 7-9, 22-25, 95-104.

assimilating the thousands who have come to settle in Canada from various lands across the seas. There seems to be a too prevalent idea that each and every male and female new-comer may, irrespective of age, after being subjected to some more or less indefinable process, which we call "assimilation," enter the ranks of full-fledged Canadian citizenship. After three years of residence here the foreigner becomes "naturalized," is given the franchise, and over his shoulders the toga of Canadian citizenship is thrown.[1] His qualifications in other respects are not for a moment considered. It matters not whether he can utter a single word of the English language. It matters not what are his ideas of the Canadian system of government. He must become a "citizen" before he can get a patent for his homestead, and thousands have eagerly signed their "crosses" in order to obtain patents for their quarter sections. Thus are they made "Canadians" in truly machine-like fashion. Surely the right to become a living link in the great earth-girdling imperial chain of the greatest Empire on earth is too lightly regarded in the apparent anxiety to "increase production" and develop "material resources."

The people of foreign countries who come to Canada after having reached maturity–the middle-aged and the aged–will never become true Canadian citizens, imbued with the highest Anglo-Saxon ideals. This should not, in fact, be expected of them. Their hearts will remain, to a very great extent, bound up with the scenes of their childhood....

...It should never be expected that the older people will become "true Canadians," and no attempt should be made to do what is an im-

possibility. It is possible, of course,...to assist them in gaining a knowledge of our language, laws, and government; but it will be practically impossible to wean them away from many of the habits and customs of their native lands; but there is an important duty to perform in seeing that the children of these newcomers are given every opportunity to receive proper training for intelligent citizenship. They, along with those who enter our country while still quite young, are the material upon which Canadians as nation-builders must work.

. . . .

A special report on the foreign-born population of Canada, as shown by the census statistics of June, 1911, has been published by the census department, and gives some interesting statistics as to the distribution, voting strength and origin of immigrants to Canada from non-British countries.

The total foreign-born population is given as 752,732, the percentage of males being 62.6 and of females 37.4. Of the total foreign-born, 62.2 per cent resided in the Western Provinces, Manitoba, Saskatchewan, Alberta, and British Columbia. The United States contributed 40.34 per cent, or 303,680, of its citizens to the population of Canada. Of European countries, Austria-Hungary comes first with a total of 121,430 immigrants, Russia second with 89,984, Norway and Sweden third with 49,194, and Germany fourth with 39,577.

Of the total foreign-born population, 344,-557, or 45.77 per cent, had become naturalized Canadians prior to the taking of the census of 1911, leaving 408,175, or 54.33 per cent, still alien citizens. Of these latter a considerable proportion have, of course, since become naturalized....

The figures show that 94,324, or 71.85 per cent, of the foreign-born naturalized were in the

[1] Since January 1, 1918, five years' residence, an "adequate knowledge" of English or French, and a good moral character, are required before Canadian and Imperial citizenship is granted.

Western Provinces; 21,022, or 16.01 per cent, in Ontario; and 2,874, or 2.19 per cent, in the Maritime Provinces. Of the 346,523 foreign-born males twenty-one and over in the Dominion, 131,289 were naturalized and 215,234 alien....

It is further interesting to note that Montreal had a total foreign-born population of 43,188, or 9.2 per cent; Toronto, 33,131, or 8.8 per cent; Winnipeg, 32,959, or 24.2 per cent; Vancouver, 27,713, or 27.6 per cent; Hamilton 7,693, or 9.4 per cent; Calgary, 9,030, or 20.6 per cent; Regina, 6,830, or 22.6 per cent; Edmonton, 5,598, or 22.5 per cent; Brantford, 2,020, or 8.7 per cent; Fort William, 4,746, or 28.7 per cent....

...The great problem of the assimilation of these non-British people lies chiefly with the Western Provinces, where they have settled in large numbers. It is quite obvious, then, that upon the manner in which the western provincial governments deal with this important and serious problem will depend the strengthening or weakening of our national structure as a result of the admission of so many thousands from foreign lands.

. . . .

The attitude of the Western Provinces in dealing with the language question may now be examined. The language of the public schools of British Columbia is English. Not many non-English have settled there, but those who have must conform to the one-language school. There are no Roman Catholic separate schools, and no religious instruction is given in the schools.

In the Province of Alberta probably the greatest progress has been made, and Canada owes a deep debt of gratitude to the far-seeing statesmen who have boldly attacked this greatest of our educational problems. In Edmonton, Calgary, Medicine Hat, and various mining centres night schools have been established under government supervision and receiving government assistance. The annual report for 1915 shows that representatives of twenty-six foreign nationalities attended these night classes.

A "supervisor of schools among foreigners" looks after the making of proper financial arrangements in the establishing of public schools in the first instance; the securing of the proper performance of the duties of trustees in carrying on the ordinary business of the school; the securing of regularly qualified teachers and the carrying on of work according to English standards and in the English language. *This supervisor is himself English-speaking.* In Manitoba ...a similar arrangement has recently been made, while in Saskatchewan representatives of the French, German, and Ruthenian nationalities act in the capacity of organizers of school districts in foreign communities.

Robert Fletcher, the present Alberta supervisor, appears to have thoroughly grasped the importance of educating the New-Canadians of that province. In his last report he says: "The task imposed on the school is not a light one. The ordinary country school in the English settlements is commonly said to be handicapped against efficient work by sparse population, bad roads, etc. If we add to this an adult population with no knowledge of our language or of our institutional life and with a natural desire for the conservation of their mother tongue, which amounts to a fear of losing it, some idea may be formed of what the common school in foreign settlements has to do."

There are now about one hundred and thirty schools in Alberta, the majority of whose ratepayers are Ruthenian, but the whole area populated by these people is dominated, as is the whole province, by the state school. Official trustees are appointed where efficient local men cannot be found to manage the affairs of the schools, and this "immediate substitution of experience for inexperience in the solving of rural school difficulties" has largely been the cause of success in Alberta.

. . . .

In Saskatchewan the school law is somewhat similar to that of Alberta, but there has been considerable difference in administration. The enforcement of compulsory attendance in rural districts has until recently been left altogether to the discretion of local school boards, and they have done little or nothing to enforce regularity. Owing to the heavy tide of imm.gration to this province during the past ten years, schools have been organized at the rate of one a day for every school day, and the supply of qualified teachers for "foreign" schools has by no means been equal to the demand.

A School Attendance Act was introduced in 1917 which should remedy conditions, and henceforth yearly schools will be insisted upon throughout thickly-populated rural districts of the province.

The following section of the School Act represents the language concessions granted in Saskatchewan:

"All schools shall be taught in the English language, [1] but it shall be permissible for the board of any district to cause a primary course to be taught in the French language.

"The board of any district may, subject to the regulations of the department, employ *one or more competent persons to give instruction in any language other than English* in the school to all pupils whose parents or guardians have signified a willingness that they should receive the same, but *such course of instruction shall not supersede or in any way interfere with the instruction by the teacher in charge of the school* as re-

quired by the regulations of the department and this Act.

"The board shall have power to raise the money necessary to pay *the salaries of such instructors*, and all costs, charges and expenses of such course of instruction shall be collected by a *special rate to be imposed upon the parents or guardians."* (Sec. 177.)...

The only authorized texts printed in foreign languages are certain French and German readers, so that any attempt to teach pupils to *read* any other foreign language in the public schools of Saskatchewan must meet with little success.

. . . .

In Manitoba, prior to the coming into office of the present administration, educational conditions among the "foreigners" in many districts were deplorable, but under the present Minister of Education, Doctor Thornton, rapid strides are being made in the teaching of the English language. On June 30th, 1915, there were 126 French bi-lingual schools in Manitoba, and these employed 234 teachers; 61 German bi-lingual schools employing 73 teachers, and 11 Ruthenian and Polish bi-lingual schools with 114 teachers. These numbers represented exactly one-fourth of the rural schools in the province. The enrolment numbered 16,720, or one-sixth of the total enrolment of the whole province. The reason for the existence of these schools is found in section 258 of the Manitoba School Act, which runs thus: "When ten of the pupils of any school speak the French language, or any language other than English as their native language, the teaching of such pupils shall be conducted in French, or such other language, and English upon the bilingual system."

As a result of this unwise legislation thousands of children have grown up in this province in comparative ignorance of the English language, and had not the present administration been imbued with a patriotic spirit of radical reform the result to many of the rising generation in Manitoba would have been disastrous.

....

From what has been said it is apparent that considerable progress has been made towards the introduction of a common language in our western schools. It may also be inferred that much yet remains to be done before the foundation stone of our new national life is well and truly laid. That this will be done–and well done–no one need doubt, as there are scores of patriotic men and women who are consecrating their lives to this great and noble task; and the supreme need at present is an addition to their number, which will undoubtedly be realized as the urgency of the appeal makes itself more strongly felt.

A further word of admonition may not be out of place. It is surely manifest that the greatest agency in racial assimilation is the common or public school. This is the great melting-pot into which must be placed these divers racial groups, and from which will eventually emerge the pure gold of Canadian citizenship. For two outstanding reasons only the common school can accomplish this splendid work of racial unification. In the first place the Church, the only other great socializing agency, stands divided, and, unfortunately, denominational sects are prone to regard each other's activities with considerable suspicion; in the second place, the common school exerts its supreme influence over youthful minds at their most impressionable stage of development. In an efficient common school system, thoroughly efficient in every sense of the term, lies the satisfactory solution of this great national problem. For manifest reasons the ele-

B.3 Source: *The Globe* (Toronto), 26 February 1916
¹Italics inserted by the writer.–ED.

mentary parochial school, with its disintegrating influences and elements of separatism, must also prove a detrimental factor in the achievement of this great end.

B.3 Bilingualism Rejected

Regulation 17 was intended...to make provision for the imparting of a sound education in English to every child attending the public or separate schools of the Province. It provided, in effect, that French might be used as the language of instruction for young children in the two lowest forms, but that thereafter English should be the language of instruction for all children, whether French or English speaking. To prevent French-speaking children from remaining ignorant of French grammar and literature provision was made for the instruction of senior pupils for one hour a day in French, English remaining the official language of instruction. Special provision was made for the training of bilingual teachers and the inspection of bilingual schools by English-speaking inspectors, to the end that there should be no evasion of the law....

Regulation 17 might have been generally recognized as the basis of a working agreement between the French and English speaking people in the bilingual districts had the quarrel...over the language issue not taken place at the very time when, in Quebec, Mr. Bourassa, Mr. Lavergne, and their followers were proclaiming the principles of Nationalism. The school dispute in Ontario has been used to illustrate the "wrongs" of the French-Canadian people. Bourassa declares that the French in Ontario have the same legal right to use their language as the English minority of Quebec. In a pamphlet issued from the press of Le Devoir in the spring of 1914, he said: "Let the English in Quebec remember that their rights in matters of education, whether religious or linguistic, rest on exactly the same constitutional basis as those of the French in Ontario." Turning from the legal to the utilitarian aspect, the Nationalist leader declares that: "The French-Canadians should persistently preach and practise the doctrine that the knowledge of both French and English is a necessity in this country."

Stated in this way, Mr. Bourassa's claim is entirely inadmissible, and will be resisted to the utmost by the English-speaking people of Ontario, irrespective of their political affiliations. No one denies the right of the French-Canadian people to use their own language in the Legislature, courts, and schools of the Province of Quebec. They are self-governing in the Provincial sphere, and doubtless have a very large power to restrict and hamper the use of the English language if they are so minded. The people of Ontario do not concede that in this Province any rights were conferred on the French-Canadian people which entitle them to regard French as an official language to be spoken at will in the Legislature, the courts, and the schools on an equality with English.

Ontario is not bilingual. There is but one official language, and that is English. It is desirable that French be taught far more commonly than it has been heretofore in the schools and colleges of the Province, because that would make for national good-will in a country a fourth of whose population is of French ancestry and language. But when Mr. Bourassa declares for "the principle of equality of rights for both races all over the land" he makes a demand that, if pressed, will cleave the Dominion asunder, and in the end lead to the sweeping away of many privileges now enjoyed by minorities in the various Provinces. Canada is not going to be a bilingual country in the sense in which Belgium is. Quebec is likely to be bilingual for all time, but Ontario is firmly resolved to maintain English as the official language in matters pertaining to the public life of the Province. Education is one of the most vital of the affairs under control of the Provincial authorities, and the electors of Ontario are not going to recede from the position that, either by Regulation 17 or by some other sufficient provision, every child educated in the public and separate schools of the Province–no matter what its racial origin–shall secure an English education enabling it to take its place in the community life of this country, in which three-fourths of the people habitually use English in business and social life. That is the irreducible minimum of the majority....

C. The National School Question Revived: the 1960s

In the 1960s many of the basic institutions of the Canadian nation were re-examined, including the prevailing (English-speaking) definition of Canadian nationality itself. The most serious challenge came from Quebec, where a revitalized nationalism demanded equality for French Canadians either in or out of Confederation. Clearly, a new concept of "national identity" was needed to unify the country. In 1963, the federal government appointed a Royal Commission on Bilingualism and Biculturalism to "recommend what steps should be taken to develop the Canadian Confederation on the basis of an equal partnership between the two founding races". One of the Commission's recommendations was a ringing appeal for equal partnership in education. Once again the public schools were expected to help shape a particular kind of Canadian nation–the very issue which so embittered Canadian relations a half century earlier. But, as the Commissioners pointed out, in the 1960s English Canadians were prepared to make compromises they had rejected before (document C.1).

Meanwhile, the revival of French-Canadian nationalism was producing repercussions in Quebec schools. For over a century Quebec's dual system of public education had allowed her English-speaking minority nearly complete autonomy in the administration of its schools. This privileged position was the standard against which French-speaking minorities in the other provinces measured their losses. Then in 1969 came Bills 62 and 63 dealing respectively with the reorganization of school administration in Montreal and the languages of instruction in Quebec public schools. To many Québécois these were only the first timid steps on the way to cultural autonomy (document C.2). To some English-speaking Canadians, however, these measures posed a threat to the future of the English-Canadian culture (document C.3). Was the English language in danger in Quebec schools at the very time the French language was gaining some measure of official recognition throughout Canada? Or was it only a case of the French- and English-speaking minorities for the first time receiving equal treatment by provincial majorities?

Biculturalism, however, was not the only national issue facing the schools in the 1960s. The Royal Commission on Bilingualism and Biculturalism also recommended that the public schools undertake the preservation of "non-British, non-French" cultures and languages (document C.4). The idea of multicultural schools, of course, was in sharp contrast to the nineteenth-century purpose of assimilation. The shift was partly due to the logic of the argument that one could hardly deny other minority cultures the basic right to exist while promoting the claims of the minority French culture to official status. But it was also a response to the new militancy of the non-British, non-French minority groups themselves. One such group was the native peoples, who were organizing to demand that the nation's schools also recognize *their* culture and *their* needs (document C.5).

C.1 Equal Partnership in Education

A.   The Implications of Equal Partnership[1]

The aims of education are as diverse as the aims of society itself, for in the final analysis they

C.1 Source: Canada, *Report of the Royal Commission on Bilingualism and Biculturalism*, vol. 2 (1968), 7-11, 73-126.
Ed's Note: Some of the original footnotes have been omitted.

A pupil in the school at Frobisher Bay, Northwest Territories, 1965-66.

are determined by the values accepted by the society. The values stressed have varied greatly over the years…but in every case they were consistent with the social purposes of the educational authorities. Any proposal for change in our educational systems must therefore be ultimately based on our view of what Canada is or should be.

Our terms of reference make it clear that the Canadian Confederation should recognize the principle of equality between English-speaking and French-speaking Canadians. This concept of equal partnership is the mainspring of our terms of reference. As we noted in the General Introduction to our *Report*, equal partnership is an ideal, an absolute, which can never be fully or finally achieved. It is nonetheless possible to propose measures which can reduce the present gulf between reality and this ideal. Equal partnership must be seen as one of the fundamental values of our Confederation and all institutions should reflect and foster this equality.

Equal partnership in education implies equivalent educational opportunities for Francophones and Anglophones alike, whether they belong to the majority or the minority in their province. More specifically, it implies a special concern for the minority. The majority, by force of numbers, is able to develop its educational system in response to its own needs. The minority, on the other hand, can draw attention to its special needs but it must rely on the understanding and generosity of the majority if it is to have access to an educational regime which reflects these needs. Educational systems devised in the past to meet the requirements of the linguistic majority in the English-speaking provinces must be equally responsive to those of the minority.

Minorities, whether French or English, inevitably give priority to their own language. If the majority language is the sole language of instruction in the provincial schools, the survival of the minority as a linguistic group is menaced. Almost by definition a minority is exposed to a social environment in which the majority language is always present. The school must counterbalance this environment and must give priority to the minority language if the mother tongue is to become an adequate instrument of communication. Language is also the key to cultural development. Language and culture are not synonymous, but the vitality of the language is a necessary condition for the complete preservation of a culture.

. . . .

The departments of Education in the English-speaking provinces have never based their programmes on the right of Canadian parents to educate their children in the official language of their choice. Each of the provinces responded to the needs of the minority group in its own way. Those concessions allowed in the English-speaking provinces were made in response to persistent pressures from the Francophone minorities. The result was a lack of co-ordination and very limited opportunities in French-language education in these provinces….

The French-speaking minorities have expressed increasing dissatisfaction over the last few years and, as a result, the provincial governments have introduced new measures or policies. At the same time, the evidence of dissatisfaction and the many recent innovations are salutary reminders that the controversy over the place of the minorities within the existing school systems has not yet been resolved. Therefore, the first step towards understanding what needs to be done is to examine the present situation within the existing systems.

Ontario

The modus vivendi that followed the disputes over Regulation 17 permitted the use of French as a language of instruction without clearly defining the nature of "bilingual" schools. Even today it is impossible to speak with assurance of the extent to which French is used in these elementary schools in Ontario, because each school establishes its own pattern. There have been changes in recent years and a greater use of French as a language of instruction has been permitted in both elementary and secondary schools. This toleration and even encouragement of French has had obvious limitations. French-language schools or classes could not be an integral part of a provincial school system which remained oriented towards the education of the English-speaking majority. Either the system would have to be restructured to give adequate recognition to both languages, or French-language schools and classes would have to be organized into a separate French-language system.

On May 30, 1968, the provincial minister of Education introduced legislation which he could legitimately describe as "historic." The bills to which the minister referred provide for French-language schools or classes at both the elementary and secondary levels. Instead of an almost clandestine modus vivendi, French is to be permitted as the legal language of instruction in elementary schools, and for the first time it will also be permitted as the normal language of instruction in secondary schools. The legislation is intended to ensure that French-speaking students will have the opportunity of receiving their education in French. It thus accords with the principle enunciated in the first Book of our *Report*–that Anglophone and Francophone parents should have the right to have their children educated in their own language–and represents a significant forward step.... In future, when 10 or more Francophone ratepayers submit a written request and when there are enough students to justify it [30], the school board is required to provide classes or even a school in which French will be the language of instruction. What in the past has been a privilege will in future be a legal right.... The language of instruction will be French for all subjects. English as a subject of instruction will be obligatory from Grade V....

The proposed French-language secondary schools...will provide composite secondary [education] in places where the enrolment will be large enough, and French-language sections within a school where a separate institution is not justified. English will be a compulsory subject, but all other subjects will be taught in French. English-language schools will still be able to offer the *cours de français* and to teach Latin, geography, and history in French if there are enough Francophone students to form a separate class. The minister of Education has defined as the objectives of this legislation "a complete command of the French language and culture" as well as "a complementary and adequate knowledge of English."

[This] recent legislation marks a dramatic change in educational policy. Provincial authorities have tended to emphasize the diversification of educational opportunities at the secondary level, and spokesmen for the Francophone minority have stressed the importance of instruction in the mother tongue. The proposed French-language schools may make it possible to combine these two objectives. Agreement has been reached on the language of instruction. It is now possible to concentrate on providing an education in French which will be equivalent in academic standards and in variety to the education now provided in English.

New Brunswick

The province of New Brunswick deserves special attention in our study of minority-language education. Here the Francophone minority–most of whom are Acadians–can scarcely be considered a minority in the same terms as Francophones in the other English-speaking provinces. Francophones form more than one-third of the total New Brunswick population, and are an overwhelming majority in many counties. As a group they are quite distinct from other Francophone Canadians....

Today New Brunswick is of special interest because dramatic changes are being introduced. But these changes are being introduced so rapidly that no one can speak with assurance about the new system being created. A pattern of a French-language education for the Acadians from elementary school to university seems to be emerging, although there are still some gaps and some policies which have not yet been fully implemented....

Most of the French-speaking children of New Brunswick attend elementary schools in which French is the language of instruction. In communities with a significant majority of Acadians, public schools have probably always been French, although there is no precise information because the statistics of the department of Education do not distinguish between schools on the basis of the language of instruction. In communities with an Acadian minority, the struggle to obtain French-language education has been long and difficult. The department of Education permits but does not guarantee French-language schools. The decision rests with the local authorities....

Today these minority-language schools provide a predominantly French environment for the pupils but until the 1950's the official purpose of these schools was to teach the children to study in English. Although this objective was not always explicit, it can be deduced from two facts– only English textbooks were provided, apart from those used for the teaching of French, and the students were expected to go on to public secondary schools where English was the language of instruction. Over the last two decades, however, the official policy has changed. Today almost all the textbooks, apart from those used for the teaching of English, are in French, although many of them are translations from English. Examinations may be taken in French, and the language of instruction is French. The major difference between the curricula of English- and French-language schools is that English is taught from the first year in the French-language schools, but French is not introduced until the fifth year in the English-language schools. Francophone children are required to study the same material as the other students in the province, and at the same time are expected to acquire a higher degree of competence in the second language.

Why has the official concept of "bilingual" schools in the province shifted from predominantly English-language to predominantly French-language schools? There is no simple answer to this question....The official acceptance of French-language elementary schools in recent years can probably be accounted for by the recognition of the need for improving the educational level among Acadians and a greater willingness to accept their aspirations to preserve their language.

At the secondary level, generalizations on minority-language schools are more difficult because bilingual secondary schools are a recent development in New Brunswick. Two decades ago, Francophones might be grouped together in separate classes in the school, but with minor exceptions they used the same textbooks and wrote the same examinations as English-speaking students and the language of instruction–at least officially–was English. Since that time, significant steps have been taken to provide a complete education in French for French-speaking children. In 1949 special textbooks were adopted for the teaching of French to Acadian students in public secondary schools; a year later a special programme for the teaching of English was introduced. In 1959 permission was given to teach history in French; a Quebec history textbook was officially approved and examinations could be written in French. In 1965 the department of Education announced that mathematics and science could also be taught in French–always, of course, at the option of the local school authorities. These changes suggest that what is now being developed in New Brunswick is a bilingual secondary school curriculum in which textbooks, examinations, and the language of instruction will be predominantly French....

In 1963 a new school was opened–the Vanier High School for Francophone students–in which all classes permitted in French are taught in French. The significance of this development can be seen from the decision of the provincial department of Education two years later to allow students at this school to study physics from a French textbook and to let them write the examination in French as an experiment. The establishment of a bilingual high school, by grouping the Francophones together, has drawn attention to their special needs and has made it possible to test new programmes designed to meet these needs.

The University of Moncton is one of the key institutions in the developing system of education for the French-speaking citizens of New Brunswick. The establishment of this university was recommended in 1962 by the Deutsch Commission, which pointed out that "There is no reason to suppose that the French-speaking high school graduate is less interested in higher education than his English-speaking counterpart. Indeed, the available evidence indicates that the rates for continuation to higher education among English-speaking and French-speaking high school graduates are now approximately equal."

The creation of the University of Moncton was a recognition of the special needs of Francophone students at the university level. The new campus is being built, and already the central role of this institution in Acadian education can be seen: it is expected to train the teachers for the French-language elementary and secondary schools. The establishment of the university made possible a predominantly French-language public education from elementary to university level. Its creation drew attention to the incongruity of a secondary school system in which English was still the predominant language of instruction and doubtless accelerated the changes already referred to in the secondary programme.

The Four Western Provinces

The French-speaking minorities of the four western provinces differ in many ways from those of the other provinces. They naturally share many of the characteristics of their English-speaking western neighbours. They belong to a relatively new society which took shape with the coming of the railway and mass migration to the Prairies, even though some Francophones in the West are descended from fur-traders and settlers of an earlier era. On the Pacific coast, Francophones are often recent arrivals, having moved from the Prairies like many other West Coast residents. As part of a broader migration pattern, the French-speaking Canadians in the West are more widely dispersed and there are no large areas comparable to counties in Ontario and New Brunswick where they form a dominant majority. And at the same time that western Francophones tend to have closer contacts with Anglophones, they are also more remote from the centre of French-speaking society, the province of Quebec.

Even more important, western Francophones are only one linguistic or cultural minority among many, and often not the largest minority group. In every English-speaking province from Ontario to the Atlantic–including Newfoundland–the Francophones are by far the largest minority group. In the West they are outnumbered by Canadians of Ukrainian mother tongue in each of the three Prairie provinces, by Canadians of German mother tongue in all four western provinces, and are only slightly more numerous than some groups of other mother tongues. In the West, therefore, seen as a regional group, they appear as part of a larger minority situation. At an early stage in their history the western provinces were faced with the problem of creating common political and social institutions for citizens with a multiplicity of languages and traditions. Almost inevitably English was adopted–often with the warm approval of members of other language groups–as the common language to make such institutions possible and workable. In the eyes of many westerners, French-speaking Canadians were a minority group just like any other, and were subjected to many of the same pressures.

Even in the western provinces, however, the Francophones have received some special recognition. In education, equality of opportunity is still usually interpreted to mean the opportunity to learn English and then compete on equal terms with other English-speaking Canadians. But recognition has been given to French-speaking students and there is no comparable recognition for other language groups. In the three Prairie provinces, for example, there is an official programme of French for these students for one school period each day, beginning in the first grade.

British Columbia

In British Columbia, French-speaking Canadians until very recently received no official recognition in the school system. There are no publicly supported denominational schools and so there has been no concentration of French-speaking children in separate Roman Catholic schools. In addition, the Francophones are predominantly urban, so few public schools have a largely Francophone student body. Since children from French-language homes have almost invariably learned English before going to school, English can be and is the language of instruction from the first grade. There are three private schools financed by French Canadian parishes in the Vancouver area, and the experience in these schools is that the children of French-speaking parents are often more at ease in English than in French. Thus, administrators of the public schools in the province saw no reason to adapt the curriculum or the language of instruction for the benefit of French-speaking students.

For many Francophones in the province, the pervasiveness of English is seen as a threat to French even as a second language for their children, and the school system has been the focus of their efforts to preserve their mother tongue at least to that degree. The Francophone community in Vancouver has been strengthened by the arrival of new families from Quebec but it has always had to depend on financial assistance from Quebec and on teaching orders in Quebec to keep the parochial schools open. In 1965 the Fédération canadienne-française de la Colombie-

Britannique proposed that the provincial government should in effect replace these parochial schools by public, non-denominational schools in which French should be a language of instruction. In a speech delivered on October 18, 1967, Premier Bennett, while insisting that there would be but one school system in British Columbia, left the way open for school boards to establish classes in which French would be the language of instruction where the demand was sufficient. The Fédération canadienne-française accordingly presented a brief to the Board of School Trustees of Coquitlam on behalf of the Francophone population of Maillardville, requesting a programme of French instruction. The Coquitlam School Board advised the Fédération on March 1, 1968, that their request had been approved, and a request for the necessary authorization forwarded to the minister of Education. The text of the resolution stated:

"That the Board wishes authority from the Department to proceed with an experimental project in French language instruction in September 1968, and the acceptance of the normal costs of operating classes as shareable expenses of the Board.

That the Board proposes to establish one or more kindergarten classes to be instructed through the medium of the French language, with the prospect further of establishing a similar program to carry children through the three primary years of elementary school.

That in the course of development of the four-year program such as indicated above, directions for later development will become apparent."

On July 24, 1968, the chairman of the Coquitlam School Board announced that approval had been granted by the provincial government to proceed

with this programme, subject to certain conditions. Therefore, it is apparent that, in British Columbia, as elsewhere in Canada, the place of French as a language of instruction in the school is being reappraised.

Alberta

There have been "bilingual" schools in Alberta for many years. These schools may be classified as public or separate schools but, whatever the official designation, the student body is usually Roman Catholic and Francophone. The provincial School Act states that "all schools shall be taught in the English language," but this was qualified by a section of the Act allowing a school board to authorize instruction in French under certain conditions. The language usage in these "bilingual" schools was described in the annual report of the provincial department of Education for 1952:

"Eight of the Superintendents reported that there are bilingual schools in their divisions in which French is used as the language in which instruction is given during a part of the school day.... In schools where all of the pupils in Grade I are members of French-speaking families, French is used almost entirely in the teaching of this class in the early part of the school year, and to a decreasing extent in the latter part of the first year. The standard plan for Grade II is that French may be used for teaching for half of the school day. In Grades III to IX the daily period for instruction in French is one hour. In one of the reports [the Superintendent noted] a tendency to exceed these time-limitations, which are as given in the authorized Primary Course in French for Bi-lingual Schools.... As the pupils come to the senior grades there are evident benefits to the pupils from their reading, oral work, composition and grammar studies in both English and French. ... In general, the teachers in the bilingual schools show a very favorable aptitude for the work which they carry on in two languages."

French thus has a privileged position in Alberta schools compared to other minority languages, since no other language is authorized as a language of instruction. Even French-speaking students, however, are taught mainly in English after two or three years in school, and are expected to compete on equal terms with English-speaking students. In subsequent years, however, a limited amount of French is taught in the classroom with the objective of helping Franco-Albertans retain the use of their mother tongue....

...the policy of the department of Education continues to give French a special status. A primary course in languages other than English or French has recently been authorized, but French remains the only minority language which can be continued after the early grades. An amendment to the School Act in 1964 confirmed this situation and made it more precise. By this amendment French may be the language of instruction in the first two grades, although English is to be taught for at least one hour a day; in the third grade, teaching in French is permitted for a maximum of two hours a day and in subsequent grades in French courses in literature and grammar, for not more than one hour a day.[1] Provision for this instruction in French is dependent on the approval of local school boards. We were assured by Francophone educators from Alberta who appeared before us at our public hearings that the provincial officials were increasingly sympathetic

to the teaching of French in "bilingual" schools. At the same time, these educators agreed that Francophone children in Alberta must learn English. As in many other provinces, both the departmental officials and the minority appear to be agreed on the need to teach the two languages in the minority-language schools and the differences of opinion that do arise represent differences of emphasis.

Saskatchewan

In Saskatchewan schools the recognition given to the French language is much more limited. The first grade was once considered a transitional year in French-speaking communities, with French being used as the major language of instruction. In 1931, however, the School Act was amended to read that "English shall be the sole language of instruction and no language other than English shall be taught during school hours." The same amendment did allow the teaching of French as a subject for one hour a day but was careful to state that "such teaching shall consist of French reading, French grammar and French composition." This created an anomalous situation: French could be taught but presumably it had to be taught in English. After considerable pressure from French-speaking parents, the Act was amended in 1967 to allow French to be "taught or used as the language of instruction" for one hour a day. This use of French is more restricted than that allowed in Alberta schools, but it does give French a status which no other minority language has in Saskatchewan.

[1]Since this writing, an act to amend the School Law in Alberta (Bill 34) was passed on April 4, 1968, providing that: the board of a district or division may by resolution authorize that French be used as a language of instruction in addition to the English language, in its school or schools in Grades I to XII inclusive but in that case
    a) in Grades I and II at least an hour each day shall be devoted to instruction in English
    b) in Grades above II the total period of time in which French

is used as a language of instruction shall not exceed 50 per cent of the total period of time devoted to classroom instruction each day, and
    c) the Board and all schools of a district or division using French as a language of instruction pursuant to clause (b) shall comply with any regulation that the Lieutenant Governor in Council may make governing the organization and application of the use of French as a language of instruction.

As in Alberta, the course of study for this special French programme began as a result of the initiative of French Canadian voluntary organizations. The Association culturelle franco-canadienne de la Saskatchewan and the Association des commissaires d'écoles franco-canadiennes developed and administered both the programme and the examinations. The course was an addition to the standard curriculum, although it could be taught during school hours. At one time no academic credit was given for this programme, even at the high school level, although credit was given to those who took the provincial French programme designed for students studying French as a second language. In 1958, however, the provincial government accorded academic recognition to the ACEFC programme at the high school level and has subsequently assumed some of the financial and administrative responsibility for the programme.

This special French programme is permitted by the School Act, but once again it can be offered in a school only with the authorization of the local school board. Again it appeared that the number of students taking the course would be reduced when school districts were consolidated, and Francophone leaders complained that the boundaries of the larger districts were drawn with little regard to ethnic factors. They feared that the Anglophone majorities in the larger districts would show little sympathy for the desire of the Francophone minority to study their language, but a few years of experience have modified these fears. The consolidated schools do provide a predominantly English milieu, in contrast to the smaller "bilingual" schools, but the larger student body also makes it possible to place French-speaking students in separate classes. Although no accurate statistics are available, it is generally agreed that at least as many students are following the special French programme now as before the consolidation of the school districts....

...the provincial government appointed a committee later in the year to inquire into the existing programmes of French instruction and to assess the educational implications of instruction in languages other than English in the provincial schools. The committee reported in July of 1966. It argued that restrictions on teaching in languages other than English were originally imposed because of the great need for all children to learn English, but that today this justification is no longer valid because most children entering Grade I can speak English. The committee considered that, of the languages other than English, French deserved a special status because of its national and international utility. Nevertheless, the committee did not recommend sweeping changes in the curriculum. It did point out the anomaly of restricting the French programme to the study of reading, grammar, and composition in view of the present emphasis on oral French, and proposed an amendment to the School Act to allow French to be used as a language of instruction during the period set aside for the French programme. It also suggested that the department and the school boards should make a special effort to offer this programme wherever it was administratively feasible. The committee did approve the idea of experimental programmes in which instruction in French might exceed one hour a day, but on the whole its recommendations implied only minor changes in the existing situation. Its report suggests, however, that there is some sympathy for the demands of the Francophone minority in the province and, as we have noted, the provincial government has already adopted the proposal that French be permitted as a language of instruction for one hour a day...

Manitoba

The status of French as a language of instruction in the public schools is changing even more rapidly in Manitoba than in Saskatchewan or Alberta. The situation in Manitoba has differed in part for historical reasons. As we have seen, provincially supported denominational schools disappeared in the 1890's, but after a prolonged controversy the Laurier-Greenway compromise allowed a period of religious instruction in a language other than English in "bilingual" schools. There was no special status for French in this arrangement and, when the provincial government abolished the "bilingual" schools in 1916, all languages of instruction other than English, including French, officially disappeared. Until 1967 the law still gave no special recognition to French; the Public School Act stated that English was to be the language of instruction and other languages might be used only during a period of religious teaching or a period authorized in the programme of studies for the teaching of a second language.

. . . .

In 1967, an amendment to the provincial School Act significantly changed the status of French in Manitoba schools. French is now officially accepted as a language of instruction, and may be used as such for as much as one-half of the school day. But the exercise of this right is subject to certain restrictions: the school board must first submit a proposal for teaching in French, stating the subjects to be taught and the number of hours involved, and the minister of Education has absolute discretion to approve, modify, or reject the proposal. But even if school boards and the minister of Education show enthusiasm for the increased use of French as a language of instruction, a great deal must be done before the legislation can have any significant effect. Textbooks and teaching aids in French will be required, and trained teachers who can teach other subjects in French must be available. The new amendment suggests that the provincial government intends to extend the use of French in minority-language schools but it is still too early to assess all the implications of the new policy, and it will be some years before the policy can be effectively implemented. It is clear, however, that the way has been opened to provide Franco-Manitobans with greater access to an education in their mother tongue in the public school system.

C.2 Quebec: National Schools

Is our new "National Assembly" going to give its blessing [through Bill 63[1]] to a long-established fact: the massive anglicization of New Quebecers? Does it intend to speed up the trend and make it irreversible? True, the English-speaking minority (and apparently to belong to it, it suffices to choose an English school) will immediately be asked to improve the teaching of French in its educational institutions so that young Anglo-Quebecers will have "a suitable knowledge of the language of the majority". In short, by our own consent, the immigrant to Quebec would be provided with the framework for becoming English-speaking, provided he could understand French. Elsewhere, the law

[1] Bill 63 required that courses be taught in French, but if, upon enrolment of a child, the parent requested that courses be given in English, the school board was to provide them in English. If the school board found it impossible to provide English courses, it was to refer the matter to the minister. If the minister decided the courses were necessary, he would authorize the extra cost of transporting the child to an English school. The legislation also required that the minister ensure that the French language curriculum be such that all children would acquire a working knowledge of French. It would be necessary to pass French examinations in order to graduate. -ED.

C.2 Source: Jean-Marc Leger, "Must we rush headlong toward suicide?", *Le Devoir* (Montreal), 26 November 1968.

generally steps in to correct any imbalance detrimental to the weak; here it would step in to reinforce this weakness. To the economic and social factors that literally push the newcomer towards the English language, the law would add the guarantee of its protection. This is called giving official blessing to the "free choice" between the English and the French school....

It is already predictable that most of the future immigrants recruited by the new Quebec Immigration Department will swell the ranks of the English-speaking minority at our expense. This is sheer suicide.

Some will say: "But Quebec is 'bilingual'". This is wrong: in the field of education, there is nothing in the Constitution to provide for, let alone require, two languages of instruction. Respect for religious differences is the only requirement. Even supposing that a century-old precedent had to be maintained on the basis of moral and political arguments, it could only apply to people who are English by origin, to those who are in fact "ex-Britishers". What "acquired right" to English-language schools can be claimed by the mass of immigrants who have come here since the Second World War and who are settling here everyday?

Here we are at the very core of the problem of the survival of the French language in Quebec; we are at the crossroads where population factors, and socio-cultural factors meet. No country in the world, even the most powerful, will tolerate on its own soil an immigration that will weaken it, that will threaten its very existence.

A law confirming the right to English-language schools in Quebec for all those who want them would constitute a decisive stage in the process of renunciation and decline of the Franco-Quebec community. Added to the centralist offensive of the Federal government, such a step

would be the death blow to what seemed to be, since 1960, a national awakening.

C.3 The English-language Minority in Quebec

In introducing Bill 62 the government has indicated its preference for the unification of the system. I said at the beginning that the situation is extremely complex and I recognize that a rapid review of the history in this way may do little to relieve the confusion, but I thought it necessary to provide this background in order to make certain points which are:

(1)   Until 1964 there was a complete division of school administration on a confessional basis at all levels up to the provincial cabinet.

(2)   In effect, with the important exception of the English Catholic schools, this division resulted largely in a separate system of French and English schools, with each language group having full control over all aspects of the running of its schools.

(3)   The English Catholics have been permitted, by many of the Catholic school commissions, almost full curriculum control. This has been purely a matter of tolerance, but its effect was to afford a high degree of control over their own teaching by all the English-speaking schools. Thus, administratively, the system has been confessional. Functionally it has been divided along language lines.

(4)   Bill 60 [1964] changed the structure at the government level placing the powers previously accorded to the Protestant and Catholic committees in the hands of the ministry.

(5)   The changes at the lower levels set forth in

C.3 Source: H. Rocke Robertson (Principal, McGill University) in an Address to the Montreal Rotary Club as reported in the *Montreal Star*, 19 November 1969.

Bills 62 and 63 do not provide any clear influence, let alone guarantee, of control by a minority over the pedagogical aspects of its schools, over the language of instruction, the curriculum or the hiring of teachers.

The engagement and distribution of teachers and decisions about the curriculum are matters dealt with, it appears by the reading of Bill 62, by the school board–a body of which two thirds is elected by the people in the school municipality and one-third representing indirectly the schools.

It is possible that the schools of the minority (be they English or French) in any municipality might not have any voice at all in the vital decisions that the school board has to make–nor, under this system, would there be any administrative officer at the board level, or above, assigned to deal with the business of the minority.

(6) It appears that in eight of the school municipalities on the Island of Montreal (set up under Bill 62) the vast majority of people are French-speaking and presumably their school boards will be predominantly, if not entirely, French-speaking. Yet in all these districts there are, at present, schools for English-speaking students and these schools may have little to say about their own affairs and no formal liaison with English-speaking schools in other municipalities.

The same situation applies, of course, and would be equally unsatisfactory, to the French-speaking schools in the two municipalities in which there is a preponderance of English-speaking citizens.

There are no provisions in this Bill dealing with education in the English language, and such as are to be found in Bill 63 are confusing and far from reassuring.

(7) The effect of this bill, then in short, is to remove from the English-speaking people of the province, the ability to control the teaching in their schools, a privilege which they have exercised from the beginning.

· ·

I have to say bluntly that one of my main reasons for supporting a plan that gives the English-speaking people a real say in how their children are taught is that I believe that, unless they have a far greater say than Bill 62 would give them, their language and their culture "will, sooner or later, disappear from Quebec."

Having said this I cannot but note that it is strange that at one and the same time both the French-speaking and the English-speaking people in Quebec should be fearful that they were about to be submerged. It is a sad commentary on our state of confidence in this community.

The fear on the one hand is derived from the facts that the birthrate of the French is declining at an alarming rate and that new-comers opt for the English language. On the other hand the fear is that the methods that may be used to preserve the French language and culture may have dire results for the English language and culture in Quebec....

There isn't any doubt that there is now a real challenge to the English-speaking people in Quebec. It is expressed in obvious form by the unilingualists–they make no bones about it–"speak French or get out" is pretty plain talk! It is inherent in the separatist movement for I think it unlikely that they could sustain a state hospitable to the English if ever they were to achieve their goal.

It appears in the daily reiterations of criticism of the English, their past and present activities–or inactivities. These outbursts are never answered, never countered by anyone–least of all the English themselves, and the challenge increases. And it is, indeed has for a long time, been evident in a relatively subtle way, in the actions of the government,–actions which are designed purely to boost the French side, which have the (probably inadvertent) result of harming the English interests–relatively and absolutely. I have observed this in connection with the inequitable financing of universities and have spoken about it in public on a number of occasions.

. . . .

In suggesting as I have done that Bill 62 should be greatly amended I am not calling for a move that would lead to (as the minister put it in a speech recently) a crumbling of the government structures and the dispersion of educational inheritance in Quebec.

I am calling for the protection of a culture that not only has a full right in this province, but which can join with the other to the real benefit of all–a combination that can bring the greatest strength to Quebec and to Canada–and I consider the interests of the two inseparable.

C.4 Multiculturalism and the Schools

Schools are the formal means by which a society transmits its knowledge, skills, languages, and culture from one generation to the next. Canada's public school systems are primarily concerned with the transmission of knowledge that is essential to all citizens, including knowledge about Canadian institutions, the traditions and circumstances that have shaped them, and the two official languages. Since those of British and French ethnic origin are the main groups in Canada, it is appropriate that the British and French cultures dominate in the public schools. But public schools can also provide an instrument for safeguarding the contribution of other cultures.

Because of the interdependence of language

C.4 Source: Canada, *Report of the Royal Commission on Bilingualism and Biculturalism*, vol. 4 (1969), 137-139.

and culture we must consider the teaching of languages other than English and French in the educational system as an important aspect of any programme to preserve the cultures of those of non-British, non-French origin. Such teaching can have the additional benefit of increasing the country's linguistic resources–resources important to any modern country and especially to one that wishes to play a role in the international community.

There are two aspects to the question of teaching languages other than the two official languages in Canada. On the one hand, there is the need to preserve the languages and cultures of those who have been in Canada for many generations. On the other hand, there is the need to preserve the languages and cultures of new immigrants while also integrating them into Canadian society. Obviously these two aspects require different techniques. Programmes that would be appropriate for teaching languages to the children of those who have been here for many generations would not be suitable for immigrants' children, who must also learn one of the official languages as their working language, as well as the other official language....

In considering the question of educational policy we have been guided by three general principles. First, members of non-British, non-French cultural groups should have opportunities to maintain their own languages and cultures within the educational system if they indicate sufficient interest in doing so. Of course, population concentration, continuing immigration, and the different historical background of the various groups, both in their homelands and in Canada, all raise important practical considerations in the application of this principle. Second, where public support is concerned, the question of language and cultural maintenance must be seen

The schoolroom at the
Sturgeon Creek
Hutterite Colony,
Headingly, Manitoba,
1954.

within the broader context of the question of bilingualism and biculturalism in Canada as a whole; for example, the learning of third languages should not be carried on at the expense of public support for learning the second official language. Third, since the elementary school years are the most vital ones for the purpose of maintaining languages, the most extensive effort should be made at this level.

C.5 The Case for Native Education

What should and what can education do for the native peoples...who once provided completely and happily for themselves?

1.   *Education*–Education is not the only key to a better tomorrow but it is a vital part of a total effort required to improve the lives of the native peoples. New schools, well equipped, well staffed, cannot alone combat lack of employment, poor housing, limited medical care, prejudice, lack of equality, a poor self-image–but must be a major part of a well co-ordinated and well-integrated attack on the ills facing the native peoples...an attack which must be *with* and *not for* the people concerned.

2.   An underlining factor missing from education is the *need for the native peoples to be recognized* as those who have a cultural identity, who belong to different nations (cree, ojibway, six nations, delaware), who are alike and who are different–who have histories, who have a past, a present, and must have a future, who are not "just Indians". There is the need for the recognition of a history and a culture which belong to not just the native peoples, but belong to the people of this country–for this country, its history and its cultures began before 1492. Recognition for the cultural identity for each native person

C.5 Source: Union of Ontario Indians, "Education of the Native Peoples of Ontario" (Toronto, 1971), pp. 4-7.

must be inherent in any educational program. This recognition must be evident in the classroom to help the child realize his own cultural identity, to grow in strength and security and security in his Indianness.

3.   To be successful, education for native children must involve the parents of these children and those parents must have some responsibility for the education of their children. In some reserve communities, there are school committees, but the oldest have existed for only one generation of elementary school children–16 years. School committees not only do not exist on every reserve but lack powers of authority and responsibility. This must be changed. If bands are to have self-administration this must include education as well as roads, housing welfare and water. The degree of success of children in schools reflects the degree of involvement and the degree of responsibility of parents in the education of their children.

4.   *The teachers* who work with Indian children should have the best of qualifications, should be ready and capable of change to meet the needs of the children relative to the child and his environment, must have knowledge and understanding of the community and of the people who are the community. Teachers should be oriented *before* they are sent into a native community. Any training given to teachers who are going into native communities must be such that it prepares them for these children....It would be preferable if the teachers were of native descent but a good teacher will be accepted by children of any community if the teacher comes to help the child in his growth. Teachers going into native communities should be prepared to stay for two years if this is acceptable both to the teacher and the community. The people of the community

should have involvement in the selection of the teachers who will be going into that community. The community must be prepared to welcome the teacher and to help her feel at home. Teachers often feel inadequate in a community where the culture is different. Because the teacher should understand the cultural differences, it is the responsibility of the community to help the teacher realize these differences.

5. *The curriculum* followed in any community includes the school, the programs, the texts, the courses, all that is needed and used to help a child to learn. The curriculum in a native community must be one of flexibility and relativity–it cannot be an urban non-native culture impressed on the child and his native culture.

The language of the classroom should be the language of the community. If the language of the community is a native language then the child should start school in his own language and at a later date (age 8 or 9) should begin in English. This will encourage the child and leave with him positive memories when he is a young adult whereby he will be strengthened in his cultural identity.

This means that the teacher should be fluent in the language of the community in which he will teach. There should be an opportunity in communities to encourage the learning to read and write in that native language, as well as the rediscovery by the young of their own language. This does not mean that English or French should not be taught but that English or French should not be taught at the expense of the native language of the children or of the community.

The printed matter in the classroom should be that which is relative and relevant to the people to this community. Books for the teaching of reading should be those which are meaningful to the children of an Indian community. The printed

matter should include the use of both languages–the native and the English or French.

Items which should be included in the program include–

a) *Civics*– the governmental processes of the community chief, council, band, band clerk, superintendent, as well as the civics of the province and the nation. Other items such as the Indian Act, the Treaty and Treaties which directly or indirectly fit the community should be known and understood.

b) *The geography* of the local community and reserve should be a major item of study. The location of other native communities in the province and in Canada could form the basis of learning in which the child would learn to which nation the people of the communities belong. This would develop a link of knowledge and understanding of other groups, lands and nations.

c) *History* should include the story of the people, of that reserve, of that band, of that nation.

d) *The culture* should be taught in the school by the teacher and *with the co-operation and help of the people of the community*. This would include the native religions and art forms (dancing, chanting, drumming, crafts, painting, songs) and the value system of the people of that community.

e) *Human Relations* should be taught whereby the child will learn of his and other native peoples, of white people, of the world beyond the native community.

6. *Schools for elementary children* should be at home in the native community. Small children should not be required to travel great distances to residential schools or to schools in an urban non-Indian community. *The secondary schools* in major centres should be prepared to receive

the student coming more than should children
be prepared to enter the high school. There
should be involvement on the part of the secondary school staff with the housing and social accommodation of the student and not just with his
academic role. There should be courses in Indian
culture and language in secondary schools. Strong
consideration should be given to the creation
of a secondary school located in a native community to which native students may go and this
secondary school would be equivalent to any
secondary school in this province....Serious
thought should be given to the creation...of a
cultural *centre for native students* whereby they
could attend and learn of their own culture by
nation and by nations so that they could create a
new expression based upon a knowledge and
understanding of their inherited past. Urgent
consideration must be given to providing educational opportunities to *young adults* who have
dropped out of school and who wish to return; to
older adults who want or need to upgrade their
skills in reading, writing, mathematics, to the
old people who wish to learn of the new and who
wish to be of use in the teaching of the young.
Those who return to education must be treated
as adults and not as children.

7.   The program called integration or joint
school programs must be made into a program of
bi-culturism at both the elementary and secondary schools whereby the native student finds within the school that which says, "it is good to be an
Indian"; which permits him to choose from both
cultures; which permits him to choose the path
along which he will develop as a person and as a
student. This *would include the teaching to non-
native children of the culture of their native
brothers and sisters....*

VI

Expanding
The Public Schools:
The New Education,
1890-1920

By the end of the century, many aspects of Victorian education were drawing criticism. Because the nature of Canadian society was undergoing fundamental changes, it was increasingly believed that the curricula, methods, and purposes of nineteenth-century education would have to be expanded if the public schools were to serve their public functions to the fullest. From town and country, from within the school and from without, came a call for new subjects and new methods more appropriate to the needs of the day. In short, new conditions required a new education.

The new conditions that were to influence the course of educational development arose from the rapid (and unplanned) growth of the city and the factory. By the end of the century, it was obvious that together they were changing the economic and social lives of thousands of Canadians. Workshops and manufacturies had existed throughout the country for years, but the methods of production in large, specialized factories were different from those in the small, privately-owned enterprises operating in small towns. By the turn of the century, when one-third of the Canadian work force was employed in factory occupations, it was obvious that not only was the rural orientation of society shifting in favour of the city and the factory, but that the nature of industrialism was itself in transition. Such vast changes in the economic order demanded changes in the educational system. How, for example, could the schools help train an agricultural population for industrial pursuits?

Meanwhile the cities were growing by leaps and bounds. In the space of a generation (1881-1911) the combined populations of Halifax, Montreal, Toronto, and Winnipeg tripled. By 1890 the first skyscrapers appeared, and a yard of frontage on Toronto's downtown King Street cost as much as a good farm. In 1908 over half of Ontario's population were urbanites and in 1921 the census showed a similar situation fast approaching throughout the country. As the cities expanded so did the urban problems that were also symptomatic of a new age. Much in evidence were the old social and moral problems of neglected children, juvenile crime, drunkenness, and the squalor of poverty; concentrated and highly conspicuous in their urban setting, these problems demanded an immediate response. Surely there was work here for the schools.

Although many Canadians were engaged in non-agricultural occupations (over 58 per cent in 1900), Canada was regarded by many of its citizens as a country whose moral and social traditions derived from a rural and agricultural heritage. But the tremendous growth of cities and manufacturing, together with a declining rural population in eastern Canada, threatened to sap this traditional pillar of society. Thus, the schools were presented with another problem. Could an educational program be devised for rural people which would strengthen rural institutions and help stem the exodus to the cities? Could rural schools be improved to provide equal educational opportunity to country and town children alike?

All these problems seemed beyond the scope of the traditional school.

Dissatisfaction with the narrow range of Victorian education was not confined to critics outside the schools. On the inside, educators were becoming increasingly impatient with the formalistic, academic mould that had hardened around much of Victorian education. Influenced by theorists like Friedrich Froebel, Johann Herbart, and John Dewey, and by the

A.   Education and Industrialization

educational psychology of William James, Canadian schoolmen were anxious to supplement the basic-skills and mental-discipline routines with subjects and methods more attuned to the new educational theories that emphasized the importance of the individual child's activity, growth, experience, and apperception. Many educators wanted to shift from the academic universalism of the mental discipline tradition to the more practical particularism of a child-centred program, which was more appropriate to the student's interests, environment, and even his future vocation. This new theory raised relevance to an educational virtue, and allowed educators to promote the new "practical" subjects and methods with enthusiasm and conviction.

And so the stage for the New Education was set: social and economic conditions calling for change in the schools, and a new educational theory ready to accommodate it.

As Canada became more industrialized toward the end of the nineteenth century, there was growing concern over the lack of "practical instruction" in the schools. Previously, industrial discipline had been received outside the school in the workplace, but changed industrial conditions were rendering these apprenticeship methods obsolete. Everyone, it seemed,–manufacturers, workmen, and many educators–agreed that the public schools as instruments of the state should assume a larger responsibility in preparing people for occupations more appropriate to the new economy (documents A.I and A.2). By the early twentieth century the concern for educational reform became a political issue. New governments came to power in Ontario (1905) and Quebec (1906) on platforms containing promises of more practical education in the public schools. According to a Quebec cabinet minister "the triumph of the Liberal party...was due to its programme....of which the basic ideas were: education in the province and the development of the natural resources".[1] Later, two other provinces and the federal government each appointed Royal Commissions to study how technical education could be provided and financed.

In the schools, the first response was to add to the traditional curriculum a new course called Manual Training (document A.3). As a school subject, Manual Training had two advantages: it was both a practical and a cultural subject, so it could be taught in the elementary school where most people completed their education, but where, it was agreed, specialized industrial training had no place. Secondly, it was comparatively cheap, requiring only a few hand tools and none of the expensive

[1] *Montreal Star,* 13 December, 1909, p. 7.

Manual Training
Classroom, Ottawa,
1901-02.

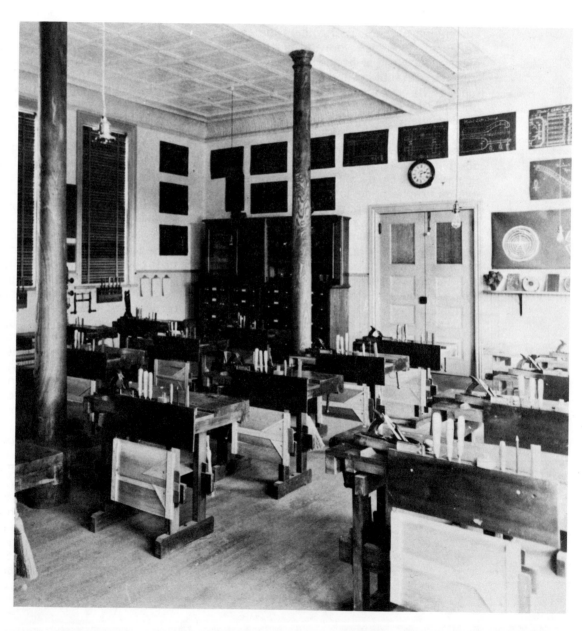

equipment necessary for technical education. The subject of Manual Training was introduced into the public schools of Ontario and Nova Scotia in the 1880s and '90s. But the real Manual Training movement got underway in the early years of the twentieth century, when the Montreal philanthropist, Sir William C. Macdonald, donated money to set up wood-working shops in selected schools from Prince Edward Island to British Columbia. For three years he maintained these centres, paying all expenses and even importing qualified teachers to staff them. The centres were later taken over and expanded by the provincial Departments of Education. As a result, by 1910 over 20,000 boys (and girls) were taking Manual Training as part of their regular school program.

But Manual Training was not industrial training; it was only a preparation for it. Therefore, the next task of the schools was to provide specialized training at the secondary level. In 1911 Ontario began to develop a technical school system under the terms of her new Industrial Education Act. Beginnings were made in other provinces as well. By the time the outbreak of World War I curtailed further expansion, technical schools had been established in Montreal, Halifax, Toronto, and Winnipeg. Technical education facilities, however, were expensive, and little was done until federal financial assistance was made available after 1919 (document A.4).

The call for more practical education reached beyond the elementary and secondary schools to penetrate the academic halls of the universities. Often that call was answered by merely replacing the Latin and Greek Classics with the English and French variety. But where the economic needs and problems of the people making up the university's constituency were widely shared and well defined, as was the case in the prairie provinces, the desire to "help with concrete practical problems" could develop into a fully-fledged public service program (document A.5).

A.1 A Plea for Practical Education

There are no adequate facilities provided whereby the workingman can become conversant with that instruction necessary to fit him to become a good artisan, well up in the practice and theory of his business.

The necessity for practical instruction of this nature is more apparent now than formerly, owing to the change in the system of working. The old plan of apprenticeship, by which a young man was taught his trade, has disappeared, and we have nothing in our industrial system to take its place.

To be successful competitors with foreign manufacturers we must have workmen as highly skilled in their respective callings as those with whom they have to compete. To do so, the same facilities must be provided to give the cultivation and training necessary to acquire skill and knowledge as the workmen of other countries have.

The time has apparently arrived when the State should extend the present school system by providing technical and industrial training schools for the youth of our working classes, where, under competent instructors (who should be practical men in the branches taught), those choosing mechanical callings can obtain a thorough theoretical knowledge of their business, as well as practical skill. A very general unanimity as to the desirability of this training will be found in the evidence in all places visited by the Com-

A.1 Source: Royal Commission on the Relations of Capital and Labor in Canada, *Report* (Ottawa, 1889), 1, pp. 119-21.

mission, the manufacturers and the mechanics alike expressing a wish that something should be done to meet this want. There is some difference of opinion as to how these schools can be made effective...

· ·

There were many witnesses who had given close attention to this subject and who were well qualified to give an opinion on the matter. They stated that some change was imperative but that the teaching should begin with the lowest classes and be continued right through every grade in the school. One witness says: "I believe that the proper place for the training of the hand is in the lower classes in schools, where all are attending. What I urge is manual or industrial training, such as the training of the hand to make it expert, and the training of the head to make it clear and definite in controlling the hand, together with some slight training in the use of tools, which should be done without teaching any particular trade." On the same subject another witness says: "I do not think the aim of industrial education should be to make men skilled mechanics, but to make them see the principles underlying mechanical operations, rather than to perform the operation skilfully. We should not aim at that in school any more than we should teach a boy at the agricultural college to draw a straight furrow with the plough." Another says: "In the common schools we have no education which is worth anything, which does not educate the boy perfectly. We should train him to use his hand, his mind and his eye together, and when we thoroughly train him to do that, when he is turned out he will be able to learn any trade." A great many others are agreed that a change like the above is a necessity; not alone because of the advantages it would give to those learning trades, but that it would tend to create a desire in the minds of children to select

industrial in preference to professional or commercial pursuits. One thing all are agreed upon, viz., that the present system unfits the scholar for mechanical life. As an Ontario witness says: "The fact of the matter is, that to my mind the public school unfits a boy for learning a trade. We are bringing up a nation of shopkeepers. To teach a boy to earn a living by the use of his hands is the proper way in this country." Stronger testimony than this it would be difficult to procure, and it is to be noticed that the witnesses engaged in all mechanical callings, who gave evidence on this subject, strongly corroborated the testimony alluded to. There can be no doubt that the proper authorities must solve this question in a practical manner, with as little delay as possible. We must see that the education that the children are receiving is one adapted to our industrial condition. It would be a misfortune to the country at large to continue in the present line. An effort should be made to instil in the minds of the young a preference for industrial avocations rather than the overstocked professional and commercial callings. But while we agree as to the desirability of such a course as is outlined in the evidence referred to, we are of the opinion that in order to obtain the full benefit to be derived from such training it is absolutely necessary that the teaching should be carried on after the pupils leave the schools. It is obvious that the knowledge acquired in the primary schools must of necessity be of the most elementary character, designed rather to create a taste for mechanics in the mind of the scholar than to be of practical use in life. The plan adopted in England, and on the continent of Europe, of establishing secondary schools, where a full technical course is given, having a direct bearing on the trade selected by the scholar, is the one we would recommend as being best suited to the wants of our people. Very full and complete reports as to the efficiency of this system are to be found in the report of the Royal Commission on Technical Instruction in Great Britain (1881). These schools, besides giving a full science course during the day to those who can afford to attend the classes, provide evening instruction for mechanics and apprentices, and, so far, have been eagerly taken advantage of by those for whose benefit they were established. This plan has the hearty endorsation of the workingmen throughout the Dominion, and would be welcomed by them as supplying a want now keenly felt. This Commission, therefore, recommends: 1st. The rearranging of the curriculum in the public schools, with a view of making the instruction more practical. 2nd. The establishment of technical schools, with evening classes attached–

A.   Because children should deal chiefly with real things during the first years of school life.

B.   Because using real things is the most certain way of exercising the child's intellectual faculties.

C.   Because it is the right of every one to receive such an education as will best fit him for the proper performance of his duties, in whatever sphere he may labor.

D.   Because the system of apprenticeship has been discontinued.

E.   Because improving the mechanical skill of the industrial classes must add largely to the wealth and prosperity of the nation.

F.   Because the great increase in the use of delicate and intricate machinery in manufacturing demands a more thorough industrial and technical training on the part of those who are to use the machines.

G.   Because it will increase the prosperity of the working classes and will elevate their social position.

H.   Because the moral effects of such training

are good. Improving a workingman's position will make him more contented and happy.

A.2 Needed: A New Product for a New Age

The author of this article was a Halifax schoolteacher.

At no time in the world's history has there been such intense industrial and commerical activity as there is now. In nearly every part of the habitable globe, the warehouse with its bales of merchandise may be seen, and busy traders striving with each other for a monopoly of the markets. Nor is it the strife between local traders only. Cheap and rapid means of transportation have made all nations neighbours and it frequently happens that articles are consumed in the antipodes of the country in which they were produced. By the use of cold storage even the New Zealander and the Canadian are able to compete with the European in the fruit market of London.

The greatness of a nation is not now measured by its power to conquer, but by its power to produce, and the boast of a people is in the extent of their trade. The mighty men of the land are no longer the orators and the philosophers but the millionaires. They are the pride of the nation, the ideals of the young, and the hope of the parents is not that their boy may grow up to be a leader in thought but in business. The general demand of the time, from parents and people at home and abroad, is for business men, men capable of successfully managing stock companies with any amount of capital.

The ideal products of the school have not been business men, but professional men, and a

A.2 Source: G. R. Marshall, "What the Teacher Can Do for the Farmer", Dominion Educational Association *Proceedings* (1901), p. 99.

study that tended to fit a man to earn a livelihood was rather looked upon with disfavour. The public complained that college graduates who did not enter the learned professions, were not, after four years of study, better prepared to earn their living than their companions...who had spent less time at their books.

A.3 The First Response: Manual Training

The author of this document was one of the Manual Training teachers brought from England by the Macdonald Fund.

In my experience in pioneer work in Manual Training here and in England, I have found that the subject appeals to different people from widely different standpoints. The utilitarian is perhaps the commonest aspect in which Manual Training is liable to be regarded. Now, accepting the ordinary use of the term, it must be clearly understood, that while the training in technical skill, manual dexterity and practical work is of the utmost value in after life for utilitarian purposes, yet if this were its sole aim and purpose it would certainly be open to question whether so much valuable time should be devoted to it during the years when the child is being developed and its character being formed. Manual Training, however, bases its claims not on its utilitarian bearing, strong as that may be, but on its fitness as a formative and disciplinary training of the mind, the will and the body, or the intellect, the emotions and the physical powers.

...It is to the intimate connection between the hand and the brain that Manual Training owes its chief value. The brain of a human being, together with the rest of the body, is subject to cer-

tain laws of growth, that is to say their growth and development depend largely on the due exercise of their functions. As everyone knows, a limb or portion of the body unused for a time, becomes atrophied and helpless, but by constant, regular exercise the body is strengthened and developed more and more. Now the power and efficiency of a human brain depend then upon the proper development of its cells, by suitable exercise, to the point at which they become functionally active. The notion that a large brain necessarily meant power of thought and action was long ago dispelled and it was shown instead that its efficiency depended as much on its thorough organization, its healthy development, as on its size or weight. The portion of the brain known to physiologists as the "motor area", depends for its growth on the proper exercise of the organs of the body, and muscular exercise, whether ordinary labour, gymnastics, play or Manual Training is absolutely necessary for that growth.

. . . .

To come now to what is perhaps one of the most important attributes claimed for Manual Training, its effects on the development of moral character. At first sight this may seem to be abrogating to the subject something in no way connected with it....I will try and show why we claim for Manual Training a distinct value along this line. First, I will deal with the question of accuracy, for the lack of accurate thought, a weak and flabby method of approaching vital questions, is one of the most glaring evils of the world to-day. In the Manual Training room there is no approximation, the thing is *right* or *wrong*, and it is delightful indeed to see aroused in a boy's mind a direct appreciation of truth and accuracy very early in his Manual Training experience. In the concrete work of the Manual Training room, the results of deviation from exactitude are at once apparent

A.3 Source: T. B. Kidner, "Manual Training", Dominion Educational Association *Proceedings* (1901), pp. 121-30.

to the child, as they are, I venture to say, in no other subject of school work. The simple operation of sawing a piece of wood to a given length becomes a most potent and effectual argument, appealing directly to the child if he is wrong, and while perhaps to the boy it may at first mean simply the spoiling of his piece of work, it involves a fresh effort, a more careful concentration of his powers, if his next attempt is to be successful. We have heard so often that "if we sow an act, we reap a habit," that like a good deal of proverbial philosophy it is in danger of losing its force, but in such acts of striving towards accuracy and truth, even though it be but in apparently simple things, the child is laying a foundation for the growth of moral character, learning to set for himself a standard of right and wrong. Again, I said just now that the will power, the power of inhibition, is largely developed by Manual Training. The man who has not learned to control himself in small actions, cannot effectively control his passions and desires. Much of our crime is the direct result of want of proper education, want of proper training of inhibitory powers in youth. The sense of power, of having accomplished something, which comes to the boy on the successful completion of his piece of work, is a means of forming and strengthening his character whose value cannot be over-estimated....

Habits of independence and self-reliance are formed and fostered by the individual character of the work. The boy is face to face with his own difficulties, and these he has to strive to overcome by himself alone. No amount of "copying" will help him; as I said at the beginning, "he has to do for himself" and this alone marks a tremendous difference in this and some other subjects of school work. Owing to the necessity of keeping large classes at some dead level, at some medium pace, in many of the ordinary school

subjects the teacher is compelled to "mark time" with his smarter pupils and to unduly press the backward ones. In the Manual Training room this is not the case, the smart boy goes on without waiting for the medium ones and the dullards, not wasting his time forming bad habits and getting into mischief perhaps; while the boy who is slow and awkward with his work goes slowly and performs simpler tasks, but, and this is most important, has to do them thoroughly and well. This individual character of the work as opposed to the class teaching in vogue in other subjects is one of the best possible aids in the formation of character....

In the cultivation of habits of industry, of concentration and of perseverance, Manual Training plays an important part. All visitors to Manual Training rooms, especially those in the habit of visiting other school rooms, are struck with the earnest absorption of the boys in their tasks; from its nature the work appeals to them, and their minds and hearts are concentrated on reaching the goal of the completed exercise.

The training in habits of order given by this work is of undoubted value in every day life, and the inculcation of such habits necessarily follows carefully planned, systematic, step by step work in which the child can clearly follow the sequence for himself. Cleanliness and neatness are other important attributes of hand work, and while these perhaps may be looked after in the ordinary school work, they are an essential part of the work in the Manual Training room.

As a preparation for specialised technical instruction in after years, Manual Training is most valuable, for while it must be clearly understood that in no sense can Manual Training be regarded as trade teaching, yet the dexterity and skill of hand and eye developed in the boy and the power of making and interpreting a working drawing, form an admirable basis on which trade instruction can afterwards be given. In England, the mistake was made of establishing the great technical or trade training schools before Manual Training had been made a part of the elementary school system, and their efforts were largely wasted at first because the almost exclusively literary character of the common school curriculum had not provided a suitable basis on which the special technical teaching could be carried forward.

The distinction between the productive workshop and the Manual Training room is important, for to the casual observer the fact that wood and woodworking tools are being used would seem to indicate that some sort of trade work is being carried on, but the aims of the Manual Training room are entirely different. To the workman the objective is the article to be produced, and the methods are of secondary importance, while in the Manual Training room, the *doing* and not the thing when done is of prime importance to the teacher of Manual Training, who has in view, not the production of an article, but the development of a human being.

A.4 The Second Response: Vocational Training

The Technical Education Act of 1919 provided ten million dollars for the promotion and establishment of technical education in Canada. This subsidy was to be used for the purchase or rental of land, buildings, furniture and equipment, the administration of programmes, teachers' salaries, teacher training and maintenance of plant and equipment. The Act excluded techni-

A.4 Source: Peter F. Bargen, ed., *The Canadian Secondary Schools and Manpower Development* (Toronto, The Canadian Superintendent: 1966), pp. 16-18.

cal education for persons under 14 years of age, as well as courses at college level, thereby eliminating assistance for elementary schools and technical or engineering colleges. Occupational instruction in religious or privately owned schools was excluded as well as projects supported by the Agricultural Instruction Act. No money was provided for manual training.

In the ten-year period from 1919 to 1929, enrolments in educational courses under the Technical Education Act increased 100 per cent from 60,546 to 121,252 students.

Federal involvement in the field of education (a provincial responsibility under the British North America Act) was justified on the basis of (a) the need of an industrial nation for an adequate supply of skilled workers, (b) provision of equality of educational opportunity, and (c) the high cost, to local and provincial authorities, of providing adequate training programmes and facilities....

The Agricultural and Technical School in Charlottetown built with assistance under this Act, offered a variety of full-time and short courses in a wide range of subjects. In New Brunswick, the Saint John Vocational School was established as well as a number of composite schools. Itinerant teachers travelled throughout the province offering short intensive courses to fishermen, auto mechanics and farmers in such subjects as gas engines, automotive electricity and oxyacetylene welding.

Trade training was offered at a number of centres throughout the province of Quebec. As an orientation programme each boy spent two weeks in the machine shop, woodworking, foundry and blacksmithing areas before deciding upon the area in which he wished to specialize. There is little information about training programmes which operated in Quebec under the Act. Perhaps this scarcity is due to the lack of a full-time Director of Vocational Education in Quebec during most of the period from 1919 to 1929.

Because of the extensive training programmes begun under the Industrial Education Act of 1911, the province of Ontario was in the best position to take full advantage of federal financial assistance. Many day vocational schools were established, both full time and part time, a number of co-operative training schemes for apprentices and extension work was offered throughout the province.

The Province of Manitoba, as well as providing day vocational classes and evening courses in a variety of subjects, made use of federal funds for the expansion of correspondence course training. Day and evening classes were operated in the Province of Saskatchewan, particularly in relation to the field of agriculture.

Tangible evidence of federal financial assistance in the Province of Alberta was seen in the establishment and operation of the Provincial Institute of Technology and Art in Calgary. This centre was used for veterans' training immediately after the war. However, during the 1920's it adapted its programme to meet a wide variety of needs in the Province of Alberta. Courses, both of vocational and pre-vocational nature, were offered in secondary schools, especially in Edmonton and Calgary.

An extensive programme of day and evening vocational classes was operated in the Province of British Columbia.

A.5 The Response of the University: Community Service

The Sphere of the University

What is the sphere of the university? Its watchword is service–service of the state in the things that make for happiness and virtue as well as in the things that make for wealth. No form of that service is too mean or too exalted for the university. It is as fitting for the university, through correspondence classes, extension courses, supervision of farmers' clubs, travelling libraries, women's institutes or musical tests to place within the reach of the solitary student, the distant townsman, the farmer in his hours of leisure or the mothers and daughters in the home the opportunities for adding to their stores of knowledge and enjoyment, as it is that the university should foster researches into the properties of radium or the causes and cure of swamp fever; provided, of course, that it is better fitted than any other existing agency for carrying on that particular work.

. . . .

Extension Work

The Summer School work is but one of the many forms of Extension Work undertaken by the University. During the past year the number of Short Courses of instruction in Agriculture for farmers has increased from 34 to 59, and the number of Junior Exhibitions for Boys and Girls from 50 to 100. The work for women has rapidly expanded. The University is attempting to stimulate the establishment of local libraries by means of small grants which the community must at least duplicate, and by offering to procure such books as may be desired.

Our Extension Work hitherto has developed mainly along agricultural lines, and the results have been excellent. The Grain Growers recently have had under consideration large plans for educational work of a more varied character –studies in Economics, History, Literature, as well as in topics more closely connected with Agriculture, and debates, illustrated lectures,

A.5 Source: University of Saskatchewan, *The President's Report*, 1908-09, p. 11; *ibid.*, 1916-17, pp. 3-4.

reading circles with library facilities, which have been attempted elsewhere with excellent results. We should bear in mind that whatever stimulates the interest, quickens the intelligence and broadens the outlook of a people will contribute to its economic improvement, no less than to its intellectual and social betterment. The Danish Folk High Schools, which made the language, literature, history, music and art of the homeland the centre of their studies, have, so their leading men declare, been largely responsible for the economic revolution which has been wrought in that country within a generation.

I can picture no greater blessing to this province than groups of men and women, young and old, in every village, hamlet and rural community gathering together for mutual instruction and entertainment through discussion, lecture courses, musical and literary entertainments. The community centre where Grain Growers, Homemakers, benevolent societies meet, will have its local library, its piano or organ, possibly its band, its singing school, its lecture hall, its club room, may be its gymnasium, where the young may get as much as their elders.

We have to-day scattered throughout Saskatchewan groups of men and women who have come from homes in other lands where they were surrounded with all that an old and highly developed social life could give them. They bring great gifts and accomplishments to us. If we in turn can give them the opportunity, they will enrich our life and at the same time add to their own happiness. If we delay for one or two generations, we may never recover the opportunity. Other lands, when at our stage of development, permitted this neglect and to-day they are suffering for it.

B. Education and Changing Social Conditions

Altered industrial conditions called for a readjustment of the social as well as the economic purposes of the school. Traditionally, the family, the farm, and the local community provided the environment that taught the child all he had to know of life. But with the rise of industrialization came the rapid growth of large towns and cities, and urban life, it was believed, destroyed many of those aspects of family and community life so essential to the full development of the child (document B.1). As a result, new institutions had to be devised, and old ones like the public schools readjusted, to assume the functions of socialization that had once been looked after elsewhere (document B.2).

As the towns and cities grew, the rural population declined proportionately. Even in the first decade of the twentieth century, when tens of thousands of "settlers" immigrated to the west, the urban population grew three times as fast as the rural. The rapid growth of large urban centres and the accompanying flow of population from the country to the city were not viewed dispassionately; to many people they posed serious threats to the traditional social and moral foundations of society. Here, then, were new purposes for the rural schools–to help build an environment that would reaffirm the values of country living and discourage the trend to "rural depopulation".

These purposes could be achieved in two ways. One was to introduce into the rural schools new subjects and experiences–Agriculture, Nature Study, School Gardens–which, it was believed, would make the schools more relevant to country life (document B.3). The other way–the consolidation of rural school sections into larger units–was a more radical approach to the problem, and, in the long run, had more lasting effects. Consolidation was based on the assumption that not only the rural curriculum but rural educational facilities in general were inadequate. Uniting small school sections into more efficient units was a way to achieve equal educational opportunity for rural youth (document B.4). But it was a long-term project involving changes in the basic organization of the public school systems, and it would not happen overnight.

These new economic and social purposes of the school were stated before the outbreak of World War I. The idealism generated by war, however, produced yet another purpose: the nation's schools had a civic responsibility to further the cause of democracy (document B.5). The capability of the school to achieve all these purposes, however, was impaired so long as school attendance was a casual affair and limited for most to a few short years. As one Minister of Education put it, "no matter what modifications may be made in the courses of study in the elementary schools, it is impossible to teach under age 14 all that a boy or girl ought to learn for effective citizenship, or for a life work". Thus, two aims of the New Education were the enforcement of compulsory attendance laws and a school-leaving age high enough to give everyone an opportunity to receive one or two years of secondary education (document B.6).

The Household Science Room, Galt Collegiate Institute, 1908.

B.1   The Social Challenge of the City

The fact is that in our city life we are facing conditions that are undermining the home. So little is this understood and yet so important are the consequences that I venture to give at length a most admirable treatment of the whole subject. This is taken from Hunter's[1] work on "Poverty" …which we should like to induce everyone to read.

"A few decades ago in England and America, practically the entire life of parents and children–whether working, playing, or learning–was in and about the home, and even now in certain backward industrial countries this is likewise true. The mass of people lived in small towns, or hamlets, as they might better be called, since that word in itself conveys the idea of home. There were a few large towns, but most of the population was grouped in these small rural communities. Nearly all work was done by hand-manufacture. Horse-power, water-power, and hand-power were the bases of the industry. The home fields raised the foodstuffs; killing, cooking, baking, brewing, smithing, forging, spinning, and weaving were home occupations. The home had its own water supply; the home supplied its own defence; the home took precautions against disease and cared for the sick and even the insane. Social gatherings took place in the fields near the home or in the house itself. The children received practically their entire education either in the home or in the adjoining fields. Certainly in those days the child received his best education under the supervision of his own parents. The entire

[1]Robert Hunter, *Poverty*, New York, 1904.

B.1 Source: J. S. Woodsworth, *My Neighbour, A Study in City Conditions, A Plea for Social Service* (Toronto, 1911), pp. 116-20.

schooling, which was necessarily restricted to the teaching of the three R's, did not average in 1800 more than eighty-two days for each person. The children were nearly always in the sight of their parents. Both parents worked, and the children worked also; but the parents could stop in their work at any time for the purpose of instructing the children. In a word, the home was the centre of the moral, educational, industrial and social life.

"In most of the countries of Western Europe and America, this is now all changed. Except in a few belated industries, the domestic workshop no longer exists, even in the country; industrial processes, except of course, agriculture, are now carried on by large, well-organized groups of employees, in offices, factories, mills, and mines, sometimes of enormous size. Steam and electricity have displaced hand, water and horse power, as the motive forces of industry. The individual workshop has given way to large co-operative methods of work. Hamlets have grown into factory towns, and the towns into cities. Millions of people in all parts of Western Europe have emigrated from their homes and fields in the rural districts to the crowded centres of industry. We have now, on an enormous scale, co-operative production, a minutely organized division of labor and great aggregations of working people laboring together in the houses of industry and dwelling together in the huge tenements of our cities. No revolution was ever before known that so completely and rapidly revolutionized the life and work of the people as this one of the last century.

"When this revolution brought into the world large cities and a new industrial life, it at the same time destroyed what has been described as the Home. In our largest cities *this* home no longer exists. The economic development of the last hundred years has destroyed it and left in its stead a mere shadow of what was once the source of all things essential to the world. The mills, factories, abattoirs, breweries and bakeries took from the home the various trades, the state supplied the defence, and the city the water supply; the sanitarium, the surgeon, and the alienist took precaution against disease and replaced home remedies by skilled practice and medical science; the sick have hospital care, the schools undertake the instruction of the child, and the factory, etc., the technical training. The home is now a few rooms in a crowded tenement or apartment house. The fields have diminished to the commons, the commons to yards, and the yards to courts and light shafts; the tenement has become yardless. Little or nothing has replaced the social losses of the home, and the same may be said of the possibilities for recreation, which were lost with the fields and commons. A few settlements have endeavored to supply opportunities for keeping alive the neighborhood feeling; a few playgrounds have come to supply the recreative needs; but the losses have been serious and as yet there are no sufficient substitutes. The rapidity with which this revolution has occurred is almost unbelievable. There are men now living who have seen the working out of the whole industrial process.

"Every one of these changes has had its effect upon the child. Although, in the working out of this process, the child was never thought of, the revolution has vitally changed the environment and conditions of child life. We are in an era of great cities, and in a few years the mass of our population will live in cities. In these changes from the home to the factory, from the cottage to the tenement, and from the country to the city, the needs of childhood have been forgotten.

. . . .

"To a very large extent [the child] has been left to readjust himself, and the result is a series of really appalling problems. His father now leaves the home and goes to the factory; he may not watch his father at work or work with him– and it would not be good for him if he could– until he himself is old enough to become a labourer. He is in the city instead of in the country. He has lost the playgrounds which nature lavishly furnished–the hills, valleys, woodland, the thousand varieties of plants and animals, the streams, the blue sky over all, even the starry night. Bored by the homeless tenement, he finds himself on an asphalt pavement, in a crowded street, amid roars of excitement–in a playground alive with business with which he must not interfere. But he plays; the street is interesting, garbage boxes and lamp-posts have a place in his games, and the child is happy, God bless him.

"These changes in the living and working conditions of the people and these changes in the environment of the child demand new agencies for the care of the child, and a series of important readjustments of the social and educational institutions to the altered economic conditions. Certain social institutions have already readjusted themselves, but the distinctly educational institutions have been slow to change."

B.2 The Social Value of Practical Training: Homemakers and Wage Earners

Changes in industrial conditions demand a readjustment of educational methods and courses of study. When the home was a manufacturing centre, from which the necessaries of life were produced, little was demanded of the elementary school except a knowledge of the three R's.

B.2 Source: (Adelaide Hoodless), *Report to the Minister of Education, Ontario, on Trade Schools in Relation to Elementary Education* (Toronto, 1909), pp. 3-5.

As the social and educational influence of construction, composition, and the stimulus of responsibility were removed to the shop and factory, and specialized work took the place of a general knowledge, women were deprived of the interesting and character building elements which were their birthright.

That circumstances compelled women to follow the various industries into shop and factory, without either mental or technical training, accounts, in a large measure, for the lower standard of efficiency, lower wages, and consequent social deterioration of women wage-earners. That this is a serious social and economic matter is beyond question.

Gradually people are awakening to the fact that a child cannot be educated much above his social environment, therefore education, to be of the highest value, must take into consideration the fundamental characteristics, physical, mental and moral, which are established in early life and are due entirely to the home influence and environment.

Whether the homemaker has been, or is a wage-earner, or woman of independent means, the responsibility is the same, and the influence upon the class she represents of equal importance. The standard of honour, obedience to laws, service to humanity, sense of justice, respect for good work and the many other qualities which make the good citizen, be he mayor or mechanic, are directly due to the home training and early influences.

To neglect the education of the wage-earners is to promote a lower social standard. In a recent magazine article on "The slums as a national asset," the writer clearly shows that the terrible condition of many wage-earners in the larger cities is the direct outcome of neglect and short-sighted legislation.

Active measures are being taken to correct the evils, chief of which is ignorance of the first essentials of decent living, and which is a menace to a community. The discovery of disease germs and other scientific investigations have awakened the more intelligent to a sense of danger, and, as a result, we have Pure Food Laws, Sanitary Inspectors, Public Baths (in some places) and other social benefits.

All these measures are good so far as they go, but until the authorities recognize the fact that legislation can never take the place of education in right living, they are working under a sad handicap, both social and economic.

Psychologists, and others interested in the study of the human mind, tell us men and women do not think alike. From this standpoint it is easily seen why institutions directly controlled by men, the schools, for instance, are one-sided.

. . . .

The writer has followed very closely...the various discussions which have taken place among manufacturers, Boards of Trade, special committees, and other organizations concerning technical education, as reported from time to time in the daily newspapers.

Not once has there appeared even a reference to the woman wage-earner. The extremely limited provision made in a few schools for instruction in domestic science and sewing is all the consideration allowed for the vast army of women workers. Even domestic science falls far short of proper recognition as a social factor.

The public school should be a great social force. The child must be taught the value of service, and how to perform his part in the world. This cannot be done theoretically, but must be done by combining the ability to know and to do. What connection is there between the school, the home, and the community?

. . . .

What becomes of all the girls released from school at fourteen or fifteen years of age? What has the school done to make them of value to employers of labour? The home industries are limited and the active, self-dependent girl must seek employment elsewhere. What is her position, socially and morally, during the years in which she is trying to acquire sufficient proficiency to earn a decent living wage?

Statisticians and social reformers tell us that the criminal and social outcasts are largely recruited from this class. It is reasonable that such consequences should follow where struggling incompetence causes discouragement before sufficient skill is developed to command living wages. This is where the trade school comes in as an organized apprenticeship, enabling the pupil to learn a trade under social and moral conditions which will carry her through the two or three years, which may be called the transition period between girlhood and womanhood, and sending her into the field of labour, a self-respecting, intelligent worker, conscious of her duty to her employer and to herself.

The Trade School idea is the outcome of the various experiments in technical education, and is the extension of elementary education on the lines over which the majority of pupils attending the public schools will travel...

. . . .

In the rural school it should lead to a knowledge of farming, gardening, poultry raising, and other agricultural pursuits. In the manufacturing centres with the industries established, the result of such schools should be towards higher standards of living (not more elaborate) and the development of a more intelligent, earnest, and capable worker. In the smaller places it has been suggested that high schools should adjust their courses so as to meet the needs of the majority.

B.3 Education for Rural Communities: Agriculture in the Schools

For fifteen years and more in my reports and in my circular letters, I have endeavored to convince the school commissions and the teachers of the advantage of giving some notions of agriculture to the pupils of the rural schools, even to the youngest. The Department of Public Instruction has had, during the last nine years, agricultural lectures given to the pupils of the normal schools, and in the pedagogical congresses the boys' academies in the country have been advised not to give the sons of the farmers a purely commercial education which might have the effect of detaching them from the soil and inducing them to prefer the life of the office and store to the work in the fields. Some teachers have certainly yielded too much to the manifest desire of the parents to have their children prepared for the commercial professions rather than for agriculture.

But in this connection a movement is on foot which should be encouraged. I speak of the initiative taken by the school commissioners of the village of Saint-Casimir, in the county of Portneuf. Impressed with the needs of the rural population, and animated with enlightened zeal, these gentlemen inaugurated last May, in a certain measure, the practical teaching of agriculture in the academy of their municipality. This educational institution has for its professors the Christian Brothers belonging to the institution which published the manual "l'Agriculture à l'école" (agriculture in the school) specially written for the primary schools of the province. These educators acceded with pleasure to the request of

B.3 Source: *Report of the Superintendent of Public Instruction for the Province of Quebec*, 1912-13, pp. xiii-xiv.

the commissioners and accepted the services of Mr. J. C. Magnan, a graduate of the Oka institute, and residing at Saint-Casimir. This young agriculturist has given to the pupils of the academy some theoretical and practical lessons in agriculture and has commenced in the institution the organisation of an agricultural library and museum.

This happy initiative taken by the commissioners of Saint-Casimir is to be commended, and this endeavor, if prudently directed and encouraged, may greatly benefit the rural population interested by helping to arrest the depopulation of the country to the profit of the cities. The primary school should be the preparatory class for the entrance of the children of the farmer to the schools of agriculture; we should have elementary and secondary instruction in the agri-

cultural domain, just as we have it in literature, in pedagogy and in household science. At the same time it is necessary to proceed with wisdom to the methodical organisation of agricultural teaching, and not leave the school commissions to act in an isolated way, without a plan ripened by specialists, or under the influence of persons of little experience.

The greatly increased grants of the government of the province, united with the generous allocations of the federal government for the benefit of the farmers, will hasten certainly the development of agricultural industry and forward the education that it requires. It belongs to the committees of the Council of Public Instruction to amend the courses of study in the sense of the new needs.

In speaking of Agriculture in the school, I

The school garden, George Jay Elementary School, Victoria, British Columbia, 1910.

learn that the work of school gardens, inaugurated in 1905, the same year as agricultural lectures in the normal schools, continues its ascendant progress. Last year, 234 schools situated in 35 counties, possessed these gardens and the number of pupils receiving instruction in horticulture was 7,740. The parents of the children, says Mr. Dalaire in his report, show themselves generally favourable to this means of making school more esteemed, and some municipalities make sacrifices to enlarge and embellish the school grounds.

The normal schools contribute also with ardor to the success of this work. I may mention in particular Jacques-Cartier School, at Montreal, where more than 50 pupils are engaged in garden cultivation. I had the pleasure of visiting these gardens and learning how favorably disposed the pupils are to the work, in order to make themselves more prepared to take charge of the rural schools.

The necessary manual labor in the gardens is accomplished in the recess hours and, writes the Rev. Abbé Desrosiers, "far from injuring the studies, this labor has contributed to develop among our young professors that spirit of personal initiative which counteracts the idleness which has well been called the curse of our age.... Let us hope that they will remain enthusiastic for agriculture, and that they will endeavor, by means of rational agricultural teaching or by the establishment of school gardens, to stop the exodus from country to city".

B.4 Education for Rural Communities: Consolidation of Schools

Interest in rural education is steadily growing. The country-life movement, which for many years has barely managed to keep alive and which has always been more or less confined to a discussion of theories growing out of the publication of statistics relative to our rural population, now seems to be gathering force. This revival of interest in rural affairs is widespread in Canada and the United States, and is manifesting itself generally in improved methods of production, better business management, and a desire on the part of the farming population for greater participation in the affairs of the country at large. With this rural awakening there is bound to come a greater appreciation of the value of education, and consequently dissatisfaction with the old form of rural school organization–the ungraded country school. Already in certain parts of the Province the movement towards improvement in education through reorganization and consolidation of school districts is well under way. On Vancouver Island the Municipalities of Duncan and North Cowichan have been united for school purposes and have got off to a very good start. Four of the one-roomed schools of North Cowichan–those nearest to the City of Duncan–were closed, and the pupils are being transported in vans to the central school at Duncan. The consolidation of the Municipality of Spallumcheen with the City of Armstrong for school purposes has also been effected, and steps have been taken to erect a new school at Armstrong to accommodate all of the children attending school from both city and municipality. More recently the question has come up for discussion at Chilliwack, and there seems to be a growing sentiment throughout the city and the adjoining muncipality in favour of a complete reorganization of their local system. In several other districts the same problem is being faced and is re-

B.4 Source: J. W. Gibson, Director of Elementary Agricultural Education, in 48th Annual Report of the Public Schools of the Province of British Columbia, 1918-19, by the Superintendent of Education. pp. 47-48.

ceiving serious consideration. "Better education under improved conditions" seems to be the main thought in the minds of people everywhere who think along educational lines or who manifest any sign of interest in the future welfare of the country.

This reorganization of rural schools will undoubtedly result in improved instruction in all branches, but it will be particularly advantageous in connection with the teaching of elementary agriculture, manual training, and domestic science. Under the new system it will be possible to have such up-to-date equipment and such improved conditions for teaching these special subjects as are obviously impossible under the old system of small, ungraded schools. With the enlarging of the unit of organization for rural consolidated schools and the added facilities for better teaching, will also come an ever-changing field of usefulness for the school itself. Courses of instruction will be improved and brought more into harmony with the best life and interests of rural people, the people themselves will find new avenues of educational and social interest opening up for them, and these will all centre around their most important institution–the school. A resolution which was passed at the 1918 annual meeting of the New Brunswick Farmers' and Dairymen's Association goes to show that the question of a more modern type of rural education is in demand in the East as well as in the West. The resolution reads as follows:-

"Whereas a big majority of the children attending the public schools of this Province are sons and daughters of farmers:

"And whereas the instruction being given in said schools is very largely of an abstract character and tends to make said children in favour of professional occupations, which further tends to increase the population of the towns and cities:

"And whereas, if the curriculums of said schools of this Province were to contain some more concrete form of education regarding agricultural matters, it would tend to increase the desires of said children toward agricultural pursuits and also to increase the population of the farms:

"Therefore, be it *Resolved*, That the Farmers' and Dairymen's Association of New Brunswick is of the opinion that a larger measure of instruction in said public schools about local conditions and activities in the country relative to agricultural pursuits is desirable, and that the efforts of the pupils, particularly in rural districts, should be directed in a greater degree by the teacher through practical methods of training, so as to cause the children to acquire a clearer, stronger, and more intelligent interest in the greatest of all industries in the Province."

B.5　Education for Democracy

In the earlier days of the war the term "Reconstruction" was used to express a return to the conditions of July, 1914. The practical tasks of reconstruction were the two related problems of *demobilization* and *restoration*–how to get men as quickly as possible from their war positions in the army or in industry back into their old niches in civil life, and how to free employers and employed from the restrictions and control of war with a view to restoring the methods of the past. But as time went on and the deeper lessons of the struggle were being impressed on men's souls, the word *reconstruction* took on a deeper meaning. Men sought for more than a simple return to pre-war conditions. There grew the ideal of a better world after the war. By war achievements there was developed an enlarged sense of what is

B.5 Source: *Report of the Minister of Education, Province of Ontario*, 1918, pp. 5-7.

possible and a quickened sense of what is just. Not the old conditions but better conditions for all, is the aim of a true reconstruction.

. . . .

The importance of education has received fresh illustration from the world cataclysm of war. We have seen on a colossal scale the power of education over the souls and minds of men. It has been able to poison the springs of national life, to change and degrade national ideals, to minister to a monstrous vanity and egotism. Education, applied with persistence and pedantic pertinacity, is the most formidable instrument in the modern world for the control of conduct and the moulding of purpose. We have seen also that the application of science to industry and commerce can enormously develop the markets of a nation and increase its wealth. Technical and industrial education is a necessity if a country is to hold its own in world competition. Nothing but the best product sold and pushed in the most effective way can win a world market. This best product can be secured only by the best management and the most skilled labour, and these once more are linked with education. We have accepted as one of the aims of the war the making of the world safe for democracy. We believe that this on the whole is the noblest and safest form of government. But we equally realize that if the world is to be safe *under* democracy, then democracy must be intelligent. Of all forms of government, democracy can least afford to neglect universal education.

. . . .

We construe education to mean more than the impartation of knowledge and the training of the mind. Its broad scope covers bodily health and fitness, mental culture, devotion of spirit and social efficiency. The German educationalists thought of civilization in terms of intellect; the British in terms of character. Which ideal is the safe and worthier, history has already pronounced. Efficiency in itself is no more moral than lightning. From what motive does it spring? To what aim is it directed? The proper place of efficiency is as the servant of a moral ideal. Apart from such an ideal, efficiency may be an evil and wicked instrument which in the end works woeful disaster.

B.6   Extending Education to the Adolescent

Rightly or wrongly, the schools are being looked to, on the one hand, for the development of the character of the youth and, on the other, for a training in efficiency. If the schools are to accept the responsibility, the possibilities and limitations should be clearly recognized, and the conditions of attendance and organization should be such as to make it possible to realize these ends.

The elementary school has an important function to play in character formation, because the tendency to conceive and to realize ends begins with the spontaneity of the infant in the kindergarten and is nurtured by intelligent and sympathetic methods in dealing at every stage with every question, exercise, and problem presented to the learner: the teacher who throws his pupil during the earlier stages on his responsibility, and leads him to work from interest and motive, is laying the foundation for a purposeful life. Yet if the child's schooling closes at the end of the elementary school period, the chief opportunity for character direction is lost to the school, because the significant aims and purposes of life do not begin to take shape until the youth enters

B.6 Source: F. W. Merchant (Director of Technical Education), in
Report of the Minister of Education, Province of Ontario,
1918, pp. 25-27.

upon the period of adolescence. If the school is to be held responsible in a large measure for the development of national character, it follows that it must take an important part in guiding and controlling the youth during this critical and formative period.

On the efficiency side, too, the training given in an elementary school cannot be said to be sufficient, whether the question is regarded from the standpoint of the academic training necessary as a basis of civic intelligence or from the standpoint of an adequate educational equipment for useful service in a commercial, agricultural, or industrial vocation. This statement is not to be construed as a reflection on elementary school systems; much of what has been demanded of the elementary schools in this and other countries cannot be realized in any system, however perfect, within the present age limitations of compulsory attendance. Most of the criticisms levelled at the elementary schools have resulted from a failure to realize the actual possibilities of education within this period, and many of the mistakes in school organization, especially in the line of congesting courses of study, have been made in the endeavour to modify school conditions to meet such criticisms.

These considerations have turned the minds of those who are looking to education as a means for moral and social advancement to the importance of utilizing much more fully the period between fourteen and eighteen years of age for the training of the youth. Attention has been drawn particularly to what secondary schools have accomplished for the very small fraction of the youth of the country who have been fortunate enough to continue their education in such institutions. The necessity for making some form of advanced training more universal is becoming very generally realized in all countries.

How shall the period of education be extended for all children? This is probably the leading educational problem that the progress of the times is forcing upon the attention of educators and administrators. Several solutions have been proposed and a variety of experiments have been undertaken. Roughly speaking, these solutions and experiments fall into two classes, first, voluntary plans; second, compulsory schemes for extending the period of full-time or part-time schooling beyond present limitations. Naturally, voluntary plans were the first to be tried. By giving a deeper interest to school studies it has been sought to induce a larger proportion of children to extend their education. The efforts have been directed mainly along two lines. The curriculum of the elementary school has been enriched by connecting the traditional subjects in a more vital way with typical forms of life's activities, and an appeal has been made to the natural impulse of the youth for a life career, in the organization of a new type of school, which is intended to bridge the gulf between the elementary schools and employments. In these two ways, by vitalizing the curriculum of the elementary schools and by the organization of vocational schools, the effort has been made to extend the period of education for an increased number of children. But these plans have been found to be exceedingly slow in their operation. They may raise by a few points the percentage of attendance at secondary schools, but as a means of reversing the figures and changing the eighty or ninety per cent of non-attendance to a corresponding percentage of attendance at advanced classes, they must be regarded as a failure.

The causes which lead children to drop out of school at the early stages continue to operate in spite of the attractions of more interesting courses of study. The necessity for earning a

C. The New Pedagogy

livelihood is forced upon a number of children at an early age, and possibly the natural desire for an adventure into the life of the adult and for the independence which employment gives causes even a larger number to leave school than economic pressure. These causes are effective even when distaste for school is removed.

It is now very generally conceded that the only adequate means of carrying out any comprehensive scheme for the further extension of general education is through some form of compulsory legislation. Legislation of this kind either has been adopted or is being considered by educational administrators in most countries where advanced systems are established.

Like the economic and social aspects of the New Education, its pedagogical dimension began as a reaction against the constrictions and limitations of the nineteenth-century public school: perceptive teachers had long been disturbed by the formalism of content and method that thrived under the dual regime of mental discipline theory and administrative centralization. They wanted to replace an abstract, bookish, and impersonal concept of education with a new kind of learning based more on the student's interest and ability, and more closely related to his personal experiences and social environment. In the nineteenth century, these pedagogical reformers presented their case for a "new education" by referring to their personal experience and to the example of those outstanding teachers of the past whose names commanded respect (document C.1).

In the early twentieth century, the case against academic formalism was greatly strengthened by the findings of the new science of psychology. The innovative teacher could now buttress his empirical conclusions with the laws of science. And many of those laws lent themselves unequivocally to the cause of pedagogical reform. Among the most telling in this respect were those which provided a scientific learning theory directly opposed to the old transfer of training doctrine so essential to the mental discipline view of education (document C.2). Meanwhile, another branch of psychology, Child Study, added to the reformers' arsenal by claiming that a child's education had to take into account his individual progress through various stages of mental and physical development (document C.3).

Finally, the new pedagogy reflected the

desire of some schoolmen to make the public schools responsive to the needs of society, as these were perceived around the turn of the century. To many educators, this meant discarding the narrow traditions of the past and adopting new methods and new subjects more attuned to the child's present interests and his future responsibilities as a worker and a citizen. The school could meet the social and economic demands placed upon it only by instituting curricular changes that amounted to a new pedagogy (document C.4).

These new ideas were not universally accepted, but as a result of the sustained attack upon the "old education", the principles of the new pedagogy did succeed in becoming the conventional wisdom of many leading Canadian educators by 1920. Two such men were

J. H. Putman of Ontario and G. W. Weir of British Columbia. For both, the early years of the century constituted the formative beginnings of careers that would significantly influence the direction of Canadian education. Commissioned in 1924 to survey the British Columbia school system and suggest measures for its improvement, they produced a historic report that anticipated the shape of educational reform for years to come. Turning their backs on mental discipline and all its works, they advocated the adoption of a more "rational school practice" in keeping with the teachings of Child Psychology, the "sociological theories" of John Dewey, and the "demands and needs of an ever-evolving social background" (document C.5).

A "New Education" kindergarten at the Toronto Model School, c.1898.

C.1 Educational Reform Within the School

The motto of the "Old Education" is "Knowledge is power". And so it is. But the experience of centuries has proven that knowledge is not the greatest power. The omniscient man is not always the omnipotent man. In the realm of mind the scholar is often distanced by his inferior in knowledge. The motto of the "New Education" is, "Activity and growth are power". A good saying it is, too, but not entirely novel. Its essence was one of the apothegms of Comenius, the distinguished educational reformer of the seventeenth century, "We learn to do by doing". The "Old Education" stored the mind with knowledge, useful and useless, and only incidentally trained the mind. The "New Education" puts training in the first place and makes the acquisition of knowledge incidental.

The "Old Education" was devoted to the study of books. Too often the text-books were used as an end rather than as a means. "How far have you been in Sangster's Arithmetic?" and "How far have you learned in Bullion's Grammar?" were common queries of the school-master in the old days, and these queries betrayed the educational aims of the questioner. Quantity was everything; growth was little or nothing. The "New Education" is devoted more to things than to books. Text-books are used, but only as repositories of knowledge to be consulted as occasion requires–that is, they are used not as an end but as a means of acquisition and improvement.

The "Old Education" was fond of *memoriter* recitation. In fact, "learning the lesson" was the be-all and the end-all of the schoolroom. How many a woe-begone victim has felt the weight of some martinet's wrath because of ignominious failure in reciting some precious morsel like this: "A Relative Pronoun, or, more properly, a conjunctive pronoun, is one which, in addition to being a substitute for the name of a person or thing, connects its clause with the antecedent, which it is introduced to describe or modify!" To repeat words correctly was everything; to understand them was of secondary importance. In all branches of study definitions had to be carefully memorized as a basis for future work. The "New Education" reverses all this. What Coleridge calls "parrotry" is reduced to a very comfortable minimum. Definitions have their place, but if they are memorized it is at the final rather than at the initial stage in the pursuit of a study or topic. Original human thought takes the place of imitative jargon. Intelligible facts displace unintelligible rules and definitions.

The "Old Education" was eminently subjective, dealing largely in abstractions. The "New Education" employs objective methods, preferring the presentation of truth in the concrete.

The "Old Education" began its work with the unseen and the unfamiliar, and dangerously taxed the weak reflective faculties. The "New Education" begins with the seen and the common and gradually develops the reflective faculties by reference to knowledge already obtained by the strong and active perceptive faculties of the child. The former system initiated the tyro in geography by forcing him to commit to memory the names of the countries and the capitals of Europe; the latter leads him on a happy jaunt over his immediate environment. The former asks the little head to carry the names of all the bones in the skeleton of a rhinoceros; the latter shows to fascinated investigators the anatomy of a leaf. The former taught our infant lips to lisp the dimensions of ancient Babylon, and the name of Jupi-

C.1 Source: J. E. Wetherell, "Conservatism and Reform in Education Methods", Ontario Teachers' Association *Proceedings* (1886), pp. 85-88.

ter's grandmother; the latter opens dull ears to the melody of birds, and unfilms dull eyes to behold the glory of the heavens. The wail of Carlyle will find an echo in many hearts; "For many years," says he, "it has been one of my most constant regrets that no schoolmaster of mine had a knowledge of natural history so far at least as to have taught me the grasses that grow by the wayside, and the little winged and wingless neighbours that are continually meeting me with a salutation which I cannot answer, as things are. Why did not somebody teach me the constellations too, and make me at home in the starry heavens which are always overhead, and which I do not half know to this day?"

The old system of tuition was marked by mechanical routine; the new boasts of almost complete absence of machinery, of infinite variety of programme, of multiplicity and attractiveness of devices. On the one hand joyless thraldom and lifeless monotony; on the other continual novelty and an exhilarating sense of freedom.

In the old order of things each subject in the curriculum was regarded as a distinct entity, and was entirely isolated. The order of things requires that the subjects should be so co-ordinated and studied together, that each as far as possible may be the ally of some other. Thus geography is the handmaid of history. Thus reading, writing, spelling and composition go hand in hand as far as possible. The spelling-book is discarded as a useless educational tool; and English composition, which had its fortnightly terrors in the past, has become the most seductive of school occupations and is practised every day in the year.

In the old days among teachers there was common a most pernicious though benevolent vice, the vice of talking too much–called by someone the "didactic disease". The teacher was prone to tell everything, to explain everything, leaving the pupil little to do but everything to learn. The new method–if I may call it new–a method practised so persistently and successfully by Dr. Arnold[1]–is, that the pupil should do the maximum of original work and that the teacher should give him the minimum of assistance; in other words, the pupil must think and show results, the teacher must study to hold his own tongue as much as possible.

The "Old Education" was not only faulty, it was also one-sided. Certain faculties of the mind were exercised, while the body and the heart were neglected. One of the ruling principles of the "New Education" is, "Harmoniously develop the whole being, the mental, the moral, the physical."

The "Old Education" carried the military idea into the schools and taught by squads, and companies, and battalions; and the "boding tremblers" were apparently under good discipline, but it was the discipline of subjection and fear, not the discipline of freedom and love. The "New Education" carries the method of the Great Teacher into the schools and pays much attention to individuals. The former system attended to the aggregation and almost neglected the unit. The latter studies the peculiarities of each child and adapts its teachings to his past experiences and his existing attitude: and thus the dull pupil receives, as he should, more attention than the brilliant pupil.

The "Old Education" made much of examinations. The passing of examinations was the goal in all grades of schools. The preparation for examinations was the constant and debasing toil. The examinations, like the text-books, instead of being kept in their proper place as a useful means for a desirable end, usurped the exalted place of the end itself. The "New Education" puts written

[1]Thomas Arnold (1795-1842), headmaster of Rugby School, England.

tests in their proper and secondary place. Examinations and promotions are not continually before the pupil's mind; and when written examinations are held, their old use is abandoned. The questions are such as test not so much the pupil's knowledge as his power of doing.

C.2 Educational Reform and Thorndike's Laws of Learning

Those of us whose professional training dates back to the pre-Thorndike[1] era remember well the laws of learning which were dinned incessantly in our ears. "Proceed from the simple to the complex." "Start with the concrete and end in the abstract." "Proceed from the empirical to the rational." "Create a pleasurable excitement in the pupils." "The genesis of knowledge in the individual must follow the same course as the genesis of knowledge in the race." "In education the process of self-development should be encouraged to the fullest extent."

Dear old Pestalozzi! Dear old Spencer! Yet though we smile patronizingly upon them to-day, they in their time played their parts and played them well. If it were not for the scientific scepticism of a Thorndike we should still be dictating their laws as the last words in educational wisdom. Perhaps the next generation will smile pityingly upon us, and, for the sake of educational progress, we hope that they will. Yet we cannot but believe that we are on more solid ground than were our forebears.
. . . .

The first law to emerge was the law of effect. Thorndike, it will be remembered, in his early

[1]Edward Lee Thorndike, 1874-1949. Professor of Educational Psychology, Teachers College, Columbia, 1901-1940.

C.2 Source: Peter Sandiford (Professor of Education, University of Toronto), "Contributions to the Laws of Learning", *Teachers College Record, 27,* 6(February, 1926), pp. 523-31.

animal experiments used original satisfiers such as food to the hungry cat, company to the lonely chicken, as rewards for certain actions. He took the law for granted as so many before him had done. Gradually, however, it became one of his most important principles of education. In his *Educational Psychology*, 1903, we learn that "the work of education is to make the outcome of desirable activities pleasurable and to inhibit their opposites by discomfort." In *Elements of Psychology*, 1905, the principle is explicitly stated in the law of habit-formation. "Any mental state or act which in a given situation produces satisfaction becomes associated with that situation, so that when the situation recurs the act is more likely than before to recur also." And conversely for discomfort. The educational applications are found in *Principles of Teaching*, 1906. "Put together what you wish to have go together. Reward good impulses. Conversely; keep apart what you wish to have separate. Let undesirable impulses bring discomfort." When *Animal Intelligence* appears in 1911 the law was called the "law of effect" and as such was embodied, with slightly altered wording, in the three-volume *Educational Psychology* of 1913.

The "law of exercise" also appeared in *Animal Intelligence* with a supplementary one designated the "law of instinct." In the later *Educational Psychology* the law of instinct is replaced by the "law of readiness," so now the laws of learning according to Thorndike may be said to be (1) the law of readiness; (2) the law of exercise which comprises the laws of use and disuse; and (3) the law of effect. Subsidiary to these main laws are the laws of (a) multiple-response or varied reaction; (b) attitudes, dispositions, preadjustments or "sets"; (c) partial or piecemeal activity of a situation; and (d) associative shifting. These four subsidiary laws or principles, like the three major laws, grew out of the experiments in animal learning.

· ·

Throughout the whole of Thorndike's work on learning the words, situation, bond and response, symbolized in S $\longmapsto$ R, occur. They are not rigidly defined but no one doubts that he uses them as the behaviorists (Watson, for example) use them. The behaviorist uses stimulus as it is used in physiology, as a relatively simple factor (e.g., light waves of different length) influencing the responses of organisms. When these factors are more complex (as in the environment of a social world) they are called situations. Situations, therefore, are the total mass of stimulating factors which lead organisms, including man, to react as a whole. Response is similarly to be understood. The response may be simple or complex. If it is complex a better word to use would be reaction, but response is now general for both. Bond or connection is to be regarded as having its physical basis in the central nervous system. The whole of the law of the prophets regarding learning is summed up in S $\longmapsto$ R.

In no field has Thorndike's genius shone so brightly as in that concerned with formal or general discipline–the influence of improvement in one mental function upon the efficiency of other functions....The tradition of ages was challenged. After a great number of experiments upon the result of training in estimating areas, lengths, and in various forms of observation or perception upon slightly different forms, Thorndike and Woodworth concluded that:

"Improvement in any single mental function need not improve the ability in functions commonly called by the same name. It may injure it.

"Improvement in any single mental function rarely brings about equal improvement in

any other function, no matter how similar, for the working of every mental function-group is conditioned by the nature of the data in each particular case."

The educational world was immediately up in arms. Scores of experiments were designed to confirm or refute these findings. On the whole, Thorndike's position was maintained and accepted, although identity of ideal was added by Bagley. The three generally accepted identities became those of matter, method, and aim. But Thorndike had given the doctrine of formal training its death blow. There might be general discipline, but it was certainly much less than was supposed. It was advisable, on the whole, to train the mental function directly rather than to trust to indirect methods.

C.3 The Influence of Child Study on Educational Reform

At times progress is so gradual, changes are so imperceptible, new applications of old principles push themselves forward so quietly as not to attract much attention. It is only by contrast with what obtained a number of years before that the extent of the changes and the decided advancement which has been made in recent years are realized.

In education we are at present passing through such a stage of imperceptible progress. Yet when we contrast what is now regarded as educationally sound in theory and practice with what was so accounted twenty or twenty-five years ago, the progress made is marvellous, especially so in our educational practice, whether in teaching or discipline. To show the connec-

C.3 Source: William Scott (Normal School, Toronto), "What Child Study has done for the Teaching World", Dominion Educational Association *Proceedings* (1901), pp. 282-90.

tion between this era of progress and Child-Study is the purpose of this paper.

The Child-Study movement began in America in 1879, with the publication of the measurement of the height and weight of several thousand school children of Boston, and was followed in 1880 by a little work known as the *Content of Children's Minds* by Dr. Stanley Hall.[1] Since then much earnest attention together with much that is foolish and useless has been devoted to Child-Study. However, the wise investigators have so dominated the foolish ones that this subject has so fully demonstrated its right to be recognized as an educational force that I will not say a word about its uses and how it should be pursued, except incidentally, but will try to point out what it has done and is doing for education and educational principles and practice.

Child-Study has freshened and heightened our interest in children. The child is now understood as never before. The child like every other growing thing must be placed in congenial surroundings. Child-Study has supplied these. Teachers are now much more earnest and sympathetic than formerly. There is much less perfunctory work now than ever before. This is true of those who study their children and of those who do not, for the former have compelled the latter to adopt a more rational form of school methods and school management.

The interest thus awakened is not confined to teachers only, but school authorities, legislators, and even the masses of the people, all find themselves impelled to take more interest in education. What is the meaning of Mothers' Clubs, Mothers' Congresses, Mothers' Reading Circles, Art Leagues, but increased interest in children?

[1]G. S. Hall, 1846-1924. President and Professor of Psychology, Clark University, 1888-1920.

Dr. Stanley Hall says that the movement has increased matrimony and the desire to rear children.

· ·

Child-Study has shown that the strongest potential capacity in the child is that for action. Hence, if we would do our full duty to our pupils, we must minister to their activities. In this connection we have not yet fully realized our possibilities. We are not yet fully training children to become men and women of action, but are still paralyzing their love of action by feeding them on words. Observation points to the fact that this capacity for action takes the direction of imitation, and hence every one who comes within the ken of the child becomes his teacher. Hence the necessity of watching the child's environment, for imitative actions affect the motor-nerve cells so as to tend to reproduce themselves unconsciously. The child thus becomes linked to his past in his manners, his speech, his modes of thought, etc. Hence to be fittingly cared for during this imitative period there must be ingrained in every nerve cell a tendency to actions of a right kind. Neither teachers nor parents yet realize the supreme importance of the simple pedagogical law. This explains the necessity of repetition in such subjects as Spelling, Tables, Pronunciation, etc., and just here Psycho-physical experiment shows that in such exercises the now rejected simultaneous method plays an important part in fixing the thing to be remembered. The only precaution to be taken is to see that the answer is necessarily simultaneous, and that the individual is giving attention to the general repetition. This is the simplest way of making the motor memory so perfect that the brain is left to attend to higher things.

· ·

Again, while the observing, questioning, and reading which teachers now do because of the study of children's interests, have added, each day, new life to the teacher and the school; and while this has individualized the mass and the class has ceased to be a herd; and while it is seen as the Irishman said of women that children are "all alike in being different", yet we are far from having solved the problem of how to treat the children of a class of fifty as distinct individuals so as not to retard the progress of those anxious to go on, nor goad on those not ready to advance. This problem is now before the educational world clearly, owing to the recognition of the rights of individuals due to Child-Study. How this problem is to be solved is for the educators of the present as yet a riddle. Yet the fact that it is recognized as a great and serious educational problem is a mark of great advancement. How great or how far we have advanced can scarcely be realized even by one who remembers that Comenius gravely maintained that it is not only possible for one teacher to instruct several hundred children at once, but that it is essential for the best interests of both the teacher and the children that he should do so.

. . . .

Child-Study has shown the crucial importance of the period of adolescence. It has shown that at this period, youths are vulnerable to all kinds of temptation, and that the older generation must at this time give the younger its most consummate care; that this is the time when the soul grows fastest and most; that now new sympathies are awakened and reverberate the widest; that now is the time when youth is most susceptible of culture and development.

. . . .

Child-Study is causing us to realize that school is made for the child–not the child for the school.

We have not realized the thought yet. The idea is, however, floating about, and sooner or later will crystallize itself in action. A good many fine systems and uniform ways of doing things will then receive their quietus. Is not this already bearing fruit? Already there is a revolt all along the line against uniform promotion examinations. These and other school hindrances will disappear just as soon as school authorities recognize that the school is for the pupil and not for the teacher or trustees.

C.4 Pedagogical Reform: New Purposes Demand New Subjects

To be able to properly value any new movement of a social character, especially if it be widely extended, one has to take account of preceeding and accompanying conditions. If he can thus estimate the causal elements at their proper worth, he is in a position to judge regarding the effects that may reasonably be looked for. In our complex civilization with its interlacing connections, no one event stands apart from others, and that is particularly the case with any phenomenon covering a wide area and affecting many nations....modern education is the latest appearing and least developed branch of that great social and industrial revolution, which during the last half century has grown to such enormous proportions that it takes rank with the great world movements of past times, whether of conquest or religion or civilizing influence.

. . . .

C.4 Source: W. S. Ellis (Collegiate Institute, Kingston), "Educational Significance of Kindergarten, Nature Study and Manual Training", Dominion Educational Association *Proceedings* (1901), pp. 163-76.

The efforts made for educational progress in connection with this wave of general advancement have been chiefly along two lines, (1) the carrying on of school work in accordance with the stages of the mental growth of the normal child; (2) the discarding of a large portion of the old routine book recitation and the substituting for them lessons and methods relating to observational and constructional work. Pressure tending to bring about these changes came from two entirely different sources, and with two entirely different objects in view. On the one hand, educators who had attempted to work out the order of mental development of the child and to formulate the principles of that growth claimed for the newly proposed subjects an important place in the schools because of their influence in the gaining of mental power. On the other hand, men of keen intellect, trained in the ordinary affairs of life were impressed by the failure of the elementary school systems to give any adequate preparation for the duties that boys and girls would be called upon to perform at later periods of their lives, and enquired if there could not be introduced into these schools subjects and methods that would have a more direct relation to the after careers of the pupils. Thus the movements from these sources tended toward a point of junction from which we are watching its progress with increased energy at the present time.

. . . .

In regard to the primary and secondary school, I think the view will have to be abandoned that they exist for the production of intellectual refinement and that mental condition known as culture. That educational ideal has come down to us from times when such schools existed for the leisure class, who could afford to indulge in the luxury of a liberal education, because they had no need to make provision for earning a living, or at worst that came in the professional school after the university course. Now the conditions are altered. These schools are used by pupils who with but few exceptions, finish their education in them. In Ontario, ninety-nine children out of every hundred do not go beyond the high school and nine out of every ten of these stop with the public school course. With the new surroundings of material expansion, and the consequent demands for mental training that have been referred to, it becomes necessary to us to provide such courses of study as will give to the young men and women of the country a symmetrical, an educative and a practical outfitting for after life. Symmetrical in that it may develop regularly and equally the powers of mind and body as a whole, not simply literary faculty, mathematical ability or mechanical ingenuity. Educative in that it shall induce accurate observation, correct reasoning and good judgment with control of both mental and bodily powers, and the acquisition of that knowledge requisite for intelligently taking part in the duties that the social community requires. Practical in that the studies and methods employed, and the knowledge and facility gained, shall all bear relation to the life beyond the school-room, and shall bear on the problem of making a livelihood.

. . . .

Recent investigations in the United States, both in the country as a whole and in individual states establish these two conditions, I think, that the wage-earning power of the people is in direct proportion to the average length of school attendance; and that financial prosperity arising from greater wage-earning power leads to better general education, so that any cause which will bring about better results of school work either by prolonging the period of attendance or by increasing the effectiveness of the teaching thereby ultimately will produce greater education and greater material advancement. Then if we can adopt our school work so that it will be effective in giving to the pupils power to think clearly, and to act effectively and while doing this use exercises that appeal to the pupils as interesting and to the people as practical, we will thereby sow seed which in future years following the law of progress, will mature through the university into the best products of scholarship and culture. Kindergarten, Nature Study, Manual Training, these appeal to the child as interesting, to the public as practical, and, at the same time, furnish to the teachers effective educational instruments.

C.5 The Extent of Pedagogical Reform: The Putman-Weir Report, 1925

There is an inherent conservatism in the minds of educators and schoolmen that shows itself in a reluctance to depart from cherished theories and practices in the educational field even when these have been scientifically disproved. Studies, and the content of certain studies, have been retained in the curriculum partly because the authorities responsible for curriculum construction have been taught the same subject-matter and are reluctant to adopt anything new. Indeed, educational reform has often been pressed upon schoolmen from the outside through the protest of enlightened members of the laity whose viewpoints were less prejudiced than those of teachers had become through constant immersion in benumbing class-room practices. The needs of life are constantly changing and educational practice must undergo a gradual process of adjustment in response to

C.5 Source: J. H. Putman and G. M. Weir, *Survey of the School System* [of British Columbia] (Victoria, B.C., 1925), pp. 40-41, 44.

the demands and needs of an ever-evolving social background. In this process of growth the schoolmen should lead the way, but, as already intimated, their tendency in many cases is to lag behind until the pressure of outside opinion makes a forward movement imperative.

This state of intellectual torpor is markedly evident in certain sections and in many educational institutions of British Columbia and other provinces. Nor are the victims of this condition of inertia entirely to blame for their mental state whose explanation is chiefly to be found in the formal discipline theory of studies current almost everywhere throughout the Province. This theory, stated in terms of the discarded "faculty" psychology, stands forth as a hoary-headed idol of pedagogical iniquity before the entrances to many educational institutions of the Province and receives the unreasoning homage of not a few schoolmen and educational authorities who have not had the opportunity or disposition to keep abreast of modern educational developments.

A word regarding the import of this theory should be added. In the first place, its advocates assume that the mind is composed of certain general "faculties," such as memory, reasoning, imagination....

The theory further assumes that there may be a transfer of training, or improvement, from one field of thought to another, without specific exercise in the latter. In British Columbia, for instance, a more comprehensive study of history was frequently urged before the Survey as efficacious in improving the memory and judgment, not merely the memory for history but for things in general. Likewise, Latin is regarded as entitled to special consideration, since, among other reasons, its study is alleged to train the "faculty" of memory for effective use in practically any field of life and to develop habits or attitudes of concentration. A number of psychologists would probably accept, with reservations, the reference to habits and attitudes. Again we were told that even the admittedly obsolete parts of the subject matter of algebra, geometry, and formal grammar, from the viewpoint of their practical applications, have a high value for the training of the reasoning "faculty" and powers of logical analysis not only in school but in the actual situations of after life. The list of examples brought to the attention of the Survey might be enlarged indefinitely, but the above will suffice.

Leading modern psychologists admit that a certain transfer of training from one field to another may take place, but in much smaller degree than is usually assumed by the advocates of the formal discipline doctrine. Memory power in general, for instance, may possibly be acquired, but skill in manipulating that power, or applying it *in toto* to a specific situation, in all likelihood does not exist. Training is specific, and Professor Thorndike points out that the amount of transfer from one field to another depends on the number of *identical* elements in the two fields or in the methods of procedure. Memory power developed in the study of Latin, for instance, may be transferred to the study of history, but the effectiveness of the transfer will depend upon the number of common elements in the fields of Latin and history studied and of the identical elements in the methods of attack. The number of identical elements in the fields of Latin and Roman history, for instance, is probably greater than in the fields of Greek and trigonometry.
· ·

In British Columbia, probably to as great an extent as in any other of the Western Provinces, the doctrine of formal discipline has influenced, either consciously or unconsciously, the aca-

demic and professional side of the educational system. This doctrine has largely determined the basis for curriculum construction, and specified its limitations. New subjects of study have been added in spite of its influence and in opposition to the formal disciplinarians, whether among the teachers or laity, who are inclined to attack the inclusion of such subjects as domestic science or manual training in the same category with the time honoured classics or mathematics. The influence of this doctrine is also evident among large numbers of the ratepayers who regard education chiefly as learning out of a book. If the teacher drills incessantly on the formal parts of grammar and arithmetic or the facts of history and geography, he is, in their opinion, a good teacher. It is also to this doctrine of formal discipline that the reactionaries and conservatives in educational thought chiefly appeal as a buttress of their conservatism.
· ·

While...there is practical unanimity as to the general aim of education–to enable the child to take his place as an efficient participant in the duties and activities of life–there is a tendency to disregard Rousseau's admonition enunciated by this great visionary nearly two centuries ago and emphasized in its modern setting by present-day educators. The child should be taught, as a child, in terms of the life about him, in which he is an active and interested participant, and not merely as an adult for a future life. Education should take account of present as well as of deferred values. The greatest exponent of modern sociological theory underlying rational school practice is probably Professor John Dewey, whose viewpoint...should be constantly kept in the foreground. Education is life, not a mere preparation for life consisting in the memorization of facts and principles and the mastery of a

formal curriculum. Furthermore, life is real
throughout and no artificial distinctions between
the so-called preparation period of childhood
and the alleged realization period of adult life
should be set up. Many academic schools with
their traditional curricula and formal methods
of instruction have consistently ignored the
admonitions of such educational philosophers
as Rousseau, Dewey, and others, with the result
that failure is written across the record of their
activities....

VII

The Progress of Educational Reform 1920-1960

The one-room school
at Ochre River,
Manitoba, in 1946.

By 1920 the pattern of Canadian educational reform was emerging. Together, lay groups and professional educators had developed the rationale and were beginning to create the structure of a New Education that would greatly expand the purposes and scope of the nineteenth-century school. At the secondary level, vocational schools and technical departments were recommended as alternatives to the traditional academic, university-oriented program. In the elementary schools, "practical" subjects and child-centred methods were prescribed so that the school might relate more closely to the economic and social lives of its students. Agricultural subjects and the consolidation of rural school sections were advanced as means of enabling the country schools to serve better the needs of rural people. In some provinces the leaving age was raised and compulsory education laws passed to ensure that schools would have more time to fulfil their social and economic purposes. Meanwhile, all these developments were embraced by a new pedagogy that made them not only economically or socially desirable, but educationally valid as well.

Stating the ideals of the New Education was one thing; implementing them proved to be quite another. As the demands for educational reform came from both the society at large and the educational profession, so too did the forces of opposition. In the ranks of the schoolmen a persistent conservative tradition endured that rejected many of the service functions of the New Education and cherished instead the intellectual ideals of the academic school. Many spokesmen of the conservative tradition were influential and articulate, and their criticisms of the direction of educational reform were felt at all levels of schooling.

But the major obstacle to educational reform was a succession of adverse economic circumstances. The period of unprecedented prosperity that came in with the new century ended shortly after World War I. In the previous twenty-five years, the era of the New Education, school expenditures had increased nearly 900 per cent, but in the decade after 1920 the rate of increase declined sharply. There were several reasons for this levelling off. The 1920s were years of uneven economic growth; moreover, the prosperity of the decade was not generally shared throughout the country, but was largely confined to central Canada. At the same time, public education was forced to compete for tax dollars with new provincial and municipal responsibilities, like highways and public welfare, which were also becoming very expensive items.

If the 1920s were marred by broken economic growth, the Depression of the 1930s brought real hardship to many regions of the country. In the first three years of the decade about one third of the labour force was thrown out of work, and farm revenue was cut in half. As the money supply dried up, the schools were among the first public institutions to suffer. Provincial expenditure on education declined, and by the end of the decade the local municipalities were paying over three quarters of the total cost of public schooling. Where local authorities had to rely on bankrupt farmers for the bulk of their property taxes, the effect on the schools was nothing short of disastrous.

The worst of the Depression was over when World War II began, but then, understandably, the war effort was the country's first priority. Not until the return of peace and prosperity in the late forties and early fifties was there public money available to finance expensive changes in the school systems. Still, conditions did not favour large-scale reform. Much money had to be spent to repay the educational debts incurred over the two previous decades. Moreover, in the 1950s education budgets were strained to provide merely the basic school facilities for the burgeoning post-war population. The school crises of the 1950s were brought on by the lack of buildings and teachers, not conflicts over the means and ends of education. The most notable educational feature of the decade was probably the portable classroom.

The progress of educational reform was only slowed, not stopped. After all, the conditions that gave rise to the New Education persisted throughout the century. The schools did have to accept broader social and economic responsibilities, and they did have to accommodate the needs of an increasingly heterogeneous student population. And although economic adversity tended to weaken lay support for expensive educational change, these were years when many schoolmen, particularly those in the West, were optimistic about the potentiality of the reformed school as an agency of social progress. Thus the period was one of dynamic compromise between the forces of school reform (as defined by the New Education) and the various forces that opposed its implementation.

Railway school car, Northern Ontario, 1926.

A. Obstacles to Reform: The Conservative Tradition

When confronted with the question "What are the school's educational responsibilities and how can they be best achieved?" not all schoolmen answered in the terms of the New Education. Because the reformers had staked out the ground of the New Education as their own, those who opposed its main premises were known as conservatives. Although these conservatives were in the tradition of the "old" education, they should not be dismissed as merely an anachronistic obstruction to the cause of educational progress. Indeed, many were as dissatisfied with the soul-destroying, Gradgrind type of schooling as any reformer. But the conservatives were also dissatisfied with the New Education's methods of correcting the situation, and, in response to the question of the ultimate purposes of education, looked for guidance to another familiar but more distant star–the ideal of a Liberal Education.

The fundamental issue dividing reformers and conservatives was the location of the "real" world. To the New Educator, it was outside the school; to the conservative, however, the real world was not to be found in the transient social and economic arrangements of the hour. Rather, it was to be discovered in that enduring part of the culture that resided in the content of the traditional academic subjects–the Arts and Sciences of a liberal education. Thus, the boundaries separating the school from the hurly-burly of everyday life should be distinct; indeed, the whole purpose of the school was to impart a specialized kind of knowledge and discipline unlikely to be gained elsewhere. The reformers tended to view the world outside the school as its natural ally in the cause of education. The conservatives saw it as something to be overcome, something to be liberated from. Education was not the acquisition of specific skills and behavioral attitudes to meet the changing interests of the child or the immediate needs of society, but the gradual attainment of intellectual power which had its own universal relevance. The ultimate goal of the school, then, was to raise the student beyond his limitations in time and space to a level of awareness at once self-fulfilling and, in the broadest sense, useful. Following logically was the conclusion that the highest products of the schools were the scholars and scientists of the University.

The conservative tradition, because it perpetuated the widely accepted ideals of a liberal education, had many adherents. As the documents in this section show, the conservative attack was not confined to a specific time period, nor was it limited to any one level of public schooling. Conservative spokesmen began to defend their principles when first confronted with the New Education (document A.1), and continued their opposition throughout the century (documents A.2, A.3).

A.1 The Conservative Tradition: The Elementary School

The teacher of the old school looked after the intellectual needs of his pupils for five hours a day, and then the parent, the church, and society at large had their turn at the pupil. To-day an impartial observer would think that the five hours of school was the only period of a child's mental activity, that he remained comatose for the rest of his time–for every one with a teaching mission makes his demand of the child during these five teaching hours. The progressive doctor,

A.1 Source: Agnes Deans Cameron (Victoria, B.C.), "Parent and Teacher", Dominion Educational Association *Proceedings,* 1904, pp. 240-44.

the preacher, the moral reformer, the specialist
of varieties manifold, demand with a "stand and
deliver" insistence that his particular fad shall be
accorded a place, and withal a place of promi-
nence on our already much "enriched" school
programme.
· ·

Long ago the medical men decided that the
welfare of the country demanded that a regular
system of physical training should be introduced
into our public schools. It was done. Then the
W.C.T.U.[1] has succeeded in introducing into
the schools the formal teaching of the effects of
alcohol. A child is now to be kept in the narrow
way of self-restraint by dangling before him a
hob-nailed liver, and by intimidating him with
visions of the tobacco-heart. He trembles and
joins the Band of Hope.

The S.P.C.A. bears down upon us with the
seductive badges of the Bands of Mercy. What
more fitting place than the school-room for
teaching love for the cat on the domestic hearth
and the honest watch-dog in the back yard?
True, these faithful animals belong to the home
rather than the school. But the child can be
taught to entice them with him to the school-
room, and the "adaptable" teacher, the versatile
one, can no doubt use Carlo and the cat not only
to point a moral and adorn a tale for the S.P.C.A.
–she might make a "nature study", perhaps, of
one of them, and give a five minute anatomy
lesson on the other. Reading, writing and arithmetic are old-fashioned. They can wait.

Last year the British Columbia Council
of Women was all agog for domestic science.
When I, opening my eastern windows which look
towards the sun, saw the procession of cooking
stoves and stew pans, carpenters' benches and
jack planes heading for the school-room door,

[1] Women's Christian Temperance Union.

I lifted up a feeble wail for mercy. In this whole
Council of Women I found no friend. I was anath-
ema and ultra-conservative. I was unprogressive
and lazy. Did I not know that cooking was a good
thing, a most necessary thing? And shouldn't the
school course be enriched?

"British Columbia is a new country", says
one superintendent of education, "The children
should be taught agriculture. You see the little
fellows will study all about soils and weeds and
ensilage, and the raising of prize stock and the
rotation of crops; and then they will go home and
round the family table they will let fall crumbs of
knowledge which their fathers will pick up and
afterwards reduce to practice in their daily lives;
and so wisdom and knowledge will increase." This
is actual fact that I am stating. This argument
was used in sober earnest, and the people who
used it had the power, and the subject of agriculture was added to our school course, and the
text books were put into the hands of the children; but, alas, the books had been compiled
for Ontario, and they told of Ontario soils and
warned against Ontario weeds, and, somehow,
neither teacher nor farmer seemed to be able to
adjust them to the longitude of British Columbia,
and so agriculture dropped out of the course.
· ·

You can't open your school-room door for
a breath of fresh air without letting some one
with a mission fall in. In the primary schools the
breastworks are weak, the missionaries of the new
learning have broken in and possess the land–it
is the period there of clay-muddling and dickey-
bird drawing, one-sum-a-week, sweet thoughts,
and spelling acquired incidentally–the Fauntle-
roys mould dachshunds out of mud and the on-
looking parents imbibe the principles of high art:–
"We educate the parents through the children,"
smile the missionaries, "and school-room life

should be one long sweet song."

I suppose I will offend again when I say that I have little sympathy with that school of educators who would remove from a child's path all difficulties and make it ever for him plain sailing. The tendency to sentimentalism in our age is, I know, constantly seeking excuses for not doing unpleasant things. Text books and school journals tell us how to keep our pupils wide awake and interested so that they may need no rules. This may be very pleasant for the time being for all concerned, but there is no discipline in it. There are hard duties in citizenship, and I contend that the habit of always expecting to be pleased and interested while a child, does not help the man or woman to do earnest work in hard places. There can be no discipline unless the child learns to do unpleasant things because they are right.

. . . .

In the Primary Schools arithmetic and spelling have gone by the board; it is unpedagogic now to teach the multiplication table and spelling is to be learned incidentally. In the Grammar Schools we lead a Jekyll and Hyde existence–we strive to teach all the old subjects in the poor remnants of time left us after the innovations have had their will. In my own school ten per cent of each week is given to physical and military drill, another ten per cent is claimed at the Domestic Science and Manual Training Schools–Nature Study nibbles away its precious fraction, while music lessons, Sunday-School entertainments and social duties claim the much distracted pupils at the very stroke of the dismissal hour, and home-lessons are at a discount.

The school-room stands wide open. The teacher and the receptive children within, panting like goldfish for a little air; are they not fair game for the wise men from the East and the West and the North and the South, and the eight and twenty other points of the compass? The truth is the large numbers of children gathered daily into school-rooms form tempting fields easy of access to every hobby horse rider for the introduction of what each considers the sine qua non for reforming the world. One of the most difficult phases of the teacher's profession is the fact that the teacher more than any other worker is at the mercy of theorists. No one gets more gratuitous advice than she does. Every one you meet is willing to tell you how to do your work–they are just bubbling over with recipes of "how to do it". Parsons keep a regular supply of sermons for our use. City editors, when they run short of subjects for the Sunday sermonette, just turn their attention to "these well-paid and certainly not overworked teachers".

. . . .

Now, well do I know that I will be called an obstructionist. I see it coming by more than one determined eye in front of me, so I want clearly to define my position with regard to these Bands of Mercy, Bands of Hope, W.C.T.U.'s and S.P.C.A.'s; this sewing, sawing and swimming, straw-weaving, rope-splicing, wood-splitting, cooking, and tonic sol-fa. Some of them I know to be good in themselves, and the rest may be. But this is not the question which confronts us. Five hours is a period of time with mathematical limitations. You can't crowd something new into it, without crowding something old out. Already the ground work subjects have suffered of necessity. We have "enriched" our course at the expense of thoroughness.

We pretend to teach that which it is an impossibility, equally mental and physical, for us to teach in the limited time at our disposal. I speak not for myself. I would fain be a special pleader for the child; as his delegate, I in all earnestness ask; "Is it not time for some one to cry a halt and let the reasoning faculties draw the breath of life?"

In the school, as elsewhere in this busy world of emulation, of turmoil and competition, we attempt too much–eagerness takes the place of earnestness;–and we are out of touch with the good old-fashioned virtues of thoughtfulness and thoroughness.

A.2 The Conservative Tradition: The High School

I do not apologize for stressing the primary importance of the basic disciplines. The idea that academic subjects are only "college-preparatory" is an insidious libel on our whole educational system. I quote Professor Arthur Bestor of the University of Illinois:

> "Our civilization requires of *every* man and woman a variety of complex skills which rest upon the ability to read, write, and calculate, and upon sound knowledge of science, history...and other fundamental disciplines. Those forms of knowledge are not a mere preparation for more advanced study. They are invaluable in their own right. The student bound for college must have them, of course. But so must the high school student who does not intend to enter college. Indeed, his is the greater loss if the high school fails to give adequate training in these fundamental ways of thinking, for he can scarcely hope to acquire thereafter the intellectual skills of which he has been defrauded."

A.2 Source: Sidney Smith, "Brains Unlimited", Ontario Secondary School Teachers' Federation *Bulletin* (September, 1954), pp. 176-79 (reprinted from *Canadian Education*, June, 1954).

It is a far cry from the ideal of democracy to reserve for those who are going on to further studies the benefits of sound training in languages, mathematics, science, and history, which should be freely given to all who are capable of profiting from it, and which produces citizens who can properly be called educated men and women. A student who has as full a program of academic subjects as he can handle is not likely to be lazy or bored. It is in these subjects that the good student's brain can be really stretched.

This brings me to a more difficult question. We hear of there being so little for the mind. I suggest that perhaps another reason for a bored and lackadaisical attitude among the best of our students is that we offer them so little for the spirit. I do not mean that we should give courses in "How to be a Good Citizen" or in "Constructive Attitudes IIIb." I mean that through history and literature, through the habitual vision of greatness, it is possible to convey something of the sense of service, the spirit of dedication, that has animated the finest and best individuals of every race at every time. Particularly in the study of those times and places when the human spirit has overflowed in great creative activity and great adventure–such as Elizabethan England or fifth-century Athens– there is a contagious enthusiasm for living life in a high key, and the teacher who feels it can transmit–not to all, perhaps, but certainly to the best students–an inspiration, an enjoyment, an intellectual curiosity, and a yearning for excellence that will stand them in good stead for the rest of their lives.

. . . .

I suggest for your consideration some criteria that might indicate whether the best students are getting their fair share of attention. If a school is being judged by its failures only, and if the pressure on that school is to lessen the number of failures, without any reference to the standards that the best students could achieve, then it is likely that the best students will be neglected, because attention will be concentrated on the poor ones....

In the same way, if a teacher is taken to task for the failures to pass, and not for the failures to take high honours, then it is almost inevitable that the best students will be neglected. This emphasis produces the kind of situation mentioned by Dr. Neatby,[1] where students are encouraged to drop the basic courses and switch to soft options in order to "keep up the school average," which is a travesty of liberal education.

If time-tables are drawn up with first consideration for the peripheral options, for physical training, and for such subjects as health and guidance, and if the academic subjects are squeezed in around these as well as they may be, then the best students are being neglected. If time-tables make it difficult or impossible for the good mathematics student to get extra work in problems, or for the good language student to take Greek or German, then the best students are being neglected. It is the responsibility of every administrator to put first things first; and if catering to the best students, in ways such as I have suggested, makes the administration more difficult, the difficulties must be shouldered. The quality of education available to any student must not be vitiated by the convenience of administrators or the vagaries of the school bus.

If the intellectual atmosphere of the school depreciates "booklearning" and pays scant respect to scholarship, the best students are being most culpably neglected, because they are being deprived of the motivation to develop themselves to the utmost of their ability. I repeat what I said

[1] Hilda Neatby, *So Little for the Mind* (Toronto, 1953).

to the Ontario Secondary School Teachers' Federation in February: much current talk about education is frankly anti-intellectual. "Intellect comes to stand for whatever is rigid, utopian, and mean." There is often a suspicion that it is queer and somehow reprehensible to be brilliant. We have all heard academic achievement spoken of in contemptuous terms, and high-ranking students described as "bookworms", "swotters", or "egg-heads". I have known people to say that a second-class honour standing is the best index for success; any student so ill-advised as to take a first in his course must be a maladjusted, impractical genius, who will probably starve in a garret. I have no hesitation in saying that this anti-intellectual attitude...is dangerous, boorish, myopic, and wrong. We need never be ashamed of developing an intellectual elite. We ought rather to be ashamed of failure to challenge and to discipline first-class intellects.

A.3 The Conservative Tradition: The University

Dr. Abraham Flexner's book on Universities[1] is certainly the chief event in the current academic year in North America. For the past two or three months it has been the most discussed book in every University faculty club; and the more of the discussion that one hears the clearer it becomes that the main points in his indictment of North American Universities are sound. Admitting that much good work is done in our Universities, he charges that nevertheless they use up too much of their energies in what is really secondary school training for boys and girls and not University work at all. Further-

[1] *Universities, American, German, English* (New York: Oxford University Press, 1930).

A.3 Source: F. H. Underhill, *Canadian Forum*, II, 127 (April, 1931), pp. 252-54.

more, in their eagerness to adjust themselves to the new needs of new times, they have too easily lost their sense of values. They have tended to become "service stations for the general public," catering to every fleeting transient popular demand. They have allowed themselves to be made the "dumping ground" for all kinds of new faculties and departments, and have prided themselves on their ingenuity in devising all kinds of "*ad hoc*" courses "designed to teach tricks, devices and conventions". "Atomistic training–the provision of endless special courses, instead of a small number of opportunities that are at once deep and broad–is hostile to the development of intellectual grasp".

. . . .

No person...who is reasonably well informed about the inside of our Canadian University world, can read the book without exclaiming at almost every page how true the picture is of Canada. For all the tendencies which Dr. Flexner deplores in American Universities can be found north of the boundary line also. If they have not gone quite so far in Canada the explanation is not our loyalty to high cultural standards, but simply our poverty. We have not had the money to spend on making asses of ourselves to the same extent as have the Americans. But to the best of their financial ability our Canadian academic authorities are steadily pressing in the American direction. We also equip ourselves with schools of Commerce and Journalism. "Ad hocness" is the order of the day. The authorities who control University policy have almost everywhere capitulated to the demand for "Service", and there are few Canadian Universities in which the Director of the Extension department is not a bigger man in the eyes of the President than the most outstanding of his scholars or scientists.

Consider, for example, the University of Toronto. It has long prided itself with justice upon its honour courses in the Arts faculty. It has kept up the standard of these honour courses by a *cloaca maxima* in the form of a pass course into which are poured all the morons whom a state University cannot avoid accepting but who are not fit for honour work. Yet now it is creating a General course between the pass and the honour courses which is designed to supply teachers for the Ontario high schools who will eventually qualify as specialists in the honour course subjects!

...A couple of years ago Toronto barely escaped establishing a pass Commerce course which was to meet the demand of certain Ontario parents that their sons have a natural right to become Bachelors of Commerce whether they can meet the honour requirements or not. The Toronto Extension department is already giving night classes in Advertising, Public Speaking, Secretarial Practice, and Journalism I, II and III. Presumably by the time that the night students have got through this "Journalism III (Advanced)" the University has equipped them to enter the profession and maintain it at the high standard which is exemplified by the four Toronto newspapers. The most recent President's report from Toronto, after surveying the activities of its scientists and scholars, adds this bit of information:–"A good deal of time and attention has been given to university publicity. Articles have been written for magazines and periodicals. Items of information have been provided almost daily to the newspapers of the Dominion. It is probably safe to say that some mention of the University of Toronto appears in the papers every day in the year." How proud a great association of scientists and scholars must be to learn that every day its Extension department is on the job seeing that it gets justifiable publicity!

McGill is not a state University, but there the urge to "Service" is just as strong as at Toronto or elsewhere. On two successive days last February the *Montreal Gazette* announced: (1) that a scheme was under way to have McGill and l'Université de Montréal give popular courses in political economy and legislative work so as to raise the general standard of political intelligence in Quebec–apparently the idea was to purify Quebec politics by sprinkling a little academic rosewater; (2) that McGill, the Board of Trade, and the Civic Industrial Commission were cooperating in a civic survey of Montreal to be directed by some sociological pundit from Oklahoma, the purpose of the survey being "to bring to the fore the value of the city of Montreal as an industrial centre and reveal to leading manufacturers and industrialists the advantages of setting up industrial plants in the metropolis." And not so very long ago McGill advertised through its "Department of Extra-Mural Relations" a course of ten classes in Tap Dancing. "The course begins with the elements of Tap Dancing and proceeds to dances of various types and rhythms… Fee $8.00 ($7.00 for members of the staff of McGill University)." The sociologists will probably need something like that after they get through with their survey.

B. Obstacles to Reform: Economic and Social Conditions

The economic crisis of the Depression focused attention on another difficulty in the way of the New Education–the shortage of funds available to implement reform. Spokesmen for the New Education had long maintained that there was a positive correlation between the amount of money spent on the schools and the quality of education, and in the 1930s it seemed as if the point was incontestable. As documents B.1 and B.2 point out, educational facilities, teacher's salaries, and working conditions all deteriorated after the onset of the Depression. Maintaining any kind of standards, old or new, was difficult in these circumstances. Although the effects of the Depression were felt throughout the country, the schools of some areas were hit harder than others. On the prairies, the troubles of the 1930s were further compounded by the effects of a prolonged and withering drought, which (according to document B.3) was as destructive of the school system as it was of the wheat economy. In Newfoundland, the whole force of the island's prevailing economic conditions and social traditions combined with the effects of the Depression to hinder the establishment of "an efficient educational system" (document B.4). As all four documents make clear, there were great disparities in Canadian education: in this case not along racial or religious lines, but between regions, and between the city and the rural schools within those regions.

The shortage of educational funds did not end with the 1930s. In the next decade, World War II absorbed most of the country's energies and resources, so that there was little of either to spare for the schools. They could wait; winning the war could not. And although educational expenditure in Canada increased sub-

The school stove,
Burgeo, Newfoundland,
1967.

stantially in the 1950s, it failed to keep pace with the rising economy of the post-war years (document B.5). As a percentage of Gross National Product, the total Canadian expenditure on formal education was the same in 1958 as it was in 1931. Moreover, most of the increased funds made available through the accident of affluence were used to provide educational facilities to accommodate the children of the post-war "baby boom". As a result, the most urgent educational concerns of the 1950s had less to do with educational reform than with the very basic problems of finding school buildings and providing classroom teachers (document B.6).

B.I Disparities in Educational Revenue

Canadian educationists are agreed that the first drawback to progressive education in Canada is the small unit system of administration. This small unit consists generally of a section of a township and is known in Ontario as school sections.... The extent to which the system still prevails in Canada is shown by the following table:

	No. of units of Administration (School Boards, Trustees, etc.)	No. of Teachers in Government-controlled General Schools
Prince Edward Island	473	657
Nova Scotia	1719	3659
New Brunswick	1518	2733
Quebec	1859	17526 (Catholic) 2591 (Protestant)
Ontario	6600	20357
Manitoba	1902	4062
Saskatchewan	4923	7285
Alberta	3492	6001
British Columbia	773	3956
Canada	22,659	48,827

B.1 Source: J. W. Noseworthy, "Education–a National Responsibility", *Canadian Forum*, 18 (February 1939), 338-43.

When we consider that there is probably an average of four members per School Board in Canada, it will be seen that almost 100,000 school trustees are needed to supervise the work of fewer than 50,000 teachers.

The second major drawback to progressive education in Canada is our system of financing. Every Province has transferred the responsibility of financing education to the municipalities, while the rural municipality has in turn left the small school section to shoulder the major part of the responsibility. Here again, notwithstanding the revision and extension which our provincial educational systems have undergone since 1867, and the continuously increasing financial demands being made upon municipal and provincial governments, our system remains very much as it did at Confederation. The following table shows how Canadian schools were financed in 1935:

Local taxes	$85,423,110	84.9%
Provincial Grants	13,483,736	13.4%
Dominion Aid	3,145,792	1.7%

The greatest sufferers of this obsolescent system are the children, especially those of rural and impoverished municipalities, and the home-owners. The homeowners, rural and urban, suffer because the percentage of costs borne by local taxes is almost entirely a tax on real property. The system is particularly iniquitous for the rural taxpayer, who is paying by direct taxation for the education of future urban citizens, for it is estimated by the Dominion Bureau of Statistics that 15% of rural raised children become city residents when they reach the age of self-support....

The extent to which the small local areas are required to carry the burden of educational

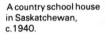

A country school house in Saskatchewan, c.1940.

costs in the province is shown as follows:

Percentage of School Revenue received from:

	(a) Local Taxation	(b) Provincial Government
Prince Edward Island	45.8	54.2
Nova Scotia	83.6	16.4
New Brunswick	82.8	17.2
Ontario	88.6	11.4
Quebec	94.3	5.7
Manitoba	85.3	14.7
Saskatchewan	78.9	21.1
Alberta	84.9	15.1
British Columbia	72.0	28.0

. . . .

Our present system of financing education has not resulted in equalization of educational opportunity, of educational facilities, nor in a fair distribution of the cost of education. The birthright of every child is equal, though not identical, educational opportunity. It is the right of every child to expect the best type of education that the resources of the state can provide, consistent with the need and capacity of the individual as a member of organized society. Education is a most important public function; this is the sole base on which its claim for public support can rest, hence, in every democracy worthy of its name, there should be provided an equality of educational opportunity. What justification can there be for providing at public expense far better educational opportunities for the future citizens of one section of the country than is provided for the citizens of other sections? The only possible limitation of educational opportunities should be those of the individual's ability and tastes, and the educational level which the state desires its citizens to reach. Educational facilities vary so widely in Canada that in certain localities modern, well-equipped, sanitary and progressive schools are found, while not over five miles away are

others where sanitation is neglected, equipment is negligible, and the only salvation of the schools is the industry and faithfulness of the teachers.

There is probably no better index of the inequality of educational opportunity than the amounts per pupil spent by the different provinces. In 1936 these amounts varied as follows:

Receipts of Province-controlled schools, 1936 (or latest year reported)

	Receipts	Average Attendance	Amount Per Pupil
P.E.I.	$ 464,895	13,140	$35.3
N.S.	3,689,909	92,279	39.9
N.B.	2,649,962	71,708	36.9
Que. (1935)	20,735,404	535,082	38.7
Ont. (1935)	40,482,922	600,440	67.4
Man.	6,623,907	115,671	57.2
Sask. (1935)	7,845,354	164,104	47.8
Alta. (1930)	9,551,849	139,155	68.64
B.C.	8,073,435	108,096	74.6

Now we do not suggest that the quality of an educational programme may be measured accurately by its cost, that one hundred dollars spent on a pupil's schooling always produces twice as good an education as fifty dollars, or that seventy-five dollars per pupil spent by one school board will buy a school programme equal in value to the product of the same amount spent by another. Such a thesis could hardly be defended. But it is undeniable that in the long run a community or nation will get about what it pays for in education. If salaries are low and classes large, a poorer type of person enters teaching than if salaries are high and classes small. And it is certain that the children in those provinces which have for years made small expenditures per capita for schools are bound to receive a poorer education than their more fortunate brothers in higher-spending provinces.

The disparity between the educational opportunities afforded the rural school pupil and the urban pupil is illustrated by the following table taken from the "Report of the Minister of Education of Ontario for 1936":

Unequal Education Opportunities:

Public School	Rural	Urban (Cities Only)
Total number of pupils enrolled	186,939	192,479
Total number of teachers	7,244	5,095
Teachers with University Training	54	355
Teachers with Auxiliary Certificates	8	130
Teachers with Manual Training Certificates	2	94
Teachers with Household Science Certificates	2	93
Average Experience of Teachers (years)	6.72	15.73
Average Salary of Male Teachers	$848	$2180
Average Salary of Female Teachers	$710	$1531
Teachers with Salaries under $600	1,687	29
Teachers with Salaries over $2000	48	1,857
Schools with Medical Inspection (%)	7	95
Number leaving School at 14 years	2,871	198

One of the gravest disadvantages of our system is the dearth of secondary schools in rural communities. It has been found almost impossible to provide the small centre with any adequate secondary school facilities beyond those of the narrowest academic type, and that only because the academic school is much less costly to operate than the vocational one. In thousands of instances secondary school work has to be taken care of by the teacher of all the public school grades in the one-room rural school. In all Canada there are only eight day technical schools in municipalities with a population under 5000.

That the task of financing and administering education is proving to be beyond the ability of the area is generally recognized. It seems to be quite evident that many of the Provinces cannot assume much larger share of the cost and at the same time support all the other social services which at present are recognized provincial responsibilities. This was made quite clear to the Rowell Commission when one Province after another deplored its inability to provide adequate educational and other social services on the present basis of taxation.

The increasing cost of provincial services in comparison with those of the Dominion Government is shown by Maxwell[1] to be as follows:

Ordinary Expenditures per capita:			
	1919	1929	1938
Federal	$35.51	$35.06	$33.60
Provincial	9.19	17.70	18.75
Bonded Debt and Treasury Bills per capita:			
Federal	$312.00	$224.00	$261.00
Provincial	37.00	90.00	117.00

In short, the development of the social services has forced the provinces to assume responsibilities which they simply cannot finance, limited as they are to "direct taxation within the province." When the depression burst upon us, they had already spent and borrowed up to the hilt, and many of them were forced to approach the Dominion Government for loans, increased subsidies and assistance in providing unemployment relief. Even with this aid, only one province has been able to finance relief on a pay-as-you-go basis, and still show a surplus of revenue over expenditures.

[1] J. A. Maxwell, *Federal Subsidies to the Provincial Governments of Canada* (Cambridge, Mass., 1937), p. 240.

Moreover, it has become abundantly evident that although the necessity for expenditure on the social services affects all provinces alike, they have very far from equal abilities to pay taxes. The natural consequence is that certain provinces can support without undue strain an adequate programme of services, while others must be taxed to the utmost to provide even a very meagre programme. This inequality is very much aggravated in times of depression, which affect the provinces very unequally.

B.2   Teaching Conditions in the 1930s: More Students, Less Money

A recent survey of unemployment among teachers reveals conditions that are antithetic to the mental well-being of the school-age citizens of Canada. Depressions notwithstanding, an efficient educational system should be the first call upon the public purse, and one must doubt the wisdom of slashing teachers' salaries, of permitting buildings and equipment to fall into disrepair or to become obsolete, or of increasing the numbers of pupils per teacher to such a ratio that scholars receive neither adequate collective or individual attention. Yet conditions of this kind prevail all across the Dominion.

. . . .

Each provincial legislature has statutes governing schools within its borders and in these statutes minimum requirements are specified. Information gathered in this present survey indicates that many of the regulations are honored in the breach, particularly in respect to–(1) ratio of pupils to teacher; (2) hours of work; (3) equipment. There is an indirect admission of lack of enforcement of regulations in the 1934 Survey of Education in Canada. Expenditures of provincial gov-

B.2 Source: "Penny Wise Education", *Canadian Forum*, 17 October, 1937, 232-34.

ernments on education...showed an approximate decline for the period 1932-1934 for the following Provinces: New Brunswick 19%; Manitoba 32%; Saskatchewan 46%; Alberta 13%; British Columbia 37%. These general reductions in expenditures included curtailments for both equipment and upkeep as well as reductions in teachers' salaries. The depressed budgets were felt much more acutely in rural than in urban schools.

The regulations for secondary schools in Ontario state that "in schools with five or more teachers the total number on the roll at any time shall not exceed an average of thirty to each teacher." This average is in many cases greatly exceeded. During recent years the number of students has continued to increase, particularly in the senior grades. For the school year 1936-37 the ratio of scholars to teachers in two Ottawa collegiates was between 36 and 37 to 1. The average throughout Ontario was approximately 34 to 1. Conditions are much worse in Public Schools where the following averages prevail: schools in cities and towns 44 to 1; in villages 42 to 1; in rural districts 32 to 1. The average in Ottawa schools of 35 to 1 implies much better conditions than prevail in many other urban centres. School Boards insist on having well qualified teachers; yet, by over-crowding, do not give the pupils a reasonable opportunity to take advantage of those qualifications. Too large a class prevents any teacher from making a careful study of the individuals of which it is comprised....It is evident from the survey that more teachers and more schools are needed. Here lies the great difficulty: schools grants have decreased considerably during the past six years. Only five secondary schools were built in Ontario between 1930 and 1935 to accommodate an increase of 9,000 pupils. For this number the teaching staff was increased by 227....

Salaries in Ontario were reduced in 1933 and again in 1934. The general level of rural salaries in 1929 for teachers was $1,000. This dropped by November 1934 to somewhere between $450 and $550. In High Schools in 1930 the average salary for men was $2,385 and for women $2,004. By 1935 these salaries had been reduced to $1,723 and $1,632 respectively. The drop in Collegiate salaries between 1930 and 1935 was from $2,890 to $2,565 for men, and from $2,424 to $2,205 for women. Even within the past year Toronto Collegiate teachers were subjected to a temporary reduction of 9%. This reduction did not create the hardship which occurred in Saskatchewan where the urban salaries suffered considerable decrease and rural salaries were reduced to an average of $505. As would be understood many received far less than this while some received only the government grant, reported to be as low as $250. New Brunswick has suffered severe reductions in educational expenditures. The medium salary received in 1934 was $474, while in 1932 it was $691. The Minimum Salaries Act in that province was suspended but was again brought into operation on July 1st, 1934. Similar reductions have taken place all through the Dominion.

. . . .

The financial aspects of the teaching profession are shown in the reductions of net expenditures for education in the various provinces during the period from 1931 to 1934. Expenditures in New Brunswick declined by half a million dollars and those of Manitoba, Saskatchewan, Alberta and British Columbia by about a million dollars each. In consequence, school properties were allowed to fall into disrepair, very limited purchases of new equipment were made, new teaching devices were neglected, and the salaries of teachers, particularly in rural sections, were slashed.

B.3 School Drought: Rural Education on the Prairies, 1936

There are two droughts in the province. With the climatic drought all are familiar; but while sun, wind, and lack of rain desolate the fields, the lack of a modern efficient school system is working a spiritual and aesthetic drought in the lives of Saskatchewan youth.

According to our Constitution, education is no concern of the Dominion Government but rests with the Provincial Government. In reality, the Saskatchewan Government shoves practically the whole burden onto the shoulders of the local authorities–municipal councils and school boards. The Department of Education is chiefly concerned with curricula, inspectors, examinations, and the provision of small money grants to the school boards. The school boards build and maintain schools, hire teachers, and raise locally the greater portion of the money required.

…Thus at present in Saskatchewan we have over 5,000 purchasing and employing agencies, 5,000 paid secretaries, paid auditors, separate bank accounts, 5,000 non-correlating, noncooperating units. The system is now cumbersome and expensive, and many evils are apparent.

The rigors of the last ten years have tried the system. The harshest tests have been applied in Saskatchewan. The consequent rapid and distressing collapse of the system in this province is appalling. The conditions actually prevalent in the majority of our rural schools will scarcely bear the light of investigation–children, undernourished and unhealthy, in dim, cold, poorly ventilated school buildings; teachers, also undernourished, poorly clothed, inadequately trained, overworked, broken in spirit and in health, living

B.3 Source: Craig M. Mooney and J. M. Braithwaite, "School Drought", *Maclean's Magazine,* I November 1937, p. 14.

on a starvation wage; slum schools and beggar teachers.

This is not true of all the schools and all the teachers, nevertheless it accurately describes hundreds of schools and hundreds of teachers–all except those in a few populous urban centres. The grossest inequalities exist.

Where the rains fall, the children are better educated and the teachers better paid than where the rains do not fall.

On tricks of climate and geography depend the child's opportunities.

The greatest indictment of the system is that it permits beautiful, luxurious schools, well equipped and well looked after on the one hand, and slum schools on the other hand, with the latter far outnumbering the former. A province-wide system which permits such an outrageous unbalance is, actually, not a system at all. The following excerpts from letters and reports, available to any parties interested, reveal a shocking state of affairs in the rural and village schools:

(1)   "At present I have been paid $12 on account of salary for this term. I have $11 board to pay. I have no suitable winter clothing such as overshoes, woollen hose, gloves. I have not even a winter coat. Last term I received $38 cash. My board, which the school board had agreed to pay, was left unpaid...During the period from Christmas to June (six months) I received approximately $45 in cash...After teaching three and one-half years, arrears of salary owing me approximate $787. In the spring of 1935 I worked for my board during May and June while teaching a heavy school, and received no salary for April, May and June of that term."

(2)   "At the present time I am in ill health, brought on by deplorable conditions under which

we must work. Our school is an old-timer; the west side of the building contains four windows which are so draughty the window blinds are kept in constant motion by the wind. The school is warmed by an old heater, the grates of which are destroyed. To keep the fire in it, the janitor, an eleven-year-old boy, has placed the lid of a lard pail over the bottom. In cold weather we pull all the seats around the stove and try to study. Some days I have not taken off my outer coat or overshoes all day....I entered the hospital as a patient December 15th, and at the present writing it is doubtful if my doctor will give me permission to return to my school March 1st."

(3)   "My contract calls for a salary of $350 per annum, but I have only been successful in obtaining the grant ($20 a month), out of which I pay $15 per month for board. The school is badly in need of repairs. There are several panes of glass needed. Here we have placed cardboard and paper patches, but these are not adequate in below zero weather....The brick work of the school needs repairing, the floor is extremely cold, and neither teacher nor pupil can do efficient work at a temperature two degrees above freezing. This is not the janitor's fault–the child certainly does his best."

(4)   "About a month ago the school was closed because there was no money to run it. There was no place for me to board, so I was obliged to stay in an empty house belonging to the municipality. I secured a cheque from the municipality for $15, but it was returned by the bank N.S.F. I was recommended by my inspector for my permanent certificate, but the Government would not grant it until my Normal School fee had been paid, nor would they accept school notes as payment. While in the district I had to board in every home

regardless of inconveniences or sickness in the homes at the time. The homeowners received $7 per month relief, and while I boarded with them no extra relief was allowed, although $18 per month was deducted from my salary and applied on their taxes."

B.4 The Effect of Local Conditions on Education: Newfoundland, 1940

The educational system of any country is in a large measure a reflection of its prevailing economic conditions and its social traditions. This is especially true of Newfoundland which because of its geographical isolation has been until recently less subject to external influences upon its life and educational system than the provinces of Canada or the states of the United States.

The basic difficulties in the development of an efficient educational system have been economic and will probably continue to be so indefinitely....the productivity of the Newfoundland economy is relatively low; the government funds available for carrying costly public services, among them education, have, therefore, been severely limited. In addition, the distribution of population in small communities, often completely isolated from one another except by sea, makes for relatively high overhead costs and small operating units in social and educational services. Moreover, the predominance of extractive industries in the economy–fishing, mining, forestry, agriculture–which require manual skill rather than book-learning or technical training, has meant that Newfoundland people have not had the incentives to those forms of education which an industrial society develops. The fishing industry

B.4 Source: R. A. MacKay and S. A. Saunders, "Education", in R. A. MacKay, ed., *Newfoundland, Economic, Diplomatic, and Strategic Studies* (Toronto: Oxford University Press, 1946), pp. 157-63.

especially tends to interfere with continuous schooling, even at the elementary level; older children are useful in many operations in the industry, and there is constant temptation in the fishing season to employ them at the expense of their schooling; the poverty of many fishing families, especially in bad seasons, may prevent the provision of shoes and clothing adequate for severe weather; and under-nourishment may undermine the health of children to the extent of interfering with regular school attendance. Considering economic conditions alone, it is little wonder that education has been an extremely difficult and complicated problem.

...One of the striking features of Newfoundland's educational system is, however, its denominational character. This has a historical explanation for Newfoundland was settled in an era when formal education was regarded generally as a function of the family and the church rather than of the state. The original stock was almost wholly Church of England folk and Roman Catholics, and the churches therefore in the early days of colonization took upon themselves the entire burden of education. It was assumed by both groups that education should at least be supervised by the church and this belief still persists, though more strongly among Roman Catholics. When, in conformity with developments in the outside world, the state began to assume responsibility, it did so by the method of grants-in-aid, as was done in England, rather than by taking over the function of education. The difficulties of Newfoundland in the way of developing institutions of local and municipal government, the fact that in many communities the church has been the only organized social institution and the local clergyman virtually the only person in the community interested in education, the readiness of religious bodies to shoulder the burden of education and the general acceptance among the people of Newfoundland of the principle of denominationalism in education have all tended to maintain the system despite the fact that the burden now being carried by the government is sufficiently important to justify one in regarding education as a government service, though it is not, of course, exclusively so.

....

The opponents of the system maintain that the denominational system tends to increase the number of small schools and that this in turn lessens the effective use of equipment and teaching personnel. Until recent decades the population was fairly well segregated along the coast on a denominational basis, but intermingling of denominations has been increased with the growth of the new industrial towns and other economic changes which have tended to shift population.

B.5 Educational Expenditure in Canada; 1931-1966
This chart presents the total expenditure on formal education and vocational training in relation to major economic indicators.

	Total expenditure as a percentage of			
Year	G.N.P.	National income	Total personal income	Per capita
1931	3.8	5.3	4.9	17
1932	4.3	6.2	5.4	16
1933	4.2	6.2	5.3	14
1934	3.5	5.0	4.4	13
1935	3.2	4.4	4.1	13
1936	3.0	4.2	4.0	13
1937	2.8	3.8	3.6	13
1938	2.9	3.8	3.7	14
1939	2.7	3.6	3.6	14
1940	2.3	3.1	3.2	14
1941	1.9	2.5	2.7	14
1942	1.6	2.0	2.2	14
1943	2.0	2.5	2.7	18
1944	1.5	1.8	1.9	14
1945	1.6	2.0	2.1	16
1946	2.4	3.0	3.0	24
1947	2.7	3.4	3.4	28
1948	2.5	3.1	3.1	29
1949	2.5	3.2	3.2	30
1950	2.6	3.3	3.5	34
1951	2.4	3.1	3.3	37
1952	2.4	3.1	3.1	40
1953	2.5	3.2	3.4	42
1954	2.9	3.7	3.9	47
1955	3.0	3.9	4.1	51
1956	3.0	3.9	4.2	57
1957	3.5	4.5	3.7	66
1958	3.8	4.9	5.0	72
1959	4.1	5.4	5.5	82
1960	4.5	5.9	5.9	91
1961	5.0	6.6	6.6	103
1962	5.6	7.4	7.4	123
1963	5.6	7.4	7.4	129
1964	5.9	8.0	8.0	146
1965	6.4	8.6	8.6	170
1966	7.0	9.3	9.4	202

B.5 Source: Dominion Bureau of Statistics, *Survey of Educational Finance, 1966*, p. 9.

B.6 The Educational Crisis of the 1950s: Providing Teachers

We are short eleven thousand teachers. By 1955 the shortage will exceed twenty-five thousand. In Newfoundland a thousand school-age children remain at home. In the prairies, thousands are taught only by correspondence. To keep the schools open, school boards have hastily recruited an assortment of unqualified men and women. There are at least eleven thousand of these substitutes in classrooms today. Some are immature teen-agers, high-school failures with no teacher training. Others have had a brief six-week "cram" course. "These people are masquerading as teachers," says Dr. M. E. LaZerte, dean emeritus of education, University of Alberta. One sixteen-year-old girl "teacher" in Quebec spent most of her classroom time reading love pulp magazines, while the children amused themselves by playing games or drawing. When her dates interfered with her job she closed the school.

These makeshift teachers have varying titles, but they usually have one thing in common: an inability to give their pupils a good education. A county superintendent near Fredericton, N.B., told me, "In the long run, I think it would be better to shut down the schools entirely." A high-school principal in the Tisdale, Sask., area says, "After a 'study supervisor' has been in charge of an elementary school for a few years you find that none of its graduates go on to high school." "They're not teachers, they're baby sitters," says Tom Parker, of the Nova Scotia Teachers' Union. Half of that province's children are receiving instruction from this type of substandard teacher.

Unqualified old people are sometimes given teaching jobs. An Ontario school employed a

B.6 Source: Sidney Katz, "The Teachers", *Maclean's Magazine,* I March 1953, pp. 9, 54.

man of eighty-seven, whose certificate was dated 1897 and who hadn't taught for thirty years.

The prestige of the teaching profession has further been lowered by the policies of most of our provincial normal schools. These training centres produce elementary-school teachers–about eighty-five percent of our total teaching force. (High-school teachers are college graduates who take an additional one year of special training at a university school of education.) To fill the empty classroom the normal schools have virtually abandoned all attempts at screening prospective teachers. One deputy minister of education told me, "We take everybody. If you haven't got a criminal record and if you haven't been certified by a psychiatrist–you're in." The vice-principal of a normal school in one of the Maritime provinces says, "No questions are asked if a person walks in and says she wants to teach." That was the same school where the nurse described some of the students as having nervous twitches, being emotionally unstable, and being "too shy to look you straight in the face when they had to talk to you."

Academic as well as personal qualifications for admission have been lowered. In the past you needed at least eight senior matriculation subjects to enroll at an Ontario normal school; now you need only five. Only fifty percent of the students at British Columbia Normal School have their complete senior matriculation, which once was insisted upon. Graduation from the normal school is just about as easy as admission. An official of an eastern normal school told me, "I can count on the fingers of one hand the number of students I've flunked in the last five years."

Such slipshod methods have discouraged many good people from becoming teachers. In one of the Maritimes normal schools the average IQ was several points below the scores made by

C. The Extent of Educational Reform

first year university students; some were in the 80s, which would make them "dull normals." In a revealing study in Alberta two groups of students were compared: those taking the one-year course to become elementary-school teachers and those taking the university course to become high-school teachers (bachelor of education degree). Half the one-year students had IQs below that of the weakest bachelor of education candidate. In tests of the one-year student's ability to understand basic principles, generalizations and rules, the average score was only eighteen percent. "Yet this is the field in which they expect to lead others within a year," comments the report. An Alberta normal school instructor told me, "The teachers I'm training are immature. They regard everything I say as sacred. When I say good-morning they write it down in their notebooks." Yet Alberta ranks as one of our most progressive provinces in teacher-training policies.

Ironically, these free-and-easy recruiting measures to boost normal-school enrollments have had the opposite effect. In the past year the number of teachers in training in Manitoba and British Columbia has decreased by one tenth. The New Brunswick Teachers' College had three hundred students in 1938; today it has one hundred and thirty-four. Many educators believe that all this points up an obvious moral: the best type of youngster gravitates toward a profession where the requirements are stiff and challenging. And fewer parents seem to want their children to become teachers. "Don't be a damn fool" was the comment of an Edmonton doctor when his son expressed a desire to teach.

When and in what form did the ideals of the New Education reach the nation's schoolrooms? Because of the regional disparities considered in the previous section, the implementation of educational reform was slow and uneven. For example, one of the basic tenets of the New Education was the necessity of bringing more schooling to more people by extending the age limit of compulsory education. But until the 1940s, two provinces and Newfoundland still lacked provincially administered compulsory attendance laws, and the school-leaving age in most of the other provinces remained at thirteen or fourteen years. On the other hand, it would be a mistake to consider the years between 1920 and 1940 as a period of educational doldrums. Much, for example, was done in the development of adult education and school extension work. Correspondence courses, radio instruction, railway school cars, all began in this period, and all were designed to bring formal instruction to those who, a generation earlier, would have had little or no contact with the school.

The New Education claimed its greatest advances in the elementary school. By the 1930s the various parts of the "new pedagogy" of the early century were refined into a more systematic educational philosophy that became known as "progressivism" (document C.I). With its scientific allusions, its humane concern for the individual, its insistence on relevancy, and its broadly democratic goals, "progressivism" became for many educators a compelling synthesis of what they should be doing in their schools. With the West showing the way, nearly every provincial department of education had revised its elementary program of studies along "progressive" lines before the end of the decade. The main technique of the

New Education in the 1930s was the "activity method", and, depending on the degree to which it was adopted, it succeeded in realizing some of the "progressive" goals (document C.2). Meanwhile, another aspect of educational reform–the concern for Child Study and educational psychology–developed into a widespread interest in mental testing, which, ironically, tended to have the effect of solidifying the rigidities of the traditional school (document C.3). While differing in some respects, both these examples of the New Education had one thing in common: they involved internal and relatively inexpensive changes that could be implemented through the initiative of school-men. Consequently, they entered the school-rooms comparatively early.

At the secondary level, change came more slowly. Not until the mid-fifties was the achievement of one central goal of the New Education–everyone in school to age 16–even approached. Yet enough students were going on to high school to necessitate some alterations. In an effort to accommodate the individual differences of those fifteen- and sixteen-year-olds who tended increasingly to finish their elementary education in the lower grades of the high school, some provinces created intermediate classes or junior high schools (document C.4). Most of the students who continued on to the regular high schools, however, had only two choices–to enter either the traditional academic courses leading to university matriculation, or (thanks to the large federal subsidies in the 1920s) one of several vocational programs. But as the school-leaving age continued its slow ascent bringing more students into the upper grades, it became obvious to many people that a much broader approach to secondary education was required

if the high school were to meet the many needs of its growing student body. In the 1940s and '50s some provinces were responding to rising enrolments by creating the "Composite School" that offered a wide variety of options to its students (document C.5).

To what extent were the reforms of the New Education realized by the 1950s? Document C.6, a review of educational developments in Quebec, illustrates how changes in public (and private) schooling in that province kept pace with industrial and social change–one of the underlying objects of the New Education. Document C.7 surveys the educational scene in 1957, and records the extent to which school consolidation, vocational education facilities, junior high schools, and composite schools were found in the rest of Canada.

C.1   The Philosophy of Progressive Education

The Philosophy Back of Progressive Education

Any adequate educational program must assist the individual child to mature from his initial state of independence to a participation in rich group life, which in a democracy includes full sharing in group living as a responsible member of society. The good life should be made available to all, both privileged and underprivileged, and one aim of a democratic society should be the elimination of an underprivileged state of existence.

Knowledge is acquired in human experience in the process of living in a culture of social groups. Living is the process of interaction between the organism and the environment.

C.1 Source: A.L. Doucette, Faculty of Education, University of Alberta, "Is Alberta Education a Failure? No...", *A.T.A. Magazine*, 23, 3(December, 1947), 8-10.

For the *experimentalist* thinker, ideas are the result of consequences in experience. Ideas, says Kilpatrick,[1] begin in social groups and have their purposes in social groups. Life experience and life expectations are the result of studying how the *human* being behaves in *human* experience.

Such moral behavior as regard for others, tolerance, even the simple experience of "taking turns", grows out of practice and experience. The test of good music is in the hearing of it, and as a result we place our stamp of approval or disapproval on it. Alternatives generally are decided in the light of tested experience. Such decisions represent the habit of weighing our thoughts or of acting thoughtfully. For the *experimentalist*, human values are the result of tested choice.

Let us list some of the principles which the experimentalist holds dear, and which are related to progressive education and to the democratic way of life:

1. Experimentalism stresses the supreme worth of the individual.
2. Experimentalism stands by the golden rule of conduct because it has been found to be practical and the result of tested experience.
3. Experimentalism advocates mutual respect between individuals, cooperation, and an active sharing of responsibility on the part of the individual in his group interaction.
4. Experimentalism stresses the freeing of intelligence and is opposed to the curbing of intelligence by a dictator or by state control.
5. Experimentalism cannot accept absolute values because they are out of the realm of tested experience.

6. Experimentalism accepts goals within experience, such goals being continuously modified by subsequent experience.
7. Experimentalism aims to train for democratic living by educating its members to manage society cooperatively.

Progressive education is a means of implementing the philosophy of experimentalism. Thinking is not limited to the intellectual. The effective use of intelligence applies to all and any phase of life, be it physical, mental, emotional or social.

But thinking must be based on data and this calls for a careful study and interpretation of facts–not the memory of facts, but rather the use of reason in the interpretation of facts. If we wish to evaluate a given social theory, for example, it is necessary to have all the facts before we are in a position to know fully the significance of such a theory. If we lack sufficient evidence, or if we are biased because of prejudice, then we are unable to give a sound judgment. Even after passing judgment on the theory, the latter must stand the pragmatic test of application in experience.

A child growing up in a culture must learn the essential elements of the culture. The function of the school is threefold: (i) it must transmit the culture, (ii) it must maintain the culture, and (iii) it must improve the culture. Our modern culture, based as it is on science and industry, is characterized by rapid change. Our schools, our curricula, and our educational methods must change in order to keep pace with the rapid development in the material, social, and spiritual phases of the culture. If our curriculum and methods are static, then we shall intensify the present cultural lag of our social and spiritual institutions behind our material institutions. The school, as a social institution, must not contribute to this social lag

[1] W. H. Kilpatrick, 1871-1965, Professor of Education, Teachers College Columbia University.

by its own lag in methods and functions. Our material and scientific achievements are far behind our man-to-man and man-to-spirit relations. We have an atom bomb, but we lack the social control to make it serve mankind profitably. We have a newer psychology of child growth and development, but our educational practices lag far behind the findings of organismic psychology, with the result that outmoded methods of faculty training and mental discipline persist in our schools of today.

Those who object to the modern school with its activities of excursions, community study, projects, problem studies, its methods of personality development and character building, are simply not up-to-date because they fail to face the educational issues demanded by a rapidly changing civilization. Our schools must prepare youth for life in a real world and not for life in the past. It is as important a function of the school to train in personality adjustment as it is to train him in abstract mathematics–probably a more important function. The school must accept the responsibility for developing social and moral attitudes, such as a regard for the rights and feelings of others and an acceptance of responsibility for the good of all. Inasmuch as our changing civilization brings ever new and challenging social problems, children must be taught to face issues, to solve problems, and to think about social issues of group living.

Such is the task which progressive educators set for themselves, and surely it is no mean task. Children must learn by living and acting. No one can learn in any other way. Learning is significant to the child if it has meaning to him and if he accepts that meaning. His learnings, his attitudes, his appreciations, his knowledge, his understandings–these build character through group activity and through individual responsibility to the group.

Such is the spirit of the classroom pervading the progressive schools. The curriculum starts where the child is.

Aims of the Progressive School

The progressive school aims to develop the social intelligence of the child in order to assist him to come to grips with the social problems of adult living, provincially, nationally, or internationally. Children should work at current problems and controversial issues in order to develop independent thinking in preparation for citizenship.

Experimentalism and progressive education utilize the scientific method and both are rooted in experience. Learning must be related to living. So, too, character is built up in living. The curriculum must be related to real life.

Experimentalism and progressive education aim at democratic education which should produce responsible, self-directed citizens who are to live in a rapidly changing world. Since such a world will always be a problem-solving world, the progressive educator upholds the experimental method and an experimentally directed curriculum.

The Curriculum

The curriculum should be based on lessons learned from a study of child behavior. The psychology of learning appropriate to progressive education will then be based on maturational growth and development of the child. Teaching procedures will recognize all aspects of the human personality as requiring development, not merely the intellectual skills, but also manual skills, bodily skills, social skills and emotional well-being.

Education

Education is co-extensive with life and includes the countless contacts with people and things in and out of school. Hence the importance of organizing the curriculum in terms of areas of living rather than in terms of rigid subject-planned zones. A progressive curriculum lays emphasis on the maintenance of health, recreation, making a living, getting an education, carrying out civic responsibilities, making a home. The curriculum aims at a broad experience in order to assist the child to later participate in all important phases of living.

C.2   Progressive Education in the Schools: The Activity Method

During the past few years schoolroom practice in the Elementary classes of the Winnipeg Public Schools, in common with that in progressive centres everywhere, has given much attention to projects, activity programmes and similar methods for obtaining results which were formerly obtained by direct drill, by definite teaching and by constant practice.

The tendency in education today is towards greater informality. Natural free expression is encouraged, developed and directed, so that every talent or interest of each child has some opportunity for expression and improvement. The happiness of the child is of paramount importance and any child is happy when interested. It is recognized that with the passing on to the school of the vastly greater part of all child training, the school has become responsible for the building of character and the development of personality in the basic essentials of social living and in the ability to meet life situations.

The teacher of beginning pupils today develops in her pupils a desire to learn to read by interesting them in some project such as the building of a "Health House," the construction of a model of a farm, or the illustration of some simple

C.2 Source: Report of the Superintendent of Winnipeg Schools, in Manitoba, Department of Education, *Report*, 1937-8, pp. 112-14.

story. In this way, concrete conceptions of words and language are built up and the translation of the word concepts to the word symbols is relatively easy because the child is thoroughly interested in the translation.

Practice and drill in reading are obtained by the use of mimeographed sheets giving directions to pupils to do things in which they are interested rather than by assigning a lesson to be read which may be entirely remote from the interests of the children.

. . . .

In the upper grades of the Elementary schools the "activity method" is being used to advantage. For example in the teaching of Geography, "Transportation in Canada" may be the immediate subject of study. In place of simply reading about transportation and reproducing what has been read, orally or in writing, the class undertakes the study as a project. Some of the class will search for information as to transportation during the days of the explorers and fur traders. This will lead to the drawing of maps showing routes taken; the calculation of distances of journeys and the time taken to make them; the making of birch-bark canoes; models of York boats, forts, Red River carts, etc. Another group will take railroad development; another transportation by river, lake, canal, and ocean; still another the development of motor car traffic including construction of highways. Lastly a group will study transportation by air naturally leading to a study of Canada's great mineral resources in the north. In this way the whole class working together will assemble models, maps, pictures and written work of their own which makes the whole study vital and real.

An activity programme of this kind is in itself so fascinating to pupils and teacher alike that a possible danger arises of losing sight of the objective to be reached by means of the activity which from the standpoint of the teacher is not an end in itself but a means to an end. It must always remain the fundamental task of the Elementary schools to provide young people with the tools of learning, proficiency in the use of which is so essential to later learning and to life. There is also a further point that must not be overlooked. Society has not reached and probably will never reach a point at which the individual is able to do only that in which he is interested or only what he would select to do from choice. Life requirements still demand obedience at times to externally imposed authority and one requires to be able to face unpleasant tasks and conquer difficult situations....

. . . .

Notwithstanding, therefore, the allure of activity programmes with their projects and other methods of undoubted value and interest, the Winnipeg Elementary schools are endeavouring to preserve a reasonable balance between the so-called "old" and the so-called "new". While trying to use what is good in the "new", they are not overlooking the "old". While using what is felt to be the best in the activity approach they are demanding the high standard of the past in the basic skills and are still doing what they can in strengthening the fibre of the young people in facing the difficult and in obedience to discipline which may at times run counter to the immediate desires and interests of the pupil.

C.3 Educational Measurement: Scientific Sorting

Much attention has been paid to the problem of the grading and promotion of pupils during the last few years, and rightly since it is intimately connected with questions of school costs, medical treatment, curricula, school plant, etc....the many comments in school surveys on age-grade tables have shown us one side of the problem. Little has been done, however, regarding the correction and, more important still, prevention of this problem.

This problem and its solution is essentially a recognition of individual differences and provision for them, with the necessity of class teaching being taken into account. The many measurements made of performance and intelligence by Courtis, Terman, and a host of others all tend to point out the great range and variety of such differences. The tendency in the past has been to consider differences in class work and in progress made through the grades as due largely to differences in health, attendance, etc., rather than to differences in natural ability.

. . . .

An account of what has been done in one school system might give a better idea of the possibilities of mental measurement follow-up work. The Alexander Taylor school has about 550 pupils in seventeen rooms, Grades I-VIII, and three other small schools, containing in all nine rooms, send nearly all of their pupils to Alexander Taylor at the end of Grade V. It is compulsory to attend school until the age of fifteen years. The course of study and the grading is very much like that of some of the Eastern states. About a third of the

C.3 Source: Charles B. Willis, Principal, Alexander Taylor Public School, Edmonton, Alberta, "The Grading and Promotion of Pupils", *Canadian Journal of Mental Hygiene*, 3, 4(January, 1922), 291-96.

pupils are foreign–Hebrew, Russian, German, and Austrian, mainly....

The follow-up work based on the [results of four years of intelligence testing] consists of: (1) extra promotions for some pupils; (2) retardation or demotion of others; (3) proper placing of new pupils; (4) especial care taken to make sure that, as pupils enter Grade I, and come up through the grades, the condition at present existing will not be repeated.

Many pupils, who were below the grade their mental age would appear to warrant were given extra promotions either by being left only a half-year in each of two successive grades or by being promoted from, for example, Grade VI in June to Grade VIII in September. During the school year 1919-20, seventy-three pupils in the Alexander Taylor school received extra promotions. Only one of these pupils failed of promotion at the end of June, 1920. From September 1, 1920, to March 1, 1921, about eighty-five pupils have been given extra promotions on the basis of intelligence, class work, etc. Of these all but three or four are doing satisfactory work.

Pupils who come in from other schools are placed by taking account of their former standing and their mental level. Some are moved up a grade, others down a grade and still others saved from demotion when they do not appear to be doing satisfactory work but the mental test shows the probability of their soon doing so. A mental level of about 12 years 9 months to 14 years 3 months is considered about right for Grade VIII at the beginning of the school year, September 1; 11 years 9 months to 13 years 3 months for Grade VII etc. Since the test was first used it has been the important or deciding factor in about 110 extra promotions and has been a means of saving about 100 children from demotion or non-promotion. Few mistakes, in fact practically none,

have been made by promoting too rapidly but doubtless many have been made by our being too cautious.

· ·

It must be kept in mind, however, that energy, persistence, regularity of attendance, class work, health, school attitude, etc., are important factors to be considered in grading. Intelligence is probably as important as all the other factors combined, and, since it is practically beyond the influence or control of the teacher and changes relatively little, is more basic. The teacher may overcome defective application on the part of the pupil but can scarcely overcome the handicap of defective mentality. If a pupil is not doing well in class, the reason should be found and proper remedies applied. If poor work is due to a lack of ability and the pupil is really doing as well as he can, he is encouraged and made to feel that he is coming on all right, but if he is found to be bright and lazy, steps are taken to bring about a change. Often the simple statement that he is not doing well, though he is bright and capable of good work and must do better, is sufficient to produce considerable improvement. It is well to remember that few pupils attain at all nearly to the success their mentality would warrant. This, no doubt, accounts for the occasional case where a pupil of average ability does excellent work or a pupil of poor ability does average work.

At present the following are being used as guide lines to aid, not as rules to be slavishly followed. Pupils who have completed Grade VI in June may be promoted to Grade VIII in September: (1) if mental age, September 1, is 14 years 3 months or above and they are in the upper 69% of the class in the June tests; (2) if mental age is 13 years 9 months to 14 years 2 months and they are in the upper 31% of the class; (3) if mental age is 13 years 3 months to 13 years 8 months and they are in the upper 7% of the class.

Grades III, IV, and V are treated similarly except that in Grade VI 12 years 3 months is substituted for 14 years 3 months in Grade VIII, etc., and the six month interval used for Grade VI is cut to 5 months for Grade IV and to 4 months for Grade III.

. . . .

The pupils in a school system should be measured by means of the National Research Group Intelligence tests, published by the World Book Company, Yonkers, New York, as early in September as possible if they have not been tested before. This, together with supervision by means of standard tests, should be the chief function of the superintendent in small cities; in large cities, a special director of measurements and supervision should take care of this work.

Pupils could be given extra promotions, etc., on the basis outlined above or, if the seven, eight, and nine year course of study were in effect, could be placed in the one of these that would, without skipping or failure, allow them to finish Grade VIII at the mental age of 14 years zero months to 15 years zero months. In extreme cases, some skipping or failure might be needed. Careful grading gives more and better education at less cost.

About 5% to 10% of any average class should be held back.

C.4 The New Intermediate Schools

Introduction–Education for Democracy

Many pupils complete their education as citizens in the Intermediate School, and all complete there the period of compulsory school attendance. There is a special connection, therefore,

C.4 Source: Alberta, Department of Education, *Programme of Studies for the Intermediate School* (Grades VII, VIII, IX)…(Edmonton, 1935), pp. 5-9.

between the Programme of the Intermediate School and the subsistence of democracy.

. . . .

Writers on education make a practice of setting forth many aims of education. In reality, there are as many aims of education in any given society as there are patterns of behaviour in that society. Every culture pattern is a legitimate aim of education in some society. Some aims, however, are more important than others at a given stage of the learner's development. Some aims, moreover, are so important at all stages that they cannot safely be left to haphazard or unduly time-consuming modes of learning. Schools were established in the first instance to facilitate the learning of things which must be learned anyway sooner or later, but which can be learned more economically and expeditiously through the specialized procedures of formal instruction than in any other way. In pioneer days it was the main funtion of schools to inculcate the three R's, because this was the only educative function that could not be performed equally well by other social institutions such as the home and the church. Through the change from a simple agrarian to a complex industrialized economy, the pattern of society and social relationships has become exceedingly intricate, with the result that the schools are now called upon to do many other things than merely to train for literacy. The schools of today have been compelled through economic and social developments to take over, in a large measure, the educative functions of other social institutions. Schools now provide a social environment for the learner in which he must react to social situations. The learner develops his capacities as an individual. He also acquires, through the attitudes and relationships induced by social behaviour, a personality that reaches out and enfolds society. The learner is part of society, and society becomes part of the learner.

. . . .

In general, one may say that the following educational trends of the present day will be found in the up-to-date school programme:

1. A broad perspective in education, with recognition not only of knowledge, but also of skills, habits, appreciations, attitudes and ideals as valid objectives. Training for literacy is not enough. The traditional view that education is book-learning still prevails, however, in socially backward communities.
2. A reaction against the mechanized routine of formal instruction, with the consequent adoption of project or enterprise procedures, and the substitution of pupil for teacher activity.
3. Recognition in the programme of training for personal and social efficiency, emotional control, and integration of personality.
4. General acceptance of the principle that the purpose of education is fundamentally social, and that an understanding of the social environment is quite as necessary as an understanding of the physical environment.
5. Belief in the ideals of democracy, and in the possibility of maintaining them through education.

The General Aim of the Intermediate School
The Intermediate School is a school for pupils of the "between ages"–pupils from eleven to fifteen years of age. It offers a distinctive programme of studies and activities specially suited to pupils who have attained the status of early adolescence. Like the elementary school, it represents an attempt to adjust the school programme and environment to the needs of an age group. Like the high school, it offers a programme of liberal-cultured studies, but with the difference that its programme is not primarily concerned with preparation for advanced academic instruction.

It is a difficult matter for most adolescents to make a wise choice from the adult occupations. Some will later go to the farm; some will go into the trades, some into business; some will find clerical or civil service positions; and some will enter the professions. But the intermediate school cannot segregate these groups. It must offer a sound "core" of instruction that is of value to all pupils, and, by way of enriching the programme, make provision for individual interests and aptitudes through elective and more or less exploratory courses. The intermediate school must be a preparatory school for pupils who will proceed to the high school; but at the same time it must serve as a "finishing school" for pupils who, for one reason or another, are unable to advance beyond Grade IX.

Many pupils who have no aptitude for academic training drop out of Grade VII or VIII with a sense of inadequacy and failure, when they could still profit from further education if it were of a kind suited to their needs. It is the proper function of the intermediate school to offer a programme that will appeal to all pupils of the adolescent group; a programme that is complete in itself and valuable in its own right, without regard to preparation for the high school; a programme that will, in effect, enable pupils who leave school to do so with a sense of accomplishment.

The intermediate school must accept responsibility for completing the education of many young citizens. It should, therefore, inculcate loyalty to the democratic ideal, and exemplify in its programme, procedures and government, the value and efficacy of that ideal. It should continue the programme, begun in the elementary school, of teaching the pupil how to examine both sides of a question, how and where to find facts, and how to use the evidence of authorities in reaching a conclusion. It should preserve and foster the spirit of personal freedom, evoked in the elementary school by the enterprise procedure.

C.5   The New High Schools

How can we get high schools which will educate everybody, or at least the majority of our citizens?

Fortunately we have come a long way towards achieving the first of two steps in the solution of the problem. We have high school accommodation for nearly everybody now.

The growth of the high school is the most notable educational achievement of the present century. Observe the gain in secondary school enrolment over a forty-year period in Ontario, the most populous province of Canada. In a period during which the population increased by roughly 60%, and elementary school enrolment by less than 20%, secondary school enrolment increased nearly 500%. If all factors were taken into account—including post-elementary classes in the public schools—the proportion of the population who received some secondary education would be found to be three times as great in 1940 as it was when the century began. For the whole of English-speaking Canada it would be close to the truth to say that in 1900 about one person in five went on to high school, whereas about three persons in five do so now.

As far as the provision of schools is concerned, we have therefore a record of which we

C.5 Source: C. E. Phillips, *New Schools for Democracy*, Behind the Headlines, Vol. 4, No. 6, published jointly by the Canadian Association for Adult Education and the Canadian Institute of International Affairs, 1944.

may be proud. True, there remains the problem of establishing high schools in the less populous rural sections of Canada; but although it is a big problem …it will be solved in the period of post-war reconstruction. Even then, however–even when rural children have the same advantages in secondary schools that city children have now –even if there are literally high schools for everybody and if everybody is made to attend them– we will not have reached the millennium.

Secondary education used to be a monopoly of the privileged few in the aristocratic type of society which prevailed a hundred or more years ago. These few were being prepared to assume positions of leadership, and they were given a distinctive type of education which marked them off from the common people....This secondary, or "higher class", education was of the type required for admission to university–consisting then exclusively of classical languages and mathematics, and now including modern languages, science, and history as well. It is the type of distinctive education–distinctive in the sense of being removed from the lives of ordinary people–that the great majority of our high schools continue to offer. And that in spite of the fact that high schools are now attended by the general public, and in spite of the fact that not one high school student in ten has any real intention of proceeding to university.

During the present century an attempt has been made to remedy this condition by providing boys and girls in urban centres with schools of an entirely different type. These are the vocational schools–commercial, technical, and, in a few cases, agricultural–which train pupils for particular jobs. Since we live in a world where making a living and getting money are matters of great concern to young people, attendance in these schools has increased tremendously and will undoubtedly continue to increase after the war. To refer again to Ontario, we find that nearly one-third of all high school pupils are enrolled in vocational courses.

But strange as it may appear, even these schools fail to hold the interest of a great many boys and girls, with the result that a great many drop out before completing a three or four years' course of training. Indeed, statistics for Ontario show that the vocational schools are even less successful than the academic schools in retaining their pupils. In 1940 there were in Ontario only 2/3 as many children enrolled in Grade XI in academic secondary schools as in Grade IX, and only 3/5 as many in Grade XI in vocational schools as in Grade IX.

Of course one reason that so many pupils leave the vocational schools before completing their course is that they have more than their share of boys and girls who are simply filling in time until they have reached the age (16 in Ontario) when the law permits them to leave school. But the very fact that many parents and teachers send these restless pupils into vocational schools shows a popular belief that vocational training is something less than a complete education and suitable for pupils of inferior ability.

Hence the plan we now follow of retaining the academic type of secondary education for some pupils and providing vocational training for other pupils has the effect of dividing young people into sheep and goats. It is a carry-over from the old aristocratic idea that only a few need be educated for leadership, while the many are given a training which fits them to be merely workers in society.

. . . .

Of course the vocational schools do offer so-called cultural subjects in addition to voca-tional training–but the focus of the pupils' attention is on the job for which he is preparing. Similarly the academic schools do offer some education of a practical nature, but most of what the pupil studies has little bearing on his life in the twentieth century....

Such are the schools we have.

So far we have fixed our attention on the faults of two different types of school. It is time now to recognize that each type has its own distinctive merits. If we can discover the merits of each and combine them, without the faults, in a single programme for one new type of school, we shall have gone a long way towards the solution of the problem.

The merit of the vocational school is its contact with reality–its concern for at least one important aspect of life in the world today. This fact needs no enlargement.

The merit of the academic school is more difficult to explain, but educationally no less vital. The old way of putting it was to say that an academic education trains the mind. Actually this is, or should be, the truth. But this worthy purpose has been defeated by superstitious faith in discredited formulae and insistence on the use of antiquated curriculum content, so that many people today laugh the very idea to scorn. It is therefore essential to clear the grounds by renouncing any such notion as that the school study of Latin, or French, or algebra, or geometry necessarily enables young people to think more clearly when they are faced with the problems of life, and similarly to reject the corresponding notion that an education without these particular subjects necessarily fails to educate in this sense. But it is true that intellectual content can be presented in such a way as to broaden a young person's interests and accustom him to thinking in important fields left untouched by the technical skills and narrowly practical knowledge of vocational training.

The school we need …is a school for making people. Like the vocational school it will offer a programme related to the needs of today–but to broad needs of people as individuals and citizens, and not merely as workers. Like the academic school, it will aim at teaching to think–but it will do this successfully by using any and every means for its purpose instead of limiting itself to the traditional content of traditional subjects. Unlike either of these schools it will be a many-sided institution offering a well-rounded education adapted to the needs of all pupils. It will not turn out sheep or goats because there will be no fanatical insistence on either a completely academic or preponderantly vocational curriculum. It will be able to produce educated persons because it will not be hampered by having to teach unwanted subject matter and being compelled to forego desirable types of guidance and instruction for lack of time.

It will be a composite school.

That this type of school is not merely a dream may be seen by announced plans for revision of the high school programme in some provinces and by current discussion of the problem. Partly for the sake of brevity, we must limit examples to Western Canada.

In Manitoba, a Committee on Articulation of High School and University has recommended a "scheme of studies for general adoption in high schools, in the hope that it may serve the needs of *all* classes of students, whether proceeding to business, home life, agriculture, or industry, or to further studies in technical and vocational schools, Normal School, or University."

This plan provides for a broad core of general education with a wide choice of other subjects and activities, including both the academic and the vocational. Moreover the plan puts less stress on subject matter requirements by adding one year to the course without increasing the content to be taught, and provides more time for activities designed to produce healthy young people with broad and keen interests. The committee which made these recommendations has the confidence of educational authorities, and there is every reason to expect that the proposals will be adopted.

In Saskatchewan, curriculum revision committees are now at work to bring the high school courses of study more into line with modern educational trends and especially to relate the work of the school more intimately with the environment. In Regina the Collegiate Institute Board has advocated the transformation of two academic high schools into composite schools and the building of a third composite school.

In Alberta it was decided seven years ago to offer only one form of high school diploma regardless of the nature of the studies pursued by the high school pupil, and indeed to prevent any pupil from limiting his studies to the strictly academic field. Obvious difficulties arose in the attempt to provide a broad and varied high school programme in small schools with one or two teachers. There is much support for the plan of providing fairly large composite high schools for all pupils with transportation facilities or dormitories to make this possible. The proposed new programme of studies, like that of Manitoba, would add one year to the length of the course without increasing proportionately the time to be spent on traditional subjects.

In British Columbia, fewer high school pupils than formerly are being compelled by circumstances and tradition to study a purely academic, or university entrance, course. "In some high schools not more than 40% of the pupils take the course for entrance to university. The reason for this is that the high school courses leading to High School Graduation attract a great number of pupils, and the High School Graduation Diploma, which requires the same number of credits as the University Entrance Certificate, is coming to be regarded as the full equivalent of University Entrance."[1]

This last quotation calls attention to a major difficulty in freeing the high school from its present shackles–the difficulty of persuading the public to recognize the value of high school graduation without the particular subjects needed for matriculation, or university entrance.

[1]Letter from the Superintendent of Education for British Columbia, June, 1944.

C.6 Educational Reform in Quebec in the 1950s

Louis Hémon, who died and was buried in this province in 1913, wrote in *Maria Chapdelaine:* "Nothing changes in the province of Quebec." That well-known saying of his has been repeated over and over again and even now it lingers in the memories of many people. But it is no longer true. If he were to come back he would be the very first to deny it, for the very face and soul of Quebec have been undergoing a great change during the past twenty years. Quebec is no longer a typical farming country; only 27 per cent of its people are living in the country, there are only about 100,000 farmers, and 73 per cent of the people live in cities. The buggy is a thing of the past; the horse and cart have become a rare oddity in country villages, and the people who drive a horse to church on Sunday in the country are stared at. More than 800,000 cars are now tearing down the roads of the province; there were only 200,000 a few years ago. An important

C.6 Source: Maurice Lebel, "Recent Reform in Education in Quebec", *Canadian Education* 3, iii (June, 1958), 35-43.

industrial and social revolution, bloodless and silent, is taking place in Quebec. According to experts in demography there will be 8,000,000 people by 1980, and only 21 per cent of them will be living in farming and rural districts.

The latest reforms in the field of education form part of the general changes that are going on in Quebec. Far from being indifferent to the industrial and social transformation, they are parallel to it, so to speak, they go hand in hand with it. Quebec is taking on a new look even in the field of education. Let us look at its most recent reforms at the different levels of education.

· ·

Compulsory education was accepted without a dissenting vote. With free and compulsory education taken for granted, school attendance is higher than ever before until the age of 14 and very strong pressure is applied nowadays to influence parents to keep their children free of charge at school as far as and including Grade XII.

· ·

One of the boldest reforms in education ever made by the present provincial government was to streamline our secondary school system, that is to say, to do away with…importation from France, to abolish the so-called superior elementary schools and replace them by public secondary schools, free of charge. As you know, there are in Quebec today 64 *collèges classiques*, 54 for boys and 10 for girls, all privately owned by the clergy and expensive to attend. These schools are frequented by some 27,000 pupils who study eight consecutive years, roughly between the ages of 12 and 20, pursuing a program of studies based mainly on languages and literatures, history and geography, science and mathematics, philosophy and psychology; these institutions, being independent of government control, prepare the sons and daughters of well-to-do people for the university. As a matter of fact, 99 per cent of those who successfully complete the eight-year course enter the university.

As a result of the reform of the public secondary school system... both public schools and classical colleges are now preparing students for the university....Enrolment in Science Faculties has increased tremendously of late, whereas enrolment in Law and Medicine does not show any remarkable increase. Last year, for the first time in Canadian history, it was from the University of Montreal that the largest number of chemists graduated. But it is only by 1960 that the full effect of this generalized public secondary school reform will be seen in our universities. The provincial Government no doubt had this in view when plans were laid for the new gigantic Faculty of Science which has just been built at the University of Montreal; according to observers and experts, this new building is the largest and best equipped of its kind in Canada today.

...More science and mathematics are being taught than ever before in [the *collèges classiques*] and in some of them intensive courses in science and mathematics are being given to first-class boys by university professors outside regular class hours. The library–these *collèges classiques* have remarkably well-stocked libraries, and I have visited almost of them–is becoming the nuclear centre of these institutions. Practically all of them are also proud of their theatres and if the theatre is so popular in Quebec these days this is due, to a very large extent, to the lead given about twenty-five years ago by these College theatres, like Saint-Laurent, Joliette, and St.-Mary's, which have helped to discover theatrical talent and to encourage public taste for good plays. The same remark applies to music, for most of the *collèges classiques* have good

concert rooms and orchestras and pupils may take advanced lessons in music, if they wish. The present popularity and revival of music is due, to a large extent, to these institutions.

· ·

If you want to see Quebec's most striking innovations in the field of education, you have to keep an eye on the specialized government schools, which now number 54. It is there that the most fundamental revolution has been taking place during the last twenty years; it is there that one may find the source of the new look Quebec's educational system is assuming. Today 15,000 students are attending these arts and crafts institutions, some of which, *L'Ecole du Meuble* of Montreal, for example, and the School of Graphic Arts, are already quite famous. Their influence is even now being felt on the labour market, in trade unions, in mines, and in industry. Our Conservatory of Music and Dramatic Art has also been completely reformed and is now producing artists and actors good enough to play and sing in Paris and London, Berlin and Moscow.

The three well-known agricultural institutes of Quebec, Macdonald College, Oka Institute, and Ste-Anne-de-la-Pocatière Faculty of Agriculture have also been undergoing tremendous changes during the last twenty years. Scientific research has been so active and successful there that even the Russians are deeply interested in the data. Quite a number of government experts from England, France, Belgium, Australia, Switzerland, Germany have been coming to Quebec lately to examine, among many other things, how the Quebec farmers are tackling and solving problems of erosion and drainage. How is it that so many farms have been cultivated with success for three centuries? That is only one of the questions that have been raised. There are many others which are treated by specialists. And the three colleges I have just mentioned, which are all government-subsidized, have drastically reformed their teaching practice and re-oriented research on very definite lines, the result of which is to be seen today. There is also one field in which less spectacular achievements have been recorded; it is in the growing number and attendance of the so-called intermediate or middle agricultural schools, with their countless winter evening courses, all given by university lecturers; they have done a lot of good to improve the tilling and enriching of the land, to modernize the general methods of farmers who are not too prone to change, to perfect their bookkeeping system and to keep them well-informed about market conditions. The government, besides sending a weekly newspaper and a monthly review to the young farmers attending these intermediate agricultural schools, gives several weekly radio talks to the younger generation on farming, botany, market prices, etc. These form a part of its program of adult education.

· ·

As regards regional or central schools, a good many reforms are afoot at the moment to extend them as much as possible throughout the province; it is a vast and complex undertaking, but quite a number of central schools are already open, thanks to the improvement and the clearing of public roads in the winter season. There is less isolation for the teachers and, as a result, teaching standards have been raised in the country especially.

At the university level a good many vital reforms have been introduced. I shall mention only those which seem to me most far-reaching. First of all, entrance requirements have been broadened in such a way that Grade XII pupils are now allowed to enter certain departments or

faculties, such as civil and electrical engineering, forestry engineering, commerce, but they are not accepted yet in law, medicine, pharmacy, dentistry, philosophy or letters. But students taking a B.A. with Latin only may enter law or medicine today. That reform is only about five years old. A good many evening extension courses have also been organized, mainly at the university of Montreal, with the result that thousands of people are flocking to them in order to obtain a degree after years of study; there is nothing of this sort at Laval University, partly because there is no demand for such courses since the population in the area is not so dense as in Montreal, and partly because Laval University does not want to undertake more than it can do. On the other hand, the evening modern language courses at Laval are extremely popular; about 350 students are taking them this year.

C.7 The Extent of Reform: Canadian Educational Institutions, 1957

Although there are variations from province to province, and within provinces, the usual pattern of education is an eleven- to thirteen-grade system of elementary and high schools, one- to three-year courses in trade schools and technical institutes at the secondary level …and universities offering three-year and longer courses in the arts and sciences and the professions. Agencies of adult education, both formal and informal, provide short- and long-term programs of study.

· ·

Newfoundland.–Newfoundland might be said to have a public denominational school system. The Deputy Minister is assisted by four Superintendents of Education, one for each of

C.7 Source: Dominion Bureau of Statistics, *Canada Year Book, 1957-58* (Ottawa, 1958), pp. 344-49.

the four main religious denominations–Anglican, Roman Catholic, Salvation Army and United Church. The Minister of Education, the Deputy Minister and the four Superintendents form a Council of Education which makes educational policy and co-ordinates the various parts of the system. One curriculum serves the schools of all denominations and teachers receive common training in the Memorial University of Newfoundland, a provincial institution.

Each denomination builds and maintains its own schools, with financial assistance from the Provincial Government. The salaries of almost all teachers are paid directly by the Province according to a provincial scale. Until recently no provision had been made for local taxation, but in 1954 legislation was passed which provided that any area might be declared taxable for school purposes. By 1955 only one area had been so declared.

Some children are admitted to school at the age of five in what is called a "pre-grade 1" class. Elementary education includes grades 1 to 8 and secondary education grades 9 to 11. Most schools teach both elementary and secondary grades. The high school curriculum is academic, leading to university entrance after grade 11. In some schools in St. John's, grade 12 studies are offered (they follow the Nova Scotia grade 12 program of studies and the pupils write Nova Scotia examinations) and a post-grade 11 commercial course is taught. An active school building program in the Province includes, for the first time, regional high schools. Few private schools are operated in Newfoundland.

Trade training is offered in the St. John's Vocational Training Institute. A provincial university to which is affiliated a theological college (Queen's) is located in St. John's. The Division of Adult Education of the Department of Educa-tion sponsors programs in both urban and rural centres.

Prince Edward Island.–Except in Charlottetown and the incorporated towns, the school boards are the only local governing authorities, and therefore collect the school tax. Teachers' salaries are provided by the Provincial Government, supplemented by the local school board.

Kindergarten classes are available in a few urban schools. The elementary school curriculum comprises grades 1 to 8 and high school grades are 9 to 12, grade 12 being the junior matriculation grade. The majority of the Island's schools are of one room and it is common for rural schools to teach grades 1 to 10, with grades 11 and 12 available in the larger centres. One junior high school has been established recently. There are a few private Roman Catholic schools in the Province.

Trade training is given in the Provincial Vocational Schools and two private business colleges provide commercial courses. The Government operates the Prince of Wales College and Normal School in Charlottetown, offering junior college and teacher-training courses, and both high school and university programs are available at St. Dunstan's College (Roman Catholic). A Director of Adult Education on the staff of the Department of Education organizes programs throughout the Province.

Nova Scotia.–The public school curriculum of Nova Scotia is in three divisions: elementary school (primary grade and grades 1 to 6), junior high school (grades 7 to 9) and senior high school (grades 10 to 12). The junior matriculation level is reached at the end of grade 11 and the senior matriculation level at the end of grade 12. Senior high schools provide commercial courses as well as a general academic course.

In recent years, numbers of rural and regional high schools, commonly offering grades 7 to 12, have been created to provide secondary school facilities outside the urban centres. The number of pupils studying by correspondence, though a relatively small proportion of the total, has increased in recent years because of the shortage of qualified teachers. There are about a score of private elementary and secondary schools in the Province, almost all of them Roman Catholic.

Vocational training is provided under the auspices of the Department of Education in two county vocational high schools, in evening vocational classes in more than 40 centres, by correspondence courses, and in eight coal-mining schools, a land survey school, a marine navigation school, a marine engineering school, and a college of art. The Department of Labour operates three Canadian Vocational Training Centres. The Nova Scotia College of Agriculture, operated under the Department of Agriculture, gives short courses in agriculture. Fisheries schools are operated by the Department of Trade and Industry. In 1955 there were seven private business colleges and nine private correspondence schools registered under the Trade Schools Regulations Act, which is administered by the Department of Education.

With the assistance of the Adult Education Division of the Department of Education, there is a province-wide program for adults which includes folk schools, evening classes, short courses and cultural services, with special emphasis on economic development. A number of the universities offer extension services.

New Brunswick.–New Brunswick has a 12-grade public school system: elementary school (grades 1 to 8) and high school (grades 9 to 12). Grade 12 is the junior matriculation grade. In two urban high schools a thirteenth grade is taught which follows the program of studies of the first-year course at the University of New Brunswick, whose examinations the pupils write. There are somewhat fewer than twenty private academic schools in the Province, most of them Roman Catholic.

In recent years facilities for secondary education have been increased by the construction of regional and rural high schools. In many of these and in urban composite high schools, there are several choices of curricula–academic, commercial, industrial, home economics and agriculture.

Vocational education is provided also in two vocational schools, in the New Brunswick Technical Institute at Moncton, in evening classes in many centres, in the Maritime Forest Ranger School, in four agricultural schools (two operated by the Department of Agriculture and two by the Department of Education), and in private business colleges of which there are about half a dozen.

Quebec.–In Quebec, education is represented in the provincial Cabinet by the Provincial Secretary rather than by a Minister of Education. Public elementary and secondary schools are controlled by a Council of Education, which is made up of two committees–one supervising Catholic education and the other supervising Protestant education. The Department of Education is headed by a Superintendent and two Deputy Ministers–one for Catholic and the other for Protestant schools–and Catholic and Protestant school systems exist side by side, each relatively independent of the other.

Private or independent schools play a much more prominent role in Quebec than in other provinces. Chief among these are the classical colleges, which number nearly a hundred. Affiliated to the French-language universities (Laval, Montreal and Sherbrooke), they offer an eight-year course, entered after completion of elementary school and leading in two four-year stages, secondary and college, to the baccalaureate degree.

The French public school curriculum was recently revised to the English pattern. In other words, a seven-year elementary school and a four- or five-year secondary school was substituted for a three-stage primary school (elementary, 1 to 7; complementary, 8 and 9; superior, 10 to 12). A classical course has also been introduced in the public secondary school, equivalent to the first four years of the classical college curriculum. The junior matriculation level in both Catholic and Protestant schools is at the end of the eleventh year.

Public vocational education is highly developed in Quebec, chiefly under the Department of Social Welfare and Youth which operates a network of arts and trades schools, technical schools, and institutes.

. . . .

Ontario.–Ontario has a thirteen-grade public school program, the junior matriculation level being reached at the end of grade 12, and senior matriculation at the end of grade 13. Commonly, elementary schools comprise grades 1 to 8, but some teach up to grade 10 and many have kindergarten classes (for four-year-olds) and kindergarten-primary classes (for five-year-olds). Secondary schools include grades 9 to 13, offering several curricula: general (academic), art, commercial, home economics and industrial.

Elementary schools under control of the Department of Education may be public or separate, all but three of the latter being Roman Catholic. A considerable number of the Roman Catholic separate schools in French-language

communities are bilingual and are staffed by teachers trained in both French and English. Secondary schools under departmental control are all public and are of five main types: collegiate institutes, high schools, continuation schools, vocational schools and composite schools....

Most vocational education at the secondary level is provided in the public secondary schools, although there is a Provincial Institute of Trades (in Toronto), and there are two agricultural schools under the Department of Agriculture, many private business colleges and a number of private trade schools. The Department of Education also operates four technical institutes with most courses at the post-secondary level.

. . . .

Manitoba.–The curriculum of Manitoba's public schools is organized in three stages: elementary (kindergarten and grades 1 to 6), junior high school (grades 7 to 9) and senior high school (grades 10 to 12). The junior matriculation level is reached at the end of grade 11, and the senior at the end of grade 12. In the larger centres there are schools of these three types while in rural areas most or all of the grades are often taught in one school. There has been little consolidation in Manitoba and many small schools still exist.

In the city of Winnipeg one of the eight senior high schools is vocational. There are composite high schools in other centres, and vocational as well as academic courses are available in a number of schools. No provision is made for separate schools in the public system but there are private or parochial schools which are inspected by officials of the Department of Education.

In addition to the vocational courses provided in the senior high schools, the Department of Education operates a trade school (Manitoba

Technical Institute) in Winnipeg, and the Department of Agriculture has an Agriculture and Home-making School in Brandon.

. . . .

Saskatchewan.–The Saskatchewan school curriculum is divided into two stages: elementary (kindergarten and grade 1 to 8) and high school (grades 9 to 12). The senior matriculation level is at the end of grade 12 and there is no leaving certificate awarded at the junior matriculation level (end of grade 11). Both public and separate (chiefly Roman Catholic) schools are under the control of the provincial Department of Education which also inspects all private elementary and most private secondary schools.

Three technical schools and an increasing number of composite high schools are included in the provincial system. A Canadian Vocational Training centre is located in Saskatoon. A government correspondence school serves a growing number of students, offering courses at all grade levels and in vocational subjects. Consolidation of school districts is proceeding in Saskatchewan but there are still many small rural schools in operation. Special attention was given to the problems of rural schooling by a provincial Royal Commission on Agriculture and Rural Life whose report on *Rural Education* was published in 1956.

Alberta.–Like Saskatchewan, Alberta has a 12-grade system ending at the senior matriculation level, and divided into public and separate schools, with, in addition, departmental inspection of private schools. The curriculum is divided into three stages: elementary school (grades 1 to 6), junior high school (grades 7 to 9) and senior high school (grades 10 to 12). Because of crowding in the schools there has been no kindergarten in the public system since 1954, but private kindergartens do operate.

A major project was completed in 1954 when the Coterminus Boundary Commission submitted its final report. For most of the settled parts of the Province, the Commission's work resulted in identical boundaries for rural school and municipal administrative areas. Centralization of school facilities has been a significant aspect of school administration in recent years, resulting in improved facilities, better qualified teachers and greater retention of pupils in high school grades.

Vocational education is provided in public high schools, many of them of the composite type; in the Provincial Institute of Technology and Art at Calgary; at three Canadian Vocational Training centres–one for trade training, one for nursing aide training and one for commercial training; at three agricultural and home economics schools operated by the Department of Agriculture; and in private trade schools and business colleges.

British Columbia.–The basic divisions in the public school system of British Columbia are: elementary school (kindergarten and grades 1 to 6), junior high school (grades 7 to 9) and senior high school (grades 10 to 13). There are, however, several combination patterns, e.g., elementary-junior high school, elementary-senior high school, junior-senior high school. The junior matriculation level is reached at the end of grade 12 and the senior matriculation level at the end of grade 13. No provision is made for the public support of separate schools but there are private schools in the Province serving minority groups. Consolidation of schools has progressed far in British Columbia.

Public vocational schools include the Vancouver Technical School, Vocational Institute and the Vancouver School of Art, all at the secondary level, two provincial trade schools and a number of private schools and business colleges.

VIII

Educational Change In the Sixties

The problems that absorbed the energies of the schoolmen in the 1960s were, in part, inherited from the fifties. The baby boom, which had flooded the elementary schools in the previous decade, threatened to inundate the secondary schools and the universities in the next. In several provinces, immigration and urbanization aggravated the situation and put extreme pressure on city and suburban school systems. Post-war prosperity, moreover, enabled more parents to keep their children in school longer. Enrolments soared at the college and secondary levels not only because of raw population growth, but because the percentage of the age group staying in school increased yearly.

The enrolment explosion alone would have caused a massive expansion of the educational system. But the sixties were also characterized by a host of new demands. For years reform-minded schoolmen had argued for a more extended secondary education for all, for better facilities for rural schools, for wider opportunities at the post-secondary level, and for more extensive pedagogical change than had yet taken place. On some issues they had been ignored by both government and public; on others, change had been slow or half-hearted. But in the sixties, the enthusiasm for change spread beyond the professionals to the society at large. A growing number of Canadians were convinced that Canada, along with the rest of the western world, was entering a new age characterized by rapid change, a highly developed technology, and a new commitment to democracy and social justice. The demands of the new era, its prophets proclaimed, would reshape our political and economic institutions. If the schools and colleges were to meet the needs of the new society, they too would have to change.

In earlier decades, swift and substantive educational reform had not been possible because of financial difficulties. In the sixties, this obstacle was removed. Since the end of World War II Canadians had enjoyed a nearly uninterrupted period of rapid economic growth. Rising national and personal wealth made it possible for the public to underwrite the costs of the educational changes that newspapers, intellectuals, politicians, and schoolmen all claimed were necessary.

This triple combination–the enrolment explosion, the host of new demands, and the availability of financial resources–was to lead to a renewed outbreak of the education mania and to alter substantially the shape of public education in Canada.

Fully extended
classroom area,
William Davis Public
School.

A. The Pressures for Change

What kinds of educational change were necessary to meet the needs of a new society? That question was discussed throughout the country, but nowhere did it meet with a more comprehensive response than in the new Quebec, emerging from the early years of the quiet revolution. And nowhere was the relationship between social and educational change delineated more clearly than in that monument to the quiet revolution, the Parent Report on education in Quebec. According to Parent, Quebec, in fact, all of Canada, was experiencing an "educational crisis" brought about by the impact of science, technology, and the new ideas abroad in the world. A new urban society was taking shape and it demanded a new kind of education. Change was particularly necessary in two broad areas: education must be democratized, and the system must provide better technical and professional training (document A.I).

These two themes dominated educational discussion during the sixties. The Parent commission, for example, was not alone in its call for the democratization of education. Journalists and sociologists–most notably, John Porter in a series of influential articles and in his book *The Vertical Mosaic*–attacked the inequalities of the educational system: the monopolization of the universities by the middle class, the odds against working-class children staying in secondary school, the regional disparities, and the gap between rural and urban school systems. Porter and others also contended that the very definition of equality of opportunity must be changed. It was no longer good enough to allow only the able or the well-off to remain in school beyond the compulsory age limit; all children must now be given the opportunity to continue their school-

ing to develop fully their interests and capacities. Arguments like these became familiar parts of policy statements, commissions of inquiry, scholarly articles, and popular journalism (document A.2).

The economic demands of the new society were of no less concern. From the late 1950s a growing number of Canadians contended that the schools and colleges were not producing the professional and technical skills needed by the new industrial state. Closely allied to this argument was the case made by a number of economists that education created wealth and should, therefore, be viewed not merely as a form of private consumption that brought economic advantage to the individual, but as a form of public investment that would stimulate national economic growth. No group put these arguments before the public more forcefully or more insistently than the Economic Council of Canada in its annual reviews of the economic needs of the country (document A.3).

A.1 Social Change and the Necessity of Educational Reform

The Scientific and Technological Revolution

During the last hundred years, science has made greater progress than in the preceding thousand. Human knowledge has advanced prodigiously on all fronts–biology, physics, the social and natural sciences, pure mathematics and the practical application of all of these. Scientific thought has been transformed and is continuing to change more rapidly. Laboratories and research centres at once vie and cooperate with

A.1 Source: *Report of the Royal Commission of Inquiry on Education in the Province of Quebec* (Parent Commission), vol. I (Quebec, 1963), pp. 60-63, 68-69, 71-72.

each other. It has been asserted–an assertion beyond the realm of proof–that the total sum of knowledge doubles in every decade. Anyone glancing through the scientific periodicals in a university library can testify to the vast number of research projects carried out each year in the various sciences. Discoveries, given concrete form in technical innovations, are put to use in industry, business and daily life. The technological era ahead of us will extend even further and deeper this empire of techniques and science over individual and social life. Modern civilization is committed to an evolution beyond anything hitherto known to man.

. . . .

In Quebec, the two World Wars stimulated new, industrial developments and accelerated existing ones. This movement has been closely linked both with scientific and technological advances and with social and intellectual ferment. Industrialization, which had begun at the end of the nineteenth century, became more widespread and diversified. Extension of the means of transportation and of hydro-electric power accompanied that of the various industries–textiles, pulp and paper, aluminum, chemical products. Employment increased and became more specialized; the traditional trades, in which an artisan, by himself alone, fashioned a finished product, were fragmented into the series of simple, repetitive tasks required by mass production. The craft as an entity was broken into a multitude of unitary bits of work. Moreover, agriculture now employs less than 15 per cent of the able-bodied population. The absolute figure for the agricultural population has likewise declined, since the mechanization of the farm has increased productivity and reduced the number of workers needed for farming. Over the last seventy-five years, the industrial revolution has multiplied jobs. It has

also acted as a brake on emigration to the United States which, at the end of the nineteenth and the beginning of the twentieth centuries, resulted from over-population in the rural areas. Today, of a farmer's four sons, only one remains on the land; the others turn to industry and the city.

. . . .

. . . a major result of advanced industrialization is the rapid increase of tertiary employments, by definition non-manual. This field includes the liberal professions, service occupations, office work, sales promotion, travel and transportation, etc. Economists point out that any country which becomes industrialized first experiences a lowering of agricultural employment and a consequent rise in industrial jobs. Once the latter have reached a stable level, the number of tertiary occupations soars. Economists and students of population trends foresee that before long, agriculture will require at most 5 to 10 per cent, industrial work 10 to 15 per cent, whereas most of the labour force, perhaps 70 to 80 per cent, will be engaged in tertiary occupations. The economic development of the Province of Quebec seems to follow this trend. Primary employment is decreasing; secondary jobs remain fairly stable; tertiary occupations are rapidly multiplying. This applies to society in general, and it applies within the factory. Here mechanization and automation require an increase in managerial staff; operational planning, the organization of work, auxiliary production services (buying, selling, forecasting, etc.) calling for greater numbers of specialists and technicians. At the same time, contemporary social life, more widespread comfort, the general extension of education, increased leisure time, broadened interest in culture and the arts have all vastly expanded existing tertiary employments and have created others. It is asserted that 25 per cent of today's school children, when they become adults, will be engaged in occupations now unknown. Today many people work in occupations that were unknown or of very minor importance, fifty years ago, such as employment dependent upon the automobile, cinema, radio, commercial aviation, television, electronics. Moreover the development of these industries has created a wide variety of new types of employment such as: mechanics, chauffeurs, technicians of all kinds, announcers, producers and a host of others. During this same period, many professions and activities, either wholly new, or now separated from older professionals, have come into existence. Among these, to name only a few, are economists, demographers, anthropologists, sociologists, personnel directors, public relations advisers, attorneys specializing in automotive, aviation or fiscal law, plastic or aesthetic surgeons.

. . . .

Ideas in Evolution

Parallel with these basic changes in living conditions, is a marked evolution in thinking. This evolution has been hastened, especially during the last thirty years, by a rapid succession of major events: the great depression, the Second World War, the cold war, the spread of communism, the division of the world into two blocs, the political independence of former colonies, the evolution of African and Asian countries, the development of nuclear arms and guided missiles. the emergence of television and space exploration, all of which have deeply upset traditional ideas.

This upheaval has put the western democracies rudely to the test. It cost the world so much to overthrow the totalitarian dictatorships that the spirit and institutions of democracy have acquired for all people a greater value than ever before. The consequent splitting of the world into two power groups has forced the West to understand the requirements of democracy, which are that the majority of citizens interest themselves in the common welfare and that they are free actively to participate in achieving it. The need to make institutions more democratic in this sense extends to other agencies than those of the State alone. It has become manifest in semi-public organizations as well as in some purely private fields. A good example is to be found in the fact that the faculty and even the student body wish to share in the management and administration of universities, and that teachers want to assist in the formulation of programmes of study. Thus there is gradually taking place a renewal of the "democratic spirit", that spirit based on respect for the rights of the human person, on the tolerance necessary for any dialogue between men, and on the concern all should have for the common good.

. . . .

As far as the State is concerned, expectations and demands become increasingly urgent. The welfare state has replaced the "police state" of the last century. It has been made to assume responsibilities which until now have rested with private initiative, simply because it is obvious that the State alone has the powers needed to apply adequately broad solutions. It alone is in a position to meet those requirements of social and distributive justice of which the modern conscience is so keenly aware. Of course safeguards must be set up against such possible abuses as the over-dependence of the individual and excesses of authority. Yet competition with the communist countries on the political, scientific and economic levels will lead to the harsh necessity for effective action in all these fields. Concerted effort will be of the essence and in this the State must play a preponderant role.

Education and Modern Society

This, then, is the context and frame of reference within which the educational system must be reassessed. During the last century, the philosophy and practice of education were radically changed by the establishment of public school systems. Now the educational revolution, at once the result and the mainspring of social development, is reflected in popular attitudes, in government policy, and in the content of curricula.

A.2 The Democratization of Education

There has been considerable expansion in Canadian education in the first half of this century. Elementary education is virtually universal. Secondary school enrolment has increased from below 5 per cent of the school enrolment in 1900, to more than 23 per cent in 1950. The duration of the pupil's school career was about eight years in 1911. In 1941 it was ten years. These data show that more opportunity is being provided for Canadians to obtain an education.

However, there is evidence that the educable potential of the country is not being adequately tapped at the level of both the secondary school and the university. The picture of the drop-out rate in Canadian schools and, by implication, their holding power has been adequately presented in recent years. J. D. Barrington Brown, President and Manager of the Polymer Corporation, presented the following data to the National Conference on Engineering, Scientific and Technical Manpower sponsored by A. V. Roe, Canada Ltd., in September 1956:

Of a sample of 10,000 children entering grade one,

(1)   some 3,200 are lost by time for entrance

A.2 Source: G. W. Bancroft, "Some Sociological Considerations on Education in Canada", *Canadian Education and Research Digest*, vol. 4, no. 1 (March, 1964), 26-28, 32.

into grade eight (in short, one third drop out in public school);

(2)   another 1,500 fail to reach grade nine;

(3)   less than half the remaining 5,300 achieve junior matriculation;

(4)   only a little over 1,000 graduate to become potential university material.

Thus two interesting pictures confront the student of Canadian education. On the one hand there is the encouraging picture of the marked expansion in education; on the other, the picture, which gives rise to grave concern, of an educational system whose capacity to provide for and retain the student is below a reassuring level. How can they be reconciled?

It would appear that while educational opportunity, as assessed in terms of conditions obtaining in 1900, has been expanding rapidly, a concurrent social and economic expansion has been taking place. Apparently the two lines of expansion have been diverging with that of educational opportunity losing ground. This adds up to serious limitation, in terms of present day demands, of educational opportunity commensurate with the educable potential of the community–a state of affairs in which, presumably, it is the average citizen who is most seriously affected. "Education for the average citizen," write researchers in the Education Division of the Dominion Bureau of Statistics, "has shown an increase; nevertheless, the education of the average person could still be raised considerably."

The term "average citizen" needs clarification. In the writer's opinion, the average citizen must be thought of in terms of such factors as his socio-economic origin, his present socio-economic status and the degree of mobility which he has experienced.

Socio-economic origin is usually determined by means of father's occupation. Some sugges-

tion of the part played by the occupation of a student's father with respect to attaining a certain level of education is contained in the following data on student mortality in Canada, presented in 1950 by the Canadian Research Committee on Practical Education:
(a) the percentage of students leaving school early in their academic career ranges from six percent in the professional group to forty-nine percent in the unskilled labour class;
(b) as far as both the early and the late leavers are concerned, the professional group loses 23 percent of its potential, the unskilled labour group 80 percent.

The above mentioned figures relate to boys only. Figures for girls show the same pattern. The findings were based on a national sample of roughly 19,000 graduates of the public school system. Thus the conclusion can be drawn: that the child in the lower occupational or socio-economic bracket suffers as far as attaining a certain level of education is concerned. This conclusion is further supported by the fact that while lack of interest was the greatest single reason for this mortality, such factors as inadequacy of family income and need to assist financially at home loomed large in the list of reasons given for leaving school.

The lack of educational opportunity may be deplored on the ground that it denies the child an opportunity for self-realization, that is, for developing to the full his potential as a human being. The following statement by Gardner Murphy shows a connection between self-realization and the process of education:

"The realization of human potentialities lies in studying the directions in which human needs may be guided, with equal attention to the learn-

ing powers of the individual and the feasible directions of cultural evolution."

The problem of self-realization is basically psychological, thus one for the psychologist to solve. However, there are vast sociological implications too. On two of these this paper will comment, namely (a) what educational opportunity–provided or denied–means for the structure of Canadian society and (b) what it means as far as coming to grips with the technological expansion of the country is concerned.

To place the problem of educational opportunity–or its lack–in its proper relationship with the structure of society, one needs to determine first what precisely the structure of society in Canada is like. Such determining focusses on questions of (a) social class–a concept which, as Christina McCall Newman writes, is "repugnant to Canadians"–(b) social or, more precisely, socio-economic mobility and, by extension, (c) the truly democratic nature of our society; for, central to the problem of democracy is the issue of equality of opportunity. The equality of *educational* opportunity is a most, if not *the* most, important strand in equality of opportunity.

. . . .

The eternal triangle in education is who shall be educated, how, and why? Educational history recounts the progress from the concept of education for the few to the democratic doctrine of education for all. Experiments in psychology have shown that education must be conducted in terms of the abilities and aptitudes of the child. Philosophically, a harmonization is needed between the demands of society on the one hand and the self-realization of the individual on the other.

Confronted with these questions each society attempts to discover answers that are true for its period and set of circumstances. Canadian educational thought would not deny to any citizen the right of a full education. Canadian educational practice must demonstrate how successfully this aim is being achieved.

A.3 Education for Economic Growth

The Supply of Highly Skilled Manpower in Canada

In Canada, as elsewhere, the impact of rising educational and skill requirements is having profound effects on the composition of the labour force. It is apparent that highly educated workers have not only created work for themselves, but also for many other workers with lesser training …the occupational groups which are increasing their share of total employment are also those in which a relatively large proportion of the workers have advanced formal education. In contrast, the occupations requiring the lowest levels of formal education are declining.

The supply of highly skilled and professional manpower will undoubtedly be a critical factor in the achievement of our economic goals in the years ahead. During our consultations with industrial firms, shortages of specialized scientific and technical manpower were often cited as an obstacle to undertaking more extensive research activities to develop and produce new industrial products. Some companies reported that the supply of engineers was a limiting factor in their present and future capital expenditure programmes. Many of these companies expected that the

A.3 Source: Economic Council of Canada, *First Annual Review: Economic Goals for Canada to 1970* (Ottawa, 1964), pp. 162-68, 181, 203.

problems of obtaining adequate numbers of highly skilled staff would become even more acute in the years ahead.

As a geographic neighbour and industrial competitor of the United States, the world's most advanced industrial country, and as an exporter of almost half of the goods which we produce, Canada has an especially urgent need to maintain adequate levels of business and technical skills. However, we are at present much less well equipped than the United States in this important area. For example, in employment outside educational institutions, Canada in 1961 had, in relative terms, approximately 40 per cent fewer scientists and engineers….

Although the number of university and college degrees granted annually in Canada has more than doubled since 1955, there has been little, if any, improvement relative to the United States….Canada added one worker to her civilian labour force for every six added in the United States, but her universities produced only one bachelor's degree for every 20 granted in the United States. The gap was much wider at the postgraduate level: for example, Canadian universities produced only one doctoral degree for every 33 granted in the United States.

. . . .

The Key Role of Immigration

Since the Second World War, the high demand for professional, technical and other highly skilled manpower in Canada has been met to a significant degree by immigration from overseas. Between 1953 and 1963, for example, slightly more than 80,000 professional and highly skilled technical workers entered Canada from outside North America. The largest portion of these workers, accounting for approximately three fifths of the total, were British. Moreover, although total overseas immigration has fluctuated widely from year to year, professional workers have been accounting for a rising share of the annual inflow.

Coincidental with the great inflow of high-level manpower from overseas, a large and growing number of professional workers have been leaving Canada each year to take up work in the United States. This increasing flow southward has been part of a substantial growth in total annual emigration to the United States and has been three to four times greater than the numbers of professional workers moving in the reverse direction. It appears, however, that the proportion which professional workers represent of total emigration to the United States has not changed appreciably during the post-war period. On the other hand, a remarkable shift has occurred in the composition of immigration from the United States, with workers in professional categories rising fairly steadily as a share of the total. Consequently, in 1963 professional workers represented approximately 40 per cent of all workers entering Canada from the United States, but only about 23 per cent of the much larger number moving in the reverse direction.

The net result of all these migration patterns has been to increase the stock of highly trained manpower in Canada and to improve the quality of the nation's labour force.

. . . .

The Outlook for the Future

Much of the recent public discussion of Canada's so-called "brain drain" has focused solely on the rate of departures to the United States and thereby ignored the very considerable numbers of highly skilled workers which Canada has received from other countries. However, it is far from certain that this pattern of a net "brain *gain*" can be maintained in the years ahead.

For one thing, it is estimated that the demands for highly skilled and professional workers in the United States will continue to grow faster than the demand for labour as a whole and possibly faster than domestic sources of supply. In these circumstances, the United States market for such workers is expected to be tight and therefore relatively attractive to Canadians. At the same time, the new and rapidly rising demands for highly skilled workers in European and other countries will make it increasingly difficult for Canada to continue to draw upon these sources on the same scale as in the past. In the United Kingdom, for example, the Robbins Committee on Higher Education has recommended that the proportion of the working population who have completed full-time higher education be nearly doubled by 1980....

. . . .

Occupational Mobility

There is an urgent need for greater occupational mobility and for improved education, training and re-training of both new entrants to, and existing members of, the labour force. This is particularly necessary in a continually and rapidly changing environment. The magnitude of these tasks has been greatly increased by the fact that many young people entering the labour force have not had either sufficient basic education or technical training to meet advancing industrial requirements. The fact that there are serious deficiencies in the existing labour force makes it all the more necessary to accelerate educational and training programmes.

. . . .

Rapid technological advance and economic change will require a high degree of adaptability over the whole range of skilled and professional manpower. Our educational and training system must both reflect and contribute to rapid adjust-

B. The Expansion of the System

ments to change which are an essential feature of dynamic industrial growth. In this context, we need greater attention to, and greater resources for, retraining programmes of all kinds–for production workers as well as for professional and managerial personnel. This is an important issue requiring the concern of management and labour, as well as public authorities. Under conditions of dynamic industrial growth in the future, there will be diminishing opportunities for employment for those who have little education and are unskilled. There will undoubtedly also be advancing levels of minimum educational requirements for many occupations and jobs. *It is vitally important that general education and training should be given a very high priority in our economic system.*

The arguments for democratization and for economic development both began from the assumption that Canadians were ill-educated, and both propounded the same remedy: more and better education for all Canadian children. The case was accepted by the public, and the result was a revolution in the structure of secondary and post-secondary education.

For fifty years "secondary education for all" meant in fact that all children would attend high school for two or three years. The senior grades were marked by massive drop-out rates as those children not intending to go on to post-secondary education left school and joined the work force. In the late fifties and early sixties, however, drop-outs ceased to be accepted as a natural phenomenon and became a "problem" posing a threat to the well-being of the nation. They were reputed to be ill-prepared for the world of work and more likely to become unemployed. They dropped out, the argument continued, because the schools failed to meet their interests and their needs. In the name of both democratization and economic growth, nearly every province reviewed and modified its high school program in order to provide a complete secondary education for all its children. A typical example of this process of revision and the reason for it is provided in document B.1 the reorganized plan introduced in Saskatchewan in the mid-sixties.

A complete secondary education for all, however, was no longer considered enough. For both economic and social reasons, far more people had to have access to post-secondary education. And for the first time in this country, education beyond high school was not equated primarily with the universities;

Canadians increasingly turned to the junior or community college as an alternative form of post-secondary education. Some of the arguments used to justify the creation of these institutions can be found in document B.2.

Perhaps the most revolutionary institutional change during the sixties took place in Quebec. The traditional dominance of the classical college over collegiate education was broken and a new kind of institution created to prepare students who had completed their secondary education for entry into the universities, the professions, and many technical vocations (document B.3).

The universities, too, experienced rapid growth. Old institutions doubled and tripled their numbers, expanded their graduate programs and their professional schools; new institutions sprang full-blown from the pocketbooks of provincial governments. Once again it needs to be emphasized that expansion was not merely a response to population growth. As the Macdonald Report on higher education in British Columbia demonstrates, it was also a response to what men believed were the economic and social imperatives of the new age (document B.4).

The Macdonald Report, however, points to an even more significant development in post-secondary education. Less concerned with particular institutions than with the development of a "system" of higher education, Macdonald proposed to create a public body responsible for planning and developing such a system throughout the province. During the sixties nearly every province moved in this direction. At first, governments acted cautiously, for it was unfamiliar territory, and academics, suspicious of any extension of government power in university affairs, responded

with alarm. Yet by the end of the decade the relationship between governments and universities had changed decisively–a change stated most laconically and starkly by the Wright Commission on higher education in Ontario (document B.5). Like the elementary schools of the 1830s and 1840s, the universities of the 1960s had come to be seen as too important to be left independent of public control and they became, in effect, part of the tertiary sector of the public system of education.

One other important structural change took place in the sixties. Arguments in favour of school consolidation had been in the air for decades. In several provinces, substantial progress had been made. In others, the typical school remained the one-room, all-grade, elementary school; the typical administrative unit, the school section trustee board. The renewed determination in the sixties to eliminate regional disparities led every province to complete its program of consolidation of both schools and school boards. Document B.6 describes the benefits of such consolidation and the progress made in several Canadian provinces during the decade.

B.1 The Reorganization of the High School Program

As employment opportunities today are few for individuals with low educational standings, the importance of bolstering the educational program for students who plan to go directly to employment becomes exceedingly important. From the 1961 census data the Dominion Bureau of Statistics has revealed that only sixty-six per

B.1 Source: *A Plan for the Reorganization of Instruction in Saskatchewan Schools*. (Saskatchewan Department of Education), October 1963, pp. 4-5.

cent of students beginning grade two enter grade eleven, only half of the sixty-six per cent eventually complete grade eleven, and less than half of these enter grade twelve. This situation is steadily improving due in part to improvements in the school system itself, but also to the scarcity of jobs for unskilled youth, which has a tendency to keep youth in school. Early drop-outs present the greatest single problem in developing a highly competent total work force. They fill the ranks of the unemployed and seldom have a sufficient educational base for specialized training in trade and technical schools.

The answer appears to be in devising a vocational program for secondary school students which is realistic in terms of the types of work available to them when they have completed their training. This indicates the need for a wider variety of courses in the business and service fields in addition to the trades and industrial crafts in which training has been concentrated heretofore.

The secondary vocational program will be designed to accommodate four groups of trainees:

1. Those who wish to prepare for entry into the institute of technology to become qualified technicians.
2. Those who wish to enter employment in the trades or other occupations directly from school, or through apprenticeship, or through further specialized training at a higher vocational school.
3. Those who wish to enter employment in business or distributive occupations or who wish more advanced training in these fields.
4. Those who are destined to leave school early and wish shorter terminal courses.

For all students except those in group 4, the vocational program is designed for a period of three years following the basic nine-year program. It should provide for the all-round devel-

opment of the individual as a member of society as well as training in his special field of interest, and it should equip the individual with a sufficiently broad educational base to enable him to advance his standing through further education and training. Transfer to the general education program from the vocational program will be possible, but some obstacles will have to be overcome.

Students in the technical course will follow a program that is strong in English, mathematics, and science, coupled with technical courses based upon and fully integrated with fields of training available at the institute of technology. In addition to becoming better prepared to take the advanced technical training these courses would likely shorten the actual period of training required at the institute of technology.

The trade and occupational training group would have the advantage of courses especially designed to facilitate their entry into employment and further training. Trade and industrial training, including agriculture, would be broadly based and although fully integrated with the more specialized institute courses, would place emphasis upon ability to learn and ability to adapt rather than on skill development. The programs would stress the basic elements common to a number of occupations, leaving the more highly specialized training for subsequent courses. This does not infer that students would receive insufficient training in the secondary vocational program to make them readily employable. Rather, there will be a deliberate attempt to ward off early obsolescence in the training program and to keep the door open to allow a trainee to move quite freely within a given family of occupations.

Most students entering training for business occupations will go directly to jobs upon completing their courses. However, the door would be open for them in the school of business at the institute of technology if they chose to take advanced training in secretarial science, accounting, or in several other related fields. In most of these advanced courses graduates in commercial work from the secondary vocational programs would receive time credit at the institute of technology.

Students in group 4, the terminal group, will be provided with a program that is designed to give them something of value to facilitate their early entry into employment. Most of their training will be spent on practical work with a minimum of time spent in the classroom on related subjects.

B.2 The Purposes of the Community College: Ontario, 1966

This statement was made by the Minister of Education (William Davis) in the Legislature, 21 May 1965.

Mr. Speaker: The introduction of this Bill providing enabling legislation for the establishment and operation of a system of Colleges of Applied Arts and Technology is an historic occasion in education in our Province.

The Bill marks a major step forward in the development of our educational system; it provides for the introduction of a new level and type of education, one which is still in keeping with our traditions and accomplishments. Above all else, it goes far towards making a reality of the promise–indeed of the stated policy–of this government to provide through education and training, not only an equality of opportunity to all sectors of our population, but the fullest possible

B.2 Source: Ontario Department of Education, *Colleges of Applied Arts and Technology: Basic Documents* (June, 1966) pp. 5, 11, 13-14.

development of each individual to the limit of his ability. In this new age of technological change and invention, also, it is essential to the continued growth and expansion of the economy of our Province, and of our nation, that adequate facilities be made generally available for the education and training of craftsmen, technicians and technologists.
. . . .

...why add another part to the structure? Well, we really have no choice; certainly not as we press forward with our reorganized programs in secondary schools. It is not feasible, nor indeed desirable, that all graduates of our high schools should go to university. The real needs of a very substantial number of our young people lie elsewhere; they would be served poorly and fare poorly in the traditional university programs. Perhaps the best summary of the situation may be found in the Report of *The Grade 13 Study Committee, 1964*, and I quote:

"The truth of the matter is that we are now in an entirely different world from that of the 1920's and 1930's, and it is necessary that we extend our educational system to meet the demands of this new world. In the past when we have faced that sort of crisis, we have solved the problems by expanding our secondary school program–in 1871, for example, when we added general education for the many to special education for the few, or in the 1920's when technical training was introduced in a considerable number of high schools. In the present crisis, the need cannot be met simply by alterations or additions at secondary school level; this time we must turn our attention to the post-secondary level, where we must create a new kind of institution that will provide, in the interests of students for whom a university course is unsuitable, a type of training which universities are not designed to offer. Fortunately, a beginning has been made in the establishment of the institutes of technology and vocational centres, but as yet these are too few in number and their offerings are too narrow in range to satisfy what is required both by the nature of our developing economy and the talents of our young people. The committee is therefore recommending the establishment of community colleges to provide these new and alternative programs."

....

As for the programs, our plans are not yet advanced to the point where I can be specific and definite. Besides, the emphasis not only could but should vary from one community to another, as local needs dictate. In general, however, one may recognize three major responsibilities of every such college:

(1)   to provide courses of types and levels beyond, or not suited to, the secondary school setting;

(2)   to meet the needs of graduates from any secondary school program, apart from those wishing to attend university; and

(3)   to meet the educational needs of adults and out-of-school youth, whether or not they are secondary school graduates.

I would hope to see the following range of offerings in most if not all Colleges of Applied Arts and Technology, the choice to be determined by local circumstances, as indicated above, and extended where a particular need exists in a community.

(a)   Engineering technician and technologist programs below university level

(b)   Semiprofessional non-engineering type programs (e.g. in the paramedical field)

(c)   High level programs in office and distributive occupations, specifically of junior and middle management level, and including courses for small business

(d)   Agricultural and agricultural-related programs, at least in rural areas, in co-operation with the Department of Agriculture

(e)   General adult education programs, including cultural and leisure time activities

(f)   Programs of recreation, including physical education

(g)   General or liberal education courses, including remedial courses in basic subjects, and often incorporated as part of the other programs (e.g. English, Mathematics, Science)

(h)   Retraining, upgrading and updating courses

(i)   Trades skills, pre-apprenticeship, and apprenticeship training

(j)   Service industry courses (e.g. for tourist industry)

(k)   Commercial courses (e.g. cost accounting, junior accounting, data processing, computer programming)

(l)   Other courses to meet local needs.

With respect to the general or liberal education courses, and the general adult education programs, I would point out that these are not thought of as university level courses. Nevertheless no able and qualified student should be prevented from going on from a College of Applied Arts and Technology to a university, and indeed such a pattern exists today for able graduates of our institutes of technology, as you may know. The university doors should always be open to capable and ambitious young men and women.

B.3   The Quebec CEGEP

Sweeping changes in the structure of post-secondary education in Quebec have been accomplished with astonishing speed. In 1964 a department of education was established. Concurrent with the publication of the second volume of the *Parent Report* in 1965, preparations were made to create a number of "instituts", later called CEGEP in the General and Vocational College Act of 1967. By 1969, twenty-three French-language colleges were in operation, and the first English language CEGEP opened in September 1969. As a rule, the CEGEP were not created afresh but were built from existing institutions. Over half of the hundred or so classical colleges have now become a part of a new CEGEP, the remainder having withdrawn from the college level in order to function exclusively within the secondary school system.

Quebec has gone beyond any other province by providing teacher training in its CEGEP, in addition to technical and pre-university programmes.

The college system provides a level between the secondary school system on the one hand and the university or employment on the other. Two-year programmes leading to various university faculties are offered. Programmes leading directly to employment are two or three years depending upon the vocation chosen. Quebec is the only province in which all students eventually must graduate from a college in order to enter a university. Initially, it was anticipated that seventy per cent of the students would elect to take occupational training whereas in actual fact three-quarters followed the university preparation route.

The term *community college* as applied in this province truly expresses a lively sense of community involvement. Each college has a board of directors consisting of nineteen members, four of whom are named by the faculty, two by the students, and four are drawn from among parents of students. In order to allow for maximum community participation, provision is made for the appointment of five other members, who are named only after consultation with other community groups. The board itself may name two members in order to ensure a proper balance between community and college representation. The principal and academic dean are also members.

Colleges have established an organization apart from government called la Fédération des CEGEP whose aim is to encourage growth in areas outside direct governmental jurisdiction.

In Quebec, colleges are supported almost entirely from provincial funds. Only in this province are students within the college system not required to pay tuition fees.

B.3 Source: Gordon Campbell, "The Community College in Canada", in R. A. Cavan, ed., *Universities and Colleges of Canada, 1970* (Ottawa, 1969), pp. 27-29.

B.4   University Expansion and Government Intervention

The following is a summary of a report on higher education written by Dr. J. B. Macdonald, at that time President of the University of British Columbia.

Kinds of Institutions Required

The resources available for higher education in this province have been centered on two main objectives: the development of the University of British Columbia at West Point Grey as an institution for students proceeding to degrees in the liberal arts, the sciences, the professions, and post graduate studies; and the development of Victoria College first as a two-year institution, then in the

B.4 Source: *The B.C. Teacher* (February, 1963), pp. 207-11.

last three years as a four-year liberal arts college, giving the degrees of the University of British Columbia. These are the only public institutions offering higher education. The two institutions mentioned, while they serve the whole province, draw most of their students from the metropolitan areas of Vancouver and Victoria. The problem of numbers of students has already been indicated. Yet British Columbia and Canada are educating too few of the suitably qualified students in the college-age group who could benefit from education beyond the high school. If we wish to maintain our cultural and economic status, then we must provide for a larger proportion of able young people, but at the same time avoid undesirable congestion in the present institutions.

I see the need for two basic kinds of institutions of higher education:
(a) Universities and four-year colleges offering degree programs and advanced training for those students who have the necessary ability and aptitude;
(b) Two-year colleges offering a variety of programs (academic and technological) of one or two years of education beyond Grade XII.

The two-year college would be a new kind of institution for this province. It would be designed for those students who plan to continue their education at a degree-granting institution; those who wish to take only one or two years of higher education (technical, academic, or a combination of both); those who are undecided about their educational future; those who by preference or for financial reasons wish to remain in their own locality. The two-year college would have its unique character and ideals and offer enough courses parallel with those of degree-granting institutions to invite the best students to pursue further studies. Although two-year colleges may differ from one another in accordance with local needs, that difference will exist mainly in the non-academic areas of their work. Such institutions could attract very able students and professors by offering courses and facilities of a distinctive character. Their academic programs must be parallel so that the best students can transfer to the University, but parallel should not mean identical.

If new two-year colleges are established at major centers of population throughout the province, much will be done to equalize educational opportunities for all young British Columbians. The University could then concentrate on the tasks for which it is best suited:
(a) Undergraduate education in the humanities, the sciences, the fine arts, and the social sciences;
(b) Advanced teaching and research connected with graduate work;
(c) Professional preparation: for example in medicine, dentistry, engineering, law, forestry, commerce, education.

In addition, we need four-year colleges offering degrees in the liberal arts, science, and education. At the moment, I see no need for more than one institution giving extremely expensive professional courses, such as medicine and engineering, and much of the advanced scientific and graduate work.

. . . .

Assistance for Higher Education

Although I have stated elsewhere that new institutions should be self-governing, it is important that provision should be made for guaranteeing the academic standards of the various regional colleges that will be established. Therefore, I propose an Academic Board which would foster the growth and academic development of new institutions; assist in gaining public support for essential facilities and resources to enable new institutions to attain the goals they set for themselves; negotiate with larger institutions to procure staff and to arrange temporary exchange of academic personnel between established institutions and new colleges; assist in arranging the transfer of students from one institution to another and in general aid new institutions in their basic planning.

The Academic Board would have no direct responsibility for the distribution of funds to the regional colleges. However, it is essential that this Board maintain close liaison with the Grants Commission, I shall propose later in this section, in order that scholarly interest may be served in an imaginative way.

If there were any indication that the academic standards of a regional college were not being maintained in line with the goals it had set for itself, the Academic Board would investigate and give assistance for correcting the situation. On occasion it might withdraw its recognition of a college, and the Grants Commission might in turn withdraw financial support through public funds. Therefore, the Academic Board would become an accrediting agency, and it would be understood that any institution eligible for public financial support would have to be approved academically by it.

The financing of two-year institutions should come from three sources: local, provincial, and federal. In order to provide for a balanced and harmonious development within the whole provincial system of higher education, and to achieve a consolidated plan for advancing our educational ideals, it is most important that responsible and effective representations be made to the Provincial Government concerning the financial support which should be given each institution. Requests by individual institutions must be considered in terms of the overall pro-

gram for higher education. Any means established should ensure the equitable distribution of funds among institutions, and at the same time ensure that the best possible use of public funds is being made by avoiding a duplication of expensive course offerings, libraries, professional schools, laboratories, and equipment for specialized teaching and research.

The kind of commission I envisage would be vested with the specific responsibility of appraising the requirements of institutions and of satisfying the government of the soundness of their proposals. Such a commission would be extremely useful as a senior advisory body to the Provincial Government, not only for immediate projects, but also for a long-range plan of continuous development of education within the province. The presence of an informed commission, commanding public respect, would increase confidence of the government itself and of the people that every precaution had been taken prior to decision.

The function of the Grants Commission would be:

(a) To analyse and appraise the needs, aims, and future plans of individual institutions in relation to the whole development of higher education in this province.

(b) To seek and gather systematically pertinent information and advice from the institutions themselves and from all available sources.

(c) To recommend to the Provincial Government policy, both long and short term, with respect to the continuing operation and financing of higher education.

(d) To receive and study the budget estimates for both capital and operating needs of each institution.

(e) To make a combined submission on behalf of all institutions to the Provincial Government for support for the operating and capital revenue of each.

(f) To exercise an executive function by distributing the funds which the Provincial Legislature assigns for higher education.

(g) To distribute the grants made by the Federal Government towards the operating revenue of institutions of higher learning.

(h) To submit an annual report to the Legislature.

I recommend a Grants Commission having the following membership:

(a) A Chairman appointed by the Lieutenant-Governor-in-Council. Because of the inseparable connection between academic and financial matters, this person should also act as chairman of the Academic Board.

(b) One member nominated for a three-year term by each of the institutions whose work the Commission embraces. The number of members will have to be increased as new institutions are established. It would be desirable if the Faculty of each institution had a voice in the appointment of the representative.

(c) An equal number appointed for a three-year term by the Lieutenant-Governor-in-Council. The choice of these members should be left to the Government, but it is suggested that they include representatives of business, labor, and the professions.

(d) A full-time, paid Executive Director, a Financial Officer, and secretarial staff who will act jointly for the Academic Board: these persons should be employees of the Commission.

B.5 The Government Role in Higher Education

Though the Wright Commission Report was not published until late 1971, it was commissioned in the spring of 1969 and reflects the problems created by university expansion during the sixties.

There has been another significant change in post-secondary education since World War II: the determining influence of governments has increased greatly. This development dramatically affects the way we evaluate the social purposes of post-secondary education. As long as our institutions performed their social roles without the support of public resources, the acceptance of those roles was a matter for institutions themselves to decide. Curiously enough, it may have been the attraction of the social roles, rather than of any goals in particular, that drew governments into the field. It was definitely the use of post-secondary education as a social escalator and, for a time, as an indispensable tool in the race with the Russians that justified the unprecedented infusion of resources into post-secondary education both in the United States and in Canada.

The significant change in Ontario, however, does not result from the kind of justifications that the government may have used to rationalize increasing its support for post-secondary education. The heart of the matter rests with the decision to make post-secondary education an area subject to public interest. The social roles of post-secondary education thereby become sanctified by the government which, in turn, inevitably becomes responsible for the performance of these roles. The reconciliation of the social purposes of post-secondary education with whatever other

B.5 Source: *Draft Report of the Commission on Post-Secondary Education in Ontario,* 1971, p. 13.

purposes there may be in society can then take place only in the political arena. Or, to put it rather bluntly, the introduction of an overwhelming public support has resulted in the politicization of post-secondary education. Since the government is the main agent of this process, it will, whether it likes it or not, bear the brunt of responsibility for whatever uses and abuses our society makes of post-secondary education.

B.6 School Consolidation in the Sixties

School Organization

Patterns of school organization have been the subject of serious study and research in both Canada and the United States for more than 40 years. Major attention has been given to the two areas of school district organization and school centralization. The pioneer form of school district organization–the local district or school section which provided a one-room school within walking distance of every home–has gradually been yielding to larger units of administration and centralized schools which could provide a wider range of educational opportunities.

"The chief function of a school district is to make it possible for the citizens of the area to provide for the organization, operation and administration of an adequate, economical, and effective educational program for those who should be educated in and through the public schools. Any district that fails to carry out this function satisfactorily is an ineffective district. The ineffectiveness may be due to the attitude of the people, to the limited size of the area, to inadequate human or economic resources, to failure to recognize

B.6 Source: Atlantic Development Board, *Profiles of Education in the Atlantic Provinces,* Background Study No. 5 (Ottawa, 1969), pp. 240-43.

or meet emerging needs, or, to any combination of these factors." (Morphet *et al.*, 1967: p. 269[1].)

Following two successful experiments with large units of administration, the Alberta government in the late 1930's introduced a complete plan for the establishment of large school divisions in the rural areas of the province. In 1965 there were 59 such large units. The provinces of British Columbia and Saskatchewan, and more recently Manitoba, Ontario and Quebec have also carried out a large-scale school district reorganization. At the present time New Brunswick is introducing its reorganization plan which divides the province into 33 large units, each including both rural and urban areas.

Table 2-23 [not reprinted] indicates the greatly decreased number of operating school boards in both the Atlantic and Western Provinces in 1966 compared with 1960. Over 600 school boards disappeared in the Atlantic Provinces, and over 1,700 in the Western Provinces during the six-year period. Since 1967 New Brunswick has the highest average number of schools under one board. Much yet remains to be done in the reorganization of school administrative units in the other Atlantic Provinces, however, particularly in Prince Edward Island and Newfoundland.

. . . .

An eventual outcome of the establishment of larger units of administration is some degree of centralization of school facilities. As reorganization of districts results in an equalization of financial resources and responsibilities, so centralization of facilities helps to equalize and extend educational opportunities. The size of school, as well as the size of school district, is an important factor in determining the degree to which professional resources can be attracted, held, and effectively utilized. A trend toward school centralization is indicated in Table 2-23 [not reprinted] which shows a reduction of 1,000 schools in the Atlantic Provinces from 1960 to 1966, and at the same time an increased school enrolment of nearly 63,000. In 1960 there was an average of four teachers per school; in 1966 the average had increased to six. The average enrolment per school was 108 in 1960 and had increased to 158 in 1967. Only a small beginning, however, has been made toward solving the important problems of school centralization.

. . . .

In relation to minimal school size Morphet has stated,

"Whenever practicable an elementary school should have sufficient pupils to warrant at least 2 teachers per grade or age group, and a junior or senior high school should have at least 100 pupils in each age group. Elementary and high schools having at least twice this minimum are usually in a position to provide a more adequate program at a more reasonable cost." (Morphet *et al.*, 1967: p: 271.)

Using Morphet's criteria, and adding one more–that not less than three grades should constitute an educational unit–the minimum size of school that might operate with any degree of efficiency and effectiveness would be a six-room school. Such a unit might be suitable for the primary grades where transportation distances were great. A six-grade elementary school organization would require a 12-room school, and an eight-grade elementary school a 16-room school. Using Morphet's criteria for high schools, the minimum size of a three-grade high school would be 300 pupils, or 12 rooms, of a four-grade high school 400 pupils or 16 rooms.

In 1966 there were 400 schools in Nova Scotia and nearly 900 in Newfoundland which would not meet the minimum standard of six rooms. Over 78,000 pupils attended these small schools. There were an additional 106 schools in Nova Scotia and 141 in Newfoundland which had six to eight rooms, accommodating another 36,000 pupils. In Nova Scotia 59 per cent of all schools had eight rooms or less in 1966, and accommodated 22 per cent of the total school population. In Newfoundland 87 per cent of all schools were in this category, accommodating 57 per cent of all pupils.

[1]E. L. Morphet, R. L. Johns and T. L. Reller, *Educational Organization and Administration* (Englewood Cliffs, N.J., 1967), 2nd. ed.

C. The Direction of Pedagogical Reform

Keeping more children in school longer was only one aspect of educational change in the sixties. The education mania also re-awakened interest in pedagogical reform: not only more schools but better schools were demanded. One response was to reaffirm the older ideals of progressivism. Most of the official and unofficial studies of the decade fell upon ideas that had been circulating for decades, refurbished them, and applied them to the needs of the sixties. No public document symbolized this tendency more than the Hall-Dennis Report in Ontario (document C.1); and few provincial educational reports have ever had its national impact. Indeed, progressive education itself had rarely had such well-publicized and unequivocal advocacy. Though there was dissent, as there always had been, progressives met a degree of support from the public they had never known before.

New learning theory and new technology, often allied to progressivism, were beginning to change the schools as well. The enthusiasm throughout Canada for "ungrading" and promotion by subject is examined in an extract from the Newfoundland Royal Commission on Education and Youth (document C.2). And for classrooms everywhere, educational technology promised–or at least, purported to promise–unlimited increases in effectiveness, flexibility, and resources (document C.3). In the late sixties, optimism ran high. The public seemed convinced that the schools and colleges could play a major role in meeting the problems of the new era, and as proof of their faith they were prepared to pay handsomely for educational expansion and reform. The professionals shared that faith and believed as well that they had the pedagogical tools to make it work.

A study group using headphones, Toronto 1969.

C.1 Progressivism Reaffirmed

We know that we do not make a dog happy by wagging his tail. To make a child learn or be ignited by an inspirational spark or become an integrated human being reaching out and upward is not done by the use of superficial gimmicks or gadgets. Leaps of the mind cannot be programmed, manipulated, or conditioned, by the most modern intensive immersion efforts. In almost a mysterious fashion, as expressed in Michelangelo's painting in the Sistine Chapel, the finger of God touches the finger of Adam at strange moments. How to inspire is not easily answered. Most of the frontiers of the mind are still unexplored; however, from empirical observation, from the history of the past, and from evidence of creative thinkers we know that the human atmosphere in which a child grows and learns, still symbolizes the greatest teaching aid since a Neanderthal father chipped a stone and showed his son how to do it.

The teacher, as a professional, should be aware of the instruments and means at his disposal to whet intellectual appetites. His personality, skills, and special experience may suit one method more readily than another. Furthermore, different methods may be required at different times with the same child in the same day; and similar methods may be found to be very effective with two children of contrasting abilities, backgrounds, and ages.

In too many schools, one sees teachers doing most of the talking. This has been the traditional method employed at schools and teachers' colleges. It was assumed that a special package of knowledge was presented at intervals by the teacher, ritualistically pumped into the children,

C.1 Source: *Living and Learning*, The Report of the Provincial Commission on the Aims and Objectives of Education in Ontario, 1968 (Hall-Dennis Report), pp. 57-60, 70-71, 76-77.

drilled, and then tested to see whether the content had taken like a vaccination. The constant buzz of a teacher's voice to a tongue-tied captive audience was accepted as desirable practice. However, in the light of present-day experience, the lecture method, used alone to transmit the overwhelming amount of knowledge pouring out every day, is far too restricting.

Children need to play. Despite the belief held by many adults that learning must be painful and serious, it is the joy and pleasure of play which often sets the stage for learning. Play provides a psychological safety zone in which children can test their competence without fear of failure. It is out of play that children develop rules of a game and a sense of order. Work and play areas are so closely interwoven in learning situations that it is often impossible to separate one from the other, and teachers aware of the learning process should not feel guilty about the fun and noisy atmosphere that may be engendered. There is nothing sinful about laughter, and serious, silent rooms are not necessarily working chambers for teaching.

Children need to be free to ask questions about the world and about themselves. Establishing 'out of bounds' areas for questioning can only lead to misconception, superstition, distorted information, and ignorance. Children's earlier questions are for the simple purpose of learning facts and the names of things ("What is it?" "What's it for?"). Then come questions about their own bodies, followed swiftly by questions growing out of their observation of many different levels of explanation.

· ·

The curriculum of the future must be child-oriented and must provide opportunities for choice within broadly defined limits. Teachers at every level, supported by qualified counsellors, will be required to guide each child along his own critically determined path, far more flexible than a computer guide, but critical in the sense that the learning programs initiated and developed will best meet the needs of each child at the time best suited to his development. Teachers will have to rely upon both their general knowledge of child development and on detailed observation of individuals to match teaching to the demands of children's various stages of development. The signs of readiness will have to be discovered and learned for all aspects of learning, so that each child's progress will be observed, recognized, stimulated, and assisted in the next stage of learning.

. . . .

One of the most important responsibilities of teachers is to help children to see order and pattern in experience. Rigid division of the curriculum into subjects tends to interrupt children's trains of thought and of interest and to hinder them from realizing the common elements in problem-solving. These are among the many reasons why most learning experiences, particularly in the early school years, should cut across the traditional subject divisions.

Activity and experience, both physical and mental, are often the best means of gaining knowledge and acquiring facts, but these facts are best retained when they are used and understood. When children are learning new patterns of behavior or new concepts, they tend both to practise them spontaneously and to seek out relevant experiences. It takes much longer than teachers have previously realized for children to master through experience new concepts or new levels of complex concepts. Only when understanding has been achieved, does consolidation follow through further learning experiences.

It is these factors which curriculum designers must keep in mind. A child-centred emphasis heralds a demand for imaginative, resourceful, and qualified teachers to create a curriculum of learning experiences on the spot. Remote curriculum constructors should wither away as anachronisms, and qualified consultants on child development, methodology, program aids, field experiences, and special learning problems should take their place as supporters and stimulators of teachers in their daily work.

Learning opportunities and program aids should be integrated so that children will not have to flit from activity to activity in their anxiety to make use of materials not available at other times of the day. As children mature, they should be capable of planning when to do work assigned to them and also have time in which to follow personal or group interests of their own choice.

Any policy which predetermines the total structure of a curriculum and attempts to impose it upon all, should be condemned. Such an approach is in complete antithesis to a learning program which seeks to develop the potential of every child.

. . . .

The Ontario *Programme of Studies for Grades 1 to 6,* first published in 1937, is the only official publication of the Department of Education which deals with aims deliberately and fully. It is of unique interest to a Committee whose terms of reference emphasize the first six years of school and whose primary concern is aims. The treatment of aims in the *Programme* provides another example of the developmental approach, but it goes much further. The simple but startling truth is that virtually every idea in it, with only one immediately noticeable exception, might have been expressed by educationally enlightened and advanced authors today.

This basic philosophy was and is in the mainstream of developing educational thought which has had its ups and downs for almost two centuries. It suffered a major set-back on this continent during and after World War II, partly because of the continuing war or cold war mentality and inability or reluctance to recruit or educate teachers for anything more than forceful instruction in facts and skills. The philosophy is current partly because its authors were far in advance of most teachers and laymen of their time. This explains the difficulty of getting the *Programme* into anything like general practice.

The aims and related philosophy of this *Programme of Studies* are very concise, and a summary of them is difficult and must be inadequate. In brief, they advocate the following: a society and school society in which the individual has opportunities for self-realization, security, and participation in decision-making. He is by implication to be educated for social responsibility, service to all, and adaptability to change, and explicitly to be educated to work and get along with others. Such education is to be effected not by precept or formal instruction but over a long period in which the school provides "meaningful social experiences in situations that require the exercise of qualities of helpfulness, self-direction and acceptance of responsibility," and the like. The atmosphere of the school must be kindly, co-operative, and purposeful. Achievement of aims depends on a program planned to take cognizance of psychological knowledge regarding child development and the learning process–a program which arouses interest and provides for pupil activity and social participation. There must be provision for individual differences, permitting some measure of success for every child. The graded school system must not be rigid and thought should be given to its modification. The

wisdom of promotion examinations, failures, and retardation is questioned. In appraising results the teacher should first look to see whether pupils are alert and living in cheerful, healthy surroundings, then satisfy himself that they are acquiring necessary skills, and above all be concerned with the interests and attitudes they are developing. The program itself "cuts across the traditional subject-by-subject arrangement."

This necessarily brief summary illustrates again the truth that progress in education is accomplished not so much by new ideas as by gaining broader acceptance of enlightened ideas and putting them into practice. Conditions are now favorable for educational advance; there is evidence of widespread progressive thought in briefs presented to the Committee, in popular journals, and in the provincial Department of Education itself. Not least in importance is the prospect of higher minimum educational requirements for teachers, a reform long advocated by the teaching profession.

. . . .

There is in education a tradition that desirable content for learning is and must be embodied in subjects. When knowledge was limited, when the concept of the interrelatedness of ideas was ignored in school curricula, and when only a select few received more than a minimum of education, there was little reason to question the value of subjects. Each of them was composed of what may be called knowledge, skills, and ideas in a particular field–all logically ordered for instructional purposes. And modern schooling that is content-oriented, or arranged around subject disciplines, seems to be based on the premise that unless subject matter is presented to a pupil in a logical sequence, or an organized pattern, he will never organize it for himself. But schooling that takes into account both the learner as an integrating organism and the subject matter pertinent to the dynamic interests of the learner cannot be organized around subjects which are patterns of the logic of other people.

The Committee supports the view that the cognitive processes through which children learn deserve prominent consideration in curriculum design. Even though only glimpses of the 'what' and 'how' of cognition are yet available from psychologists, it is this incompleteness of our understanding that requires us to be less certain, less rigid, less organized, in the arrangements we make of subject matter for children to learn. A curriculum should be so devised that the inquisitive, goal-seeking, self-reconstructing minds of children can be brought in touch with subject matter relevant to their individual interests and needs. A six-year-old is interested in counting rather than mathematics, in rain rather than science. From an early age, the student probes the frontiers of understanding, and it is only in the later stages of his learning experience that these frontiers crystallize in the form of a discipline of study with clearly defined structure and content. Thus there is a place in the more senior elements of the curriculum for subjects of instruction, at least as long as these are required for admission to higher institutions. But generally speaking, subjects, with their adjuncts of textbooks and the like, should be used primarily as resources for knowledge. They should be so used freely in designing learning activities which suit students' needs, systematically in planning studies for older children, and often selectively in topical studies which include content from several subjects.

On the other hand, it would be confusing to send pupils on voyages of discovery over one vast ocean of knowledge. The study of man, or a curriculum embracing all of life, is too formidable a sea for students to navigate without charts of some sort. To give direction to learning without imposing inflexible subject restrictions is a fundamental problem for those who design the curriculum.

Such direction can be found by basing the learning program on a number of organizing centres or areas of emphasis within the human experience, each of which is a common denominator to certain fields of learning. Three such areas are suggested here as nuclei for organized learning in our schools. With these areas as bases, the teacher and her pupils may look to subject areas, not as packages for instruction, but as repositories of information, to be used according to the interest and the needs of the learner.

The first area of emphasis offered is 'Communications,' embracing all aspects of learning that relate to man's interchange of thought. In terms of the curriculum, communication involves ability to speak and listen, to read and write, to record and to film, to paint, to dance. It also involves aspects of social studies, mathematics, business and commerce, manual arts, and almost all of man's activities in which ideas are transmitted and received. Thus the skills of debating, of reading maps, of interpreting data and ideas, and of invoicing and accounting, all become legitimate focuses for interests of learners.

A second area offered as a curriculum base is that of man and his environment. The sciences are natural elements in studies of the environment, but children must not be restricted, especially in the pre-adolescent years, to the confines of the sub-disciplines of science. The geographical elements of social studies and much of applied mathematics may be properly included in such studies. The practical aspects of agriculture, of manual arts, of home and consumer economics, and much of what is called vocational training may also be identified with this area, referred to as 'Environmental Studies.'

A third area of emphasis is concerned with man's ideas and values–those abstract yet powerful concepts which shape our lives, yet have no tangible form of their own. The search for the ideal, the constant probing of the unknown, the seeking for truth, the intuitive effort toward unity –these are humanizing values that lift man toward a nobility of thought and purpose. Among such studies one may include the fine and practical arts; and recent trends in physical education indicate a return to the Greek concept of physical arts and point to its inclusion also. Studies of philosophy should be accessible to adolescent students, and the religious ideals of various people of the world should be open for study and discussion. This area of aesthetic exploration is designated by the term 'Humanities,' and embraces studies related to human aspirations, ideals, and values.

While presenting these as areas within which the learning experience may be organized, the Committee resists the temptation to list the traditional subjects that might appear in each. To do so would defeat the purpose of such a thematic approach. The approach is intended to free teachers and pupils from the confines of structured, isolated subjects, to encourage a wider exploration of knowledge relative to each theme, and to emphasize the embracing nature of the learning experience. This is not meant to imply that studies of history, mathematics, or other well-known subjects should disappear from the curriculum. The organization does imply, however, that such disciplines should be seen as aids in the student's search for skills and understanding rather than as bodies of content to be mastered, or as organizing criteria for such purposes as timetables, evaluation, and teacher certification.

The selection of subject areas and the level of learning to which they are applied, should be the prerogative of pupils and teachers. This is not to say that individual teachers should be left entirely to their own devices in curriculum planning, but as the professional group most closely associated with the needs of pupils, they have a prior responsibility to see that these needs are met.

The teacher should be sensitive also to the child's need for a balanced learning experience, and should discourage the development of any one interest at the expense of all others.

C.2 Ungrading in the Elementary and High Schools

Recently there has been a great deal of dissatisfaction with the traditional grade system. Educators throughout the world claim that the system has failed to meet adequately individual differences in the ability to learn. It has, in many schools, become rigid and inflexible, requiring slow-learners, average students, and above-average to complete basically the same amount of curriculum content before going on to the next grade. If a child is unable to pass a set of examinations, based on the package of content assigned to the grade, then he may be required to repeat the whole year's work. If a student did extremely well in his examinations, he may be permitted to skip a grade. Many claim that both of these practices are crude and sporadic procedures which deny the fact of continuous growth. They recommend use of a non-graded system as a means of providing better education for all kinds of children–the slow learners, the slow starters, the average, and the bright.

C.2 Source: Newfoundland, *Report of the Royal Commission on Education and Youth*, 1968 (Warren Commission), vol. 2, 2-5.

There have been numerous attempts to define the non-graded system. Dr. Ian Housego states that it is the type or organization that takes into account realities about individual differences and the realities of curriculum development.[1] He lists the major characteristics as follows:

1.   The structure encourages continuous progress for each child. It makes sure that in each child's progress there are no long pauses, no gaps, and no duplications. There is instead steady progress which is related to the irregular development of the child himself.

2.   Alternatives exist for placing children who do not appear to be profiting from their present experiences. There is provision, in other words, for horizontal replacement of any given child instead of having that child repeat or skip a grade.

3.   The ungraded structure encourages a reasonable balance of success and failure in each child's school life. According to John Goodlad, one of the promoters of the system, about twenty-five per cent of the children in the grades experience about seventy-five percent of the failure that occurs.

· ·

The number of non-graded schools is increasing in Canada. The City of Hamilton has long operated a type of non-graded system known as the unit of promotion plan. Quebec and New Brunswick have taken steps towards the introduction of the system throughout these provinces. The Province of Saskatchewan is perhaps best known in Canada for developments of this kind.

In the elementary schools of Saskatchewan, the traditional grades have been eliminated and replaced by two broad divisions–the first replacing the former grades I, II, and III, and the second replacing the former grades IV, V, and VI. In each broad division, the content for the skill subjects (reading, language, and arithmetic) is set out in twelve units. Teachers are expected to handle up to three groups in a classroom, with each group progressing from unit to unit at its own particular rate of progress. Housego states that there are three possibilities when it comes to placement of a given pupil–he may be in an accelerated group, a decelerated group, or an average group.[2] There is no failure in the sense of repetition of the year's work; nor does a pupil skip large blocks of content. Students progressing at their own rate may spend two, three, or four years in each division.

There has been very little objective analysis of the non-graded plan. What there is, however, seems to indicate that the plan is superior to the graded system. We, therefore, suggest that the plan be instituted in certain selected elementary schools in the Province as a pilot project. The Commission believes that this system, or some adaptation of it, must be introduced throughout the Province in the not-too-distant future, if the rigidity of the present system is to be reduced.

We suggest that the non-graded school has a number of needs that must be met before the plan can become a reality. These include relatively small classes, a wide variety of instructional materials (including library resources and standardized tests), additional supervisory and specialist help, and a favourable attitude and adequate preparation on the part of teachers. This will clearly mean additional expenditures for many school boards.

[1] I. E. Housego, "A Definition of the Nongraded School," *Continous Progress*. Vancouver, B.C.: The British Columbia Teachers' Federation, 1966.

[2] Housego, *loc. cit.*

Promotion by Subject

The essential feature of the system of promotion by subject is that students proceed through the school by passing subjects rather than grades. When this is applied to the high school, students operate on a credit system, moving from one level of a subject to another as they become ready. Able students can move rapidly from the lower level to more advanced courses, whereas the less able progress more slowly. In any class where this scheme is followed, it will be possible to have pupils taking courses at different grade levels: a pupil for instance may be doing French at Grade X level and History at Grade IX level.

In a publication entitled *Subject Promotion*, the Protestant School Board of Greater Montreal states that the system of promotion by subject was based on two main premises:

1.   That better provision would be made for the individual differences of students, according to ability, needs, and interests.
2.   That the student's educational progress would be facilitated and strengthened educationally by progressing regularly through his programme in subjects which he passed, and by repeating only those subjects which he failed, instead of repeating all the subjects of his grade because of failure in some of them.
Complementary advantages of the system were stated to be:
1.   Better grouping of pupils into homogeneous classes, with instruction varied accordingly.
2.   The completion of certain subjects in one year instead of two, thus permitting more concentrated effort on the student's part, and a programme of fewer subjects in each year.
3.   Reduced failure and drop-out rate because of a programme better suited to each student.

The publication also made reference to the need for more and better guidance services and the importance of requiring students to continue certain subjects progressively throughout high school. This would avoid the "patchwork" accumulation of credits. The importance of providing additional clerical assistance was also stressed.

An attempt to introduce promotion by subject in the high school grades in Newfoundland was made through the Department's Division of Public Examinations in the school year 1965-66. Teachers were advised that students who had passed in any subject in Grade IX or X would be required to repeat any compulsory subject in which he had failed; he could either drop or repeat an optional subject failed.

. . . .

The Commission believes that this plan has many advantages. Unnecessary repetition should be largely eliminated in a school organized in this fashion. Whether promotion by subject will fulfill its promise has yet to be seen, but it does seem to offer bright prospects for making greater provision for individual differences among students.

C.3 The "New" High School: The Wonders of Technology

Regina's Miller Composite High School is a little like the Saskatchewan Roughriders: you don't expect such a city-slicker operation so deep in the West.

At least, not unless you know Lew Riederer, director of education for the Regina Separate School Board and mastermind behind Miller—Canada's most up-to-date high school.

Since September the new school has been

C.3 Source: Barrie Zwicker, "The Most Up-to-Date High School", *The Globe Magazine*, 7 January 1967.

ironing the bugs out of an impressive array of education-of-tomorrow techniques. It will be inaugurated officially tomorrow afternoon with a videotaped speech by John Deutsch, chairman of the Economic Council of Canada, played over part of the school's $200,000 worth of electronic gear.

Altogether, Miller–a $1,900,000 academic, technical and vocational institution–boasts $500,-000 worth of equipment, including its own closed-circuit television system. Teachers are already looking ahead to the computer scheduled to be installed in May. But these expensive items are merely means to an end.

The school's aim is to make learning an individual matter for each of its 1,053 pupils–a rare state of affairs, as most high school students would testify, although one praised in decades of lip service. Along with its equipment, Miller has or is developing:
Team teaching;
Continuous progress–with year-end examinations played down;
Steadily increasing student freedom;
Ties with universities and teachers' colleges;
A broad in-service training program for teachers (Miller has a staff of 50).

If the school is the brightest flower among Canada's secondary schools, the Saskatchewan system of education is the soil which makes it possible. The province's Department of Education has in recent years developed, without fanfare, a plan to divide schoolwork into four three-grade blocks with students free to learn at their own pace within the blocks.

Miller is making maximum use of this departure from the old rigid grade structure.

Avoidance of the impersonal nature that plagues so many high schools has been given priority. "I went out and recruited people. I told them of the philosophy of the school. If their eyes didn't sparkle, they weren't put in it," Riederer says. (His eyes sparkle.)

Riederer, members of the Separate School Board, and other school officials visited Florida, California and Nevada in a search for the best ideas on which to base the school. They read hundreds of reports and conferred with dozens of experts.

"We asked ourselves: what did we need to fit our children for life in an automated society? This is what we came up with...

"In our traditional school system we acknowledged all this need for individualization on paper, but in fact we were very far from carrying it out."

Miller is intended to synthesize the best ideas of the most advanced high schools on the continent. The Nova school near Fort Lauderdale, Florida, had the greatest impact on the trustees; Riederer took groups there twice. Unlike Miller, the Nova school, an academic marvel with an individual curriculum for nearly every student, has no technical-vocational branch.

Riederer's synthesis is so attractive that he was one of the few Canadian education officials from outside Ontario invited to appear before the province's Hall Committee on the Aims and Objectives of Education. His brief last year stressed the value of the non-graded approach to secondary education–an approach not only almost impossible under Ontario regulations, but one for which most of Ontario's high school teachers and officials lack enthusiasm.

An official of the Clark County, Nevada, school system, which leads in the continuous progress approach, is a consultant to the College of Education, Regina Campus. Riederer and his officials talk to him on his several-times-yearly visits.

This coattail consultancy is typical of Riederer's flexibility. He also brought an abundance of his own ideas to the post of director, to which he was appointed only in late 1965.

"Lighting fires under people is the key," says Riederer. "This is paramount. You cannot allow senility to set in anywhere. People like a challenge."

Miller's closed-circuit television setup is one such challenge. The staff has taken to it enthusiastically. And Kenneth Barker, co-ordinator of the school's growing data processing centre, notes that teachers have asked for an in-service program on the use of computers since he established two such courses for the students.

The students, too, face a challenge. "I don't think the students know all the facilities around the school that they can use. They're a little bewildered yet," according to Michael leVolbus, 16.

But 14-year-old Margery Linacher, who plans to teach high school science, feels she knows the value of the school's features: "The resource centre is going to be just great." (Thousands of new books for it are on order.)

The teachers are working out new ways to exploit the Miller approach and facilities.

The science department, for one, has developed short television lessons–the school has its own TV studio–on the slide rule. "We can show it over and over, giving the students a chance to practise along with the program," science teacher Lionel Brenholen points out.

Sister Catherine, who teaches social studies, is excited at the prospects of television. "Through the TV centre we are able to show various men who lived in the past and make these men come alive again."

The social studies teachers are ordering matching sets of reference books so that students, interested in a man presented on television, can pore over a detailed biography of him. They are also emphasizing role playing, in which students discover, with more impact than through lectures, how governments run.

Riederer, the man behind it all, discovered his enthusiasm for teaching as a radar instructor during a stint with the RCAF during the Second World War. "I learned I enjoyed working with people. I never felt as if I was shovelling out information. Teaching, for me, has always been thrilling."

He became a school principal after the war, joining the Separate School Board in 1955 as an assistant superintendent. He has plenty of challenges in Miller. Both he and Miller's principal say it will be at least three years before the school really takes the shape they want.
they want.

"The teachers will have to acclimatize themselves to greater freedom first and then pass it on to students," Selinger says. "Some teachers may realize they've gone too far and have to pull in their horns."

There isn't much pulling-in of horns yet. There are even plans for Miller, with the tacit approval of the province's Department of Education, to begin drawing up its own curriculum this year, incorporating the new ideas developed by its teachers in the months ahead.

Individualized learning is the key to the Miller system, and it is being pushed in a variety of ways. The large resource centre features study desks, conference rooms, a laboratory for students with reading problems, a small audio-visual supply depot and 32 carrels for individual study.

The carrels have television monitors and earphones. Students can dial a lesson or other related material, to catch up or review.

Basic to the system envisaged is the team teaching approach now being established in a number of subject areas.

Team teaching can take several forms. Often one member of the team is responsible for presenting the lesson to an extra large class while others look on with the students. After the presentation, the students study the subject on their own in greater depth and team members circulate, ready to respond to questions or to offer advice.

Sometimes more than one team member is involved in the presentation. Because the teachers specialize and have each other to rely on, the team in effect gives the students a super teacher. The teachers also absorb techniques from one another.

The school's teams will keep in touch with each other. "This dividing up of subjects has been tomfoolery. Knowledge is a meaningful whole," Selinger says.

For staff the school is reaching out into the universities and the community. Frederick Wagman, with seven years radio and television production experience, was hired to co-ordinate and encourage teacher use of Miller's audio-visual facilities.

· ·

The new science program being drawn up for use in Division IV will have richly-equipped laboratories, in which the emphasis will be on self-discovery, at its core. Students will be left alone with materials and machines to come up with the answers their predecessors were fed by text and teacher. Miller is already set up for this kind of learning.

"Without question, Miller's facilities are the most modern available," declares Saskatchewan Education Minister George Trapp. "They will provide a research vehicle for still further development and improvement of instruction at all levels."

D. The Retreat from Optimism: Towards the Seventies

With bewildering rapidity, the optimism of the middle and late sixties turned to frustration, cynicism, apathy, and occasionally, open rebellion. We expanded our facilities to meet the enrolment explosion; we now find empty seats in our schools and colleges. We expanded our facilities, as well, to meet our manpower needs; suddenly, highly trained young people cannot find jobs. We implemented pedagogical and curricular reforms; yet students seem less satisfied and parents are in revolt against the financial burdens involved. We paid our teachers more, and told them they were professionals; but we are not sure we are getting our money's worth. We reorganized our administrative systems in the name of economy and efficiency; but we seem to have created an impenetrable bureaucracy which only heightens our sense of loss of control. Some of the important components of this malaise are examined in more detail in the following extracts from a recent article by Hugh A. Stevenson (document D.1).

It is far too early to estimate the long-term impact of such disenchantment on the future of public education. It may be no more than a temporary phenomenon, a querulous period of consolidation after the rapid changes of the sixties. But it is no less possible that we have ceased to believe in the traditional justifications for the purposes and structure of public education propounded by the great schoolmen of nineteenth-century Canada and sustained by the faith and works of successive generations of Canadians.

D.1 Disenchantment
with the Schools

To put it succinctly, Canadians have no precedents for the degree of critical accord that has been reached by the combined effects of contemporary public and professional disillusionment with institutionalized education. This polarity of opinion has been strengthened by current economies and the fetish for accountability, but they have not been the only causes for it. Over a decade of debate in the mass news media has had the effect of making the public much more discerning where their own and their children's education is at stake. Similarly, educators–in particular classroom teachers–have become more accustomed to questioning the innovations which theorists, commissions and civil servants suggest they implement. The varied reactions to such reforms as those advocated in *Living and Learning* illustrate the point.[2] At the same time, educators have become more vocal in their criticisms when non-educational factors, usually political considerations, stand in the way of implementing reforms for which there is general acceptance among members of the profession.

Some recent, random examples of public and professional disdain will illustrate its depth and provide a basis for exploring some of the probable results of this apparently new crisis in Canadian education. They may also provide sample evidence upon which to judge whether or not it is realistic or rather alarmist to suggest that the results of this convergence of contemporary opinion which may be seen as a casual alliance based on dissatisfaction should be described as a spectre.

A great deal of publicity has centered on rising militancy among teachers with regard to salary increases. While teachers insist that their professional organizations are not unions, trade union tactics such as working to rule, short-term walkouts, protest marches and strikes are the ones to which they resort against intransigent school boards. It is difficult to be unsympathetic to teachers if there is truth in their charges that 'Manitoba Teachers' Salaries...' are indeed 'Equal to Janitors'.[3] But one wonders where their professional judgement lies when their leaders resort to threats like 'Maybe it's about time mothers taught their own daughters how to cook and fathers informed their sons about family life and industrial arts'–after pointing out that teacher-trustee relations are bound to deteriorate because of the 'incompatibility of political and technical decisions.' However, the teachers may be right when they argue 'the public must accept the blame for current conflicts as it demands ever-increasing services from education while, at the same time, displaying increasing reluctance to pay for these services.'[4] In any event, these examples leave little doubt about the depth of teachers' discontent with the education establishment.

. . . .

[2]Readers are encouraged to consult: BRIAN CRITTENDEN (ed.), *Means and Ends in Education,* O.I.S.E. Occasional Papers 2 (Toronto, 1969); JAMES DALY, *Education or Molasses? A Critical Look at the Hall-Dennis Report* (Ancaster 1969); and one which includes the views of parents, Research and Publication Committee of the Ontario School Inspectors' Association, *Reactions to Hall-Dennis: A Collection of Comments from the Point of View of the Secondary School* (Toronto, 1969). Daily newspapers for the period following publication of the Report serve as another less academic source of positive and negative reactions.

D.1 Source: Hugh A. Stevenson, "Public and Professional Disenchantment: The Spectre of a New Crisis in Canadian Education", *Lakehead University Review*, 4, no. 2 (Fall, 1971), pp. 83-99.

[3]E. KOWALCHUK, "Manitoba Teachers' Salaries Equal to Janitors", *The Teacher*, (January 15, 1971), p. 7.

[4]E. KOWALCHUK, "Militancy on the Rise", *Manitoba Teacher*, XLVIII, No. 7 (1970), p. 7.

Lack of money, however, is not the only issue that disturbs educators. Relations with trustees and provincial educational officials have also deteriorated on fundamental educational grounds. It is hardly an accident that one finds a savagely critical article entitled, 'The Curriculum Committee that Never Was' deploring the phoney participation of teachers in planning, printed in a teachers' journal beside a platitudinous one by a Department of Education official lauding the democratic, consultative process, which clearly does not work well, as sound policy for the foreseeable future.[9] Seldom do teachers' concerns for the poor and for the need for such things as better special education facilities, capture the fancy of the public and receive the respect they deserve. Nevertheless, it is encouraging to find a magazine like *Saturday Night* printing an article entitled 'The Sickening Servility of the Kids in High Schools' written by a young teacher. Perhaps it is a little too much to expect the public to see in it the terrible teaching conditions which many young educators face when they begin work in over-institutionalized systems.[10] Or is it? Direct appeals for public sympathy through popular media aimed at securing support for reforms are not the exclusive preserve of establishment spokesmen and politicians. And such appeals by teachers are not by any means always designed as public relations ploys to help secure more adequate salaries.

In their attempts to improve education, teachers have begun to abandon the posture of crying meekly in their beer when confronted with difficulties and have become not only more militant, but also more indignant. An Alberta teacher summed it up nicely when he wrote challenging his colleagues:

"To be innovators we must first be scholars, which is what we most desire to make of our students. Innovation then becomes a state of mind, not a system. McLuhan, while he explored the inherent messages in light bulbs ignored the major educational media–us! We must become our own message. In the meantime, we must stop acting like social directors on the *Titanic*."[11]

Thus far, the new degree of unanimity in the nature and direction of critical comment which I am suggesting has grown up between complaining professionals and disgruntled members of the general public, such as parents and other public pressure groups, may seem rather tenuous. But contemporary public opinion also shows clear evidence of becoming more indignant at the unsolved problems which seem to be chronic with education. Rising costs are always a matter of concern, but so is financial retrenchment when parents and their children see innovations and specialized facilities disintegrate because of lack of funds. Religious and ethnic minorities are understandably unhappy when their interpretation of equal opportunity and constitutional rights cannot be fulfilled. Also, ratepayers have begun to question seriously the adequacy and fairness of our educational taxation system, not merely the high cost of education. More than a decade of lively, critical discussion in the public news media

[9]BLAIR NEATBY, "The Curriculum Committee That Never Was", *The Canadian Journal of History and Social Science*, V, No. 3 (1970), pp. 59-64; and J. K. Crossley, "Planning for a More Creative Curriculum: Curriculum Development Policy-1970", *ibid*., pp. 19-23. In Alberta improvements have been made in this situation. There members of curriculum committees are now nominated and trained by the Alberta Teachers' Association.

[10]JOHN THOMAS, "The Sickening Servility of the Kids in High Schools", *Saturday Night* (March, 1971), pp. 17-20.

[11]DON ROBERTSON, "What Happened to 'Think and Do'?" *A.T.A. Magazine*, LI, No.4 (April 1971), p. 39.

has educated Canadians to probe beyond the surface of educational questions for the fundamental issues. The result has been growing pressure on educators to improve their services. It is significant, however, that public demands for improvement are not exclusively directed toward teachers–those establishment figures such as administrators and politicians who control the system have become subjected to a degree of public watchfulness to which they find it increasingly difficult to become accustomed. In this respect, the masters have become the target of criticism by both practising teachers and those who are served by the educational system.

. . . .

How strong can public confidence remain when parents and taxpayers read articles pointing up educational abuses like a school board's having purchased 'enough chalk, paper, benches and gymnastic equipment to last at least 15 years'[15] and one in *Macleans* called 'Class of 71: The Graduates Nobody Wants' which suggests that 'Even in boom times we won't need the number of graduates we now have' and that 'We'll never need them again'?[16] All across the country the educational implications of the crisis in the Canadian book publishing industry have been made very clear to the public.

In the maritimes new magazines like *The Mysterious East* regularly point out educational problems. A recent issue commented on *Living and Learning:*

"In its introduction, that Report contains a crystallization of the reason that liberal reform of public education was to prove a failure. On page

five, the authors quote hopefully from the United Nations Universal Declaration of Human Rights: 'Parents have a prior right to choose the kind of education that shall be given to their children.' On the very next page, the report obliterates any ideas that the authors might take that assertion seriously, stating categorically that '...the small school and the local school board have outlived their day. The complexities of modern education demand larger units of instruction and administration.'"[17]

Meanwhile, Calgary and West Vancouver parents make attempts to secure community control of schools, to abolish school boundaries, to adopt a policy of client-choice of schools; *Chatelaine* wants to know why all the schools cannot be used by people after school hours; educators survey the topics that are discussed at school board meetings to isolate areas of neglect for more attention; and *Weekend Magazine* asks parents how obsolete their child's school is and how inferior is his education?[18]

Even conservative, long-established magazines like the *Atlantic Advocate* editorialize for national standards in education and in the same issue publish a companion article by a layman advocating that universities be abolished.[19] With regard to higher education. Hilda Neatby pro-

[15]"Fire School Officials, Quebec Report Urges", *The Globe and Mail,* Toronto, 4.3.71.

[16]BARBARA FRUM, "Class of '71", *Macleans* (June, 1971), pp. 19-25.

[17]RUSSELL HUNT, "Pruning the Public Schools", *The Mysterious East* (May-June, 1971), p. 31.

[18]"Client Choice In Schools", *Lions Gate Times*, West Vancouver, 11.5.70; ROBERT M. STAMP, "Let's Abolish School Boundaries", *A.T.A. Magazine*, LI, No. 1 (September-October, 1970, pp. 38-39; E. A. HOLDAWAY, "What Topics Are Discussed At School Board Meetings", *School Progress*, XXXIX, No. 4 (April, 1970, pp. 44-45; JOCELYN DINGMAN, "Why Can't We All Use the Schools After School?" *Chatelaine*, XLIII, No. 9 (September, 1970, pp. 29ff; ROBERT MCKEOWN (Assisted by John Young), "Your Child is Getting An Inferior Education. How Obsolete is Your School?", *Weekend Magazine*, XX, No. 37 (September 12, 1970, pp. 4-7.

vided the counter-point in a speech that did not receive such wide circulation:

"The public, which has been so admiring and indulgent, appears now to be losing its faith, not so much in the universities as institutions, but in the essential thing without which a university has no character. On January 15 last, I read this headline in the *Globe and Mail*: 'Higher University Tuition Fees Predicted With the End of Education For Its Own Sake.' I mentally commented on the sin of misleading headlines, but I was wrong. The article began, '"The heyday of education for its own sake is over, particularly at the post-secondary level", according to the chairman of the Economic Council of Canada.'

I am quite prepared to think that this expression was carelessly used; that what was meant was 'school for the sake of going to school,' the university as a pleasant way of life between high school and marriage, with or without a job. But I find it alarming that the expression can be carelessly used, because 'education for its own sake' represents something without which civilization and perhaps even technology cannot endure."[20]

The 'new crisis' which I am suggesting exists, is fundamentally an institutional one. Russell Hunt, writing in *The Mysterious East*, describes it succinctly: 'A large, centralized, uniform system of public education, it is becoming increasingly clear, simply cannot be responsive to the different demands and needs of individual parents and students.'[21] One might add teachers too. In a similar vein, and one which also serves as an example of the media feeding a disenchanted public's appetite for criticism and direct solutions, one need only examine the meteoric career and consult the writings of Ivan Illich. The June 19, 1971 issue of *Saturday Review*, which is read widely in Canada, contained an article by Illich, his final statement on education, entitled 'The Alternative to Schooling.'[22] The cover of the issue was devoted to a quotation from Illich which summarized and propagandized his point of view: 'We can disestablish schools or we can de-school culture.' 'Final statements' of course are very tempting–they are an excellent way of feeding a hungry public, ravenous for solutions and really innovative reforms, nothing but cake. As the educational editor of *Saturday Review*, in the same issue that carried Illich's 'final statement' rightly pointed out:

"Perhaps, during the 1970's we will learn to innovate in a fashion that brings true change in the classroom, and will remember that the objective is not merely to substitute a new orthodoxy for the old."[23]

Recent popular and professional literature would seem to confirm the view that public education is in the midst of a genuinely new crisis brought about by an informal alliance of complaint between educators and the general public. Never before has confidence in Canadian public education sunk so low, for such good reasons after so much intelligent discussion. A monumental confrontation is brewing with ingredients of disen-

[19]J. B. (The Editor), "The Need For National Standards in Education", *The Atlantic Advocate* (May, 1970), p. 16; and GEORGE CRUICK-SHANK, "It's High Time We Did Away With Universities!" *ibid.*, pp. 19-21.

[20]HILDA NEATBY, "Sorrows of a University", *Queen's University Alumni Review*, XLV, No. 3 (May-June, 1971), p. 68.

[21]HUNT, p. 31. For an interesting discussion of student and political reactions within Quebec to this fundamental problem see: "CEGEPS, Charlebois, Chartrand: The Quebec Revolution Now", in W. E. Mann (ed.), *Social and Cultural Change in Canada*, II (Toronto, 1970), pp. 200-210.

[22]pp. 44-48, 59-60.

[23]JAMES CASS, "New Orthodoxies for Old", *Saturday Review* (June 19, 1971), p. 39.

chantment that are becoming uglier and more dangerous with alarming rapidity. Economic depression notwithstanding, confidence in public education will not be restored by political attempts to reduce spending alone. Such measures are comically too little and too late. For example, in Ontario, the Minister of Education recently announced details of a major study of educational costs that will take a year and a half to complete, and was instituted roughly a year or more after the financial difficulty had become apparent to anyone who read a daily newspaper.[24]

. . . .

At this point in the discussion, one should begin to feel very uneasy because traditional solutions are not working and that means our education system, organized on traditionally accepted democratic grounds, is in very serious trouble. Educational commissions as problem-solving mechanisms seem not to serve very useful purposes in modern society. They are too often established too much after the fact, and politicians are under no obligation to implement their recommendations. About the only reliable accomplishment one can anoint them with is that Commissions continue to serve as an expensive device to stimulate still more public and professional discussion. However, that function is no longer likely to restore public confidence if recommendations come too late and do not receive official attention. As a safety valve for hostile public opinion the device has largely lost its former value. Also, when other old solutions like instant economies will not quiet public and professional criticism the politician is in dire jeopardy of losing both his power and his control of institutionalized education. It is easy to see why 'either–or' solutions such as those proposed by Illich have

a tantalizing appeal. The very foundation of public education is on the firing line–both professionals and laymen seem unwilling to keep faith with a politically led, organizational hierarchy when it no longer works effectively. With the exceptions of blind loyalty or ignorance, which are pretty much one and the same thing, it is difficult to see why taxpayers and professional educators should not demand radical improvements from their common enemy, the highly bureaucratized system.

The solutions to intensified public and professional disillusionment would seem to rest with extensive institutional reforms–if the institution is to survive. When one considers the possible alternatives, 'spectre' defined as a 'haunting presentment of ruin' does not seem too strong a word to describe the situation. The depth and breadth of criticism is not likely to abate if governments employ fence-mending tactics to accomplish short-term solutions. Where this has been tried, little but scorn has resulted. Tightening legal and professional controls will simply further irritate the educators who are already angry; it would also represent a reversal of ten years of increasing freedom to innovate and teach creatively. The latter would infuriate the public half of the critical alliance by denying educational aspirations now expected by society. Whatever combination of these alternatives might be tried, it seems logical to conclude that Canadian public education as an institution may well fail.

It surely will end in ruin if professional and public attitudes toward it continue to deteriorate at the rate they have in the last two years. A public funeral is likely to be staged if schools cannot adjust to the skill requirements of a highly industrialized economy and insecurity of employment becomes chronic. And thoughtful educators will attend *en masse* if public schools become

[24]DELL BELL, "School Cost Study May Take 1½ Years", *The London Free Press*, 6.30.71.

Further Reading

so vocational in their outlook that the aspects of education necessary to achieve a fuller and richer life through less pragmatic pursuits of the mind and spirit are neglected in favour of job training and extensive acquiescence to the exigencies of the marketplace.[27]

Time is a factor too–it is a luxury we do not have and cannot buy at any price to allow a leisurely search for solutions. If they are to be found, it must be done without seriously interrupting the education of thousands of young people. Too much time has been lost because we have not adjusted to our contemporary environment quickly enough; what remains must be used effectively for study and then application of new modes with comparatively little room for error.

The student of the history of education in Canada is soon confronted with the problem of finding source material. There is not an extensive secondary literature on the subject; some regions –Ontario, for example–have no book-length studies that claim to deal comprehensively with the development of educational thought and practice. Similarly, many important themes, like the growth of industrial education in Quebec, also await their historian. There is a fairly extensive literature in the journals, but even some of the best of these tend to be highly specialized studies, demanding that much be brought to them. As for primary sources, these are often unobtainable for the student. Few libraries carry more than a smattering of out-of-province department of education *Reports*, and the various provincial educational association reports and teachers' journals are equally hard to locate. The purpose of this guide to further reading is to draw attention to some of the more accessible literature. It does not contain references to primary source material or theses.

To find what is available, a student might begin by consulting the various bibliographical aids. None of them is complete, but all are helpful. Raymond Tanghe, *Bibliography of Canadian Bibliographies* (Toronto: University of Toronto Press, 1960) and its *Supplement* contain some educational material. Much more specific is Canada, D.B.S., Educational Division, *A Bibliographical Guide to Canadian Education* (Ottawa, 1964). By far the most complete in their field and two of the best general sources available are Robin S. Harris and Arthur Tremblay, *A Bibliography of Higher Education in Canada* (Toronto: University of Toronto Press, 1960) and its *Supplement* (1965). Alan H. Child, "The History of Canadian Education: A Bibliographical Note", *Social History*, vol. 8 (Nov.,

[27]For an interesting sociological discussion of some of these problems see: DANIEL W. ROSSIDES, "The Functional Adaptation of Canadian Education", in *Society as a Functional Process* (Toronto, 1968), pp. 232-237.

1971), 105-117 is also worth consulting, as is D. Myers, "Education", in R. Fulford, D. Godfrey, A. Rotstein, eds., *Read Canadian* (Toronto: James Lewis and Samuel, 1972), 182-93. A valuable source of educational writing in the early twentieth century is Albert H. Smith, *A Bibliography of Canadian Education*, Bulletin 10 of the Department of Educational Research, University of Toronto (Toronto: University of Toronto Press, 1938). Cumulative educational bibliographies for the later period can be found in several journals not directly connected with Canadian education.Some of the best of these are: *The Canadian Historical Review, Revue d'histoire de l'Amérique francaise, Culture* (ceased publication in 1970 and the *History of Education Quarterly*. After 1965 the best reference for

books, reports, pamphlets and periodical articles on education published in Canada is the *Canadian Education Index*. Most of the 200 odd newsletters, magazines, reports and journals that make up Canada's "education press" are classified in Julius Friesen, *America's Education Press, A Classified List of Educational Publications issued in the United States and Canada* (Syracuse, N.Y.: Educational Press Association of America, 1969).

There are several general histories of Canadian education. The most comprehensive is J. D. Wilson, R. M. Stamp, L.-P. Audet, eds., *Canadian Education: A History* (Scarborough: Prentice-Hall, 1970), but C. E. Phillips, *The Development of Education in Canada* (Toronto: W. J. Gage, 1957), is still useful. Both have biblio-

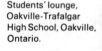

Students' lounge, Oakville-Trafalgar High School, Oakville, Ontario.

graphies. Much shorter accounts can be found in F. Henry Johnson, *A Brief History of Canadian Education* (Toronto: McGraw-Hill, 1968), and in the very basic Joseph Katz, *Society, Schools and Progress in Canada* (Toronto: Pergamon Press, 1969). Statistics relating to the use and financing of Canadian public schools can be found in Canada, D.B.S., *Canada Year Book* from 1905 to the present.

Each province has its own school system, but there are histories for only a few of them. Some of these are: F. W. Rowe, *The Development of Education in Newfoundland* (Toronto: Ryerson Press, 1964); K. F. C. MacNaughton, *The Development of the Theory and Practice of Education in New Brunswick, 1784-1900* (Fredericton: University of New Brunswick, 1946); Louis-Philippe Audet, *Histoire de l'enseignement au Québec, 1608-1971*, 2 vols. (Toronto: Holt, Rinehart & Winston, 1972); John W. Chalmers, *Schools of the Foothills Province* (Toronto: University of Toronto Press, 1967); F. Henry Johnson, *A History of Public Education in British Columbia* (Vancouver: U.B.C. Publications Centre, 1964). For those provinces that have no book-length studies, the student may refer to articles and theses. There are brief accounts of the history of education of the Maritime provinces in Adam Shortt and Arthur G. Doughty, eds., *Canada and its Provinces*, vol. 14, published in 1914. Bruce C. Fergusson, *The Inauguration of the Free School System in Nova Scotia* (Halifax: Public Archives of Nova Scotia, 1964) provides an introduction to nineteenth-century developments in that province, and Sister Mary Olga, "The Impact of Religion and Politics in the Structure of Education in Prince Edward Island", Canadian Association Foundations of Education *Report of the Annual Meeting* (1967) is an excellent treatment of some

significant educational problems in P.E.I. There is no adequate history of education for Ontario. Robin S. Harris, *Quiet Evolution: A Study of the Educational System of Ontario* (Toronto: University of Toronto Press, 1967) is a brief overview. The massive J. G. Hodgins, *Documentary History of Education in Upper Canada*, 28 vols. (Toronto: Education Department, 1896-1910) is a storehouse of information for the Ryerson years, while W. G. Fleming, *Ontario's Educative Society,* 7 vols. (Toronto: University of Toronto Press, 1971-72) is an intensive examination of the post-World War II period. Unfortunately, in the published literature the educational histories of Manitoba and Saskatchewan generally begin and end with the "Manitoba School Question, 1890-1896" and the "Autonomy Question" of 1905. Very brief surveys of nineteenth-century developments in these two provinces are available in *Canada and Its Provinces*, vol. 20 (1914), and C. C. Lingard, *Territorial Government in Canada* (Toronto: University of Toronto Press, 1946).

The emigrants who came to New France and later to British North America brought with them the educational traditions of their homeland, which in turn helped to shape the schools of colonial Canada. What were those traditions? The best single source is Philippe Ariès, *Centuries of Childhood: A Social History of Family Life* (New York: Vintage Books, 1962). Although it draws its subject matter mostly from France in the fifteenth to the eighteenth centuries, the sheer brilliance of the book casts light on many areas outside its immediate scope. The French educational tradition can be examined specifically in Georges Snyders, *La pédagogie en France aux XVIIe et XVIIIe siècles* (Paris: Les Presses universitaires de France, 1905). The English heritage is available in T. L. Jarman, *Landmarks in the History of Education* (London: John

Murray, 1963), and Brian Simon, *Studies in the History of Education, 1780-1870* (London: Lawrence and Wishart, 1960). The Scottish tradition can be viewed nearly in its entirety in James Scotland, *The History of Scottish Education*, 2 vols. (London: University of London Press, 1969), and Donald H. Akenson, *The Irish Education Experiment: The National System of Education in the Nineteenth Century* (London: Routledge, 1970) is an insightful account of the development of schools in Ireland. There is a multitude of books on the history of education in the United States. Among the best of those that describe the educational heritage early American settlers in this country might have brought with them are: Bernard Bailyn, *Education in the Forming of American Society* (New York: Random House, 1960), Lawrence Cremin, *American Education; The Colonial Experience, 1607-1783* (New York: Harper and Row, 1970). R. Freeman Butts & Lawrence Cremin, *A History of Education in American Culture* (New York: Holt, Reinhart & Winston, 1953) is an adequate survey of the later period.

There are a number of issues associated with the development of public school systems in Canada. Each has its own literature, but unfortunately, not every geographical region is adequately represented. Two views of the "education mania" that started it all are presented in Marcel Lajeunesse, "Espoirs et illusions d'une réforme scolaire au Québec du XIXe siècle", *Culture*, vol. 31, no. 2 (June, 1970), 149-159, and Susan E. Houston, "Politics, Schools, and Social Change in Upper Canada", *Canadian Historical Review*, vol. 53, no. 3 (September, 1972), 249-271. The kinds of systems created can be viewed from various angles. Louis-Philippe Audet, *Histoire du Conseil de l'Instruction Publique: 1856-1964* (Montréal: Editions Lémeac,

1964) examines the public system from the vantage point of the central authority. The justifications for centralization in Ontario are considered in R. D. Gidney, "Centralization and Education: The Origins of an Ontario Tradition", *Journal of Canadian Studies*, vol. 7, no. 4 (November, 1972). James Fraser, *Report…on the Common School Systems of the United States and of the Provinces of Upper and Lower Canada* (London, 1866) is a contemporary overview presented with the detachment of an outsider. Other useful sources of information on the development of the public school systems are the biographies of the men who were instrumental in their creation and growth. The best known of these is C. B. Sissons, *Egerton Ryerson, His Life and Letters*, 2 vols. (Toronto: Clarke, Irwin, 1937 and 1947). Some of the others are: Jean-Baptiste Meilleur, *Mémorial de l'Education du Bas-Canada* (Québec, 1876); R. Dawson, ed., *Fifty Years at Work in Canada; Scientific and Educational: Being Autobiographical Notes by Sir William Dawson* (London: Ballantyne, 1901); P. L. McCreath, "Charles Tupper and the Politics of Education in Nova Scotia", *Nova Scotia Historical Quarterly*, vol. 1, no. 3 (September, 1971, 203-224; R. S. Patterson, "F. W. G. Haultain. Educational Statesman of the Canadian West", *Alberta Journal of Educational Research*, vol. 8, no. 2 (June, 1962), 85-93; and F. Henry Johnson, *John Jessop: Goldseeker and Educator* (Vancouver: Mitchell Press, 1971). Unfortunately, there is no biography of the influential Maritime educator, T. H. Rand.

In the early part of the nineteenth century the responsibility for education was shared in part by both the church and the state. But it was an uneasy partnership. The problems of church-state relations and their educational ramifications in early Ontario are examined in John S.

Moir, *Church and State in Canada West* (Toronto: University of Toronto Press, 1959). The church-state controversy was also an issue in Quebec, and it is well presented in two articles, one each by Fernand Ouellet and Patrice Garant in Pierre W. Bélanger et Guy Rocher, eds., *École et Société au Québec* (Montréal: Editions H. M. H., 1970). Marcel Lajeunesse, "L'évêque Bourget et l'instruction publique au Bas-Canada, 1840-1846", *Revue d'histoire de l'Amérique Française*, vol. 23, no. 1 (juin, 1969), 35-52 is a more detailed study of the issue in a critical period. The unique Newfoundland solution to the church-state question is presented in F. Jones, "Religion, Education and Politics in Newfoundland, 1836-1875", *Journal of the Canadian Church Historical Society*, vol. 12, no. 4 (December, 1970), 63-76.

Outside of Quebec (and especially later in the century) the church-state controversy generally centred around the Roman Catholic Church in conflict with a Protestant-oriented provincial government. The issue then became one of minority rights for Catholics. The best general survey of this aspect of the question is C. B. Sissons, *Church and State in Canada* (Toronto: Ryerson Press, 1959). There are also many good regional studies such as George A. Rawlyk and Ruth Hafter, *Acadian Education in Nova Scotia, An Historical Survey to 1965* (Studies of the Royal Commission on Bilingualism and Biculturalism, 1970), and F. A. Walker, *Catholic Education and Politics in Ontario* (Toronto: Thomas Nelson, 1964). The case for the Catholics in Manitoba is well argued in Lovell Clark, ed., *The Manitoba School Question: Majority Rule or Minority Rights?* (Toronto: Copp Clark, 1968), and Craig Brown, ed., *Minorities, Schools, and Politics*, Canadian Historical Readings, no. 7 (Toronto: University of Toronto Press, 1969),

has chapters on the plight of the Catholics in the West and the Territories.

The educational problems of minorities loom large in the history of the public schools. C. B. Sissons, *Bilingual Schools in Canada* (Toronto: J. M. Dent, 1917) is still a useful survey of the problems involved in trying to secure a French-language education outside of Quebec. Its value is enhanced, however, if it is balanced with L. Groulx, *L'Enseignement français au Canada* (Montréal: Librairie Granger Frères, 1934). A more specialized study deserving mention is C. J. Jaenen, "French Public Education in Manitoba", *Revue de l'Université d'Ottawa*, vol. 38, no. 1 (jan.-mars, 1968), 19-34. Another sizeable minority is made up of English-speaking Quebeckers, and a history of their schools in a predominantly French Catholic province is available in W. P. Percival, *Across the Years, A Century of Education in the Province of Quebec* (Montreal: Gazette Printing Company, 1946). Some of the educational problems that other minority groups have met, and in many cases still face, are discussed in H. B. Hawthorne, ed., *A Survey of the Contemporary Indians of Canada* (Ottawa: Indian Affairs Branch, 1967); G. F. G. Stanley, "The Métis and the Conflict of Cultures in Western Canada", *Canadian Historical Review*, vol. 28, no. 4 (December, 1947), 428-433; E. K. Francis, "The Mennonite School Problem in Manitoba", *Mennonite Quarterly Review*, vol. 27, no. 3 (July, 1953), 204-237; F. Henry Johnson, "The Doukhobors of British Columbia: The History of a Sectarian Problem in Education", *Queen's Quarterly*, vol. 70, no. 4 (Winter, 1964), 528-541; R. W. Winks, "Negro School Segregation in Ontario and Nova Scotia", *Canadian Historical Review*, vol. 50, no. 2 (June, 1969), 164-191. J. W. Chalmers,"Strangers in Our Midst", *Alberta Historical Review*, vol. 16, no. 1

(Winter, 1968), 18-23 is a discussion of education among the Ukrainian immigrants to Alberta.

The history of technical education in most provinces still lies buried in theses or the various Ministers of Education *Reports*. A beginning has been made, however, in Ontario with R. M. Stamp, "Urban Industrial Change and Curriculum Reform in Early Twentieth Century Ontario" in R. D. Heyman, R. F. Lawson, and R. M. Stamp, *Studies in Educational Change* (Toronto: Holt, Rinehart and Winston, 1972) and in D. A. Lawr, "Agricultural Education in Nineteenth-Century Ontario: An Idea in Search of an Institution", *The History of Education Quarterly*, vol. II, no. 4 (Fall, 1972). The best source for federal involvement in technical education is still D. Clendenning, "A Review of Federal Legislation Relating to Technical and Vocational Education in Canada", mimeographed by the Department of Labour, Ottawa, 1965.

There are a number of ways of approaching the sources of twentieth-century educational thought and practice. One of the most interesting is through the biographical works of the men who were actually involved in the day-to-day affairs of public education. Some of these include: *G. Fred; The Story of G. Fred McNally recorded by H. T. Coutts and B. E. Walker* (Don Mills: J. M. Dent, 1964), J. H. Putman, *Fifty years at School, An Educationist Looks at Life* (Toronto: Clarke, Irwin, 1938), John G. Althouse, *Addresses...,* edited by K. B. McCool (Toronto: Gage, 1958), and Watson Kirkconnel, *A Canadian Headmaster* (Toronto: Clarke, Irwin, 1935). Donalda Dickie, *The Enterprise School in Theory and Practice* (Toronto: Gage, 1940) is a good statement of the purposes and methods adopted by many "progressive" educators of the period. Another source is the educational statements of people outside the public school systems, usually members of the university community. These sources tend to be more ideological than the schoolmen's accounts of their stewardship, and they are certainly more critical. Some of the most incisive of these are Hilda Neatby, *So Little for the Mind* (Toronto: Clarke, Irwin, 1953), Northrop Frye, ed., *Design For Learning* (Toronto: University of Toronto Press, 1962), R. M. Dawson's comments in Nova Scotia, *Report of the Royal Commission on Provincial Development and Rehabilitation*, vol. 1, pt. V (1944), Frank F. MacKinnon, *The Politics of Education...,* (Toronto: University of Toronto Press, 1960), and A. I. Wittenburg, *The Prime Imperatives, Priorities in Education* (Toronto: Clarke, Irwin, 1968). In Quebec, events later proved that essays by two "outsiders" (in spirit if not in fact) anticipated the shape of things to come: Georges-Henri Lévesque, *Humanisme et sciences sociales* (Toronto: University of Toronto Press, 1953) and [Jean-Paul Desbiens] *The Impertinences of Brother Anonymous* (Montreal: Harvest House, 1962).

The journals of the provincial teachers associations are fruitful sources of educational opinion throughout the twentieth century, particularly the *B.C. Teacher* and the *A.T.A. Magazine. The School*, published by the Ontario College of Education (1912-1948), kept abreast of developments across the country.

A productive source for the post-World War II period is the *Reports* of the various commissions and committees appointed by provincial authorities to investigate their public school systems and recommend ways for their improvement. Some of the most influential of these are referred to above in Chapter VIII. Other important studies include British Columbia, *Report of the Royal Commission on education* (1960) and Alberta, *Royal Commission on Education* (1959).

Both represent rather conservative statements. Much more reform-minded are British Columbia Teachers' Federation, *Report of the Commission on Education* (1968) and Alberta, *Report of the Commission on Educational Planning* (1972). Comments on a wide variety of topics from many different viewpoints can be found in the Quance Lecture Series published annually by Gage since 1949.

Public education is best understood in the context of the society that created and uses it. By far the best source on the relation of the schools to the prevailing social structure is John Porter, *The Vertical Mosaic* (Toronto: University of Toronto Press, 1965). John R. Seeley, R. A. Sim and E. W. Loosley, *Crestwood Heights, A Study of the Culture of Suburban Life* (Toronto: University of Toronto Press, 1956) contains a study of the socialization function of the school in a modern middle-class suburb. The relationship between educational provision and economic development is examined in O. J. Firestone, *Industry and Education* (Ottawa: University of Ottawa Press, 1969).

There are three collections of readings which, taken together, present a wide spectrum of viewpoints on Canadian education in the 1960s. The most complete of these is H. A. Stevenson, R. M. Stamp, J. D. Wilson, eds., *The Best of Times, The Worst of Times, Contemporary Issues in Canadian Education* (Toronto: Holt, Rinehart and Winston, 1972). A. Malik, ed., *Social Foundations of Canadian Education* (Scarborough: Prentice-Hall, 1969) reprints a few of the most representative essays of the decade. The material in N. Byrne and J. Quarter, eds., *Must Schools Fail, The Growing Debate in Canadian Education* (Toronto: McClelland and Stewart, 1972) is more critical. Anthony Burton,

The Horn and the Beanstalk, Problems and Possibilities in Canadian Education (Toronto: Holt, Rinehart and Winston, 1972) is a short monograph that attemps to bring a radical analysis to the problems of the public school.

Acknowledgements

Grateful acknowledgement is made to the following for permission to use the copyrighted material indicated below. Every reasonable care has been taken to acknowledge copyright information correctly. The publisher would welcome information that will enable him to correct any errors or omissions in succeeding printings.

The ATA Magazine: For "Is Alberta Education a failure" by A. L. Doucette, which appeared in the December 1947 issue of The ATA Magazine, Volume 28, Number 3.

Association of Universities and Colleges of Canada: For "The Community College in Canada" from *Universities and Colleges in Canada* 1970.

Sidney Katz: For "The Teachers" which appeared in *Maclean's Magazine*, March 1953.

Lakehead University Review: For "Public and Professional Disenchantment: The Spectre of a New Crisis in Canadian Education" by Hugh Stevenson from *Lakehead University Review* IV No. 2 (Fall 1971).

LeDevoir: For "Must We Rush Headlong Toward Suicide?" by Jean-Marc Leger in *LeDevoir* issue of November 26, 1968.

John B. Macdonald: For "Higher Education in British Columbia and a Plan for the Future".

The Macmillan Company of Canada Limited: For "Investment in Canadian Youth" by John Cheal.

McGraw-Hill Ryerson Limited: For "The Canadian Secondary Schools and Manpower Development" edited by Peter Bargen.

H. Rocke Robertson: For "Address to the Montreal Rotary Club" on 19 November 1969.

Teachers College Record: For "Contributions to the Laws of Learning" by Peter Sandiford from *Teachers College Record* XXVII, 6 February 1926.

Union of Ontario Indians: For "Education of the Native Peoples of Ontario" 1971.

The United Society for the Propagation of the Gospel: For the letter of the Revd. George Archbold, to Bishop of Quebec, 2 April 1838.

University of Toronto Press: For "My Neighbour, A Study in City Conditions" by J. W. Woodsworth, first published by Methodist Young People's Forward Movement 1911.

Max Braithwaite and C. M. Mooney: For "School Drought" which appeared in the November 1937 issue of *Maclean's Magazine.*

The Canadian Education Association: For "Some Sociological Considerations in Education in Canada" by G. W. Bancroft from *Canadian Education and Research Digest*, March, 1964. For "Recent Reforms in Education in Quebec" by Maurice Lebel from *Canadian Education*, June, 1958. For "Brains Unlimited" by Sidney Smith from *Canadian Education*, June 1954, Volume 9, No. 3.

Canadian Forum: For "Penny Wise Education" from *Canadian Forum*, XVII issue of October 1937. For "Education–a National Responsibility" by J. W. Noseworthy in *Canadian Forum*, XVIII issue of February 1939. For untitled article by F. H. Underhill on the universities from *Canadian Forum*, XI issue of April 1931.

Canadian Institute of International Affairs and Canadian Association for Adult Education: For "Behind the Headlines" by C. E. Phillips.

Canadian Mental Health Association: For "The Grading and Promotion of Pupils" by Charles B. Willis which appeared in the *Canadian Journal of Mental Hygiene*, issue III, 4, January 1922.

Dalhousie Review: For "The Little White Schoolhouse" by E. W. Nichols from issue V, 1925-26.

J. M. Dent & Sons (Canada Limited): For "The Education of the New Canadian" by J. T. M. Anderson.

The Globe & Mail: For "The Most Up-to-date High School" by Barrie Zwicker from *The Globe Magazine*, 7 January 1967.

Photo Sources

John Ross Robertson Collection.
Metropolitan Toronto Central Library;
Jesuit College and Church, Quebec, 1761,
drawn by Mr. Short and published by Act
of Parliament, 1761.
"March of Intellect", sketched by William
Elliott in Adelaide Township, Middlesex
County, Ontario, in 1845.
Red River Settlement, 1858.
Dalhousie College — the first building.

Board of School Trustees, School District
No. 61, Victoria, British Columbia:
George Jay Elementary School, 1910.
The school garden.

Ontario Archives:
Devlin School, 1904.
Rainy River District.
Ontario Normal College and Collegiate
Institute, Hamilton, c.1901.
Plan No. 3 from *The School House: Its
Architecture, Arrangements, and Discipline,
with additional Papers on Various Subjects,*
edited by J. George Hodgins, M.A. and
printed for the Department of Public
Instruction for Upper Canada, 1857-58.
Railway school car, 1926.
Manual Training classroom, Ottawa, 1901-02.

Archives of Saskatchewan:
A country school house.

Historical Collection, Toronto Board of
Education Centre Library:
Collecting for the Red Cross, Charles G.
Fraser, principal, in front of Manning Avenue
School, 1916.
Household Science Room, Galt Collegiate
Institute, 1908. Picture taken from the

Report of the Minister of Education for
Ontario, 1908.
A "New Education" kindergarten, Toronto
Model School, c.1898.

Information Canada Phototheque:
Hutterite school, photo by Chris Lund
Ochre River, photo by John Drieman

John de Visser:
Frobisher Bay, Northwest Territories
The school stove, Newfoundland
Loretto Abbey
Study of Educational Facilities, Metropolitan
Toronto School Board

Students with Headphones, from SEF E2:
Educational Specifications and User
Requirements for Intermediate Schools,
1969.

Edward Jones:
Oakville-Trafalgar High School

Hans Geerling Photography:
William Davis Public School

Index

(See also Table of Contents)